Ending the Era

of

Fanaticism

Spiritualizing the World, vol 10

Ending the Era

of

Fanaticism

KIM MICHAELS

MORE TO LIFE PUBLISHING

www.morepublish.com

For foreign and translation rights,

contact: info@ morepublish.com

ISBN: 978-87-93297-70-8

Cover art by Sandra Singer

For more information: *www.ascendedmasterlight.com and www.transcendencetoolbox.com*

Content

INTRODUCTION

This book belongs to the series *Spiritualizing the World*. The books in this series are given by the ascended masters as workbooks that provide the knowledge and practical tools we need in order to make a contribution to solving concrete world problems. This book contains the knowledge and the tools we need in order to end the era where the fanatical mindset has such a dominant influence on earth. These books do not contain foundational knowledge about ascended masters and their teachings. In order to make the most efficient use of this book, you need to have a general knowledge of the following topics:

- You need to know who the ascended masters are, how they give their teachings and how you can make the best use of them on a personal and planetary level. You can find extensive teachings on this in the books: *How You Can Help Change the World* and *The Power of Self*.

- You need to know how the earth functions as a cosmic schoolroom. You need to know your own role and the authority you have as a spiritual being in embodiment. You need to know the role of the ascended masters and how only we who are in embodiment can give them the authority to use their unlimited power to affect change on earth. You can find more on these topics in the first book in this series: *How You Can Help Change the World*.

• You need to know how to use the practical tools given by the ascended masters. You can find more on this topic in: *How You Can Help Change the World* and on the website: *www.transcendencetoolbox.com.*

• You need to know about the existence and methods of the dark forces who are ultimately responsible for creating problems on earth. You can find foundational teachings on this in: *Cosmology of Evil.*

How to use this book

There is no one way of using the teachings and tools in this book. However, if you want to make a significant contribution to solving world problems, it is suggested that you start by following this program:

• You read one of the chapters in the book completely in order to increase your understanding of the topic.

• You give the invocation associated with that chapter once a day for nine days while studying the same chapter again.

The reasoning behind this program is that the chapters in the book form a progression. As you give an invocation for one chapter, you are also clearing your own consciousness from certain energies and illusions. This makes it easier for you to absorb and apply the teachings from the next chapter.

You can, of course, also read the book all the way through and then select one or more invocation(s) that you give several times. It is always more powerful to give an invocation once a day for nine or 33 days.

Because some of the invocations in this book are quite long, they have been divided into two or more parts. It takes about 15-20 minutes to give each part. If you prefer, you can give all of the parts for one invocation in succession. In that case, you do not need to give the sealing after the first invocation or the preamble to the next. You give a preamble in the beginning, continue through the parts and give a sealing in the end.

1 | MODERN DEMOCRACIES MUST MOVE BEYOND FANATICISM

I AM the Ascended Master Mother Mary, and it is my privilege to open this conference and bid you all welcome here to this place. What is a place? Does it really matter where you have a conference? Well, yes and no. It does not matter in the sense that the right place to commune with the ascended masters is always in the heart. On the other hand, it is of course important to have conferences in certain places where we can shatter certain energy matrices that are not of the light, or we can have an impact on the collective consciousness.

That is why we are grateful to have a conference here on the European continent that has, in the past, been the cradle of so much fanaticism. Naturally my beloved, the concept of fanaticism is something that all people on earth are aware of but that hardly anyone understands. If you search on the Internet or look up in a dictionary to find the meaning of the word fanaticism, you will often find a definition that says something like "fanaticism – the act of being fanatical." What does that tell you exactly? Well, not very much, does it? You will see that even psychologists who have studied this phenomenon for some time have difficulty in defining exactly what fanaticism is.

Many people reinforce fanaticism

Now, the first thing that I want to bring to your attention here (for you to make calls on, and be aware of) is that there is a tendency, in worldly psychology or in all fields of society that deal with fanaticism, to look at the extreme manifestations of fanaticism. Here on the European continent, you naturally always have psychologists reach back to Adolph Hitler as the example of a very fanatical person, and how he managed to get so many among the German population to go into the fanatical mindset. The problem with taking this approach is that it actually reinforces fanaticism. It does this in a very subtle way that few people are aware of.

You see my beloved, going back to Sigmund Freud, he set a tone for modern psychology, for what became known as the "Science of Psychology" by focusing on studying abnormal psychology. So many psychologists have then looked at the topic of fanaticism, looked at the more extreme manifestations of fanaticism (such as Hitler) and they have studied this from the same vantage point as traditional psychology. This is abnormal, fanaticism is something abnormal, something extreme. The problem with taking this approach is that you then automatically create a division where you say: "Certain people are in such an extreme state of mind that they are fanatics. But most people are not in such an extreme state of mind, and therefore, they are not fanatics. They are not in a fanatical state of mind." If you look at this, including how many of the nations of Europe look back at the time of Hitler, you will see that there is a tendency for many people to feel: "We are normal but these people are fanatics."

Many, here in this country of Holland, look at the German people and Hitler as clearly being fanatical. They think that because the people here in the Netherlands are so open, so tolerant, certainly we are not fanatics. Many people would be greatly offended if they were told that they were fanatics, which of course is what I intend to do later.

Dividing human beings into groups

The problem here is simple. You create a division of humankind into two groups, and then you say: "We are the normal people, they are the fanatics." You are pointing the finger at somebody else. What was the essential dynamic of Hitler's Germany? It was exactly the same. We are dividing humanity into two groups, the Aryan Germans and the Jews. They are the bad people, and they are the ones we need to get rid of. The mindset behind this is very simple. There is a problem in the world, but the problem is not with us, the problem is with those other people. In order to solve the problem, we need to change those other people.

Now, grant you, Hitler's solution, *final* solution of killing all the Jews, was extreme and was fanatical. Certainly the actions of ISIS of blowing up people and killing them is also extreme. What needs to be recognized is that fanaticism does not start in the extreme. It starts in what many people call "normal" and then it gradually becomes extreme. If you are totally honest and looking at Germany in the 1920's and 1930's up until the rise of Hitler, you cannot say that the majority of Germans were in a fanatical state of mind. There is no way you can say this and be honest and objective. You can of course see that there was a certain psychological mechanism in the German people, which had the potential to evolve into the fanaticism you saw after the rise of Hitler.

If you are honest and objective, you cannot say that this state of mind or this psychological mechanism was only found in the Germans. There were special circumstances, in the sense that the Germans were very upset over the conclusion of the First World War and the Treaty of Versailles. Nevertheless, if you are looking at just the mindset of the people and not the outer circumstances, you will see that many other nations in Europe and around the world had a very similar mechanism in a majority of the population.

Identifying the problem as "out there"

It is precisely this mechanism, you see, that is a problem. You are not taking responsibility for the problem and saying: "What can *we* do? How can we change ourselves to solve the problem?" You identify that the problem is out there with other people and they are the ones who have to change. If you look honestly at history, you will see how many examples there are of people that you would call "normal" from a psychological evaluation, but who (when there were certain circumstances that manifested) they became willing to kill other people. Before these circumstances manifested, they were what you call "normal human beings." They are not necessarily aggressive and certainly not willing to kill others. But when certain circumstances changed, then all of a sudden, now people are willing to kill other human beings.

I know that there are people out there, my beloved, who want to define fanaticism by saying that when you are willing to kill other human beings, you are in a fanatical state of mind. If you are not willing to kill, then you are not a fanatic. That is too simplistic of a definition. It certainly is not a definition that will allow you to ever remove fanaticism from the earth. As I said, the essence of fanaticism is that you point the finger at somebody else and you say: "They are the problem. They are the ones who have to change." You can never remove fanaticism if you are in that same state of mind. If you isolate certain people, label them as fanatics, point the finger and say: "They are the ones who are the problem, they are the ones who have to change," you will not remove fanaticism. Not only will you not *remove* fanaticism, you will *reinforce* fanaticism.

There are people, here in Holland and certainly in other nations, who think that they are being so open and tolerant that what they are doing is the opposite of fanaticism. When they then look at the people who are extremists, and label them as fanatics, by this very mental act (and emotional act) they are reinforcing the consciousness of fanaticism that exists.

Fanaticism is a state of mind present everywhere

We need to become aware that fanaticism is, first of all, and this is our first definition of fanaticism: a state of mind. It is not a state of mind that is exclusive to some people or even a few people. It is a state of mind that is present in all populations around the world. Even in what you call the modern democracies (that often see themselves as having risen above fanaticism) you find the state of mind that is the cradle, the wellspring, of fanaticism. It is the seed of fanaticism.

You find this, not in all people in the modern democracies, but you find it in the majority of the population. You find this very psychological mechanism, this state of mind. What is this state of mind? Well, it is very simply this. You think you know something. You think you have an opinion, a belief, and you think that *it could never be replaced by a higher understanding*.

You may see this in a religious setting where they believe they have received some Divine revelation from a superior God, and this is now the ultimate, absolute truth. Because it came from the superior God who is supposedly perfect, it could never be improved upon or expanded. You have the people who believe that the Bible is the literal word of God, and that it was given 2,000 or more years ago in its perfect form, and that God has had nothing to say to humankind for the past 2,000 years. Because he gave everything that he wanted to give and that needed to be given and it is perfect, and it is absolute, it could never be improved upon. Well, anybody who has this state of mind is in a state of fanaticism. This is the very mindset of fanaticism because you hold a certain belief, and you believe that it could never be improved upon.

Now, look at the political setting where you have the most obvious example in Marxism. Marx has stated, not just an opinion, not just an observation, not just a theory, but he has tuned in to the infallible historical mechanism that brings society forward. Therefore, what he is stating is historical necessity. It could never be improved upon. It could never be changed because it is an absolute, infallible truth.

Now, you take science. You see that science itself is an ongoing process, a never-ending process. The essence of science, as it was given by Saint Germain and other ascended masters, is that we never believe that we have the final truth and the final understanding. We are always open to making observations, to making experiments, and whenever we see something that our current theories cannot explain or we see a contradiction, then we know here is something to investigate.

What have some people done with science? They have (in their eagerness to disprove religion, which was one infallible belief system) created scientific Materialism, which they now claim is another infallible belief system. The scientific materialists look down upon religious people and think religious people are fanatics, but: "We materialists, we are the ones who know the truth." They do not see that they are in the exact same state of mind. They are in the exact same state of mind as the religious people that they so despise. They also believe they have an absolute truth that could never be expanded upon. It could never be replaced by a higher understanding because it is an absolute fact proven by science that there is nothing beyond the material universe, and this could never be proven wrong.

Of course, it can never be proven wrong when you are not looking. If you are not looking beyond the material universe, how will you ever prove that there is something beyond the material universe—and scientific materialists are not looking. They are trying to do everything they can to prevent the real scientists from looking. They do not want anyone to see that they are wrong.

Defining where not to look

How do they fail to see that this is the exact same mindset as medieval Catholics who did not want Galileo or Kepler or the other astronomers to prove that the Catholic doctrine was wrong? How do they not see that they are doing the exact same thing that they so despise in religious people? Well, because they are in a mindset of fanaticism, and fanaticism blinds you. When you think that you have an absolute infallible truth that could never be improved upon, then the only way to uphold this belief (the sense of security that you get from this belief) is to define that there are certain areas where you are not looking.

You are not looking in areas that could disprove your infallible belief. The Catholics did not believe that they needed to look outside of church doctrine or the Bible. The materialists do not need to look outside the material universe. They do not need to look at consciousness. They do not need to look at the findings of quantum physics or at least not interpret them in a logical way. They are in the exact same fanatical mindset.

You see people who have gone into this state of almost an extreme form of agnosticism where they say: "Oh, nobody can know the truth. There is no truth we can know. Therefore, any idea is as good as any other idea, because it's all just ideas." That is also a state of fanaticism because what do they do? They say: "Well, we are the only ones who have really understood the essence of the world, while all of these other people, the religious people, the political people, the materialists, all those who are certain that they have the only truth, they are the ones who are wrong. *They* are the fanatics."

The fight or flight mentality

Again, it reinforces the division between different groups of people. The essence of the fanatical mindset is that you hold a belief that cannot, that you believe *could* not be expanded upon. What does it do? Well, first of all, it creates a division between you and all those who do not share your belief, all those who do not agree with you. They are outside of your group. They are *out there* and you are *in here*. There is *us* versus *them*.

What also happens is that you automatically create this sense of threat. You know very well (and you observe very well) that not everybody agrees with you. You almost cannot live in this world without realizing that there has been progress in history and knowledge has been expanded. It is very hard not to realize at some level of your being that there is a potential that new knowledge could be developed that would overturn your infallible belief. Therefore, you go into a state of mind where you are threatened. You are threatened by anyone who could overthrow your sense of security that your belief is infallible.

This means that you then go into a "fight or flight" reaction where you are seeking to escape those who could challenge your belief. If you cannot escape it, then you are willing to fight them. If you look at people based on this evaluation, you could say that the vast majority of the people around the world are in this particular mindset that I have labeled as "the seed of fanaticism." They are in this "fight or flight" mode.

Now, in many of the modern democracies, people have transcended the willingness to kill others in order to defend their beliefs. I am not saying that it is very likely that you could get the majority of the people in Holland, England, Denmark or even Germany to start a crusade fighting those who are threatening their beliefs, whatever that belief might be. They have transcended it. They have gone out of the fight mode, but they are still in flight mode, in the sense that they attempt to escape or ignore anything that threatens their worldview, their sense that they have a certain understanding of the world.

What you see here is that you have all people in the same mindset, but some are in the flight mode and are seeking to ignore or explain away anything that might disturb their sense of security. Then, there are some people who are still (because they have not evolved enough on a spiritual or mental level) in fight mode, and they are willing to fight those who threaten their beliefs.

Conflict between Europeans and Muslims

You can see in the European nations how, for decades, there was a certain sense of peace and tranquility in many European nations because the people were in a certain state of mind. There was a certain agreement, a collective agreement, on how we look at the world. There may have been some disagreements here and there, but there was a certain agreement and a certain tolerance where everybody could tolerate each other.

This was not real harmony, this was not real resolution. You can see this by a very simple fact. Look at how people have reacted when they had an influx of refugees from Muslim countries. The European nations had a certain conformity, most people were either Lutheran Christians or they were agnostics or they did not speak about religion. When the Muslims come in, who are very devout with their faith, people in Europe, many people, felt threatened by this. This shows you that they are still in flight mode, because as long as they could ignore that there were other religions, they were not disturbed by it. When those religions come knocking on their doorstep, then they become disturbed. They do not necessarily become violent, although a few have done it, but the majority certainly have not become violent. Nevertheless, they would much rather see these Muslims just go back where they came from. You see this in every country. This demonstrates that they are in flight mode. They have not risen to the next level where they have actually transcended the fanatical mindset.

What you see of course in the Middle East, in many of the Muslim nations, is that there is still a majority of the people there who are in fight mode. It is not enough for them to try and run away from those who threaten their religion, they have to do something violent about it. They have to fight them somehow.

It is obvious that people in Europe, who have transcended this state, will look at this and say: "Well, these people are fanatics, we are not." Now, look at the history of Europe. Why have you transcended the fight mode, the willingness to kill others, those who threaten your beliefs? Well, why have you transcended it in Europe? Because you saw the very extreme manifestation of this exemplified by Hitler and the Nazis. If you had not had the example of Hitler and the Nazis in Europe, do you think Europe would have been where it is today? There is absolutely no way that the European nations could have been as peaceful as they have been if they had not had this example from their own backyard, so to speak, where they could not ignore it. What does that mean? Does that mean that you as Europeans can say: "You in the Arab world, you should have learned from what Hitler did and have overcome your fanaticism, your extremism, your willingness to kill?"

Well, yeah, they *could* have. They really could have, because naturally it was not a strictly European phenomenon. It was something that had worldwide ramifications, and certainly could be a learning lesson for people around the world. They *could* have learned from that. But if you look at it realistically, you can see they have not. Given that we have talked to you about the School of Hard Knocks, what do they need to go through? Well, they need to go through their own version somehow of this, whether it is

ISIS or an even worse manifestation that can come up in coming years or even a decade or so. They might need to go through the School of Hard Knocks and see this. It is possible that it could be transcended, but they may need to act out what you in Europe had acted out for you in order to see it and come to the point where they say: "We cannot allow this to happen again. Therefore, we need to change."

Dealing with the uncertainty of the world

Now, let me go to an even broader perspective here. We have before talked about the fact that we are not looking to get all people in the world to accept ascended master teachings. We are looking to get people to accept certain ideas. We are not looking for you who are ascended master students to go out there and convert everybody to believe in ascended master teachings. We are looking for you to help project into the collective consciousness certain ideas that can shift the collective consciousness so people can see what they are ready for, what they are ready to see at the three higher levels, the identity, mental and emotional level, but it has not broken through to the physical. That is where your calls can have, as we have said many times, a tremendous impact where you can help trigger a shift so that suddenly there is that almost a wave that goes through the collective consciousness, and suddenly everybody turns in the same direction and they say: "Oh yes, this is obvious. Why didn't we see it before?"

Speaking from a completely neutral, universal perspective here, we can simply look at this psychology that I have mentioned, the psychological mechanism. Why is it that people need to feel that they have certain beliefs, a certain understanding of the world, that is absolutely infallible, and therefore could not be improved upon? It could not be wrong. Why do people need to feel this?

Well, in most universal terms, we can say that if you look at the world, you can see that the world is an uncertain place. None of you know what could happen. You could be struck by lightning. You could be hit by a bicycle (if you live in Amsterdam and walk down the street) and many other things can happen. You see that life on earth (and you do not even need to talk about earth being an unnatural planet and fallen beings, the dark forces and all this), you can just simply observe that life on earth presents people with a certain uncertainty. There is a certain uncertainty in life. You cannot predict everything. You cannot know what is going to happen.

You cannot control everything. People cannot know what could happen, but they have a certain sense that bad things *could* happen.

Dealing with uncertainty is a major need

What has not really been recognized by the science of psychology, but which could very quickly be recognized, is that this is one of the major needs that people have. Now, you take the American psychologist, Maslow, he set up a pyramid of needs. You have the physiological needs, the safety and security needs, love and belonging needs, you have esteem needs, and then on the top, you have self-actualization needs.

Maslow divided these into two categories, the lowest four he called the *deficit* needs, and the top of the pyramid, the self-actualization needs, were *being* needs, as he called it. You have here a model that says that the lower needs in the pyramid are needs that people are not aware of if they are met. When they are not met, they become very, very dominant in people's minds. The physiological needs, well, you have a need to eat. Try not to eat for several hours and see how all of your higher needs that you might have (of what kind of career and what to talk to your friends about), see how all of these higher needs gradually fade away and your stomach takes up a prominent position in your consciousness. This simply demonstrates what Maslow said: When these lower needs are not met, they take up a very prominent position in people's minds, and it becomes very, very urgent that they are fulfilled.

One of these physiological needs is obviously the need to survive. We can go a little bit further than Maslow did and say that the need to survive physically, to be protected against sudden and violent death, also ties in with the safety needs. Therefore, we see that, yes, people have certain purely physical needs. When your body is hungry, or when it needs to sleep, those needs need to be fulfilled. Really, what is driving human beings primarily is not the *physiological* needs, it is the *psychological* needs.

You have a very strong psychological need to have some sense of security about the future. You need to have some sense that you are not going to be killed at any moment. Now, if you go back several hundred years, just two or three hundred years here on the European continent, you will see that these were much more violent times than you can even imagine today. As many as two thirds of all male adults had knife wounds, those who survived. Many have died from being in various kinds of fights or conflicts, not necessarily wars but certainly including wars. The likelihood of surviving to old age was much lower back then because you were more likely to incur a violent death or being wounded. This gave a sense of insecurity that you can barely imagine today in these affluent European countries that have a much more peaceful state than was there two or three hundred years ago in the same countries.

If you go back to that time (or even further back when it was an even more violent time), you will see that people had a very, very deep psychological need to feel some kind of security about the future. It is difficult for you to imagine, those of you who have not experienced it (but some of you of course have experienced it) that if you are facing death, or you fear that you could be facing death any moment, it is very, very difficult to engage in life. It is very, very difficult to do many of the things you call normal daily activities, if you are afraid that you could die tomorrow.

If you go back to that time (where people had reason to be afraid that they could die tomorrow or be physically attacked), then you will see that the overriding psychological need that people had back then was the need to have some sense of security about the future, some sense of how they could avoid a violent and sudden death. If they did not have this, they could not function psychologically in their daily lives, they could not do many of the things you call normal daily activities.

You can see today that people who have depression or various kinds of mental disturbances or illnesses, they become unable to take care of these ordinary few daily tasks because there is a certain insecurity in their beings. It can be caused by different things, I grant you, but nevertheless, my point is: Insecurity about the future makes it very difficult to function in your daily life.

The most basic human need relates to the future

What did people have to do back then? They faced a situation that most of you who have grown up in the more modern countries have not had to face. You have not had to physically protect yourself because you have gradually achieved a society where society does that for you. Society makes sure that you are not likely to be attacked, you are not likely to have somebody invade your home, or have somebody come up to you on the street and stick a knife into you, and those kinds of things. Back then, when that was a possibility, a real possibility, people had to do something.

Therefore, we can say that Maslow's needs are of course very valid. But if you step back from Maslow's pyramid, you see that there is actually one underlying human need, that we could argue is the most fundamental, the deepest human need. The reason why it is the deepest human need is that if you look at animals, you will know that an animal is not concerned about the future. It does not have the ability to think in time the way human beings can do. A cow is not going to be angry with another cow because it kicked it three weeks ago. You do know they are not going to have those kinds of arguments in the cow stable, where the cows are blaming each other for what they did in the past. They just move on, they just chew the cud and move on. Arguably an advantage of being a cow, but nevertheless, does not help you much since you are stuck in a human body.

How do you then get out of this in a human body? Well, you have to recognize that as a human being, you have the ability to operate with past, present and future. You remember what happened in the past, and you have a tendency to use what happened in the past to project what might happen in the future. It is this very ability that gives you the "ability" to worry about the future, to fear for the future.

This is one of the most basic differences between animals and humans. This means that the deepest, the most basic, human need is to have that sense of security about the future, *some* sense of security about the future. How do you then produce this security about the future? Look at history. You can look at so many of the ideas, ideologies, beliefs, political philosophies and religious philosophies that have appeared in history. They have all had this one underlying purpose of giving people some sense of security about the future. They have the future somewhat under their control because they feel that they can predict what might happen.

How the Catholic church met the basic need

You look at medieval Catholicism. What was the reason that this became accepted by so many people? Why do so many people accept the Catholic church? Why did they stay in the Catholic church? Why did they not rebel against it? Well, yes, you can point to all kinds of outer reasons that the church suppressed all other forms of knowledge, that the people were heavily suppressed by the kings, the noble class and the priesthood. You can point to all of these physiological, physical, material, historical reasons, but underlying it all is the psychological mechanism that the Catholic church, for several centuries, actually fulfilled the most basic human need. The Catholic church gave people a sense of security about the future, not about what would happen here on earth, because the Catholic church basically said that life on earth is beyond repair. But if you believe in the church and follow our rituals, then your life on earth, which you know is just a short time, it is not really what matters. Because if you follow us, we will guarantee you that you will go to heaven and have a wonderful life in heaven for all eternity. The price of submitting to the church hierarchy and the church doctrines for a short, few decades here on earth seemed reasonable compared to an eternity in some wonderful heaven where you did not have the insecurity you have on earth.

Do you see there was a reason why the Catholic church had so many followers? Because it offered people some sense of security. What did Marxism do? It also offered people a sense of security that historical necessity shows that all countries will become communist. Therefore, those who are already in a communist country, they know they have history on their side. They know, therefore, that their society will move towards the communist utopia. It may not be there now. There may not be bread in the stores, and we may have to stand in line for several hours to get basic necessities, but we are on the way towards it.

You see how what you had in previous ages was that you still had these very insecure conditions in the world and you had institutions in society that could not necessarily do something about those conditions, but they could at least promise you a better future that was not so far away. Now, to some degree, the Catholic church also promised people some sense of security in their daily lives. Because people believed that they could pray to a saint or to Mother Mary, and then, as the wish-fulfilling God, they would appear and give them what they wanted or protect them from evil. Then, this could also give them a sense of security that allowed them to function. It was a fragile sense of security, and for many people, it was shattered when violent events happened to them, but there was some sense of it.

Same thing in communist countries, everybody was almost in the same boat and were equally poor and that gave people some sense of security. They could not lose what they had. They could not lose their job. It was a lousy job and the pay was lousy. As the old joke goes: "We pretend to work, and they pretend to pay us." Nevertheless, you could not do worse than this. You knew the minimum of what you had and it gave people that sense of security.

Security in modern democracies

What you see in the modern democracies is that you have now shifted the equation somewhat. Because you now have countries where there is a certain physical safety. For most people, yes, you can become ill, yes, you could have an accident. But you are not likely to be exposed to some violent event and therefore, you can pretty much predict that, yes, you can go to school and get an education. Then, you can get a job. You can buy yourself a house. You can spend the next 30 years paying off your mortgage on the house, and working in the same job, or you could even grow and attain a promotion. But you can pretty much plot your life, the rest of your life. You can have a certain reasonable sense of confidence that your life will go the way you planned. This gives people that sense of security where they feel they have their lives under control.

We might say that the basic dynamic of life for a human being on a planet like earth is that there is a certain uncertainty in life, but that people have a need to explain how life works in order to give them a sense of certainty, a sense of security, a sense of being able to predict the future. In being able to predict the future, you have a sense of being in control of the future. This is the basic psychological mechanism. It is still there in the modern democracies today. The same psychological mechanism is there. It is not quite as urgent anymore.

You see how, if you go back several centuries to when times were more violent, people knew that it was very difficult to get security about their physical situation in this world, in the physical world. Therefore, they were more open to those who promised them some utopia in the future. Now, you have societies where people do not have that sense of fear about the physical world, they feel more secure in the physical world. That is why you see that many people in the modern democracies are not so attached to religion anymore. They are not concerned about religion. They do not go to church. It does not offer them anything because they feel they have the security in their daily lives and in the physical world.

Then, look how fragile that sense is. Look how many people, if they are exposed to an accident, if they fall ill, their faith, their sense of security is shattered. Now, they go through various kinds of crises of explaining this because they have not gone beyond that basic sense of security. Why have people not gone beyond it? Well, it is explained by Maslow. The lower needs, once people feel they are satisfied to a sufficient degree, people forget about them. You see what has happened in the modern democracies, people still have a need to feel they have the world under control. Because of the very stable, peaceful, outer circumstances that they have, they feel that this need has been fulfilled to a critical degree and therefore they forget about it.

They do not think about religion, or they do not think about death, or they do not think about what could happen. They do not have a need to think more deeply about the deeper questions of life. That is why so many people, when they then face a life-threatening illness, or when they become old and death is approaching, they cannot deal with these questions, the fundamental questions. They do not know how to deal with them. This plunges them into a crisis of some sort, even an identity crisis, or certainly a mental and emotional one. This is really what has happened in many of the affluent nations.

The natural progression of history

You also see of course that there is a growing tendency that challenges this. Because you see, in all of the modern democracies, all of the affluent societies, a growing number of people who go into depression or mental illness. You see a growing awareness that mental illness is becoming a greater and greater problem for these modern democracies. These affluent nations that have, now for decades, had material welfare but they have not made a transition, which is natural, if you look at the progression of history and see how societies have progressed.

There was, if you go back to what I have just said here, a time where the danger of physical harm was very prominent. You have created societies where that danger of physical harm disappeared, then poverty became a big issue. As long as you are fearing that you could be killed tomorrow by the Huns invading from the East, you are not so concerned about being poor. You are more concerned about being alive. Once you do not fear for your safety, you become concerned about the poor and now you want material security, material welfare.

That is what the modern democracies have provided over the last several decades. For a couple of generations, maybe 100 years or more, they have been focused on providing this physical, material welfare. If the materialists' claim that there is nothing beyond the material universe was true, then all people in these rich affluent nations should have become deliriously happy because they have all the material welfare they could want. The materialist paradigm basically says that human beings, the consciousness of human beings, is a product of the physical bodies. If the physical body has all of its needs met, people should be happy. That is the consequence of the materialist paradigm.

Now, since anyone can observe that this is not happening, then you have to question the materialist paradigm. You can see that the very fact that there is a rise in mental illness means that society has an explanation problem. There is something here you cannot explain. This goes back to what I said is the seed of fanaticism.

Anybody who is willing to observe society and see the rise in mental illness can see how even children down to an early age are suicidal or have various kinds of problems. If we are responsible, modern societies, we have to look at this phenomenon and say: We have not fulfilled our responsibility to our citizens. Because even though we have provided them material welfare, we can now see that this is not enough. It is not enough for people to be happy and function well in society. Therefore, we must begin to ask ourselves, why is it not enough? What have we been missing in our approach so far? What is the next logical step in the evolution of society?

The next logical step of course is that you focus on psychological well-being, what makes people happy. It is not the physical conditions that automatically makes people happy. What is it? That is where you then start to look at this.

From security to fanaticism

You can now say that, well, many of the modern democracies achieved a very high state of affluence back in the 1960s. That was also when you had the youth rebellion, the student rebellion, the whole hippie movement of people looking for an alternative lifestyle. That was really the start of what you might call the New Age phenomenon. In a sense, you could say that in the 1960s, the modern democracies had the opportunity to transition from focusing on material welfare to starting to use their material affluence to focus on spiritual well-being.

Why did not societies do that? Well, they did not do it for one particular reason and it can be explained by one word: fanaticism. Not the fanaticism that you see in Hitler, or ISIS, but the more widespread fanaticism that I started out talking about where people have a belief that they think could not be expanded. Therefore, they resist expanding their understanding of life. They do not want to expand their understanding of life. They do not want to know more than they know because it will threaten their sense of security, their sense of equilibrium.

What people had achieved back in the 1960s was that, from a material viewpoint, both in terms of material security and material affluence, they had achieved what was sufficient for many people. They achieved the sense that they felt secure about the future. This gave them that sense of equilibrium where they felt that they could exist in the world, they could look at the rest of their life with some sense of confidence. This was based on them accepting a certain view of life and their very sense of equilibrium is tied to their view of life.

That is why they do not want to question that view of life. They do not want to see those who question it. That is why you saw so many people in the 1960s who reacted with such negativity and closed-mindedness to their own children who questioned their materialist lifestyle and explored other possibilities. You saw how, incredibly, you cannot really say violent in a physical way, but certainly violent in an emotional, mental way, the reaction was. Think back to four musicians in England, called the Beatles, who were considered extremely provocative. Why? Because their hair was two or three centimeters longer than what was the norm at the time.

Look at society today. Would society get upset because somebody had a little bit longer hair? No, but back in the 1960s, people were completely disturbed by some people wearing a little bit longer hair than what was considered normal. This shows you just how fragile their sense of equilibrium was.

My beloved, there is a certain mindset here that is the seed of fanaticism. The question is, what does it take to go from that sort of passive state of equilibrium towards what you would normally call a fanatical state of mind, the more extreme aspects of fanaticism? In other words, you have the more passive aspect of fanaticism, you have the more active or aggressive states of fanaticism, what does it take to move from one to the other? It is a gradual scale and it is simply a matter of how fragile is your sense of equilibrium. How easily could it be threatened by something that upset the applecart? The more fragile your sense of equilibrium is, the more likely you are to move towards the more extreme manifestations of fanaticism.

I am not here trying to defend the Beatles but by the very fact that the reaction you saw to something as relatively insignificant as somebody letting their hair grow longer, you see how fragile people's sense of equilibrium was back in the 1960s. Of course, it has something to do with the fact that the Second World War was not so far away, many people were still alive who had experienced the war. They knew that something could happen, there could be another war. Therefore, in order to hold on to their ability to function, their sense of equilibrium, they became very, very attached to their worldview, and they did not want to see anything that threatened it. That is why the modern democracies did not make that transition from the focus on material welfare to psychological well-being.

The older generation that resists change

This is why you have the influx of Muslim immigrants in these modern democracies. Because they were not willing to question their sense of equilibrium on their own, they enrolled themselves in the School of Hard Knocks. Now comes somebody whom they see as being in a fanatical state of mind but what are the Muslims really here to do? They are here to challenge the fanaticism of the Europeans who do not want to question their basic outlook on life. They do not want to question this materialist view of life that it is enough to take care of people's material needs, and then, they should automatically be happy.

You have so many people today in society who have led the good material life all of their adult lives. They are now towards the end of their lives, they are beginning to retire or they have retired. They have, so to speak, sold their soul on the corporate altar. They have played the good game. They have worked their jobs, paid their houses, bought their cars. They are now retired, or they are close to retirement, and they feel that because they worked all of their lives and saved their money, and this and that, they are entitled to live their retirement years the way they plan to live them, and nothing should upset the applecart.

You have really a generational gap here where you have many, many young people who are open to changes in society, who are open to the need to focus more on psychological well-being because they are experiencing various psychological issues. Then, you have the older people who may also have psychological issues, but who are denying them or pushing them away if at all possible. They do not want society to change because they want to live out their lives with the sense of equilibrium that they have had all of their lives. You really have this very, very deep fundamental tension in the western democracies and you see it coming out in many ways.

You see it in the extreme reaction to Muslims where people feel so threatened by this. You see how there are countries where they do not want anybody who is different to come in. You have these movements that are the extreme right-wing movements that want to shut out immigrants. They want to shut out foreigners. They do not want people from Eastern Europe to come and work in these countries because they are different. They think in a different way.

It really goes back to this whole attempt to avoid having your equilibrium threatened by removing diversity. Where does that come from, my beloved? Well, you know that it comes from the fallen beings. Of course, you cannot make most people accept that. What you *can* make most people accept is that the very unwillingness to have people who are different come into your society and point out that you have a need to change, the very unwillingness to do this, is exactly what you saw outpictured in the Nazi regime and their attempt to kill the Jews.

From material welfare to well-being

You see here that it is possible for people to shift very quickly and realize some of these things I have talked about: the need to shift from material welfare to psychological well-being. Many, many young people have already made this shift in their own minds. Of course, they are not the ones who have influence in society yet because they are not old enough. They have not risen to positions in politics, the media, science or elsewhere. They have the psychological issues. Why do they have the psychological issues? Well, here is something that will be a little more difficult for people to accept, but at least it is something that some people, and a growing number of people, are open to. It is a matter of saying: "What kind of beings are human beings?" As I have said here, if you look at what is happening (just look at the fact that material affluence does not automatically produce happiness), you can draw the conclusion.

Human beings are *psychological* beings. Everything that really happens in your lives, everything you do, it revolves around something in your psyche. That is why you do what you do. Why did Hitler do what he did? It revolved around something in his psychology. Why do you do what you do? Again, why does everybody do what they do? It revolves around their psychology. Now, once you start taking an honest look at people's psychology, you see that society has an explanation problem again. What can explain the incredible complexity? Now, most people (especially the older generation who have lived the materialistic lifestyle) they have no experience of looking into their own psychology. As more and more people begin to actually do this, you realize how complex human beings are, how many layers there are to the human psyche. You really have to ask yourself: "How is that possible?" You can, if you are willing, and scientists could very easily do this, look at people. You can take a certain person, look at the psychological issues that person has that his psychologists know about. You can go back to look at the person's childhood and say: "Can we explain this person's very complex psychology by what he has experienced in this lifetime in terms of his environment, his parents, his family background? Can we explain the complexity of the psyche based on this?" Then, a neutral scientific observation would say: "No, we can't. We cannot explain why people are so complex."

You will all know this, you who have worked on your psychology, you will know how complex it is. You will know that you can look back at your own childhoods and see there was not such a big trauma. At least for many of you, there was not such a big trauma in your childhood that it explains some of these deep things you have coming up, that we have seen come up in your psyche. So what does explain it? Well, that people have lived before, that reincarnation is a reality.

Reincarnation explains psychological problems

You can go back in history, you can see how the Catholic church deliberately took reincarnation out of Christianity, took out all mention of reincarnation. It was done for clearly political reasons that have no relevance whatsoever to today's world. You can begin to use science to study this phenomenon and say: "Is there something here?" If this was done in a neutral, objective manner, it would not be that impossible, or that far into the future, that many psychologists could make the shift and say: "Well, whether we believe in reincarnation or not, we need to accept here that people's psychology is very complex, and we can't help people by only considering their present lifetime. Even if we don't accept that reincarnation is real, we still have to accept that by doing regression therapy, for example, we can actually help people resolve some of these deep traumas in their psyches. And if it works for the patients, why shouldn't we use it?" This could then bring this shift that could gradually pave the way for an understanding of why you have so many young people in these affluent nations that have psychological issues.

You can take two approaches here. You can say that, well, if you go back several decades, people considered it very traumatic to go to a psychologist. Many of the people that I talk about, who have lived their materialistic lifestyle and are retiring now, would never consider going to a psychologist because of the attitude that was there. You had to be very, very extreme, very, very crazy to go to a psychologist. You have people who are denying the value of it but you cannot deny that in the younger generation, even children, you have many more people who not only have psychological issues, but who are willing to do something about them.

On the one hand, you could say there *were* psychological issues two generations ago, but people just did not recognize it, they did not acknowledge it and they did not seek help for it. In a sense, you could ask yourself: "Were there more psychological issues back then than there is today?" Maybe there were quite a few that were just not recognized.

Nevertheless, most psychologists would recognize (those who have been in their jobs for just two or three decades) and would say: "There has been an increase in the number of psychological issues, at least what people seek help for." When you ask yourself this, you can say: "But why is it then that these nations who have taken care of the material welfare, why are these nations seeing this increase in psychological problems?" Again, you can take one explanation and say: "Well, it's all explained by Maslow."

Maslow set up a pyramid of needs and he said that you first have to fulfill the lower needs to a critical degree. Once a lower need is fulfilled, you can move on and focus on the higher needs. You have the physiological, the safety and security needs, the love and belonging needs and the esteem needs. Once people have fulfilled them to a critical degree, as you have seen in the affluent nations, it is natural for them to focus on the higher needs, the being needs, the self-actualization needs.

You could say that people acknowledging that they have psychological issues, and people being willing to seek help to do something about them, it is just a natural progression of the fact that their lower needs have been met, and now they are focused on these higher needs. Of course, this will not explain everything. Because if you look at it just statistically, you should say that this still does not explain why there are an increasing number of younger people and even children who are displaying these psychological issues. In order to really explain this and be able to help people with it, you need to incorporate reincarnation.

You can take a very broad view and you can say: "Well, when you understand reincarnation, you understand that you get a different perspective on Maslow's pyramid of needs." Instead of just looking at one lifetime, you could say that there are people who are at different levels of Maslow's pyramid. You can see that there are people in the world who are still focused primarily on their physiological needs, they are focused around the physical body and its needs. Then, there are people for whom the main focus of their lives is safety and security needs. Many of these people are what you see in the extreme Muslims who are willing to kill others to maintain their sense of security that they have the only true religion. Then, you can see other people who are focused on the love and belonging needs. You can see other people who are focused on esteem needs and being recognized by society and other people. Even what you see on Facebook where you see people feel that they have satisfied their esteem needs if they have a certain amount of friends, or if they have so many followers on Instagram, or so many viewers on YouTube, and this and that. These are actually people who are using this social media to fulfill these needs that they have. If this can help them come to the point where they have fulfilled that need to a critical degree and can move on, then it is not necessarily an un-spiritual process.

What you can say here is that among humankind, you will find a certain group of people who have worked through the deficit needs, who have gotten all of the love and belonging, all of the esteem, all of the security that they needed as souls. They have worked through these in past lifetimes. In the lifetime that they are now in, they are ready to focus on their self-actualization needs, their higher needs, their being needs. They are ready to focus on actualizing themselves. If you were such a soul that were ready to focus on your self-actualization needs, in which type of country would you want to embody? Well, you would not really embody in a poor country in Africa, would you? Because you would be forced to focus on your physiological survival. Neither would you embody in the Middle East because you would be so focused on safety, security, or love and belonging needs that you could not focus on self-actualization. The only place you can really embody, if you have reached a certain level of soul maturity, is the affluent democracies.

The increase in depression

In the affluent democracies, there is the possibility that you can take care of your material needs in a fairly basic manner, and therefore have time left over to focus on self-esteem needs. The problem is of course that these affluent democracies have not moved on from the 1960s to where they have shifted the paradigm to focus on psychological well-being.

Here you have all of these souls who are embodying in these nations, thinking that this is where they can work on their self-actualization needs, but they receive absolutely no help from society. They receive no understanding of psychology, no awareness that there is a certain possibility of expanding your psychology, raising your consciousness, healing your psychological wounds. They become very, very dissatisfied. They feel they have no sense of purpose in life because they cannot find purpose in living a materialistic lifestyle. That is not why they are in embodiment, but society does not offer them anything, so they go into depression.

If society had a different paradigm where people had help, and had the concept that they could grow (they could expand their awareness, they could raise their consciousness) these people would not be seeking help from psychologists. They would be dealing with their self-actualization needs on their own because that is the only way to fulfill your self-actualization needs. You see that there is a shift here where society could shift and recognize that we are not meeting these peoples needs, and we need a different paradigm in order to do it.

Now, you could of course also take a more narrow view and say: Well, if we recognize reincarnation, and if we then dare to look at the history of Europe, what can we see? We can see that the people who are embodying today who are now young people, or in their 20s or 30s, could very well have been alive during the Second World War. They might very well have been soldiers who were killed. They might very well have been civilians who had their houses bombed. They might very well have been in various very, very unpleasant situations that gave them deep psychological trauma.

You can say that, if we are responsible here in Europe and look at our past, we need to have a way where we can help people overcome the traumas that they might have received in their past lives here in Europe. It is simply natural that we fulfill this need, given our history. If we are to continue to grow and raise our awareness and overcome the past, how could this be done unless people heal their wounds so they can let go of the past?

You have the concept in the Bible that the sins of the fathers are visited upon the third and fourth generation. This can really only be understood through reincarnation where you see that the generation of the fathers may have done something that caused the children to have severe psychological trauma that they carry with them for several generations. There could very easily be (not necessarily tomorrow, but certainly in the foreseeable future) a shift where people began to look at this. Even if they do not accept reincarnation, they can say: "Well, can the concept that people have lived before and could have received traumas in a past life, can that help us help people resolve these traumas so they can actually be free of them? The psychologist may not believe in past lives, but if the patient believes in it, and is helped by regression to a past life, then is not that still very much what we should be doing in order to pursue psychological well-being?"

My beloved, as I realize, the dinner bell is ringing. I will limit my remarks for today and therefore leave something for the other masters to talk about tonight and in the days to come. With this, my beloved, I am very grateful for your attention. I know this is the first day. I know some of you were looking for a soft start. You probably did not quite get that. Nevertheless, I am very grateful to have had this platform for you to direct this into the collective consciousness in the many countries from which you have come to this conference.

My beloved, there is a shaft, a pillar of light coming down from me and the ascended realm through you here and radiating out in all the directions from which you have come. For this, I am very grateful. I am grateful for those who will, in coming years, use these tools and these invocations and these dictations to again direct that energy that can shift the collective consciousness so that people suddenly wake up and say: "Oh, this is obvious." It is obvious to *you,* and by the very fact that it became obvious to you, you can see how it can become obvious to others as well.

2 | INVOKING THE MOVEMENT BEYOND FANATICISM (PART 1)

In the name of the I AM THAT I AM, Jesus Christ, I use the authority that I have as a being in embodiment on earth to call upon Mother Mary to reinforce my calls and use my chakras to project the statements in this invocation into the collective consciousness and awaken people to the fact that the modern democracies need to overcome all remnants of the fanatical mindset. Awaken people to the reality that we are spiritual beings and that we can co-create a new future by working with the ascended masters. I especially call for …

[Make your own calls here.]

Part 1

1. Mother Mary, shatter the energetic matrix that prevents people from seeing that the concept of fanaticism is something that all people are aware of, but that hardly anyone understands. Even psychologists find it difficult to define fanaticism.

O blessed Mary, Mother mine,
there is no greater love than thine,
as we are one in heart and mind,
my place in hierarchy I find.

O Mother Mary, generate,
the song that does accelerate,
the earth into a higher state,
all matter does now scintillate.

2. Mother Mary, shatter the energetic matrix that prevents people from seeing that there is a tendency, in both psychology and society, to look at the extreme manifestations of fanaticism.

I came to earth from heaven sent,
as I am in embodiment,
I use Divine authority,
commanding you to set earth free.

O Mother Mary, generate,
the song that does accelerate,
the earth into a higher state,
all matter does now scintillate.

3. Mother Mary, shatter the energetic matrix that prevents people from seeing that the problem with this approach is that it actually reinforces fanaticism in a subtle way that few people are aware of.

I call now in God's sacred name,
for you to use your Mother Flame,
to burn all fear-based energy,
restoring sacred harmony.

O Mother Mary, generate,
the song that does accelerate,
the earth into a higher state,
all matter does now scintillate.

4. Mother Mary, shatter the energetic matrix that prevents people from seeing that psychologists tend to think that fanatics are in an extreme state of mind, whereas those who are not as extreme are not fanatics.

> Your sacred name I hereby praise,
> collective consciousness you raise,
> no more of fear and doubt and shame,
> consume it with your Mother Flame.

> **O Mother Mary, generate,**
> **the song that does accelerate,**
> **the earth into a higher state,**
> **all matter does now scintillate.**

5. Mother Mary, shatter the energetic matrix that prevents people from seeing that this creates a division of humankind into two groups, the normal people and the fanatics.

> All darkness from the earth you purge,
> your light moves as a mighty surge,
> no force of darkness can now stop,
> the spiral that goes only up.

> **O Mother Mary, generate,**
> **the song that does accelerate,**
> **the earth into a higher state,**
> **all matter does now scintillate.**

6. Mother Mary, shatter the energetic matrix that prevents people from seeing that this causes those who think they are normal to point the finger at others. And this is exactly the same dynamic as in Hitler's Germany.

> All elemental life you bless,
> removing from them man-made stress,
> the nature spirits are now free,
> outpicturing Divine decree.

> **O Mother Mary, generate,**
> **the song that does accelerate,**

the earth into a higher state,
all matter does now scintillate.

7. Mother Mary, shatter the energetic matrix that prevents people from seeing that the mindset behind this is that there is a problem in the world, but the problem is not with us, the problem is with those other people. In order to solve the problem, we need to change those other people.

I raise my voice and take my stand,
a stop to war I do command,
no more shall warring scar the earth,
a golden age is given birth.

O Mother Mary, generate,
the song that does accelerate,
the earth into a higher state,
all matter does now scintillate.

8. Mother Mary, shatter the energetic matrix that prevents people from seeing that fanaticism does not start in the extreme. It starts in what many people call "normal" and then it gradually becomes extreme.

As Mother Earth is free at last,
disasters belong to the past,
your Mother Light is so intense,
that matter is now far less dense.

O Mother Mary, generate,
the song that does accelerate,
the earth into a higher state,
all matter does now scintillate.

9. Mother Mary, shatter the energetic matrix that prevents people from seeing that there was a certain psychological mechanism in the German people, which Hitler developed into fanaticism. Yet many other nations in Europe and around the world had a similar mechanism in a majority of the population.

In Mother Light the earth is pure,
the upward spiral will endure,
prosperity is now the norm,
God's vision manifest as form.

**O Mother Mary, generate,
the song that does accelerate,
the earth into a higher state,
all matter does now scintillate.**

Part 2

1. Mother Mary, shatter the energetic matrix that prevents people from seeing that the problem is that we are not taking responsibility for the problem and saying: "How can we change ourselves to solve the problem?" We identify that the problem is out there with other people and they are the ones who have to change.

O blessed Mary, Mother mine,
there is no greater love than thine,
as we are one in heart and mind,
my place in hierarchy I find.

**O Mother Mary, generate,
the song that does accelerate,
the earth into a higher state,
all matter does now scintillate.**

2. Mother Mary, shatter the energetic matrix that prevents people from seeing how many examples there are of people that were "normal," but who became willing to kill other people when certain circumstances manifested.

I came to earth from heaven sent,
as I am in embodiment,
I use Divine authority,
commanding you to set earth free.

O Mother Mary, generate,
the song that does accelerate,
the earth into a higher state,
all matter does now scintillate.

3. Mother Mary, shatter the energetic matrix that prevents people from seeing that some people want to define fanaticism by saying that when you are willing to kill other human beings, you are in a fanatical state of mind. If you are not willing to kill, then you are not a fanatic.

I call now in God's sacred name,
for you to use your Mother Flame,
to burn all fear-based energy,
restoring sacred harmony.

O Mother Mary, generate,
the song that does accelerate,
the earth into a higher state,
all matter does now scintillate.

4. Mother Mary, shatter the energetic matrix that prevents people from seeing that this is too simplistic of a definition. It is not a definition that will allow us to remove fanaticism from the earth.

Your sacred name I hereby praise,
collective consciousness you raise,
no more of fear and doubt and shame,
consume it with your Mother Flame.

O Mother Mary, generate,
the song that does accelerate,
the earth into a higher state,
all matter does now scintillate.

5. Mother Mary, shatter the energetic matrix that prevents people from seeing that the essence of fanaticism is that we point the finger at somebody else and say: "They are the problem. They are the ones who have to change." We can never remove fanaticism if we are in that same state of mind.

All darkness from the earth you purge,
your light moves as a mighty surge,
no force of darkness can now stop,
the spiral that goes only up.

O Mother Mary, generate,
the song that does accelerate,
the earth into a higher state,
all matter does now scintillate.

6. Mother Mary, shatter the energetic matrix that prevents people from seeing that if we isolate certain people, label them as fanatics, point the finger and say: "They are the ones who are the problem. They are the ones who have to change," we will not remove fanaticism, we will *reinforce* fanaticism.

All elemental life you bless,
removing from them man-made stress,
the nature spirits are now free,
outpicturing Divine decree.

O Mother Mary, generate,
the song that does accelerate,
the earth into a higher state,
all matter does now scintillate.

7. Mother Mary, shatter the energetic matrix that prevents people from seeing that some people think they are so open and tolerant that what they are doing is the opposite of fanaticism. When they look at the people who are extremists and label them as fanatics, they are reinforcing the consciousness of fanaticism.

I raise my voice and take my stand,
a stop to war I do command,
no more shall warring scar the earth,
a golden age is given birth.

O Mother Mary, generate,
the song that does accelerate,

**the earth into a higher state,
all matter does now scintillate.**

8. Mother Mary, shatter the energetic matrix that prevents people from seeing that one definition of fanaticism is that it is a state of mind. It is not a state of mind that is exclusive to some people or even a few people. It is a state of mind that is present in all populations around the world.

As Mother Earth is free at last,
disasters belong to the past,
your Mother Light is so intense,
that matter is now far less dense.

**O Mother Mary, generate,
the song that does accelerate,
the earth into a higher state,
all matter does now scintillate.**

9. Mother Mary, shatter the energetic matrix that prevents people from seeing that even in the modern democracies (that often see themselves as having risen above fanaticism) we find the state of mind that is the cradle of fanaticism.

In Mother Light the earth is pure,
the upward spiral will endure,
prosperity is now the norm,
God's vision manifest as form.

**O Mother Mary, generate,
the song that does accelerate,
the earth into a higher state,
all matter does now scintillate.**

Part 3

1. Mother Mary, shatter the energetic matrix that prevents people from seeing that the majority of the population have this psychological mechanism

where we think we know something. We think we have an opinion, a belief, and we think that *it could never be replaced by a higher understanding*.

> O blessed Mary, Mother mine,
> there is no greater love than thine,
> as we are one in heart and mind,
> my place in hierarchy I find.

> **O Mother Mary, generate,**
> **the song that does accelerate,**
> **the earth into a higher state,**
> **all matter does now scintillate.**

2. Mother Mary, shatter the energetic matrix that prevents people from seeing this in a religious setting where people believe they have received some Divine revelation from a superior God, and it could never be improved upon or expanded.

> I came to earth from heaven sent,
> as I am in embodiment,
> I use Divine authority,
> commanding you to set earth free.

> **O Mother Mary, generate,**
> **the song that does accelerate,**
> **the earth into a higher state,**
> **all matter does now scintillate.**

3. Mother Mary, shatter the energetic matrix that prevents people from seeing this in a political setting, for example in the belief that Karl Marx stated, not just an opinion but an infallible historical mechanism that brings society forward. It could never be changed because it is an absolute, infallible truth.

> I call now in God's sacred name,
> for you to use your Mother Flame,
> to burn all fear-based energy,
> restoring sacred harmony.

O Mother Mary, generate,
the song that does accelerate,
the earth into a higher state,
all matter does now scintillate.

4. Mother Mary, shatter the energetic matrix that prevents people from seeing that people who wanted to disprove religion created scientific Materialism, which they now claim is another infallible belief system.

Your sacred name I hereby praise,
collective consciousness you raise,
no more of fear and doubt and shame,
consume it with your Mother Flame.

O Mother Mary, generate,
the song that does accelerate,
the earth into a higher state,
all matter does now scintillate.

5. Mother Mary, shatter the energetic matrix that prevents people from seeing that scientific materialists look down upon religious people and think religious people are fanatics, but: "We, materialists, we are the ones who know the truth." They do not see that they are in the exact same state of mind as the religious people they so despise.

All darkness from the earth you purge,
your light moves as a mighty surge,
no force of darkness can now stop,
the spiral that goes only up.

O Mother Mary, generate,
the song that does accelerate,
the earth into a higher state,
all matter does now scintillate.

6. Mother Mary, shatter the energetic matrix that prevents people from seeing that materialists also believe they have an absolute truth that could never be expanded upon. They think it could never be replaced by a higher understanding because it is an absolute fact proven by science that there

is nothing beyond the material universe, and this could never be proven wrong.

> All elemental life you bless,
> removing from them man-made stress,
> the nature spirits are now free,
> outpicturing Divine decree.
>
> **O Mother Mary, generate,**
> **the song that does accelerate,**
> **the earth into a higher state,**
> **all matter does now scintillate.**

7. Mother Mary, shatter the energetic matrix that prevents people from seeing that something can never be proven wrong when we are not looking. If we are not looking beyond the material universe, how will we ever prove that there is something beyond the material universe?

> I raise my voice and take my stand,
> a stop to war I do command,
> no more shall warring scar the earth,
> a golden age is given birth.
>
> **O Mother Mary, generate,**
> **the song that does accelerate,**
> **the earth into a higher state,**
> **all matter does now scintillate.**

8. Mother Mary, shatter the energetic matrix that prevents people from seeing that scientific materialists are not looking. They are trying to do everything they can to prevent the real scientists from looking. They do not want anyone to see that they are wrong.

> As Mother Earth is free at last,
> disasters belong to the past,
> your Mother Light is so intense,
> that matter is now far less dense.

**O Mother Mary, generate,
the song that does accelerate,
the earth into a higher state,
all matter does now scintillate.**

9. Mother Mary, shatter the energetic matrix that prevents people from seeing that this is the exact same mindset of medieval Catholics who did not want Galileo, Kepler or other astronomers to prove that the Catholic doctrine was wrong.

In Mother Light the earth is pure,
the upward spiral will endure,
prosperity is now the norm,
God's vision manifest as form.

**O Mother Mary, generate,
the song that does accelerate,
the earth into a higher state,
all matter does now scintillate.**

Part 4

1. Mother Mary, shatter the energetic matrix that prevents people from seeing that fanaticism blinds us. When we think we have an absolute infallible truth that could never be improved upon, then the only way to uphold this belief is to define that there are certain areas where we are not looking.

O blessed Mary, Mother mine,
there is no greater love than thine,
as we are one in heart and mind,
my place in hierarchy I find.

**O Mother Mary, generate,
the song that does accelerate,
the earth into a higher state,
all matter does now scintillate.**

2. Mother Mary, shatter the energetic matrix that prevents people from seeing that fanatics are not looking in areas that could disprove their infallible beliefs. Catholics did not believe they needed to look outside of church doctrine. Materialists do not need to look outside of the material universe. They are in the exact same fanatical mindset.

> I came to earth from heaven sent,
> as I am in embodiment,
> I use Divine authority,
> commanding you to set earth free.

> **O Mother Mary, generate,**
> **the song that does accelerate,**
> **the earth into a higher state,**
> **all matter does now scintillate.**

3. Mother Mary, shatter the energetic matrix that prevents people from seeing that some people go into an extreme form of agnosticism where they say: "Oh, nobody can know the truth. There is no truth we can know. Therefore, any idea is as good as any other idea, because it's all just ideas."

> I call now in God's sacred name,
> for you to use your Mother Flame,
> to burn all fear-based energy,
> restoring sacred harmony.

> **O Mother Mary, generate,**
> **the song that does accelerate,**
> **the earth into a higher state,**
> **all matter does now scintillate.**

4. Mother Mary, shatter the energetic matrix that prevents people from seeing that this is also a state of fanaticism because they say: "Well, we are the only ones who have really understood the essence of the world. The religious people, the political people, the materialists, all those who are certain that they have the only truth, they are the ones who are wrong. They are the fanatics."

Your sacred name I hereby praise,
collective consciousness you raise,
no more of fear and doubt and shame,
consume it with your Mother Flame.

O Mother Mary, generate,
the song that does accelerate,
the earth into a higher state,
all matter does now scintillate.

5. Mother Mary, shatter the energetic matrix that prevents people from seeing that the essence of the fanatical mindset is that we hold a belief that we believe could not be expanded upon.

All darkness from the earth you purge,
your light moves as a mighty surge,
no force of darkness can now stop,
the spiral that goes only up.

O Mother Mary, generate,
the song that does accelerate,
the earth into a higher state,
all matter does now scintillate.

6. Mother Mary, shatter the energetic matrix that prevents people from seeing that this creates a division between us and all those who do not share our belief, all those who do not agree with us. They are outside of our group. They are *out there* and we are *in here*. There is *us* versus *them*.

All elemental life you bless,
removing from them man-made stress,
the nature spirits are now free,
outpicturing Divine decree.

O Mother Mary, generate,
the song that does accelerate,
the earth into a higher state,
all matter does now scintillate.

7. Mother Mary, shatter the energetic matrix that prevents people from seeing that this automatically creates the sense of threat. We know that not everybody agrees with us. We know knowledge has been expanded. There is a potential that new knowledge could be developed that would overturn our infallible belief.

I raise my voice and take my stand,
a stop to war I do command,
no more shall warring scar the earth,
a golden age is given birth.

**O Mother Mary, generate,
the song that does accelerate,
the earth into a higher state,
all matter does now scintillate.**

8. Mother Mary, shatter the energetic matrix that prevents people from seeing that we now go into a state of mind where we are threatened. We are threatened by anyone who could overthrow our sense of security that our belief is infallible.

As Mother Earth is free at last,
disasters belong to the past,
your Mother Light is so intense,
that matter is now far less dense.

**O Mother Mary, generate,
the song that does accelerate,
the earth into a higher state,
all matter does now scintillate.**

9. Mother Mary, shatter the energetic matrix that prevents people from seeing that this means we go into a "fight or flight" reaction where we are seeking to escape those who could challenge our belief. If we cannot escape it, then we are willing to fight them. The vast majority of the people around the world are in the mindset that is the seed of fanaticism, namely "fight or flight" mode.

In Mother Light the earth is pure,
the upward spiral will endure,
prosperity is now the norm,
God's vision manifest as form.

O Mother Mary, generate,
the song that does accelerate,
the earth into a higher state,
all matter does now scintillate.

Sealing

In the name of the I AM THAT I AM, I accept that Archangel Michael, Astrea and Shiva form an impenetrable shield around myself and all constructive people, sealing us from all fear-based energies in all four octaves. I accept that the Light of God is consuming and transforming all fear-based energies that make up the dark forces working against ending the era of fanaticism on earth!

3 | INVOKING THE MOVEMENT BEYOND FANATICISM (PART 2)

In the name of the I AM THAT I AM, Jesus Christ, I use the authority that I have as a being in embodiment on earth to call upon Mother Mary to reinforce my calls and use my chakras to project the statements in this invocation into the collective consciousness and awaken people to the fact that the modern democracies need to overcome all remnants of the fanatical mindset. Awaken people to the reality that we are spiritual beings and that we can co-create a new future by working with the ascended masters. I especially call for …

[Make your own calls here.]

Part 1

1. Mother Mary, shatter the energetic matrix that prevents people from seeing that in many of the modern democracies, people have transcended the willingness to kill others in order to defend their beliefs. We have gone out of the fight mode, but we are still in flight mode. We attempt to escape

or ignore anything that threatens our worldview, our sense that we have a certain understanding of the world.

> O blessed Mary, Mother mine,
> there is no greater love than thine,
> as we are one in heart and mind,
> my place in hierarchy I find.

> **O Mother Mary, generate,**
> **the song that does accelerate,**
> **the earth into a higher state,**
> **all matter does now scintillate.**

2. Mother Mary, shatter the energetic matrix that prevents people from seeing that all people are in the same mindset. Some are in flight mode and are seeking to ignore anything that disturbs their sense of security. Some are still in fight mode, and they are willing to fight those who threaten their beliefs.

> I came to earth from heaven sent,
> as I am in embodiment,
> I use Divine authority,
> commanding you to set earth free.

> **O Mother Mary, generate,**
> **the song that does accelerate,**
> **the earth into a higher state,**
> **all matter does now scintillate.**

3. Mother Mary, shatter the energetic matrix that prevents people from seeing that in many European nations there was a sense of peace because the people were in a certain state of mind. There was a collective agreement and a certain tolerance where everybody could tolerate each other.

> I call now in God's sacred name,
> for you to use your Mother Flame,
> to burn all fear-based energy,
> restoring sacred harmony.

**O Mother Mary, generate,
the song that does accelerate,
the earth into a higher state,
all matter does now scintillate.**

4. Mother Mary, shatter the energetic matrix that prevents people from seeing that this was not real harmony or resolution. This is demonstrated by how people have reacted when they had an influx of refugees from Muslim countries. Many people felt threatened by Muslims being so religious.

Your sacred name I hereby praise,
collective consciousness you raise,
no more of fear and doubt and shame,
consume it with your Mother Flame.

**O Mother Mary, generate,
the song that does accelerate,
the earth into a higher state,
all matter does now scintillate.**

5. Mother Mary, shatter the energetic matrix that prevents people from seeing that many people are still in flight mode. When they could ignore that there were other religions, they were not disturbed by it. When those religions came knocking on their doorstep, then they became disturbed.

All darkness from the earth you purge,
your light moves as a mighty surge,
no force of darkness can now stop,
the spiral that goes only up.

**O Mother Mary, generate,
the song that does accelerate,
the earth into a higher state,
all matter does now scintillate.**

6. Mother Mary, shatter the energetic matrix that prevents people from seeing that although people have not become violent, many would much rather see the Muslims go back where they came from. This demonstrates that they are in flight mode and have not transcended the fanatical mindset.

All elemental life you bless,
removing from them man-made stress,
the nature spirits are now free,
outpicturing Divine decree.

O Mother Mary, generate,
the song that does accelerate,
the earth into a higher state,
all matter does now scintillate.

7. Mother Mary, shatter the energetic matrix that prevents people from seeing that in many Muslim nations, a majority of the people are in fight mode. It is not enough for them to try and run away from those who threaten their religion, they have to do something violent about it. They have to fight them.

I raise my voice and take my stand,
a stop to war I do command,
no more shall warring scar the earth,
a golden age is given birth.

O Mother Mary, generate,
the song that does accelerate,
the earth into a higher state,
all matter does now scintillate.

8. Mother Mary, shatter the energetic matrix that prevents people from seeing that in Europe people have transcended the fight mode because they saw the extreme manifestation of this exemplified by Hitler and the Nazis. If people had not had the example of Hitler and the Nazis in Europe, where would Europe have been today?

As Mother Earth is free at last,
disasters belong to the past,
your Mother Light is so intense,
that matter is now far less dense.

O Mother Mary, generate,
the song that does accelerate,

**the earth into a higher state,
all matter does now scintillate.**

9. Mother Mary, shatter the energetic matrix that prevents people from seeing that people in Muslim nations may have to go through their own extreme manifestations in order to come to the point where they say: "We cannot allow this to happen again. Therefore, we need to change."

In Mother Light the earth is pure,
the upward spiral will endure,
prosperity is now the norm,
God's vision manifest as form.

**O Mother Mary, generate,
the song that does accelerate,
the earth into a higher state,
all matter does now scintillate.**

Part 2

1. Mother Mary, shatter the energetic matrix that prevents people from seeing that the world is so uncertain that it is difficult for us to live with this psychologically. Seeking to deal with the uncertainty is what sets the stage for fanaticism.

O blessed Mary, Mother mine,
there is no greater love than thine,
as we are one in heart and mind,
my place in hierarchy I find.

**O Mother Mary, generate,
the song that does accelerate,
the earth into a higher state,
all matter does now scintillate.**

2. Mother Mary, shatter the energetic matrix that prevents people from seeing that because the world is an uncertain place, we need to feel that we

have certain beliefs, a certain understanding of the world, that is infallible and could not be improved upon.

> I came to earth from heaven sent,
> as I am in embodiment,
> I use Divine authority,
> commanding you to set earth free.

> **O Mother Mary, generate,**
> **the song that does accelerate,**
> **the earth into a higher state,**
> **all matter does now scintillate.**

3. Mother Mary, shatter the energetic matrix that prevents people from seeing that life on earth presents us with a certain uncertainty. There is a certain uncertainty in life. We cannot know what could happen, but we have a certain sense that bad things *could* happen.

> I call now in God's sacred name,
> for you to use your Mother Flame,
> to burn all fear-based energy,
> restoring sacred harmony.

> **O Mother Mary, generate,**
> **the song that does accelerate,**
> **the earth into a higher state,**
> **all matter does now scintillate.**

4. Mother Mary, shatter the energetic matrix that prevents people from seeing that one of the major needs we have is to find a certainty that helps us live with uncertainty.

> Your sacred name I hereby praise,
> collective consciousness you raise,
> no more of fear and doubt and shame,
> consume it with your Mother Flame.

> **O Mother Mary, generate,**
> **the song that does accelerate,**

**the earth into a higher state,
all matter does now scintillate.**

5. Mother Mary, shatter the energetic matrix that prevents people from seeing that this is a *deficit* need, and when it is not met, it takes up a prominent position in our consciousness.

All darkness from the earth you purge,
your light moves as a mighty surge,
no force of darkness can now stop,
the spiral that goes only up.

**O Mother Mary, generate,
the song that does accelerate,
the earth into a higher state,
all matter does now scintillate.**

6. Mother Mary, shatter the energetic matrix that prevents people from seeing that although we have certain purely physical needs, what is driving human beings is not the *physiological* needs, it is the *psychological* needs.

All elemental life you bless,
removing from them man-made stress,
the nature spirits are now free,
outpicturing Divine decree.

**O Mother Mary, generate,
the song that does accelerate,
the earth into a higher state,
all matter does now scintillate.**

7. Mother Mary, shatter the energetic matrix that prevents people from seeing that we have a very strong psychological need to have some sense of security about the future. Insecurity about the future makes it very difficult to function in our daily lives.

I raise my voice and take my stand,
a stop to war I do command,

no more shall warring scar the earth,
a golden age is given birth.

O Mother Mary, generate,
the song that does accelerate,
the earth into a higher state,
all matter does now scintillate.

8. Mother Mary, shatter the energetic matrix that prevents people from seeing that the most fundamental human need springs from our ability to operate with past, present and future.

As Mother Earth is free at last,
disasters belong to the past,
your Mother Light is so intense,
that matter is now far less dense.

O Mother Mary, generate,
the song that does accelerate,
the earth into a higher state,
all matter does now scintillate.

9. Mother Mary, shatter the energetic matrix that prevents people from seeing that we remember what happened in the past, and we have a tendency to use what happened in the past to project what might happen in the future. It is this very ability that gives us the "ability" to worry about the future, to fear for the future.

In Mother Light the earth is pure,
the upward spiral will endure,
prosperity is now the norm,
God's vision manifest as form.

O Mother Mary, generate,
the song that does accelerate,
the earth into a higher state,
all matter does now scintillate.

Part 3

1. Mother Mary, shatter the energetic matrix that prevents people from seeing that the deepest, the most basic, human need is to have some sense of security about the future.

> O blessed Mary, Mother mine,
> there is no greater love than thine,
> as we are one in heart and mind,
> my place in hierarchy I find.

> **O Mother Mary, generate,**
> **the song that does accelerate,**
> **the earth into a higher state,**
> **all matter does now scintillate.**

2. Mother Mary, shatter the energetic matrix that prevents people from seeing that we produce this security through ideas, ideologies, beliefs, political and religious philosophies that give us some sense of having the future under our control, because we feel that we can predict what might happen.

> I came to earth from heaven sent,
> as I am in embodiment,
> I use Divine authority,
> commanding you to set earth free.

> **O Mother Mary, generate,**
> **the song that does accelerate,**
> **the earth into a higher state,**
> **all matter does now scintillate.**

3. Mother Mary, shatter the energetic matrix that prevents people from seeing that the Catholic church fulfilled this need by making people believe that no matter what happened here on earth, they would go to heaven after this lifetime.

> I call now in God's sacred name,
> for you to use your Mother Flame,

to burn all fear-based energy,
restoring sacred harmony.

O Mother Mary, generate,
the song that does accelerate,
the earth into a higher state,
all matter does now scintillate.

4. Mother Mary, shatter the energetic matrix that prevents people from seeing that Marxism offered people a sense of security because historical necessity shows that all countries will become communist. Therefore, those who are already in a communist country, know they have history on their side.

Your sacred name I hereby praise,
collective consciousness you raise,
no more of fear and doubt and shame,
consume it with your Mother Flame.

O Mother Mary, generate,
the song that does accelerate,
the earth into a higher state,
all matter does now scintillate.

5. Mother Mary, shatter the energetic matrix that prevents people from seeing that in the modern democracies, we have a certain physical safety. We can plot our lives and have a reasonable sense of confidence that our lives will go the way we planned. This gives people that sense of security where they feel they have their lives under control.

All darkness from the earth you purge,
your light moves as a mighty surge,
no force of darkness can now stop,
the spiral that goes only up.

O Mother Mary, generate,
the song that does accelerate,
the earth into a higher state,
all matter does now scintillate.

6. Mother Mary, shatter the energetic matrix that prevents people from seeing that the basic dynamic of life is that there is a certain uncertainty in life, but that people have a need to explain how life works in order to give them a sense of certainty, a sense of security, a sense of being able to predict the future.

> All elemental life you bless,
> removing from them man-made stress,
> the nature spirits are now free,
> outpicturing Divine decree.

> **O Mother Mary, generate,**
> **the song that does accelerate,**
> **the earth into a higher state,**
> **all matter does now scintillate.**

7. Mother Mary, shatter the energetic matrix that prevents people from seeing that in the modern democracies, people still have a need to feel they have the world under control. Because of the very stable, peaceful, outer circumstances, they feel this need has been fulfilled to a critical degree and therefore they forget about it.

> I raise my voice and take my stand,
> a stop to war I do command,
> no more shall warring scar the earth,
> a golden age is given birth.

> **O Mother Mary, generate,**
> **the song that does accelerate,**
> **the earth into a higher state,**
> **all matter does now scintillate.**

8. Mother Mary, shatter the energetic matrix that prevents people from seeing that people do not have to think more deeply about the deeper questions of life. That is why so many people, when they face a crisis, cannot deal with these fundamental questions.

> As Mother Earth is free at last,
> disasters belong to the past,

your Mother Light is so intense,
that matter is now far less dense.

**O Mother Mary, generate,
the song that does accelerate,
the earth into a higher state,
all matter does now scintillate.**

9. Mother Mary, shatter the energetic matrix that prevents people from seeing that in many of the affluent nations a growing number of people go into depression or mental illness.

In Mother Light the earth is pure,
the upward spiral will endure,
prosperity is now the norm,
God's vision manifest as form.

**O Mother Mary, generate,
the song that does accelerate,
the earth into a higher state,
all matter does now scintillate.**

Part 4

1. Mother Mary, shatter the energetic matrix that prevents people from seeing that mental illness is becoming a greater and greater problem because modern democracies have been focused on providing physical, material welfare.

O blessed Mary, Mother mine,
there is no greater love than thine,
as we are one in heart and mind,
my place in hierarchy I find.

**O Mother Mary, generate,
the song that does accelerate,**

the earth into a higher state,
all matter does now scintillate.

2. Mother Mary, shatter the energetic matrix that prevents people from seeing that if the materialists' claim that there is nothing beyond the material universe was true, then all people in the rich affluent nations should have become happy because they have all the material welfare they could want.

I came to earth from heaven sent,
as I am in embodiment,
I use Divine authority,
commanding you to set earth free.

O Mother Mary, generate,
the song that does accelerate,
the earth into a higher state,
all matter does now scintillate.

3. Mother Mary, shatter the energetic matrix that prevents people from seeing that the materialist paradigm says that the consciousness of human beings is a product of the physical bodies. If the physical body has all of its needs met, people should be happy. That is the consequence of the materialist paradigm.

I call now in God's sacred name,
for you to use your Mother Flame,
to burn all fear-based energy,
restoring sacred harmony.

O Mother Mary, generate,
the song that does accelerate,
the earth into a higher state,
all matter does now scintillate.

4. Mother Mary, shatter the energetic matrix that prevents people from seeing that since this is not happening, we have to question the materialist paradigm. The very fact that there is a rise in mental illness means that

society has an explanation problem. This goes back to the mindset that is the seed of fanaticism.

Your sacred name I hereby praise,
collective consciousness you raise,
no more of fear and doubt and shame,
consume it with your Mother Flame.

O Mother Mary, generate,
the song that does accelerate,
the earth into a higher state,
all matter does now scintillate.

5. Mother Mary, shatter the energetic matrix that prevents people from seeing that if we are responsible, modern societies, we have to look at the rise in mental illness and say: We have not fulfilled our responsibility to our citizens.

All darkness from the earth you purge,
your light moves as a mighty surge,
no force of darkness can now stop,
the spiral that goes only up.

O Mother Mary, generate,
the song that does accelerate,
the earth into a higher state,
all matter does now scintillate.

6. Mother Mary, shatter the energetic matrix that prevents people from seeing that even though we have provided people material welfare, we can now see that this is not enough. It is not enough for people to be happy and function well in society.

All elemental life you bless,
removing from them man-made stress,
the nature spirits are now free,
outpicturing Divine decree.

O Mother Mary, generate,
the song that does accelerate,
the earth into a higher state,
all matter does now scintillate.

7. Mother Mary, shatter the energetic matrix that prevents people from seeing that the next logical step is that we focus on psychological well-being, what makes people happy. It is not the physical conditions that automatically makes people happy so we need to understand what does.

I raise my voice and take my stand,
a stop to war I do command,
no more shall warring scar the earth,
a golden age is given birth.

O Mother Mary, generate,
the song that does accelerate,
the earth into a higher state,
all matter does now scintillate.

8. Mother Mary, shatter the energetic matrix that prevents people from seeing that in the 1960s, the modern democracies had the opportunity to transition from focusing on material welfare to starting to use our material affluence to focus on spiritual well-being.

As Mother Earth is free at last,
disasters belong to the past,
your Mother Light is so intense,
that matter is now far less dense.

O Mother Mary, generate,
the song that does accelerate,
the earth into a higher state,
all matter does now scintillate.

9. Mother Mary, shatter the energetic matrix that prevents people from seeing that societies did not do that because of fanaticism. This was not extreme fanaticism, but the more widespread fanaticism where people

have a belief that they think could not be expanded. Therefore, they resist expanding their understanding of life.

> In Mother Light the earth is pure,
> the upward spiral will endure,
> prosperity is now the norm,
> God's vision manifest as form.

> **O Mother Mary, generate,**
> **the song that does accelerate,**
> **the earth into a higher state,**
> **all matter does now scintillate.**

Sealing

In the name of the I AM THAT I AM, I accept that Archangel Michael, Astrea and Shiva form an impenetrable shield around myself and all constructive people, sealing us from all fear-based energies in all four octaves. I accept that the Light of God is consuming and transforming all fear-based energies that make up the dark forces working against ending the era of fanaticism on earth!

4 | INVOKING THE MOVEMENT BEYOND FANATICISM (PART 3)

In the name of the I AM THAT I AM, Jesus Christ, I use the authority that I have as a being in embodiment on earth to call upon Mother Mary to reinforce my calls and use my chakras to project the statements in this invocation into the collective consciousness and awaken people to the fact that the modern democracies need to overcome all remnants of the fanatical mindset. Awaken people to the reality that we are spiritual beings and that we can co-create a new future by working with the ascended masters. I especially call for …

[Make your own calls here.]

Part 1

1. Mother Mary, shatter the energetic matrix that prevents people from seeing that in the 1960s many people had achieved the sense that they felt secure about the future. This gave them that sense of equilibrium where they felt they could look at the rest of their lives with some confidence.

O blessed Mary, Mother mine,
there is no greater love than thine,
as we are one in heart and mind,
my place in hierarchy I find.

**O Mother Mary, generate,
the song that does accelerate,
the earth into a higher state,
all matter does now scintillate.**

2. Mother Mary, shatter the energetic matrix that prevents people from seeing that this is why so many people in the 1960s reacted with such closed-mindedness to their own children who questioned their materialist lifestyle and explored other possibilities.

I came to earth from heaven sent,
as I am in embodiment,
I use Divine authority,
commanding you to set earth free.

**O Mother Mary, generate,
the song that does accelerate,
the earth into a higher state,
all matter does now scintillate.**

3. Mother Mary, shatter the energetic matrix that prevents people from seeing that this mindset is the seed of fanaticism. What does it take to go from that passive state of equilibrium towards the more extreme aspects of fanaticism?

I call now in God's sacred name,
for you to use your Mother Flame,
to burn all fear-based energy,
restoring sacred harmony.

**O Mother Mary, generate,
the song that does accelerate,
the earth into a higher state,
all matter does now scintillate.**

4. Mother Mary, shatter the energetic matrix that prevents people from seeing that there is a passive aspect of fanaticism, and the more active or aggressive states of fanaticism.

> Your sacred name I hereby praise,
> collective consciousness you raise,
> no more of fear and doubt and shame,
> consume it with your Mother Flame.

> **O Mother Mary, generate,**
> **the song that does accelerate,**
> **the earth into a higher state,**
> **all matter does now scintillate.**

5. Mother Mary, shatter the energetic matrix that prevents people from seeing that moving from one to the other is a gradual scale and it is a matter of how fragile people's sense of equilibrium is.

> All darkness from the earth you purge,
> your light moves as a mighty surge,
> no force of darkness can now stop,
> the spiral that goes only up.

> **O Mother Mary, generate,**
> **the song that does accelerate,**
> **the earth into a higher state,**
> **all matter does now scintillate.**

6. Mother Mary, shatter the energetic matrix that prevents people from seeing that the more fragile is our sense of equilibrium, the more likely we are to move towards the more extreme manifestations of fanaticism.

> All elemental life you bless,
> removing from them man-made stress,
> the nature spirits are now free,
> outpicturing Divine decree.

> **O Mother Mary, generate,**
> **the song that does accelerate,**

**the earth into a higher state,
all matter does now scintillate.**

7. Mother Mary, shatter the energetic matrix that prevents people from seeing that we have the influx of Muslim immigrants in the modern democracies because we have not been willing to question the sense of equilibrium on our own. Thus, we have enrolled ourselves in the School of Hard Knocks.

I raise my voice and take my stand,
a stop to war I do command,
no more shall warring scar the earth,
a golden age is given birth.

**O Mother Mary, generate,
the song that does accelerate,
the earth into a higher state,
all matter does now scintillate.**

8. Mother Mary, shatter the energetic matrix that prevents people from seeing that Muslims are here to challenge the fanaticism of the Europeans who do not want to question the materialist view of life that it is enough to take care of people's material needs, and then they should automatically be happy.

As Mother Earth is free at last,
disasters belong to the past,
your Mother Light is so intense,
that matter is now far less dense.

**O Mother Mary, generate,
the song that does accelerate,
the earth into a higher state,
all matter does now scintillate.**

9. Mother Mary, shatter the energetic matrix that prevents people from seeing that many people have played the materialistic game and feel they are entitled to live their retirement years the way they plan to live them, and nothing should upset the applecart.

In Mother Light the earth is pure,
the upward spiral will endure,
prosperity is now the norm,
God's vision manifest as form.

**O Mother Mary, generate,
the song that does accelerate,
the earth into a higher state,
all matter does now scintillate.**

Part 2

1. Mother Mary, shatter the energetic matrix that prevents people from seeing that many young people are open to changes in society, are open to the need to focus more on psychological well-being because they are experiencing various psychological issues.

O blessed Mary, Mother mine,
there is no greater love than thine,
as we are one in heart and mind,
my place in hierarchy I find.

**O Mother Mary, generate,
the song that does accelerate,
the earth into a higher state,
all matter does now scintillate.**

2. Mother Mary, shatter the energetic matrix that prevents people from seeing that the older people may also have psychological issues, but they are denying them or pushing them away if at all possible. They do not want society to change because they want to live out their lives with the sense of equilibrium they have.

I came to earth from heaven sent,
as I am in embodiment,
I use Divine authority,
commanding you to set earth free.

O Mother Mary, generate,
the song that does accelerate,
the earth into a higher state,
all matter does now scintillate.

3. Mother Mary, shatter the energetic matrix that prevents people from seeing that we have this fundamental tension in the western democracies and it is coming out in people's reaction to those who are different.

I call now in God's sacred name,
for you to use your Mother Flame,
to burn all fear-based energy,
restoring sacred harmony.

O Mother Mary, generate,
the song that does accelerate,
the earth into a higher state,
all matter does now scintillate.

4. Mother Mary, shatter the energetic matrix that prevents people from seeing that this comes from an attempt to avoid having our equilibrium threatened by removing diversity.

Your sacred name I hereby praise,
collective consciousness you raise,
no more of fear and doubt and shame,
consume it with your Mother Flame.

O Mother Mary, generate,
the song that does accelerate,
the earth into a higher state,
all matter does now scintillate.

5. Mother Mary, shatter the energetic matrix that prevents people from seeing that the unwillingness to have people who are different come into our society and point out that we have to change is exactly what we saw outpictured in the Nazi regime and their attempt to kill the Jews.

All darkness from the earth you purge,
your light moves as a mighty surge,
no force of darkness can now stop,
the spiral that goes only up.

O Mother Mary, generate,
the song that does accelerate,
the earth into a higher state,
all matter does now scintillate.

6. Mother Mary, shatter the energetic matrix that prevents people from seeing that the fact that material affluence does not automatically produce happiness means we human beings are psychological beings. Everything that happens in our lives, everything we do, revolves around something in our psyches.

All elemental life you bless,
removing from them man-made stress,
the nature spirits are now free,
outpicturing Divine decree.

O Mother Mary, generate,
the song that does accelerate,
the earth into a higher state,
all matter does now scintillate.

7. Mother Mary, shatter the energetic matrix that prevents people from seeing that when we look into our own psychology, we realize how complex human beings are, how many layers there are to the human psyche.

I raise my voice and take my stand,
a stop to war I do command,
no more shall warring scar the earth,
a golden age is given birth.

O Mother Mary, generate,
the song that does accelerate,
the earth into a higher state,
all matter does now scintillate.

8. Mother Mary, shatter the energetic matrix that prevents people from seeing that we cannot explain a person's complex psychology by what he has experienced in this lifetime. The only explanation is that people have lived before, that reincarnation is a reality.

> As Mother Earth is free at last,
> disasters belong to the past,
> your Mother Light is so intense,
> that matter is now far less dense.

> **O Mother Mary, generate,**
> **the song that does accelerate,**
> **the earth into a higher state,**
> **all matter does now scintillate.**

9. Mother Mary, shatter the energetic matrix that prevents people from seeing that by using science to study this phenomenon, we would conclude that even if we don't accept that reincarnation is real, we can help people resolve some of their deep traumas by seeing them as created before this lifetime.

> In Mother Light the earth is pure,
> the upward spiral will endure,
> prosperity is now the norm,
> God's vision manifest as form.

> **O Mother Mary, generate,**
> **the song that does accelerate,**
> **the earth into a higher state,**
> **all matter does now scintillate.**

Part 3

1. Mother Mary, shatter the energetic matrix that prevents people from seeing that reincarnation explains why we have so many young people in the affluent nations that have psychological issues.

O blessed Mary, Mother mine,
there is no greater love than thine,
as we are one in heart and mind,
my place in hierarchy I find.

**O Mother Mary, generate,
the song that does accelerate,
the earth into a higher state,
all matter does now scintillate.**

2. Mother Mary, shatter the energetic matrix that prevents people from seeing that the nations who have taken care of the material welfare are seeing this increase in psychological problems because they attract people who are ready to work on their psychology and their need for self-actualization.

I came to earth from heaven sent,
as I am in embodiment,
I use Divine authority,
commanding you to set earth free.

**O Mother Mary, generate,
the song that does accelerate,
the earth into a higher state,
all matter does now scintillate.**

3. Mother Mary, shatter the energetic matrix that prevents people from seeing that people acknowledging that they have psychological issues is just a natural progression of the fact that their lower needs have been met, and now they are focused on the higher needs.

I call now in God's sacred name,
for you to use your Mother Flame,
to burn all fear-based energy,
restoring sacred harmony.

**O Mother Mary, generate,
the song that does accelerate,
the earth into a higher state,
all matter does now scintillate.**

4. Mother Mary, shatter the energetic matrix that prevents people from seeing that when we understand reincarnation, we realize that some people are still focused on lower needs, but more and more people are moving on to the need for self-actualization.

> Your sacred name I hereby praise,
> collective consciousness you raise,
> no more of fear and doubt and shame,
> consume it with your Mother Flame.

> **O Mother Mary, generate,**
> **the song that does accelerate,**
> **the earth into a higher state,**
> **all matter does now scintillate.**

5. Mother Mary, shatter the energetic matrix that prevents people from seeing that souls who are ready to work on self-actualization often choose to embody in the affluent democracies where they have time left over to focus on self-esteem needs.

> All darkness from the earth you purge,
> your light moves as a mighty surge,
> no force of darkness can now stop,
> the spiral that goes only up.

> **O Mother Mary, generate,**
> **the song that does accelerate,**
> **the earth into a higher state,**
> **all matter does now scintillate.**

6. Mother Mary, shatter the energetic matrix that prevents people from seeing that the problem is that these affluent democracies have not moved on from the 1960s to where they have shifted the paradigm to focus on psychological well-being.

> All elemental life you bless,
> removing from them man-made stress,
> the nature spirits are now free,
> outpicturing Divine decree.

**O Mother Mary, generate,
the song that does accelerate,
the earth into a higher state,
all matter does now scintillate.**

7. Mother Mary, shatter the energetic matrix that prevents people from seeing that we now have souls who are ready to work on self-actualization needs, but they receive no help from society. Therefore, they become dissatisfied and have no sense of purpose in life because they cannot find purpose in living a materialistic lifestyle.

I raise my voice and take my stand,
a stop to war I do command,
no more shall warring scar the earth,
a golden age is given birth.

**O Mother Mary, generate,
the song that does accelerate,
the earth into a higher state,
all matter does now scintillate.**

8. Mother Mary, shatter the energetic matrix that prevents people from seeing that if society had a different paradigm where people had help, they would not be seeking help from psychologists. They would be dealing with their self-actualization needs on their own because that is the only way to fulfill our self-actualization needs.

As Mother Earth is free at last,
disasters belong to the past,
your Mother Light is so intense,
that matter is now far less dense.

**O Mother Mary, generate,
the song that does accelerate,
the earth into a higher state,
all matter does now scintillate.**

9. Mother Mary, shatter the energetic matrix that prevents people from seeing that society could shift and recognize that we are not meeting these peoples needs, and we need a different paradigm in order to do it.

> In Mother Light the earth is pure,
> the upward spiral will endure,
> prosperity is now the norm,
> God's vision manifest as form.

> **O Mother Mary, generate,**
> **the song that does accelerate,**
> **the earth into a higher state,**
> **all matter does now scintillate.**

Part 4

1. Mother Mary, shatter the energetic matrix that prevents people from seeing that when we recognize reincarnation, and look at the history of Europe, we see that the people who are embodying today could very well have been alive during the Second World War.

> O blessed Mary, Mother mine,
> there is no greater love than thine,
> as we are one in heart and mind,
> my place in hierarchy I find.

> **O Mother Mary, generate,**
> **the song that does accelerate,**
> **the earth into a higher state,**
> **all matter does now scintillate.**

2. Mother Mary, shatter the energetic matrix that prevents people from seeing that many young people might have been soldiers or civilians who were killed or experienced very unpleasant situations that gave them deep psychological trauma.

I came to earth from heaven sent,
as I am in embodiment,
I use Divine authority,
commanding you to set earth free.

O Mother Mary, generate,
the song that does accelerate,
the earth into a higher state,
all matter does now scintillate.

3. Mother Mary, shatter the energetic matrix that prevents people from seeing that if we are responsible in Europe and look at our past, we need to have a way where we can help people overcome the traumas that they might have received in their past lives in Europe.

I call now in God's sacred name,
for you to use your Mother Flame,
to burn all fear-based energy,
restoring sacred harmony.

O Mother Mary, generate,
the song that does accelerate,
the earth into a higher state,
all matter does now scintillate.

4. Mother Mary, shatter the energetic matrix that prevents people from seeing that it is only natural that we fulfill this need, given our history.

Your sacred name I hereby praise,
collective consciousness you raise,
no more of fear and doubt and shame,
consume it with your Mother Flame.

O Mother Mary, generate,
the song that does accelerate,
the earth into a higher state,
all matter does now scintillate.

5. Mother Mary, shatter the energetic matrix that prevents people from seeing that if we are to continue to grow and raise our awareness and overcome the past, how could this be done unless people heal their wounds so they can let go of the past?

> All darkness from the earth you purge,
> your light moves as a mighty surge,
> no force of darkness can now stop,
> the spiral that goes only up.

> **O Mother Mary, generate,**
> **the song that does accelerate,**
> **the earth into a higher state,**
> **all matter does now scintillate.**

6. Mother Mary, shatter the energetic matrix that prevents people from seeing that the generation of the fathers may have done something that caused the children to have severe psychological trauma that they carry with them for several lifetimes.

> All elemental life you bless,
> removing from them man-made stress,
> the nature spirits are now free,
> outpicturing Divine decree.

> **O Mother Mary, generate,**
> **the song that does accelerate,**
> **the earth into a higher state,**
> **all matter does now scintillate.**

7. Mother Mary, shatter the energetic matrix that prevents people from seeing that we need to make a shift and say: "Well, can the concept that people have lived before and could have received traumas in a past life, can that help people resolve these traumas so they can be free of them?"

> I raise my voice and take my stand,
> a stop to war I do command,
> no more shall warring scar the earth,
> a golden age is given birth.

**O Mother Mary, generate,
the song that does accelerate,
the earth into a higher state,
all matter does now scintillate.**

8. Mother Mary, shatter the energetic matrix that prevents people from seeing that even if a psychologist does not believe in past lives, but the patient believes in it, and is helped by regression to a past life, then is not that still very much what we should be doing in order to pursue psychological well-being?

As Mother Earth is free at last,
disasters belong to the past,
your Mother Light is so intense,
that matter is now far less dense.

**O Mother Mary, generate,
the song that does accelerate,
the earth into a higher state,
all matter does now scintillate.**

9. Mother Mary, I accept the shaft, the pillar of light coming down from you and the ascended realm through me and radiating out in all the directions and shifting the collective consciousness so that people suddenly wake up and say: "Oh, it is obvious that we need to change."

In Mother Light the earth is pure,
the upward spiral will endure,
prosperity is now the norm,
God's vision manifest as form.

**O Mother Mary, generate,
the song that does accelerate,
the earth into a higher state,
all matter does now scintillate.**

Sealing

In the name of the I AM THAT I AM, I accept that Archangel Michael, Astrea and Shiva form an impenetrable shield around myself and all constructive people, sealing us from all fear-based energies in all four octaves. I accept that the Light of God is consuming and transforming all fear-based energies that make up the dark forces working against ending the era of fanaticism on earth!

5 | YOU ARE NOT POWERLESS TO DEAL WITH FANATICISM

I AM the Ascended Master MORE, and I wish to continue Mother Mary's discourse and some of the remarks that she made. My beloved, you look at planet earth, you look at how people resist change. You look at how they want to hold on to what gives them a sense of equilibrium, a sense that they have the uncertainty of the physical universe somewhat under control. What basis is there really for thinking that if you can prevent change, you can maintain control?

You look at all of these people who have a certain belief system, a certain worldview. They believe it gives them absolute and infallible knowledge. They do not believe that it could ever be expanded upon, whether it comes from some divine revelation, scientific revelation or political revelation. They resist any knowledge that could change or challenge their view of life. What basis do you really have, on a planet like earth, for thinking this is even possible?

Worldviews come and go

Look at history. Look at all the changes that have happened. Just look back over the last couple of thousand years here in the western world. You can go back to the Roman Empire. They had a certain worldview. Most people today have not really bothered to think about the Roman worldview, but they had a certain view of the universe, with themselves firmly in the center. They believed they were a superior civilization that had a right to rule the world, and that they lived in the center of the world, and that they basically had conquered most of the known world. They believed they had absolute knowledge, that it could never be expanded upon, that this was something final. Does anybody care today what the Romans believed 2,000 years ago? Has their worldview not been obliterated by time? Is there anybody today who sits there and thinks: "Oh, I wish we could go back to the Roman worldview and all believe what they believed back then."

Then, look at the medieval worldview, the so-called Dark Ages, of how they had certain beliefs, certain ideas, among them that the earth was flat, that it was the center of the universe. If you sailed out over the oceans, you would fall off the edge, and there would be dragons eating you. Does anyone miss that worldview today? Does anyone think: "Oh, we should go back to this?" Look at all the people in later periods. Look even in modern times, the Marxist worldview. Well, yes, there may be a few people who think we should go back to this, but do the majority of the people around the world think we should go back to the Cold War days and the division of the world into a communist and a capitalist camp?

When you look at reality, when you look at history, is there any basis for thinking that you could create a worldview that would last for eternity? You may say: "Well, the Bible is several thousand years old and there are still people who believe in these scriptures." I would say to you: "Is that really so?" You take a fundamentalist Christian in the United States today who claims that the Bible is the Word of God, the literal Word of God, and that it is perfect, and it could never change, and it will stand the test of time. He might say: "Well, the first books in the Bible were given so many thousands of years ago, and we still believe in them today. Therefore, they have stood the test of time." I can assure you that if you went back to when the first people received the first books of the Bible and looked at their worldview and their mindset, you could see that perhaps the words have survived, but the way people looked at those words, *that* has not survived. It was such a different worldview they had back then that you cannot even imagine it in the modern world.

The irony of fundamentalist Christianity being, of course, that before the scientific era there were no fundamentalist Christians. Even in medieval times, people did not take the Bible literally as the fundamentalist

Christians do. It was actually only after the advent of science, and specifically Materialism, that there was a shift in the collective consciousness where people started to take things very literally, instead of looking at their symbolic value. The fundamentalist worldview is not as old as the Bible, and it will not stand the test of time.

People do not want to go back to the past

You look, my beloved, at all of the people in the world (yourselves among them, most of you) who have experimented with various forms of diets. There is the Atkins diet, there is the Keto diet, there is the "supercalifragilisticexpialidosius-diet" and many other diets. Including the Paleolithic diet where people try to eat like they did in the Stone Age. Well, if you want to eat like they did in the Stone Age, why do you not go back and find yourself a nice cave somewhere, and find some old furs and dress in them and live in that cave? Then, you could really eat like they did in the old days. Go out there with your spear and your club and hunt for food, gather berries, and then come home and try to prepare a meal from this.

You see that there may be people who look back to the past and think that there is something original that was better than what we have today. But when it really comes down to it, they do not want to go back and live in the past. Most people, and certainly most people in the modern democracies, would not want to go back to live in the past. If you acknowledge (and this is one of these shifts that can happen in the collective consciousness) that you do not want to go back and live in the past, you can ask yourself why that is. The reason that you do not want to go back to the past is that you acknowledge, you experience, that there has been progress. We can always debate whether something is good or bad, but there has been progress compared to 200 years ago, 2,000 years ago, 10,000 years ago. Humankind has made progress.

Progress is based on increasing knowledge

Now, why have you made progress? Why has humanity made progress in that time? What is the difference between the Stone Age and today? Why did not the Stone Age have, for example, the technology that you take for granted today and that is one of the reasons why people do not want to go back to the Stone Age? Well, because in the Stone Age they did not have the knowledge that this technology is based on. So what is all progress based on? It is based on an expansion of knowledge. People know more, and knowing more is the basis for progress. It has been that way throughout history. Knowing more allows you to make progress. If you do not know more, if you keep holding on to the same knowledge and do not expand your knowledge, you will stay in the same place you are at. Knowledge is power.

If you recognize that knowledge is the key to progress, or rather, expanding your knowledge is the key to progress, why would you hold on to your present worldview and beliefs? Why would you get yourself in a state of mind where you believe that you have some absolute knowledge that could never be expanded upon? If your knowledge could not be expanded upon, that would mean you could not progress beyond your current level, at least in that area of life.

Very, very simple logic. Not beyond the average person in the modern democracies to acknowledge this, and therefore take this step further and say: "Well, why do we human beings have this tendency to hold on to a certain worldview, a certain knowledge, and think it is absolute?" Then, they can realize, as Mother Mary so eloquently explained, the entire security dynamic of the need for security, and your tendency to feel that when you have a certain knowledge that is absolute or infallible, then you have some control over the universe.

When you acknowledge this, then you can again take a look at history and see how all ideas have eventually been changed, perhaps even overturned, by the progress of time. Therefore, you can say: "Okay, if I really want security, does it make any sense to try and base my sense of security on an idea that could be changed anytime?" You would, if you went back in time, see that when people believed that the earth was flat, and that it was the center of the universe, these two beliefs were part of what gave them a sense of security. They felt they could explain how the universe worked and this gave them that sense of equilibrium. Now, you can see that those beliefs have been overturned. Therefore, you can see that basing your sense of security on two beliefs that were so obviously wrong, was not a very smart move. It was not the way to get security.

The real way to get security

What is the only real way to get security? Well, it was explained by Maslow. As long as you, as a human being, are focused on, we might even say trapped in, the four lower needs, the deficit needs, what Maslow said was, you will never be at peace, you will never be happy. Let us focus here on peace of mind. How could you have the security that gives you peace of mind, as long as you are focused, your attention is focused, on the deficit needs? It cannot be done, according to Maslow, according to common sense. Why can it not be done? Because in the deficit needs, you are focusing your attention outside of yourself and thinking that you need something from outside yourself in order to fulfill your needs.

This is reasonable enough when it comes to the need for food where the body (at the current level, at least for most people) cannot sustain itself internally so you need to eat. It is reasonable enough with love and belonging where you, at a certain level, want to have the love of other people. You want to have esteem from other people at a certain level, but you are still at that point where you are very vulnerable because you think it has to come from outside yourself. You think your security has to be based on establishing certain conditions that are controlled, which means you have to try and control your own external circumstances. This means you have to try and control other people, which of course is quite difficult. Love and belonging, if you need it from other people, you need to control them. That is why you see so many people for whom what they call love is basically a control game.

You have the same thing with esteem needs where you see so many people that are in the public eye that have this need to be esteemed by society. They try to control people, they try to control what people know about them, they try to control the press and the media. They employ spin doctors and PR specialists and this and that and the next thing (image consultants and whatever you call them) in order to control how other people look at them so they can get that esteem.

You are always thinking that the fulfillment of your needs has to come from outside yourself. When you look at the planet, you look at the turbulence, you look at the insecurity that is here, you can see this is not a wise move. What did Maslow say? Well, the only way to really find inner peace is to rise to the top of the pyramid and focus on your self-actualization needs because then you do not need anything from outside yourself. What would you need from outside yourself to actualize your self? Permission from mom? Not likely, so you need nothing.

That is the beginning of security, true security, when you acknowledge this. When you rise to that level where you can begin to focus on actualizing yourself, *that* is when you stop looking outside yourself. It is when you stop pointing the finger at other people and saying: "Those people are the reason why I am not at peace with myself. So I need to change those people so I can have peace of mind." When you give that up, when you transcend that, you say: "Well, those people may be doing something that I don't really like, but I don't need to feel threatened by it, I don't need to react to it. I can actually look at myself, I can look at my own psyche, my own state of consciousness, my own reactionary patterns. By transcending these patterns, I can come to a point where these people can continue doing what they are doing because they are not affecting me, they no more have any power over me, they have no power over my state of mind." This is the ultimate state of security.

Security by flowing with change

Now, you could look at this from a slightly different angle (a perhaps less psychological angle) and say that, given how everything has changed and how the pace of change has accelerated over the past century, you can see that you cannot find security if you want to maintain a certain state on earth, if you want to maintain a certain knowledge, a certain worldview. You cannot find security by seeking to do this, you will just enter yourself into an endless fight with other people who have a different worldview and who are threatened by you having your worldview. These two groups of people who are threatened by each other can continue fighting indefinitely, as you see in the Middle East. Most people in modern democracies can quickly step up and realize: This is of course not what we want to do, it is not what we have been doing, it is not how we built our democracies, and how we built this welfare society, this affluent society that we have.

We did not build the current welfare by holding on to the poverty of the past, did we? So how did we transcend the poverty of the past? Well, we had to transcend the mindset that people had when they were living in poverty. We have a fundamentally different attitude to money and affluence today than people had a 100 years ago. Otherwise, we would not have been more affluent.

What is the real key to security? It is not to hold on to a fixed belief, but it is actually to be prepared to flow with a change in society. It is by being prepared to expand our worldview, to refine it, that we can find ultimate security. How would you possibly find ultimate security by holding on to a viewpoint that was later proven to be limited? If you can maintain the idea that your viewpoint was infallible, as they believed that the earth as the center of the universe was an infallible doctrine, then you might have a sense of security. Given that the earth is not the center of the universe, it was not real security, was it?

Giving up the dream of absolute truth

You cannot have real security by having a viewpoint that is wrong, that is out of touch with reality. Therefore, when you then acknowledge that there has been progress, you can see: Progress does not happen in huge leaps. It happens in increments. Small changes. What that means is that there is neither an almighty God, nor some law of nature that is seeking to reveal some absolute truths to humankind right now. You can go back in time and see how all of the people in these past civilizations (the Middle Age Catholics, the Romans, the Jews of the Old Testament, the Muslims, the Hindus, the this and the that) they all believed back then, 500 or 1,000 years ago, that they had some infallible knowledge. But that has been proven to be inaccurate by progress, by the movement of time.

Is it so difficult to see that we should be smarter today in the democratic countries, we should acknowledge that it does not make sense for us to strive to develop some infallible worldview? Instead, we should realize that there is some kind of process that produces progress in society but this happens increment by increment. As we human beings raise our understanding of the universe, we are able to grasp or receive a higher understanding than we had before.

In other words, human progress is an interactive process. As human beings are willing to raise their understanding, they become able to interact with something that can then give them a higher understanding. You may call it the laws of nature, or some spiritual being or ascended masters. It does not even matter what you call it, but you can see that the reason why your civilization today knows more than the civilization of 500 years ago is that there has been this gradual process where somebody expanded their mind, a few people expanded their minds, grasped a new idea. Gradually, that idea spread and became more widely accepted by the population. This then shifted people's awareness so that suddenly a new idea emerged that gave an even higher understanding of the universe and all of the knowledge for how to create more sophisticated technology, more sophisticated societies, and so on.

Embracing gradual change

The real foundation for getting psychological security is not to create or strive for a fixed viewpoint and hold on to it blindly. It is to actually embrace the process of a gradually expanding understanding. Humankind has in known history been in the process of gradually expanding its understanding of life. You can see this when you look back. Then, you can go back to previous civilizations and say: "They didn't see it. They thought they had the final knowledge and that it would never be overturned." When you can see that, why would you repeat the same mindset today that you see they had in the past and that did not work?

Naturally, you do not have the final understanding of the universe today. Naturally, humankind will gradually receive a higher and higher understanding. Your children, when they reach your age, will understand more about the universe than you do now. A hundred years from now, society will understand vastly more about the universe than your civilization understands today. When you realize that this is the driving force behind progress, you can embrace progress instead of trying to stop progress so that you can hold on to the belief that you think is the only key to your security.

Fanatics attempt to stop the clock

You see here that—what is fanaticism? It is in a sense an attempt to stop the clock, to stop progress, to stop the flow of time. This ties in to a dream that people have had for a very long time, that of the Paradise Lost.

Once upon a time, there was this wonderful edenic state, but it was lost and we are trying to get it back. Once we get it back, we will have the society that is ideal and that will stay that way indefinitely, for all eternity, or for 1,000 years, or whatever people believe. Was there ever an edenic state in the past? Well, we have talked about the fall into a dualistic state of consciousness. You could say that in a very distant past, beyond known history, there was a state of a higher form of civilization than what you have today.

Are we of the ascended masters seeking to guide you back to that state, and then once you reach it, keep you in that state indefinitely? *No, we are not.* We are not seeking to recreate some past Utopia, even though I in a previous embodiment coined that term. It was done with a fair amount of irony, referring to the contemporary societies of my day. You see that our goal is not to get you back to a lost paradise. Our goal is to help humanity make progress from here, and then go higher than any condition in the past and continue to do this. As we have now said several times, Saint Germain has plans for the Golden Age, but it is not so that he envisions that he will take society to a certain level, and then it will stay that way for the rest of the Aquarian Age. He envisions constant, steady, gradual progress throughout the 2,000 years.

Once you can recognize *that,* then you can see that you can find a different form of security. You can see that the real key to security is not *static* security but *dynamic* security. It is not a static understanding but a dynamic understanding where you are constantly flowing with the force of progress, embracing a new and higher understanding whenever it comes out, whenever it is developed. You can even start looking for it and that is how you will, in the long run, fulfill the need for security that you still have as long as you are on earth and that it has the very insecure conditions that you see in the current world.

The need for security in the modern world

It is clear that when we look at the modern democracies (and you look at the reaction to 9/11 and other terrorist acts) it is clear that before 9/11, there was a certain sense of security among many modern democracies that the Cold War was over, perhaps the era of warfare and violence was over and there would be more peaceful times. Then, that was shattered by 9/11 and other terrorist acts. By the very fact that so many of the modern democracies went into or joined the war on terror, you see that people still have a need for security even in the modern world. You have not transcended that. Even though there are more and more people in the modern democracies who have gone up to the self-actualization needs (even though they do not realize that is where they are at in consciousness), you see that people still have a need for a sense of security. You still have a certain need for a sense of equilibrium. You can look at yourselves, as ascended masters students, and you can see that you also have a need.

You can see that you are using our teachings to formulate a certain worldview that gives you a sense of what you can expect from your life, how you can protect yourself from negative events. I am not in any way criticizing this. I am not in any way criticizing anybody's worldview because if people have a worldview that gives them a sense of equilibrium, that allows them to function in their daily lives in a constructive way, then there is absolutely nothing unspiritual, there is nothing wrong, there is nothing that needs to be changed about that. Except that the only way for people to really have security is to shift into that dynamic sense where they are willing to expand their understanding.

Naturally, if you are really following the teachings of the ascended masters, you realize that we are giving progressive revelation. We are constantly giving you new things, and therefore you are willing to constantly expand your understanding. You have shifted into this dynamic quest for security. There is nothing wrong with this when you are living on a planet like this. There is nothing unspiritual about it. You need to be able to function in your daily life, and therefore you need to know that you can plan somewhat into the future. You can set things in motion that might take time to be fulfilled, but that is okay because you realize (or you have at least a fair confidence) that you have that time.

What you can do as ascended masters students is you can make these calls because there is a tension that has been building in the collective consciousness where a significant number of people (not a majority in any way, but a significant number of people) are ready to make that shift and embrace a more dynamic form of security and simply realize: We will not find security by holding on to our existing beliefs. Because it is only natural that as progress moves forward, there will be an expanded understanding of how the world works. Naturally, if we want to maintain security, we need to embrace that understanding. We always need to have the latest most advanced understanding of how the world works, instead of holding on to the flat-earth theory.

The current paradigm is not working

This is a shift that is very possible for a certain critical mass of people. This can very quickly (within a matter of a decade, or even less) begin to shift the equation in the modern democracies in many, many ways. First of all, as Mother Mary talked about, the very real problem of how do we help the growing number of people who have psychological problems, psychological illness? How can we help people with this? This can very quickly lead to a situation where people realize: Well, we have tried for decades to give them drugs that basically numb their minds. And we are realizing it is not working because there is more and more evidence that it is not working for a greater and greater number of people. Our approach to this was based on the materialistic worldview that the body is a machine, therefore the brain is the origin of the psyche, the mind, the psychic processes. Therefore, if we introduce some chemical that changes something in the brain, we should be able to change the psyche. But this is not working. When do we then make the choice: "Do we want to stop trying to help people and abandon them? Or do we want to change our paradigm so we can perhaps find a way so we actually *can* help them?" Obviously, we cannot help them based on our current paradigm because if we could, it should be working and everybody should be happy. And they are not. Therefore, when do we change the paradigm? When do we look beyond the paradigm?

Again, this is not going to be a return to the medieval times where people thought that a particular religion could give them all the answers they needed. It is never going to happen. Society, the modern democracies, are never going to become theocracies or religious societies. They are never going to have a worldview that is based on a particular religion, including the teachings of the ascended masters. That is not what we are working towards at all. There can be a certain universal recognition of certain principles that you would now call spiritual, but which could just as well be seen from a different perspective so that they come to be seen as universal, as just self-evident based on experience, based on observation.

Recognizing self-actualization needs

One of these is, as Mother Mary said, that psychologists can recognize that a growing number of people in the modern democracies have shifted into focusing on their self-actualization needs. We need to give these people some kind of path, some kind of systematic procedure, whereby they can fulfill those self-actualization needs. This means they need to be able to actualize themselves, which means we need to explore: What is a self-actualized human being? What is the human potential? What is the potential of the mind?

If our attempts to solve psychological problems by introducing chemicals into the brain, the nervous system, has not worked, what has it proven? It has somehow proven that the mind cannot be an exclusive product of the physical processes in the brain. There is more to mind than matter. Therefore, we need to develop a universal approach to this so that we can give people something that they need. It is a very simple procedure, as this messenger realized in his native country of Denmark, where you have a public health care system. If anybody goes to the doctor and says, I feel depressed, or I have this problem or that problem (such as: I think ascended masters are speaking to me), then the system is obligated to treat them, to attempt to treat these people. Whatever the system does costs money.

Now, there was a time when this messenger was a child, in the 60s and 70s, where in the Scandinavian countries, there was debate: Could the public health care system be overwhelmed by physical illness? There was a growing awareness, for example, that cigarettes cause cancer and most people were smoking. Nobody was concerned about it because there was not the knowledge of the link between smoking and cancer. People were smoking, and then when they developed lung cancer, they went to the doctor and the health care system had to pay for this. There were people who projected and said: "Well, we can see that as the population is aging, there is going to come a point where we have so many sick people that the system cannot handle it, and our economy cannot pay for it."

What did the countries do? Well, they said: Perhaps we can shift from focusing on *curing* disease to focusing on *preventing* it. They created an information campaign, for example, about the link between cancer and smoking. They created information about diet, about exercise, about heart disease, about this and that, and it has led to a drop in the number of physical diseases that people have, which means that the healthcare system has still been able to function. Right now, there are people who are beginning to realize that in the next 10 to 20 years, the biggest challenge for the public health care system will be mental illness because more and more people have depression and other illnesses.

To pay up or step up

You can see again: It is simple. Do you want to *pay* up, or do you want to *step* up? Do you want to step up to a higher approach to the problem of psychological illness? Then, you have to find a way to help people with their self-actualization needs so that they can get on a positive growth path, preferably from a young age, where they even in school learn basic things about how the human psyche works, the possibility that you yourself can develop your psyche in an active way, that you are not a victim of your upbringing or your family background. The psyche is a dynamic thing that you can take control over. You can change what you do not like in your psyche, as a bodybuilder can change certain things about his body.

You can begin then, at an early age, to start molding your psyche the way you want it. This can put people on a positive track where, first of all, they never develop severe mental illness. They do not have to go to the doctor or the psychiatrist. They do not have to go to a mental hospital. Second of all, they do not go into depression because if you have the sense that your life has a purpose, which is to expand your consciousness, to develop your consciousness, you are not as likely to be depressed as when you do not have any sense of purpose.

Or when you, as Mother Mary said, came into embodiment to raise your consciousness, but you have been given no tools so you think that a materialistic lifestyle is meaningless. Since there is no other lifestyle in your society, you think life is meaningless so you naturally become depressed. How could you not be depressed if you think life is meaningless, the life that is common in your society is meaningless?

The older generation that Mother Mary talked about, they found it to some degree meaningful to strive for a good material lifestyle. It was meaningful to them because they could see that their parents did not have it. What you need to recognize is that the children of these people have not seen their parents live in poverty. They do not care what happened a hundred years ago. They want something else. They do not want the material lifestyle that their parents have. It does not give them a sense of meaning and purpose in life. Keeping up with the Joneses is not a life purpose for the younger generation. The only way out of this is to give people that sense of purpose and you only do that by helping them develop themselves, taking command over their psyche.

Fanatics are powerless people

Then, you can begin to go even further in the democratic nations and you can recognize many, many things that we will talk about later. To pick up on what Mother Mary said, you have a situation today where you have certain cultures that clearly are in the extreme, the aggressive, fanatical mindset. Now, you can look at the Middle East, you can look at Islam, you could look at these cultures, as many people in the West have done. You can see, in a certain way (many people can see this) that it is just a matter of time. Naturally, there will be some progress, it may take a long time but inevitably, invariably, there will come a point where the current fanaticism that you see in Islam will not be there anymore. Somehow it will go away. History has proven this.

This is proven by the fact that the modern democracies have raised themselves beyond the fanaticism that they had 100, 200, 300 years ago. It is clear that this *will* happen, but as Mother Mary said, the fanatical mindset, the essence of it, is that you think the problem is "out there." The problem is outside yourself. It is these other people that are the problem and therefore the only way for you to feel secure is to change these other people. This is the background for the entire Islamic fundamentalist terrorist movement. The West is the problem. The West is a threat to Islam. The only way therefore to create the world that Islam and Allah supposedly wants is to change people in the West.

Now, you in the modern democracies can look at this and say, from a purely realistic evaluation: "If this situation is to change, who is going to change it?" We can step back, let history take its course and say: "Oh, eventually these countries, they will get over it, they will get over the Islamic fundamentalism, they will develop either a more modern version of Islam, or they will abandon Islam or whatever. Eventually they will get over it." But be realistic. How long do you think that will take? Because I can tell you it will take way over a century if nothing changes the equation that is there right now. If you take the equation that is there right now, it will take over a century before the Islamic nations, on their own, overcome this, and there could very well be several very bloody wars before that happens.

What can change the equation? Well, you need to recognize, you who say you have transcended fanaticism, what is the basic dynamic of the fanatical mindset. You look at these terrorists who are attacking you and who are throwing bombs and hijacking airplanes, and you think they are being very aggressive. You may even think they are displaying a certain power. But are they powerful people? No, because they feel threatened. They are driven by insecurity. Why are they attacking the West? Why are they not changing themselves? Because they feel powerless. *They feel powerless.*

They may appear to have a certain power, but it all springs from the sense that they are completely powerless. Why are they powerless? Because they cannot see how to change their situation. Why can they not see how to change their situation? Because they are in the fanatical mindset. They do not want to change their worldview and the worldview they have is, in many cases, based on the Sharia law that goes 500 years back. They are looking at the world the way people in the West looked at the world in medieval times and that is why they cannot manifest the progress that the western world is manifesting. Instead of being willing to learn from the West, they feel threatened by it, and now they think they have to fight the West, and destroy the West, and this and that and the next thing.

How democracies can help stop fanaticism

You can look at this in the western world and say: "They are not going to change this for a long time. What can change this?" And then you can say: "What have we gone through in our western democracies, in our modern democracies, compared to 200 years ago?" You can go back in Europe, here, where we stand, and look at the mindset that people had 200 years ago and you will see that back then, there was a very clear segmentation of society. There was the general population and then there was a very small elite who had all the power, all the privilege, all the wealth. This meant that the majority of the population felt powerless. They felt disempowered. They felt they could do nothing to improve their lives. It was the same state of disempowerment that many people in the Islamic world feel today.

Then, you can say to yourselves: "Well, how did we then make the transition from those kinds of societies to democracies?" Well, somehow, the generation that ushered in democracy, the people overcame their sense of being powerless. They took upon themselves a sense of being powerful. They realized that even though we do not own the land and we do not have the army, by the fact of our numbers, we have power. Therefore, when we demand change, the leaders will have to comply. When people took unto themselves power, society changed. Then, you can take this forward to today and say: The Arabs, the Muslims, feel powerless. After 9/11, we allowed ourselves to go into a state of mind where we felt powerless, because we felt: "What can we do about these fanatics?" That is why you were all deceived by the American government, and the people behind the American government, to go on this adventure in Iraq and Afghanistan to supposedly bring freedom and democracy through force.

You felt powerless. You may say there was tremendous power displayed by these armed forces, but it all sprang from the sense of being powerless and therefore thinking you have to change other people in order to have a sense of equilibrium. Do you not see that in America they had a sense of equilibrium, and on 9/11 it was shattered? All of the attempts to go into Afghanistan and Iraq was just an attempt to reestablish America's sense of equilibrium? They are still trying to do it today. How successful have they been? Well, they have not, and why not? Because they are trying to create a sense of peace in *their* minds by changing the minds of other people and it can never, *ever* happen.

There are enough people in the modern democracies (especially here in Europe, Australia and South Korea and other modern democracies around the world, Canada, not so much in the United States but even in the United States) who are ready to step up and see: We in the modern democracies have to take back our power and how do we do this? By changing what we *can* change: ourselves, our own state of consciousness. We do this by reexamining our paradigms and stepping up to a higher worldview that gives us our power back, because we realize that when we change our consciousness, our world *will* change.

That is how you created democracies. You had for centuries had elitist, totalitarian dictatorships and the transition to democracy happened because the people, a critical mass of people, changed their consciousness, took back their power and admitted that we have the power to do something of ourselves. We have the power to demand change when we change ourselves. This will shift our world. Therefore, you can recognize that very, very simply: When you shift your approach to Muslim fundamentalism and Muslim terrorism, when you shift your approach to life, your view of the world, when you shift into this dynamic willingness to raise your understanding of life, even going beyond the materialistic paradigm and the Christian paradigm, then your world *will* change.

Let the fanatics fight each other

You may say: "Well, how will that change the Muslims? They will still be in their fanatical mindset." Sure. But will you be the target of it? Or will they instead begin to fight amongst themselves, as they are already doing and have been doing for thousands of years? If the fighting happens down there, has your world not shifted? What you are really concerned about in the modern democracies is when they come to you with their bombs. If they blow each other up down there, you are not so concerned about it because in a democracy, you respect that other people elsewhere might want to live in a different way. If they want to blow each other up, well, why should you object to that as long as they do not blow you up?

You need to recognize that: Why have you become a target of Muslim fundamentalism? Because you have not shifted your paradigm. As Mother Mary said, most of the modern democracies should in the 1960s have shifted their paradigm away from Materialism. This has not happened and therefore, you have attracted to yourself this outplaying of your own state of consciousness.

The Muslim fundamentalists are clearly more extreme but they are really just showing you what you still have left in your own consciousness that is unrecognized and denied by most. You need to recognize here (and again this is not something the general public will recognize, but you as ascended master students can recognize it) that the School of Hard Knocks works in a very simple way. If you have a certain mindset of fanaticism, of holding on to certain beliefs, you will attract to you people who are having that same mindset in a more extreme form. Because when you see it in a more extreme form, it is more easy to see that this is fanaticism. Of course, the test then that most people have failed so far, is that they think that because the Muslims are so extreme, and are willing to kill, and we have transcended the willingness to kill, we do not have that kind of fanaticism in ourselves. But as we have now tried to tell you, you have the same dynamic. It is there in the collective consciousness, this willingness to hold on to the ideas and the absolute denial of the possibility that these ideas could be expanded upon, that you could gain a deeper understanding. This is really the essence of fanaticism and the rest is just a matter of degree.

You think, when you look at the extreme of the Muslim warriors, that this is fanaticism and what you have is not. You think there is a *qualitative* difference, a *fundamental* difference. We are talking about two different things here. They are fanatics, we just have certain opinions. It is not the opinions you have, it is how you hold on to them. It is only a matter of degree whether you hold on to them the way you do in the West or the way they do in the Middle East. It is only a matter of degree of whether you are willing to kill somebody to defend your ideas or whether you are willing to ridicule and put down those who believe differently than you believe. Or whether you want to exclude them from your countries because you cannot bear to be threatened by the fact that there are some people who are religious and you are not.

Overcoming higher levels of fanaticism in Europe

You see here, this is a shift that can happen where people will recognize that we became democracies by being willing to take back our power and to change ourselves. Our obligation, the only way we are going to really survive as democracies, is to continue to do this, continue to take back more and more power, instead of allowing somebody to make us feel disempowered. How do we do this? How do we take back power? By changing our consciousness and this is something we can do. When we start doing this, we will be able to build a more secure world that is *really* a secure world because we transcend the fanatical mindset and therefore do not have to attract to us a more extreme outpicturing of it.

Has Europe had the fanatical mindset? Well, why on earth would you have attracted Nazism on European soil if people did not have the fanatical mindset and therefore needed to see it outpictured in such an extreme form in order to get over it? What people got over in Europe after Nazism was the willingness to kill other people to defend your ideas, but that was just the *first* step. It was not the *ultimate* or *final* step. It was just overcoming the more aggressive aspect of fanaticism. The more, we might say, physical aspect of fanaticism.

Again, I am not expecting the general public to start believing in emotional, mental and identity realms, but you who are ascended master students can see that when you are taking physical action to defend your ideas by forcing other people, killing them or forcing them in other ways, that is physical. That was what Hitler outpictured, this willingness to actually take extreme physical actions in order to defend your illusion. There is also an emotional component of this where you are seeking to intimidate people at an emotional level. All of you who are spiritual people have probably experienced this when you talk to other people, such as your family members, about your spiritual beliefs and how they felt threatened by this and they try to make you either feel afraid or feel shameful or feel stupid or whatever.

Then, there is an intellectual, mental level of fanaticism where you are using mental faculties. You see this in universities, in the media, among intellectuals and so-called scientists around the world where they try to intellectually disprove or even ridicule religious beliefs, spiritual beliefs. There is even an identity level of this where you can see that, not to again harp on the Jews, but they are such an easy example. When the Jews, back in previous millennia accepted that they had the superior God and that they were the chosen people of this God, they created a state of identity-level fanaticism. It was exactly the same that the Germans had under Hitler. They were the Aryan race and by their very identity, they were better, they were superior to others.

You see that fanaticism has a physical component and that was what Europe largely overcame after the Second World War. The extreme out-picturing done by Hitler enabled most people in Europe to transcend that and realize: We simply cannot kill other people in order to defend an idea. What is lacking, what is still left to be done, is that Europe transcends the emotional, mental and identity level component of fanaticism, the willingness to defend your ideas by intimidating other people emotionally, by arguing against them, or by denying other beliefs, disproving them, or by even making you feel that you are better than others because of some characteristic.

What spiritual people can do about fanaticism

That is where, again, you as the spiritual people can be the forerunners for this and your calls can make a difference so that more and more people come to see this. It is not beyond what people can come to see in the foreseeable future, otherwise we would not bother telling you this. We are not going to tell you what can happen 200 years from now because what would be the point in you making calls for this at this point? We are telling you things that can happen within the foreseeable future, thereby hoping that you will feel empowered to do something about this. This messenger, on the last day before coming to this conference, he felt these projections against him of: "Why do you think a conference like this can make any difference? What do you think could possibly be said about fanaticism? And 50 people coming together and making invocations, what difference will this make? Look how many fanatics there are around the world. Do you really think this can make any difference?" He knew of course that these were projections, and many of you might also have felt it. You might end up feeling at some point: "What difference does it make? Here I am sitting in my little room giving these invocations, repeating these words, how could this ever make a difference?"

We are hoping that you will realize that it *will* make a difference. Therefore, you will feel empowered that you can do something about your own situation and about your life—your outer circumstances, your inner circumstances. Most of you have already proven that you can change your inner circumstances, many of you have proven how you can change your personal outer circumstances. It is just a matter of realizing that maybe not each of you alone, but the fact that there are many people around the world who give these invocations, you are empowered. You are in the possession of a tool that can, as we have explained, trigger that shift so that people suddenly see something that they could not see before and that *will* shift the equation. When enough people in the modern democracies transcend fanaticism, it will shift the equation even in the Islamic world. Therefore, you are never powerless—unless you believe you are.

How powerless are you? However powerless you believe you are. How much power do you have? However much power you can accept that you have. Because is it *your* power? Nay, as Jesus said: "I can of my own self do nothing." When you make the calls, we can unlock our power because you give us the authority to use that power. I can assure you that as the Chohan of the First Ray, I do not feel powerless at all. I look at earth and I see what power I have just as one ascended master, but knowing how many other ascended masters, Elohim and Archangels there are. If I should ever feel powerless, I just need to tune in to Archangel Michael and he will give me such a jolt of power that I could never possibly feel powerless. I look at the earth, I see this power and I see how, if we just have your authority, we can unleash that power and it *will* make a difference.

Naturally, there is always the equation of free will. As we have said many times, how free is people's free will right now when they do not see more than what they see? When you give the calls and we can unlock the power, not to *force* a change, but to set people free to see it so that they choose it. *That,* my beloved, is power. *I AM that power.* Call to me and I *will* unlock it. The call *will* compel the answer.

6 | INVOKING FREEDOM FROM FEELING POWERLESS (PART 1)

In the name of the I AM THAT I AM, Jesus Christ, I use the authority that I have as a being in embodiment on earth to call upon Master MORE to reinforce my calls and use my chakras to project the statements in this invocation into the collective consciousness and awaken people to the fact that we are not powerless to free the world from fanaticism. Awaken people to the reality that we are spiritual beings and that we can co-create a new future by working with the ascended masters. I especially call for …

[Make your own calls here.]

Part 1

1. Master MORE, shatter the energetic matrix that prevents people from seeing that we tend to resist change because we want to hold on to what gives us a sense of equilibrium, a sense that we have the uncertainty of the physical universe somewhat under control.

Master MORE, come to the fore,
we will absorb your flame of MORE.
Master MORE, our will so strong,
our power centers cleared by song.

**Master MORE, your Sacred Heart,
from this we will no more depart,
we are forever in your flow,
of Diamond Will that you bestow.**

2. Master MORE, shatter the energetic matrix that prevents people from seeing that we have a certain belief system that we believe gives us absolute and infallible knowledge. We resist any knowledge that could change or challenge our view of life.

Master MORE, your wisdom flows,
as our attunement ever grows.
Master MORE, we have a tie,
that helps us see through Serpent's lie.

**Master MORE, your Sacred Heart,
from this we will no more depart,
we are forever in your flow,
of Diamond Will that you bestow.**

3. Master MORE, shatter the energetic matrix that prevents people from seeing that on a planet like earth, we have no basis for thinking it is possible to prevent change. Change is the only constant on earth.

Master MORE, your love so pink,
there is no purer love, we think.
Master MORE, you set us free,
from all conditionality.

**Master MORE, your Sacred Heart,
from this we will no more depart,
we are forever in your flow,
of Diamond Will that you bestow.**

4. Master MORE, shatter the energetic matrix that prevents people from seeing that when we look at reality, when we look at history, there is no basis for thinking that we could create a worldview that would last for eternity.

> Master MORE, we will endure,
> your discipline that makes us pure.
> Master MORE, intentions true,
> as we are always one with you.

> **Master MORE, your Sacred Heart,**
> **from this we will no more depart,**
> **we are forever in your flow,**
> **of Diamond Will that you bestow.**

5. Master MORE, shatter the energetic matrix that prevents people from seeing that although there may be some who look back to the past and think that there is something original that was better than what we have today, we do not want to go back and live in the past.

> Master MORE, our vision raised,
> the will of God is always praised.
> Master MORE, creative will,
> raising all life higher still.

> **Master MORE, your Sacred Heart,**
> **from this we will no more depart,**
> **we are forever in your flow,**
> **of Diamond Will that you bestow.**

6. Master MORE, shatter the energetic matrix that prevents people from seeing that the reason we do not want to go back to the past is that we acknowledge that there has been progress, humankind has made progress.

> Master MORE, your peace is power,
> the demons of war it will devour.
> Master MORE, we serve all life,
> our flames consuming war and strife.

**Master MORE, your Sacred Heart,
from this we will no more depart,
we are forever in your flow,
of Diamond Will that you bestow.**

7. Master MORE, shatter the energetic matrix that prevents people from seeing that all progress is based on an expansion of knowledge. People know more, and knowing more is the basis for progress. It has been that way throughout history.

Master MORE, we are so free,
eternal bond from you we see.
Master MORE, we find rebirth,
in flow of your eternal mirth.

**Master MORE, your Sacred Heart,
from this we will no more depart,
we are forever in your flow,
of Diamond Will that you bestow.**

8. Master MORE, shatter the energetic matrix that prevents people from seeing that knowing more allows us to make progress. If we do not know more, if we keep holding on to the same knowledge and do not expand our knowledge, we will stay in the same place we are at. Knowledge is power.

Master MORE, you balance all,
the seven rays upon our call.
Master MORE, forever MORE,
we are the Spirit's open door.

**Master MORE, your Sacred Heart,
from this we will no more depart,
we are forever in your flow,
of Diamond Will that you bestow.**

9. Master MORE, shatter the energetic matrix that prevents people from seeing that when we recognize that expanding our knowledge is the key to progress, why would we hold on to our present worldview and beliefs?

Master MORE, your Presence here,
filling up the inner sphere.
Life is now a sacred flow,
God Power we on all bestow.

**Master MORE, your Sacred Heart,
from this we will no more depart,
we are forever in your flow,
of Diamond Will that you bestow.**

Part 2

1. Master MORE, shatter the energetic matrix that prevents people from seeing that if we believe that we have some absolute knowledge that could never be expanded upon, then we cannot progress beyond our current level. Very simple logic.

Master MORE, come to the fore,
we will absorb your flame of MORE.
Master MORE, our will so strong,
our power centers cleared by song.

**Master MORE, your Sacred Heart,
from this we will no more depart,
we are forever in your flow,
of Diamond Will that you bestow.**

2. Master MORE, shatter the energetic matrix that prevents people from seeing that we human beings have this tendency to hold on to a certain worldview because of our need for security. We feel that when we have infallible knowledge, then we have some control over the universe.

Master MORE, your wisdom flows,
as our attunement ever grows.
Master MORE, we have a tie,
that helps us see through Serpent's lie.

**Master MORE, your Sacred Heart,
from this we will no more depart,
we are forever in your flow,
of Diamond Will that you bestow.**

3. Master MORE, shatter the energetic matrix that prevents people from seeing that when we look at history and see how all ideas have eventually been changed, it does not make sense to try and base our sense of security on an idea that could be changed anytime.

Master MORE, your love so pink,
there is no purer love, we think.
Master MORE, you set us free,
from all conditionality.

**Master MORE, your Sacred Heart,
from this we will no more depart,
we are forever in your flow,
of Diamond Will that you bestow.**

4. Master MORE, shatter the energetic matrix that prevents people from seeing that the only real way to get security is to transcend the deficit needs defined by Maslow.

Master MORE, we will endure,
your discipline that makes us pure.
Master MORE, intentions true,
as we are always one with you.

**Master MORE, your Sacred Heart,
from this we will no more depart,
we are forever in your flow,
of Diamond Will that you bestow.**

5. Master MORE, shatter the energetic matrix that prevents people from seeing that as long as we are focused on the deficit needs, we cannot have peace of mind because we are focusing our attention outside of ourselves and thinking that we need something from outside ourselves in order to fulfill our needs.

Master MORE, our vision raised,
the will of God is always praised.
Master MORE, creative will,
raising all life higher still.

**Master MORE, your Sacred Heart,
from this we will no more depart,
we are forever in your flow,
of Diamond Will that you bestow.**

6. Master MORE, shatter the energetic matrix that prevents people from seeing that thinking that the fulfillment of our needs has to come from outside ourselves is not productive on such a turbulent planet.

Master MORE, your peace is power,
the demons of war it will devour.
Master MORE, we serve all life,
our flames consuming war and strife.

**Master MORE, your Sacred Heart,
from this we will no more depart,
we are forever in your flow,
of Diamond Will that you bestow.**

7. Master MORE, shatter the energetic matrix that prevents people from seeing that the only way to really find inner peace is to rise to the top of the pyramid and focus on our self-actualization needs because then we do not need anything from outside ourselves.

Master MORE, we are so free,
eternal bond from you we see.
Master MORE, we find rebirth,
in flow of your eternal mirth.

**Master MORE, your Sacred Heart,
from this we will no more depart,
we are forever in your flow,
of Diamond Will that you bestow.**

8. Master MORE, shatter the energetic matrix that prevents people from seeing that we need nothing from outside ourselves to actualize the self. Acknowledging this is the beginning of true security.

> Master MORE, you balance all,
> the seven rays upon our call.
> Master MORE, forever MORE,
> we are the Spirit's open door.

> **Master MORE, your Sacred Heart,**
> **from this we will no more depart,**
> **we are forever in your flow,**
> **of Diamond Will that you bestow.**

9. Master MORE, shatter the energetic matrix that prevents people from seeing that when we begin to focus on actualizing ourselves, we stop pointing the finger at other people and saying: "Those people are the reason why I am not at peace with myself. So I need to change those people so I can have peace of mind."

> Master MORE, your Presence here,
> filling up the inner sphere.
> Life is now a sacred flow,
> God Power we on all bestow.

> **Master MORE, your Sacred Heart,**
> **from this we will no more depart,**
> **we are forever in your flow,**
> **of Diamond Will that you bestow.**

Part 3

1. Master MORE, shatter the energetic matrix that prevents people from saying: "Well, those people may be doing something that I don't like, but I don't need to feel threatened by it, I don't need to react to it.

Master MORE, come to the fore,
we will absorb your flame of MORE.
Master MORE, our will so strong,
our power centers cleared by song.

**Master MORE, your Sacred Heart,
from this we will no more depart,
we are forever in your flow,
of Diamond Will that you bestow.**

2. Master MORE, shatter the energetic matrix that prevents people from saying: "I can look at my own reactionary patterns. By transcending these patterns, I can come to a point where these people can continue doing what they are doing because they have no power over my state of mind." This is the ultimate state of security.

Master MORE, your wisdom flows,
as our attunement ever grows.
Master MORE, we have a tie,
that helps us see through Serpent's lie.

**Master MORE, your Sacred Heart,
from this we will no more depart,
we are forever in your flow,
of Diamond Will that you bestow.**

3. Master MORE, shatter the energetic matrix that prevents people from seeing that given how everything has changed and how the pace of change has accelerated over the past century, we cannot find security if we want to maintain a certain state on earth or a certain worldview.

Master MORE, your love so pink,
there is no purer love, we think.
Master MORE, you set us free,
from all conditionality.

**Master MORE, your Sacred Heart,
from this we will no more depart,**

> we are forever in your flow,
> of Diamond Will that you bestow.

4. Master MORE, shatter the energetic matrix that prevents people from seeing that we cannot find security by seeking to stop change. We will put ourselves into an endless fight with other people who have a different worldview and who are threatened by us having our worldview.

> Master MORE, we will endure,
> your discipline that makes us pure.
> Master MORE, intentions true,
> as we are always one with you.

> **Master MORE, your Sacred Heart,**
> **from this we will no more depart,**
> **we are forever in your flow,**
> **of Diamond Will that you bestow.**

5. Master MORE, shatter the energetic matrix that prevents people from seeing that two groups of people who are threatened by each other can continue fighting indefinitely, yet most people in the modern democracies have transcended this.

> Master MORE, our vision raised,
> the will of God is always praised.
> Master MORE, creative will,
> raising all life higher still.

> **Master MORE, your Sacred Heart,**
> **from this we will no more depart,**
> **we are forever in your flow,**
> **of Diamond Will that you bestow.**

6. Master MORE, shatter the energetic matrix that prevents people from seeing that we did not build the current welfare by holding on to the poverty of the past. We transcended the poverty of the past by transcending the mindset that people had when they were living in poverty.

Master MORE, your peace is power,
the demons of war it will devour.
Master MORE, we serve all life,
our flames consuming war and strife.

**Master MORE, your Sacred Heart,
from this we will no more depart,
we are forever in your flow,
of Diamond Will that you bestow.**

7. Master MORE, shatter the energetic matrix that prevents people from seeing that the real key to security is to be prepared to flow with a change in society. It is by being prepared to expand our worldview, to refine it, that we can find ultimate security.

Master MORE, we are so free,
eternal bond from you we see.
Master MORE, we find rebirth,
in flow of your eternal mirth.

**Master MORE, your Sacred Heart,
from this we will no more depart,
we are forever in your flow,
of Diamond Will that you bestow.**

8. Master MORE, shatter the energetic matrix that prevents people from seeing that we cannot possibly find ultimate security by holding on to a viewpoint that will later be proven to be limited.

Master MORE, you balance all,
the seven rays upon our call.
Master MORE, forever MORE,
we are the Spirit's open door.

**Master MORE, your Sacred Heart,
from this we will no more depart,
we are forever in your flow,
of Diamond Will that you bestow.**

9. Master MORE, shatter the energetic matrix that prevents people from seeing that we cannot have real security by having a viewpoint that is out of touch with reality. Progress does not happen in huge leaps. It happens in increments.

> Master MORE, your Presence here,
> filling up the inner sphere.
> Life is now a sacred flow,
> God Power we on all bestow.

> **Master MORE, your Sacred Heart,**
> **from this we will no more depart,**
> **we are forever in your flow,**
> **of Diamond Will that you bestow.**

Part 4

1. Master MORE, shatter the energetic matrix that prevents people from seeing that there is neither an almighty God, nor some law of nature that is seeking to reveal some absolute truths to humankind.

> Master MORE, come to the fore,
> we will absorb your flame of MORE.
> Master MORE, our will so strong,
> our power centers cleared by song.

> **Master MORE, your Sacred Heart,**
> **from this we will no more depart,**
> **we are forever in your flow,**
> **of Diamond Will that you bestow.**

2. Master MORE, shatter the energetic matrix that prevents people from seeing that all of the people in past civilizations believed they had some infallible knowledge. But that has been proven to be inaccurate by progress, by the movement of time.

Master MORE, your wisdom flows,
as our attunement ever grows.
Master MORE, we have a tie,
that helps us see through Serpent's lie.

**Master MORE, your Sacred Heart,
from this we will no more depart,
we are forever in your flow,
of Diamond Will that you bestow.**

3. Master MORE, shatter the energetic matrix that prevents people from seeing that we should be smarter today in the democratic countries, we should acknowledge that it does not make sense for us to strive to develop some infallible worldview.

Master MORE, your love so pink,
there is no purer love, we think.
Master MORE, you set us free,
from all conditionality.

**Master MORE, your Sacred Heart,
from this we will no more depart,
we are forever in your flow,
of Diamond Will that you bestow.**

4. Master MORE, shatter the energetic matrix that prevents people from seeing that there is some kind of process that produces progress in society but this happens increment by increment. As we human beings raise our understanding of the universe, we are able to grasp or receive a higher understanding than we had before.

Master MORE, we will endure,
your discipline that makes us pure.
Master MORE, intentions true,
as we are always one with you.

**Master MORE, your Sacred Heart,
from this we will no more depart,**

we are forever in your flow,
of Diamond Will that you bestow.

5. Master MORE, shatter the energetic matrix that prevents people from seeing that human progress is an interactive process. As we are willing to raise our understanding, we become able to interact with something that can then give us a higher understanding.

Master MORE, our vision raised,
the will of God is always praised.
Master MORE, creative will,
raising all life higher still.

Master MORE, your Sacred Heart,
from this we will no more depart,
we are forever in your flow,
of Diamond Will that you bestow.

6. Master MORE, shatter the energetic matrix that prevents people from seeing that the reason our civilization knows more than the civilization of 500 years ago is that there has been this gradual process where a few people expanded their minds and grasped a new idea.

Master MORE, your peace is power,
the demons of war it will devour.
Master MORE, we serve all life,
our flames consuming war and strife.

Master MORE, your Sacred Heart,
from this we will no more depart,
we are forever in your flow,
of Diamond Will that you bestow.

7. Master MORE, shatter the energetic matrix that prevents people from seeing that gradually, the new idea spread and became more widely accepted by the population. This shifted people's awareness, so that suddenly a new idea emerged that gave an even higher understanding of the universe and the knowledge for how to create more sophisticated societies.

Master MORE, we are so free,
eternal bond from you we see.
Master MORE, we find rebirth,
in flow of your eternal mirth.

Master MORE, your Sacred Heart,
from this we will no more depart,
we are forever in your flow,
of Diamond Will that you bestow.

8. Master MORE, shatter the energetic matrix that prevents people from seeing that the real foundation for getting psychological security is not to create or strive for a fixed viewpoint and hold on to it blindly. It is to embrace the process of a gradually expanding understanding.

Master MORE, you balance all,
the seven rays upon our call.
Master MORE, forever MORE,
we are the Spirit's open door.

Master MORE, your Sacred Heart,
from this we will no more depart,
we are forever in your flow,
of Diamond Will that you bestow.

9. Master MORE, shatter the energetic matrix that prevents people from seeing that humankind is in the process of gradually expanding our understanding of life. Previous civilizations did not see this, but why would we repeat the same mindset today that they had in the past and that did not work?

Master MORE, your Presence here,
filling up the inner sphere.
Life is now a sacred flow,
God Power we on all bestow.

Master MORE, your Sacred Heart,
from this we will no more depart,

**we are forever in your flow,
of Diamond Will that you bestow.**

Sealing

In the name of the I AM THAT I AM, I accept that Archangel Michael, Astrea and Shiva form an impenetrable shield around myself and all constructive people, sealing us from all fear-based energies in all four octaves. I accept that the Light of God is consuming and transforming all fear-based energies that make up the dark forces working against ending the era of fanaticism on earth!

7 | INVOKING FREEDOM FROM FEELING POWERLESS (PART 2)

In the name of the I AM THAT I AM, Jesus Christ, I use the authority that I have as a being in embodiment on earth to call upon Master MORE to reinforce my calls and use my chakras to project the statements in this invocation into the collective consciousness and awaken people to the fact that we are not powerless to free the world from fanaticism. Awaken people to the reality that we are spiritual beings and that we can co-create a new future by working with the ascended masters. I especially call for …

[Make your own calls here.]

Part 1

1. Master MORE, shatter the energetic matrix that prevents people from seeing that we do not have the final understanding of the universe today. We will gradually receive a higher and higher understanding. A hundred years from now, society will understand vastly more about the universe than our civilization understands today.

Master MORE, come to the fore,
we will absorb your flame of MORE.
Master MORE, our will so strong,
our power centers cleared by song.

**Master MORE, your Sacred Heart,
from this we will no more depart,
we are forever in your flow,
of Diamond Will that you bestow.**

2. Master MORE, shatter the energetic matrix that prevents people from embracing progress instead of trying to stop progress so that we can hold on to the belief that we think is the only key to our security.

Master MORE, your wisdom flows,
as our attunement ever grows.
Master MORE, we have a tie,
that helps us see through Serpent's lie.

**Master MORE, your Sacred Heart,
from this we will no more depart,
we are forever in your flow,
of Diamond Will that you bestow.**

3. Master MORE, shatter the energetic matrix that prevents people from seeing that fanaticism is an attempt to stop the clock, to stop progress, to stop the flow of time. This ties in to the dream of the Paradise Lost.

Master MORE, your love so pink,
there is no purer love, we think.
Master MORE, you set us free,
from all conditionality.

**Master MORE, your Sacred Heart,
from this we will no more depart,
we are forever in your flow,
of Diamond Will that you bestow.**

4. Master MORE, shatter the energetic matrix that prevents people from seeing through the illusion that once upon a time, there was this wonderful Edenic state, but it was lost and we are trying to get it back. Once we get it back, we will have the ideal society.

Master MORE, we will endure,
your discipline that makes us pure.
Master MORE, intentions true,
as we are always one with you.

**Master MORE, your Sacred Heart,
from this we will no more depart,
we are forever in your flow,
of Diamond Will that you bestow.**

5. Master MORE, shatter the energetic matrix that prevents people from seeing that the goal is not to get back to a lost paradise. The goal is to help humanity make progress from here, and then go higher than any condition in the past and continue to do this.

Master MORE, our vision raised,
the will of God is always praised.
Master MORE, creative will,
raising all life higher still.

**Master MORE, your Sacred Heart,
from this we will no more depart,
we are forever in your flow,
of Diamond Will that you bestow.**

6. Master MORE, shatter the energetic matrix that prevents people from seeing that Saint Germain has plans for the Golden Age, but he does not envision that he will take society to a certain level, and then it will stay that way for the rest of the Aquarian Age. He envisions constant, steady, gradual progress throughout the 2,000 years.

Master MORE, your peace is power,
the demons of war it will devour.

Master MORE, we serve all life,
our flames consuming war and strife.

Master MORE, your Sacred Heart,
from this we will no more depart,
we are forever in your flow,
of Diamond Will that you bestow.

7. Master MORE, shatter the energetic matrix that prevents people from seeing that we can find a different form of security. The real key to security is not *static* security but *dynamic* security.

Master MORE, we are so free,
eternal bond from you we see.
Master MORE, we find rebirth,
in flow of your eternal mirth.

Master MORE, your Sacred Heart,
from this we will no more depart,
we are forever in your flow,
of Diamond Will that you bestow.

8. Master MORE, shatter the energetic matrix that prevents people from embracing a dynamic understanding where we are constantly flowing with the force of progress, embracing a new and higher understanding whenever it comes out, whenever it is developed.

Master MORE, you balance all,
the seven rays upon our call.
Master MORE, forever MORE,
we are the Spirit's open door.

Master MORE, your Sacred Heart,
from this we will no more depart,
we are forever in your flow,
of Diamond Will that you bestow.

9. Master MORE, shatter the energetic matrix that prevents people from seeing that we can even start looking for a higher understanding and that

is how we will fulfill the need for security that we still have as long as we
are on earth.

> Master MORE, your Presence here,
> filling up the inner sphere.
> Life is now a sacred flow,
> God Power we on all bestow.

> **Master MORE, your Sacred Heart,**
> **from this we will no more depart,**
> **we are forever in your flow,**
> **of Diamond Will that you bestow.**

Part 2

1. Master MORE, shatter the energetic matrix that prevents people from
seeing that before 9/11, there was a certain sense of security among many
modern democracies that the Cold War was over, perhaps the era of warfare and violence was over and there would be more peaceful times.

> Master MORE, come to the fore,
> we will absorb your flame of MORE.
> Master MORE, our will so strong,
> our power centers cleared by song.

> **Master MORE, your Sacred Heart,**
> **from this we will no more depart,**
> **we are forever in your flow,**
> **of Diamond Will that you bestow.**

2. Master MORE, shatter the energetic matrix that prevents people from
seeing that this was shattered by 9/11 and other terrorist acts. By the very
fact that so many of the modern democracies went into or joined the war
on terror, we see that people still have a need for security even in the modern world.

Master MORE, your wisdom flows,
as our attunement ever grows.
Master MORE, we have a tie,
that helps us see through Serpent's lie.

**Master MORE, your Sacred Heart,
from this we will no more depart,
we are forever in your flow,
of Diamond Will that you bestow.**

3. Master MORE, shatter the energetic matrix that prevents people from seeing that even though more and more people in the modern democracies have gone up to the self-actualization needs, people still have a need for a sense of security, a sense of equilibrium.

Master MORE, your love so pink,
there is no purer love, we think.
Master MORE, you set us free,
from all conditionality.

**Master MORE, your Sacred Heart,
from this we will no more depart,
we are forever in your flow,
of Diamond Will that you bestow.**

4. Master MORE, shatter the energetic matrix that prevents people from seeing that if people have a worldview that gives them a sense of equilibrium, that allows them to function in their daily lives in a constructive way, then there is nothing wrong with that.

Master MORE, we will endure,
your discipline that makes us pure.
Master MORE, intentions true,
as we are always one with you.

**Master MORE, your Sacred Heart,
from this we will no more depart,
we are forever in your flow,
of Diamond Will that you bestow.**

5. Master MORE, shatter the energetic matrix that prevents people from seeing that the only way for us to really have security is to shift into that dynamic sense where we are willing to expand our understanding.

Master MORE, our vision raised,
the will of God is always praised.
Master MORE, creative will,
raising all life higher still.

**Master MORE, your Sacred Heart,
from this we will no more depart,
we are forever in your flow,
of Diamond Will that you bestow.**

6. Master MORE, shatter the energetic matrix that prevents people from making the shift and embracing a more dynamic form of security and realizing: We will not find security by holding on to our existing beliefs.

Master MORE, your peace is power,
the demons of war it will devour.
Master MORE, we serve all life,
our flames consuming war and strife.

**Master MORE, your Sacred Heart,
from this we will no more depart,
we are forever in your flow,
of Diamond Will that you bestow.**

7. Master MORE, shatter the energetic matrix that prevents people from seeing that it is only natural that as progress moves forward, there will be an expanded understanding of how the world works. If we want to maintain security, we need to embrace that understanding. We always need to have the latest most advanced understanding of how the world works, instead of holding on to the flat-earth theory.

Master MORE, we are so free,
eternal bond from you we see.
Master MORE, we find rebirth,
in flow of your eternal mirth.

**Master MORE, your Sacred Heart,
from this we will no more depart,
we are forever in your flow,
of Diamond Will that you bestow.**

8. Master MORE, shatter the energetic matrix that prevents people from shifting the equation in the modern democracies and seeing the need to help the growing number of people who have psychological problems, psychological illness.

Master MORE, you balance all,
the seven rays upon our call.
Master MORE, forever MORE,
we are the Spirit's open door.

**Master MORE, your Sacred Heart,
from this we will no more depart,
we are forever in your flow,
of Diamond Will that you bestow.**

9. Master MORE, shatter the energetic matrix that prevents people from seeing that we cannot solve psychological problems through drugs. Our approach has been based on the materialistic worldview that the body is a machine, and the brain is the origin of the psyche.

Master MORE, your Presence here,
filling up the inner sphere.
Life is now a sacred flow,
God Power we on all bestow.

**Master MORE, your Sacred Heart,
from this we will no more depart,
we are forever in your flow,
of Diamond Will that you bestow.**

Part 3

1. Master MORE, shatter the energetic matrix that prevents people from seeing that we face a choice: "Do we want to stop trying to help people and abandon them? Or do we want to change our paradigm so we can find a way to help them?"

Master MORE, come to the fore,
we will absorb your flame of MORE.
Master MORE, our will so strong,
our power centers cleared by song.

Master MORE, your Sacred Heart,
from this we will no more depart,
we are forever in your flow,
of Diamond Will that you bestow.

2. Master MORE, shatter the energetic matrix that prevents people from seeing that we cannot help them based on our current paradigm because if we could, it should be working and everybody should be happy. Therefore, we need to change the paradigm, we need to look beyond the paradigm.

Master MORE, your wisdom flows,
as our attunement ever grows.
Master MORE, we have a tie,
that helps us see through Serpent's lie.

Master MORE, your Sacred Heart,
from this we will no more depart,
we are forever in your flow,
of Diamond Will that you bestow.

3. Master MORE, shatter the energetic matrix that prevents people from seeing that this is not going to be a return to the medieval times where people thought that a particular religion could give them all the answers they needed.

Master MORE, your love so pink,
there is no purer love, we think.
Master MORE, you set us free,
from all conditionality.

**Master MORE, your Sacred Heart,
from this we will no more depart,
we are forever in your flow,
of Diamond Will that you bestow.**

4. Master MORE, shatter the energetic matrix that prevents people from seeing that the modern democracies, are never going to become theocracies or religious societies. They are never going to have a worldview that is based on a particular religion, including the teachings of the ascended masters.

Master MORE, we will endure,
your discipline that makes us pure.
Master MORE, intentions true,
as we are always one with you.

**Master MORE, your Sacred Heart,
from this we will no more depart,
we are forever in your flow,
of Diamond Will that you bestow.**

5. Master MORE, shatter the energetic matrix that prevents people from seeing that there can be a universal recognition of certain principles that we would now call spiritual, but which could just as well be seen as universal, as self-evident based on experience, based on observation.

Master MORE, our vision raised,
the will of God is always praised.
Master MORE, creative will,
raising all life higher still.

**Master MORE, your Sacred Heart,
from this we will no more depart,**

we are forever in your flow,
of Diamond Will that you bestow.

6. Master MORE, shatter the energetic matrix that prevents people from seeing that a growing number of people in the modern democracies have shifted into focusing on self-actualization needs. We need to give these people a path, a systematic procedure whereby they can fulfill those needs.

Master MORE, your peace is power,
the demons of war it will devour.
Master MORE, we serve all life,
our flames consuming war and strife.

Master MORE, your Sacred Heart,
from this we will no more depart,
we are forever in your flow,
of Diamond Will that you bestow.

7. Master MORE, shatter the energetic matrix that prevents people from seeing that we need to be able to actualize ourselves, which means we need to explore: What is a self-actualized human being? What is the human potential? What is the potential of the mind?

Master MORE, we are so free,
eternal bond from you we see.
Master MORE, we find rebirth,
in flow of your eternal mirth.

Master MORE, your Sacred Heart,
from this we will no more depart,
we are forever in your flow,
of Diamond Will that you bestow.

8. Master MORE, shatter the energetic matrix that prevents people from seeing that if our attempts to solve psychological problems by introducing chemicals into the brain has not worked, this has proven that the mind cannot be an exclusive product of the physical processes in the brain.

Master MORE, you balance all,
the seven rays upon our call.
Master MORE, forever MORE,
we are the Spirit's open door.

**Master MORE, your Sacred Heart,
from this we will no more depart,
we are forever in your flow,
of Diamond Will that you bestow.**

9. Master MORE, shatter the energetic matrix that prevents people from seeing that there is more to mind than matter. We need to develop a universal approach to this so that we can give people something that they need.

Master MORE, your Presence here,
filling up the inner sphere.
Life is now a sacred flow,
God Power we on all bestow.

**Master MORE, your Sacred Heart,
from this we will no more depart,
we are forever in your flow,
of Diamond Will that you bestow.**

Part 4

1. Master MORE, shatter the energetic matrix that prevents people from seeing that we need to make a shift from focusing on *curing* mental illness to focusing on *preventing* it.

Master MORE, come to the fore,
we will absorb your flame of MORE.
Master MORE, our will so strong,
our power centers cleared by song.

Master MORE, your Sacred Heart,
from this we will no more depart,
we are forever in your flow,
of Diamond Will that you bestow.

2. Master MORE, shatter the energetic matrix that prevents people from seeing that in the next 10 to 20 years, the biggest challenge for the public health care system will be mental illness because more and more people have depression and other illnesses.

Master MORE, your wisdom flows,
as our attunement ever grows.
Master MORE, we have a tie,
that helps us see through Serpent's lie.

Master MORE, your Sacred Heart,
from this we will no more depart,
we are forever in your flow,
of Diamond Will that you bestow.

3. Master MORE, shatter the energetic matrix that prevents people from seeing that we can *pay* up or we can *step* up.

Master MORE, your love so pink,
there is no purer love, we think.
Master MORE, you set us free,
from all conditionality.

Master MORE, your Sacred Heart,
from this we will no more depart,
we are forever in your flow,
of Diamond Will that you bestow.

4. Master MORE, shatter the energetic matrix that prevents people from seeing that if we want to step up to a higher approach to the problem of psychological illness, then we have to find a way to help people with their self-actualization needs so that they can get on a positive growth path.

Master MORE, we will endure,
your discipline that makes us pure.
Master MORE, intentions true,
as we are always one with you.

Master MORE, your Sacred Heart,
from this we will no more depart,
we are forever in your flow,
of Diamond Will that you bestow.

5. Master MORE, shatter the energetic matrix that prevents people from seeing that public schools need to teach basic things about how the human psyche works, the possibility that we can develop our psyches in an active way, that we are not victims of our upbringing or family background.

Master MORE, our vision raised,
the will of God is always praised.
Master MORE, creative will,
raising all life higher still.

Master MORE, your Sacred Heart,
from this we will no more depart,
we are forever in your flow,
of Diamond Will that you bestow.

6. Master MORE, shatter the energetic matrix that prevents people from seeing that the psyche is a dynamic thing that we can take control over. We can change what we do not like in our psyche, as a bodybuilder can change certain things about the body.

Master MORE, your peace is power,
the demons of war it will devour.
Master MORE, we serve all life,
our flames consuming war and strife.

Master MORE, your Sacred Heart,
from this we will no more depart,
we are forever in your flow,
of Diamond Will that you bestow.

7. Master MORE, shatter the energetic matrix that prevents people from seeing that we can begin, at an early age, to start molding our psyche the way we want it. This can put us on a positive track where we never develop severe mental illness. We do not have to go to the doctor or the psychiatrist.

> Master MORE, we are so free,
> eternal bond from you we see.
> Master MORE, we find rebirth,
> in flow of your eternal mirth.

> **Master MORE, your Sacred Heart,**
> **from this we will no more depart,**
> **we are forever in your flow,**
> **of Diamond Will that you bestow.**

8. Master MORE, shatter the energetic matrix that prevents people from seeing that when we sense that life has a purpose, which is to expand our consciousness, we are not as likely to be depressed as when we do not have any sense of purpose.

> Master MORE, you balance all,
> the seven rays upon our call.
> Master MORE, forever MORE,
> we are the Spirit's open door.

> **Master MORE, your Sacred Heart,**
> **from this we will no more depart,**
> **we are forever in your flow,**
> **of Diamond Will that you bestow.**

9. Master MORE, shatter the energetic matrix that prevents people from seeing that some people came into embodiment to raise their consciousness, but they have been given no tools so they think that a materialistic lifestyle is meaningless and they become depressed.

> Master MORE, your Presence here,
> filling up the inner sphere.
> Life is now a sacred flow,
> God Power we on all bestow.

**Master MORE, your Sacred Heart,
from this we will no more depart,
we are forever in your flow,
of Diamond Will that you bestow.**

Part 5

1. Master MORE, shatter the energetic matrix that prevents people from seeing that the older generation found it meaningful to strive for a good material lifestyle. Yet the children of these people want something else. The material lifestyle that their parents have does not give them a sense of meaning and purpose in life.

Master MORE, come to the fore,
we will absorb your flame of MORE.
Master MORE, our will so strong,
our power centers cleared by song.

**Master MORE, your Sacred Heart,
from this we will no more depart,
we are forever in your flow,
of Diamond Will that you bestow.**

2. Master MORE, shatter the energetic matrix that prevents people from seeing that we need to give people that sense of purpose and we only do that by helping them develop themselves, taking command over their psyches.

Master MORE, your wisdom flows,
as our attunement ever grows.
Master MORE, we have a tie,
that helps us see through Serpent's lie.

**Master MORE, your Sacred Heart,
from this we will no more depart,
we are forever in your flow,
of Diamond Will that you bestow.**

3. Master MORE, shatter the energetic matrix that prevents people from seeing that certain cultures are in the extreme, the aggressive, fanatical mindset. Yet even in the Middle East and Islam, there will be some progress.

> Master MORE, your love so pink,
> there is no purer love, we think.
> Master MORE, you set us free,
> from all conditionality.
>
> **Master MORE, your Sacred Heart,**
> **from this we will no more depart,**
> **we are forever in your flow,**
> **of Diamond Will that you bestow.**

4. Master MORE, shatter the energetic matrix that prevents people from seeing that inevitably there will come a point where the current fanaticism that we see in Islam will not be there anymore. It will go away. History has proven this.

> Master MORE, we will endure,
> your discipline that makes us pure.
> Master MORE, intentions true,
> as we are always one with you.
>
> **Master MORE, your Sacred Heart,**
> **from this we will no more depart,**
> **we are forever in your flow,**
> **of Diamond Will that you bestow.**

5. Master MORE, shatter the energetic matrix that prevents people from seeing that this is proven by the fact that the modern democracies have raised themselves beyond the fanaticism that we had 100 or more years ago.

> Master MORE, our vision raised,
> the will of God is always praised.
> Master MORE, creative will,
> raising all life higher still.

**Master MORE, your Sacred Heart,
from this we will no more depart,
we are forever in your flow,
of Diamond Will that you bestow.**

6. Master MORE, shatter the energetic matrix that prevents people from seeing that while change *will* happen, the essence of the fanatical mindset is that we think the problem is "out there," outside ourselves.

Master MORE, your peace is power,
the demons of war it will devour.
Master MORE, we serve all life,
our flames consuming war and strife.

**Master MORE, your Sacred Heart,
from this we will no more depart,
we are forever in your flow,
of Diamond Will that you bestow.**

7. Master MORE, shatter the energetic matrix that prevents people from seeing that fanatics think it is these other people that are the problem and therefore the only way for them to feel secure is to change these other people.

Master MORE, we are so free,
eternal bond from you we see.
Master MORE, we find rebirth,
in flow of your eternal mirth.

**Master MORE, your Sacred Heart,
from this we will no more depart,
we are forever in your flow,
of Diamond Will that you bestow.**

8. Master MORE, shatter the energetic matrix that prevents people from seeing that this is the background for the entire Islamic fundamentalist terrorist movement: The West is the problem. The West is a threat to Islam. The only way to create the world that Islam and Allah supposedly want is to change people in the West.

Master MORE, you balance all,
the seven rays upon our call.
Master MORE, forever MORE,
we are the Spirit's open door.

**Master MORE, your Sacred Heart,
from this we will no more depart,
we are forever in your flow,
of Diamond Will that you bestow.**

9. Master MORE, shatter the energetic matrix that prevents people from seeing that in the modern democracies we can either step back and let history take its course, or we can realize that we can do something to change the equation.

Master MORE, your Presence here,
filling up the inner sphere.
Life is now a sacred flow,
God Power we on all bestow.

**Master MORE, your Sacred Heart,
from this we will no more depart,
we are forever in your flow,
of Diamond Will that you bestow.**

Sealing

In the name of the I AM THAT I AM, I accept that Archangel Michael, Astrea and Shiva form an impenetrable shield around myself and all constructive people, sealing us from all fear-based energies in all four octaves. I accept that the Light of God is consuming and transforming all fear-based energies that make up the dark forces working against ending the era of fanaticism on earth!

8 | INVOKING FREEDOM FROM FEELING POWERLESS (PART 3)

In the name of the I AM THAT I AM, Jesus Christ, I use the authority that I have as a being in embodiment on earth to call upon Master MORE to reinforce my calls and use my chakras to project the statements in this invocation into the collective consciousness and awaken people to the fact that we are not powerless to free the world from fanaticism. Awaken people to the reality that we are spiritual beings and that we can co-create a new future by working with the ascended masters. I especially call for ...

[Make your own calls here.]

Part 1

1. Master MORE, shatter the energetic matrix that prevents people from seeing that fanatics may seem very aggressive, but they are not powerful people. They are driven by insecurity.

> Master MORE, come to the fore,
> we will absorb your flame of MORE.

Master MORE, our will so strong,
our power centers cleared by song.

**Master MORE, your Sacred Heart,
from this we will no more depart,
we are forever in your flow,
of Diamond Will that you bestow.**

2. Master MORE, shatter the energetic matrix that prevents people from seeing that extremists are attacking the West because they feel powerless. *They feel powerless.*

Master MORE, your wisdom flows,
as our attunement ever grows.
Master MORE, we have a tie,
that helps us see through Serpent's lie.

**Master MORE, your Sacred Heart,
from this we will no more depart,
we are forever in your flow,
of Diamond Will that you bestow.**

3. Master MORE, shatter the energetic matrix that prevents people from seeing that fanatics are powerless because they cannot see how to change their situation. They cannot see this because they are in the fanatical mindset and do not want to change their worldview.

Master MORE, your love so pink,
there is no purer love, we think.
Master MORE, you set us free,
from all conditionality.

**Master MORE, your Sacred Heart,
from this we will no more depart,
we are forever in your flow,
of Diamond Will that you bestow.**

4. Master MORE, shatter the energetic matrix that prevents people from seeing that fanatics are looking at the world the way people in the West

looked at the world in medieval times and that is why they cannot manifest the progress that the western world is manifesting.

Master MORE, we will endure,
your discipline that makes us pure.
Master MORE, intentions true,
as we are always one with you.

**Master MORE, your Sacred Heart,
from this we will no more depart,
we are forever in your flow,
of Diamond Will that you bestow.**

5. Master MORE, shatter the energetic matrix that prevents people from seeing that in the mindset that people had 200 years ago, there was a very clear segmentation of society. There was the general population and then there was a very small elite who had all the power, all the privilege, all the wealth.

Master MORE, our vision raised,
the will of God is always praised.
Master MORE, creative will,
raising all life higher still.

**Master MORE, your Sacred Heart,
from this we will no more depart,
we are forever in your flow,
of Diamond Will that you bestow.**

6. Master MORE, shatter the energetic matrix that prevents people from seeing that in the past the majority of the population felt powerless. They felt disempowered. They felt they could do nothing to improve their lives. It was the same state of disempowerment that many people in the Islamic world feel today.

Master MORE, your peace is power,
the demons of war it will devour.
Master MORE, we serve all life,
our flames consuming war and strife.

Master MORE, your Sacred Heart,
from this we will no more depart,
we are forever in your flow,
of Diamond Will that you bestow.

7. Master MORE, shatter the energetic matrix that prevents people from seeing that the generation that ushered in democracy overcame their sense of being powerless. They took upon themselves a sense of being powerful. They realized that by the fact of our numbers, we have power. Therefore, when we demand change, the leaders will have to comply.

Master MORE, we are so free,
eternal bond from you we see.
Master MORE, we find rebirth,
in flow of your eternal mirth.

Master MORE, your Sacred Heart,
from this we will no more depart,
we are forever in your flow,
of Diamond Will that you bestow.

8. Master MORE, shatter the energetic matrix that prevents people from seeing that the Arabs, the Muslims, feel powerless. After 9/11, we allowed ourselves to go into a state of mind where we felt powerless because we felt: "What can we do about these fanatics?"

Master MORE, you balance all,
the seven rays upon our call.
Master MORE, forever MORE,
we are the Spirit's open door.

Master MORE, your Sacred Heart,
from this we will no more depart,
we are forever in your flow,
of Diamond Will that you bestow.

9. Master MORE, shatter the energetic matrix that prevents people from seeing that this is why we were deceived by the American government, and the people behind the American government, to go on this adventure

in Iraq and Afghanistan to supposedly bring freedom and democracy through force.

> Master MORE, your Presence here,
> filling up the inner sphere.
> Life is now a sacred flow,
> God Power we on all bestow.

> **Master MORE, your Sacred Heart,**
> **from this we will no more depart,**
> **we are forever in your flow,**
> **of Diamond Will that you bestow.**

Part 2

1. Master MORE, shatter the energetic matrix that prevents people from seeing that even though there was tremendous power displayed by these armed forces, it all sprang from the sense of being powerless and therefore thinking we have to change other people in order to have a sense of equilibrium.

> Master MORE, come to the fore,
> we will absorb your flame of MORE.
> Master MORE, our will so strong,
> our power centers cleared by song.

> **Master MORE, your Sacred Heart,**
> **from this we will no more depart,**
> **we are forever in your flow,**
> **of Diamond Will that you bestow.**

2. Master MORE, shatter the energetic matrix that prevents people from seeing that America's sense of equilibrium was shattered on 9/11. Going into Afghanistan and Iraq was an attempt to reestablish America's sense of equilibrium.

Master MORE, your wisdom flows,
as our attunement ever grows.
Master MORE, we have a tie,
that helps us see through Serpent's lie.

**Master MORE, your Sacred Heart,
from this we will no more depart,
we are forever in your flow,
of Diamond Will that you bestow.**

3. Master MORE, shatter the energetic matrix that prevents people from seeing that America is still trying to do it today. They have not been successful because they are trying to create a sense of peace in their minds by changing the minds of other people and it can never, *ever* happen.

Master MORE, your love so pink,
there is no purer love, we think.
Master MORE, you set us free,
from all conditionality.

**Master MORE, your Sacred Heart,
from this we will no more depart,
we are forever in your flow,
of Diamond Will that you bestow.**

4. Master MORE, shatter the energetic matrix that prevents people from stepping up and seeing: We in the modern democracies have to take back our power and how do we do this? By changing what we *can* change: ourselves, our own state of consciousness.

Master MORE, we will endure,
your discipline that makes us pure.
Master MORE, intentions true,
as we are always one with you.

**Master MORE, your Sacred Heart,
from this we will no more depart,
we are forever in your flow,
of Diamond Will that you bestow.**

5. Master MORE, shatter the energetic matrix that prevents people from seeing that we do this by reexamining our paradigms and stepping up to a higher worldview that gives us our power back, because we realize that when we change our consciousness, our world *will* change.

> Master MORE, our vision raised,
> the will of God is always praised.
> Master MORE, creative will,
> raising all life higher still.

> **Master MORE, your Sacred Heart,**
> **from this we will no more depart,**
> **we are forever in your flow,**
> **of Diamond Will that you bestow.**

6. Master MORE, shatter the energetic matrix that prevents people from seeing that this is how we created democracies. We had for centuries had elitist, totalitarian dictatorships and the transition to democracy happened because a critical mass of people changed their consciousness.

> Master MORE, your peace is power,
> the demons of war it will devour.
> Master MORE, we serve all life,
> our flames consuming war and strife.

> **Master MORE, your Sacred Heart,**
> **from this we will no more depart,**
> **we are forever in your flow,**
> **of Diamond Will that you bestow.**

7. Master MORE, shatter the energetic matrix that prevents people from seeing that people took back their power and admitted that we have the power to do something of ourselves. We have the power to demand change. When we change ourselves, this *will* shift our world.

> Master MORE, we are so free,
> eternal bond from you we see.
> Master MORE, we find rebirth,
> in flow of your eternal mirth.

**Master MORE, your Sacred Heart,
from this we will no more depart,
we are forever in your flow,
of Diamond Will that you bestow.**

8. Master MORE, shatter the energetic matrix that prevents people from seeing that when we shift our approach to Muslim fundamentalism and terrorism, then Muslims will also change.

Master MORE, you balance all,
the seven rays upon our call.
Master MORE, forever MORE,
we are the Spirit's open door.

**Master MORE, your Sacred Heart,
from this we will no more depart,
we are forever in your flow,
of Diamond Will that you bestow.**

9. Master MORE, shatter the energetic matrix that prevents people from seeing that when we shift our approach to life, our view of the world, when we shift into this dynamic willingness to raise our understanding of life, even going beyond the materialistic paradigm and the Christian paradigm, then our world *will* change.

Master MORE, your Presence here,
filling up the inner sphere.
Life is now a sacred flow,
God Power we on all bestow.

**Master MORE, your Sacred Heart,
from this we will no more depart,
we are forever in your flow,
of Diamond Will that you bestow.**

Part 3

1. Master MORE, shatter the energetic matrix that prevents people from seeing that even if the Muslims stay in their fanatical mindset, we will not be the target of it. They will instead begin to fight amongst themselves, as they are already doing and have been doing for thousands of years.

> Master MORE, come to the fore,
> we will absorb your flame of MORE.
> Master MORE, our will so strong,
> our power centers cleared by song.

> **Master MORE, your Sacred Heart,**
> **from this we will no more depart,**
> **we are forever in your flow,**
> **of Diamond Will that you bestow.**

2. Master MORE, shatter the energetic matrix that prevents people from seeing that if the fighting happens down there, our world has shifted.

> Master MORE, your wisdom flows,
> as our attunement ever grows.
> Master MORE, we have a tie,
> that helps us see through Serpent's lie.

> **Master MORE, your Sacred Heart,**
> **from this we will no more depart,**
> **we are forever in your flow,**
> **of Diamond Will that you bestow.**

3. Master MORE, shatter the energetic matrix that prevents people from seeing that if they fight amongst each other, we do not need to be concerned about it because in a democracy, we respect that other people might want to live in a different way.

> Master MORE, your love so pink,
> there is no purer love, we think.

Master MORE, you set us free,
from all conditionality.

Master MORE, your Sacred Heart,
from this we will no more depart,
we are forever in your flow,
of Diamond Will that you bestow.

4. Master MORE, shatter the energetic matrix that prevents people from seeing that we have become a target of Muslim fundamentalism because we have not shifted our paradigm. Most of the modern democracies should in the 1960s have shifted our paradigm away from Materialism. This has not happened and therefore, we have attracted to ourselves this outplaying of our own state of consciousness.

Master MORE, we will endure,
your discipline that makes us pure.
Master MORE, intentions true,
as we are always one with you.

Master MORE, your Sacred Heart,
from this we will no more depart,
we are forever in your flow,
of Diamond Will that you bestow.

5. Master MORE, shatter the energetic matrix that prevents people from seeing that the Muslim fundamentalists are clearly more extreme but they are showing us what we still have left in our own consciousness that is unrecognized and denied by most.

Master MORE, our vision raised,
the will of God is always praised.
Master MORE, creative will,
raising all life higher still.

Master MORE, your Sacred Heart,
from this we will no more depart,
we are forever in your flow,
of Diamond Will that you bestow.

6. Master MORE, shatter the energetic matrix that prevents people from seeing that the School of Hard Knocks works in a very simple way. If we have a certain mindset of fanaticism, we will attract to us people who are having that same mindset in a more extreme form.

Master MORE, your peace is power,
the demons of war it will devour.
Master MORE, we serve all life,
our flames consuming war and strife.

**Master MORE, your Sacred Heart,
from this we will no more depart,
we are forever in your flow,
of Diamond Will that you bestow.**

7. Master MORE, shatter the energetic matrix that prevents people from seeing that when we see it in a more extreme form, it is more easy to see that this is fanaticism.

Master MORE, we are so free,
eternal bond from you we see.
Master MORE, we find rebirth,
in flow of your eternal mirth.

**Master MORE, your Sacred Heart,
from this we will no more depart,
we are forever in your flow,
of Diamond Will that you bestow.**

8. Master MORE, shatter the energetic matrix that prevents people from seeing that the test we have failed so far, is that we think that because the Muslims are willing to kill, and we have transcended the willingness to kill, we do not have that kind of fanaticism in ourselves.

Master MORE, you balance all,
the seven rays upon our call.
Master MORE, forever MORE,
we are the Spirit's open door.

Master MORE, your Sacred Heart,
from this we will no more depart,
we are forever in your flow,
of Diamond Will that you bestow.

9. Master MORE, shatter the energetic matrix that prevents people from seeing that we have the same dynamic. It is there in the collective consciousness, this willingness to hold on to the ideas and the absolute denial of the possibility that these ideas could be expanded upon. This is the essence of fanaticism and the rest is just a matter of degree.

Master MORE, your Presence here,
filling up the inner sphere.
Life is now a sacred flow,
God Power we on all bestow.

Master MORE, your Sacred Heart,
from this we will no more depart,
we are forever in your flow,
of Diamond Will that you bestow.

Part 4

1. Master MORE, shatter the energetic matrix that prevents people from seeing that it is not the opinions we have, it is how we hold on to them. It is only a matter of degree whether people hold on to them the way we do in the West or the way they do in the Middle East.

Master MORE, come to the fore,
we will absorb your flame of MORE.
Master MORE, our will so strong,
our power centers cleared by song.

Master MORE, your Sacred Heart,
from this we will no more depart,
we are forever in your flow,
of Diamond Will that you bestow.

2. Master MORE, shatter the energetic matrix that prevents people from seeing that it is only a matter of degree whether we are willing to kill somebody to defend our ideas or whether we are willing to ridicule and put down those who believe differently.

Master MORE, your wisdom flows,
as our attunement ever grows.
Master MORE, we have a tie,
that helps us see through Serpent's lie.

**Master MORE, your Sacred Heart,
from this we will no more depart,
we are forever in your flow,
of Diamond Will that you bestow.**

3. Master MORE, shatter the energetic matrix that prevents people from seeing that it is also fanaticism if we want to exclude people from our countries because we cannot bear to be threatened by the fact that there are some people who are religious and we are not.

Master MORE, your love so pink,
there is no purer love, we think.
Master MORE, you set us free,
from all conditionality.

**Master MORE, your Sacred Heart,
from this we will no more depart,
we are forever in your flow,
of Diamond Will that you bestow.**

4. Master MORE, shatter the energetic matrix that prevents people from seeing that we became democracies by being willing to take back our power and to change ourselves and our obligation.

Master MORE, we will endure,
your discipline that makes us pure.
Master MORE, intentions true,
as we are always one with you.

**Master MORE, your Sacred Heart,
from this we will no more depart,
we are forever in your flow,
of Diamond Will that you bestow.**

5. Master MORE, shatter the energetic matrix that prevents people from seeing that the only way we are going to survive as democracies is to continue to do this, continue to take back more and more power, instead of allowing somebody to make us feel disempowered.

Master MORE, our vision raised,
the will of God is always praised.
Master MORE, creative will,
raising all life higher still.

**Master MORE, your Sacred Heart,
from this we will no more depart,
we are forever in your flow,
of Diamond Will that you bestow.**

6. Master MORE, shatter the energetic matrix that prevents people from seeing that we take back power by changing our consciousness and this is something we can do. When we start doing this, we will be able to build a more secure world because we transcend the fanatical mindset and therefore do not have to attract to us a more extreme outpicturing of it.

Master MORE, your peace is power,
the demons of war it will devour.
Master MORE, we serve all life,
our flames consuming war and strife.

**Master MORE, your Sacred Heart,
from this we will no more depart,
we are forever in your flow,
of Diamond Will that you bestow.**

7. Master MORE, shatter the energetic matrix that prevents people from seeing that if Europe did not have the fanatical mindset, we would not

have attracted Nazism on European soil. We needed to see it outpictured in such an extreme form in order to get over it.

> Master MORE, we are so free,
> eternal bond from you we see.
> Master MORE, we find rebirth,
> in flow of your eternal mirth.

> **Master MORE, your Sacred Heart,**
> **from this we will no more depart,**
> **we are forever in your flow,**
> **of Diamond Will that you bestow.**

8. Master MORE, shatter the energetic matrix that prevents people from seeing that what people got over in Europe after Nazism was the willingness to kill other people to defend our ideas, but that was just the *first* step. It was not the *ultimate* or *final* step. It was just overcoming the more aggressive, physical aspect of fanaticism.

> Master MORE, you balance all,
> the seven rays upon our call.
> Master MORE, forever MORE,
> we are the Spirit's open door.

> **Master MORE, your Sacred Heart,**
> **from this we will no more depart,**
> **we are forever in your flow,**
> **of Diamond Will that you bestow.**

9. Master MORE, shatter the energetic matrix that prevents people from seeing that Hitler outpictured the willingness to take extreme physical actions in order to defend our illusion.

> Master MORE, your Presence here,
> filling up the inner sphere.
> Life is now a sacred flow,
> God Power we on all bestow.

Master MORE, your Sacred Heart,
from this we will no more depart,
we are forever in your flow,
of Diamond Will that you bestow.

Part 5

1. Master MORE, shatter the energetic matrix that prevents people from seeing that there is also an emotional component to fanaticism where we are seeking to intimidate people at an emotional level.

Master MORE, come to the fore,
we will absorb your flame of MORE.
Master MORE, our will so strong,
our power centers cleared by song.

Master MORE, your Sacred Heart,
from this we will no more depart,
we are forever in your flow,
of Diamond Will that you bestow.

2. Master MORE, shatter the energetic matrix that prevents people from seeing that there is an intellectual, mental level of fanaticism where we are using mental faculties to disprove or even ridicule other beliefs.

Master MORE, your wisdom flows,
as our attunement ever grows.
Master MORE, we have a tie,
that helps us see through Serpent's lie.

Master MORE, your Sacred Heart,
from this we will no more depart,
we are forever in your flow,
of Diamond Will that you bestow.

3. Master MORE, shatter the energetic matrix that prevents people from seeing that there is an identity level of fanaticism where people decide that because of their identity, they are superior to others.

Master MORE, your love so pink,
there is no purer love, we think.
Master MORE, you set us free,
from all conditionality.

**Master MORE, your Sacred Heart,
from this we will no more depart,
we are forever in your flow,
of Diamond Will that you bestow.**

4. Master MORE, shatter the energetic matrix that prevents people from seeing that what is lacking is that Europe transcends the emotional, mental and identity level component of fanaticism, the willingness to defend our ideas by intimidating other people emotionally, by arguing against them or by making us feel that we are better than others.

Master MORE, we will endure,
your discipline that makes us pure.
Master MORE, intentions true,
as we are always one with you.

**Master MORE, your Sacred Heart,
from this we will no more depart,
we are forever in your flow,
of Diamond Will that you bestow.**

5. Master MORE, shatter the energetic matrix that prevents people from seeing that even though it may seem hopeless to change the fanatics, when enough people in the modern democracies transcend fanaticism, it will shift the equation even in the Islamic world.

Master MORE, our vision raised,
the will of God is always praised.
Master MORE, creative will,
raising all life higher still.

**Master MORE, your Sacred Heart,
from this we will no more depart,
we are forever in your flow,
of Diamond Will that you bestow.**

6. Master MORE, shatter the energetic matrix that prevents people from seeing that we are never powerless—unless we believe we are.

Master MORE, your peace is power,
the demons of war it will devour.
Master MORE, we serve all life,
our flames consuming war and strife.

**Master MORE, your Sacred Heart,
from this we will no more depart,
we are forever in your flow,
of Diamond Will that you bestow.**

7. Master MORE, shatter the energetic matrix that prevents people from seeing that we have as much power as we can accept that we have. Because it is not *our* power.

Master MORE, we are so free,
eternal bond from you we see.
Master MORE, we find rebirth,
in flow of your eternal mirth.

**Master MORE, your Sacred Heart,
from this we will no more depart,
we are forever in your flow,
of Diamond Will that you bestow.**

8. Master MORE, shatter the energetic matrix that prevents people from seeing that we who are in embodiment have the authority to decide what happens on earth and the ascended masters have the power to change anything on earth.

Master MORE, you balance all,
the seven rays upon our call.

Master MORE, forever MORE,
we are the Spirit's open door.

**Master MORE, your Sacred Heart,
from this we will no more depart,
we are forever in your flow,
of Diamond Will that you bestow.**

9. Master MORE, shatter the energetic matrix that prevents people from seeing that when we make the calls to the masters, they can unlock the power, not to force a change, but to set people free to see it so that they choose it. The call *will* compel the answer.

Master MORE, your Presence here,
filling up the inner sphere.
Life is now a sacred flow,
God Power we on all bestow.

**Master MORE, your Sacred Heart,
from this we will no more depart,
we are forever in your flow,
of Diamond Will that you bestow.**

Sealing

In the name of the I AM THAT I AM, I accept that Archangel Michael, Astrea and Shiva form an impenetrable shield around myself and all constructive people, sealing us from all fear-based energies in all four octaves. I accept that the Light of God is consuming and transforming all fear-based energies that make up the dark forces working against ending the era of fanaticism on earth!

9 | FANATICISM PREVENTS SOCIETY FROM MOVING BEYOND MATERIALISM

I AM the Ascended Master Saint Germain. I come to continue what Mother Mary and Master MORE have talked about, but I want to give it this perspective of freedom. You have in all of the modern democracies a certain consciousness that has grown over time where people believe they are free. Of course, from a certain perspective you can say that people in democratic nations *are* free. Certainly, compared to those in dictatorial nations—but are they truly free? Has their freedom gone as high as it can go? Are people as free as they could be? This is a question rarely asked. Why is it that people rarely ask that question? Well, it can again be explained by the pyramid of needs created by Maslow. He said that, once a lower need has been fulfilled to a critical degree, people no longer think about it. It simply falls out of their awareness and they do not consider it a problem.

If you go back to before the democratic era and look at these nations that are now democracies, you can see that people lived under what was essentially a dictatorship. When you are living in a dictatorship, most people will feel restricted. They will feel that they are not free. Certainly, in the feudal societies of Europe, most of the population did not feel free because they could not improve their station in life. They lived in constant poverty, their daily lives were a struggle, just to survive physically.

They clearly felt that as a limitation. There came a point where they started recognizing that they were being oppressed by the kings, by the noble class, by the power elite. There came that point where they took back their power and demanded freedom.

What happened back then was that throughout several centuries, there had been building this collective consciousness that: "We are oppressed, we want to be free." Then, you had democracies created and now that level of consciousness felt that it had gained freedom. It had gained the freedom it was longing for in the pre-democratic era. People had physical, political freedom. In a certain sense, you can say this is somewhat correct, at least because they have greater freedom than they had before.

Mental freedom is a higher level of freedom

As we have many times talked about, there is still a power elite in democratic nations that are trying to set themselves up in a position where they have power and privilege beyond the general population. They can only do this by taking freedom, privileges and abundance from the population. That is why you see this concentration of wealth in the hands of fewer and fewer people. This is a return towards even a physical form of slavery where people are not enslaved by the threat of physical violence, of being killed, but they are enslaved economically. They are enslaved to work their whole lives to pay back their mortgage and therefore pay the interest to the power elite. Nevertheless, we can still say that people in democratic nations enjoy a high level of physical, political freedom. Even to some degree economic freedom in the sense that they can live a relatively comfortable material life.

What can happen, and what has been building for some time, is a shift where people become aware that this is not enough. This level of freedom is not the highest potential for democratic nations. It can happen when you look back to what Mother Mary and Master MORE have talked about. The trigger can be the rise in mental illness. What happens when a person suffers from a mental illness or depression and therefore is incapable of functioning in a normal way? Well, is that not a state of non-freedom, of anti-freedom? It is very, very close, (in the collective consciousness the tension has been built) where a shift can happen where people start realizing that physical freedom is just one side of the equation of freedom. It is one aspect of it. We need to step higher in the democratic nations and realize that the only way to truly be free is to have freedom in the psyche. What I have before called mental freedom. *That* is true freedom.

You can have political freedom, you can have economic freedom, but if you are still trapped in some limited psychology, you are not truly free. You can see this by looking at many of these people who have used their political and physical freedom to gather more and more wealth to the point where they have more wealth than anyone could spend for the rest of this lifetime. They cannot stop there, buy themselves a vacation house somewhere and just enjoy life. They have to keep accumulating wealth. You see that the only explanation for this is that these people, even though they have *financial* independence, they do not have *psychological* independence. They are not free in their minds.

You can then see again that it is not just the elite, it is also the population. People are not free in their minds. Physical, political freedom is just the first step in the process of becoming a free human being. You really need to build on this and then say, once we have the political and economic freedom that gives us free time and free attention, then we can build on this, we can use this as a foundation. Instead of thinking it is an end in itself, we use it as a foundation for now pursuing psychological freedom, mental freedom.

It is easy to live in a dictatorship

You can see this very, very clearly in the affluent nations by the fact of the increase in mental illness, psychological problems, substance abuse. What you can realize here is that when people are oppressed, life is in a sense easy for them. If you go to the dictatorships that are still in the world, you can see that in a certain sense life for these people is easy. They have very clearly defined outer parameters that they feel powerless to change. In some cases, people come to a point where they accept conditions as they are. You can go back to communist times and see how many people had accepted that: "Oh this is how life is, there is nothing that can be done, we couldn't improve our lives beyond a certain limit. I can get this job, I can hold this job for the rest of my life, I make this income, this gives me a certain standard of living, there is nothing I can do about it." There were people who accepted this, therefore life was, in a sense, easy for them. They did not have the options to choose from. What you can do in the affluent nations is you can look at this generation that is now coming into retirement or has already retired, of the people that we have talked about that lived a materialistic lifestyle for all of their lives. They were pursuing material affluence as the main goal for their lives. You can see how many of these people have been used to working, and often working hard in order to gain more economic abundance. What happens when they retire? In many cases, they do not know what to do with themselves. They do not know what to do with the physical freedom they now have because they are not spending 40 hours or more a week on their jobs. What do they do? You see many people who have worked very hard for many years, they retire and within a year they die. It is simply because they do not know what to do with their freedom.

What you can realize based on this is that freedom actually demands something. When you have physical freedom, political freedom, economic freedom this is not an easy state to be in. There is again, if we reach back to the pre-democratic era in Europe and elsewhere, you see that there was a certain assumption in the collective consciousness. People assumed that: "If we just get free of the kings and the noble class, if we just have physical, political, economic freedom, then we will have utopia, then we will have paradise, then we will have the ideal society." What you see is that when people are feeling oppressed, they look at what is oppressing them and they think that if we got rid of that, we would be free. This is a very limited understanding of what freedom means. You can see here that after these democratic nations, after people gained that political, economic freedom this has not been as easy as people thought.

The escapism industry

You see that many people have not been able to figure out what to do with their freedom. That is why you can see that there are many things that are happening in the modern democracies that are an effect of the fact that people have not gained the psychological freedom to correspond with their physical freedom. Therefore, they do not know what to do with their physical freedom. You can see mental illness as one aspect, but you can see the entire escapism industry, as we might call it, where people instead of making a choice of what they want to do with the freedom they have, they go into seeking some kind of escape, some kind of entertainment. It can be anything from drugs and alcohol to cheap entertainment that just diverts your attention in the moment. It can be movies, it can be television, it can be computer games, it can be all kinds of things, reading books that just help you pass time.

You see that there is an entire phenomenon that has happened in the democratic nations where people now have free time. But if they are not free in their minds, they do not know what to do with their free time. There is an entire industry that has sprung up that only has one purpose, that is to help people pass their free time.

The need for a sense of purpose

What you realize is that people cannot just sit around and do nothing. You can then begin to ask yourself: "Why is that so?" It is because the human psyche has a certain mechanism. That mechanism can be understood in various ways and we have given you a deeper understanding, but what can become general knowledge, can become generally accepted within a very short time, is that the human psyche has a need to have a sense of purpose. This is something that transcends Maslow's pyramid of needs. At all levels, except the purely physiological needs, but at all of the other levels, there is an underlying need that you need to have a sense of purpose. Life must have some sense of purpose. As a human being, you cannot just live, you cannot just live in the moment, you cannot sit around and do nothing. You can train yourself, as Yogis and some monks and nuns have done, to meditate, but that requires a lot of training. In general, the human psyche is such that you cannot sit around and do nothing.

What it really comes from is that there is a need in human beings to have a sense of purpose. Where does this need come from? Well, you who are ascended master students know it comes from the fact that you are all co-creators. You have come to this earth, you have been blinded by a certain state of consciousness, but you still have some inner sense that your life has a purpose. There was a reason why you came here and you want to grow. Even in a general term, people can come to realize that human beings have a much more complex psyche than animals. Therefore, what you see in a cow (where a cow can be perfectly happy, lying in a field all day and chewing the cud), human beings (obviously, by observation) cannot be happy that way. You can see this throughout the ages. You must then come to the conclusion that a human being, in order to function well psychologically, needs a sense of purpose. As Maslow said, if the lower needs are *not* fulfilled, then these more subtle needs—you are not even aware of them. You do not have attention left over to focus on these more subtle needs. As we have said, if you are really hungry, the purpose of life is not a big concern for you. The purpose of life right then is to get some food. When you have satisfied the lower needs, the physiological needs, the safety and security needs, then the need for a sense of purpose begins to come to the foreground. The more free time you have, the more important becomes that need for purpose.

This means that if the democratic nations want to do what we have talked about, want to help people overcome their psychological problems, then you need to find a way to give people a sense of purpose. It is the only way to truly move to a point where the welfare system does not become overburdened by people with psychological illnesses because people can deal with it themselves. You cannot really deal with your psychology unless you have a sense of purpose.

A simple sense of purpose can be, as Master MORE talked about, that you recognize that there is a path whereby you can develop your psyche, you can grow, you can transcend your consciousness, you can reach higher levels of consciousness. This can be one sense of purpose, but another sense of purpose can be that you help other people, that you do something for other people, that you use the free time that you have, the abundance that you have, to help other people. It can be in your own nation, it can be in other nations, but that can also give people a sense of purpose that reaches beyond yourself.

In a sense we can say that, if we go a little bit further, what is the sense of purpose you need? What can give you a sense of purpose? In reality, what the human psyche needs is a sense of purpose that reaches beyond the psyche itself.

The problem of narcissism

We have talked about what we have called the second law of thermodynamics where a closed system begins to self-destruct. This is not something that is beyond what people in general (and certainly the more mature people, the top 10%) can begin to understand. If you actually look at humanity, if you look at people, you can see that there are people who have become narcissists. There is a growing awareness of narcissism as a problem in society. The essence of a narcissist is that this is a person who becomes, from a psychological perspective, a closed system.

You can take the more extreme example of Adolph Hitler, who was both a narcissist and a psychopath and any other thing you can imagine. You can look at this and you can see that his psychology was a closed system. He did not believe that there was any God above him that he needed to listen to, he did not believe he needed to listen to his own advisors and generals, and certainly not the people. He became a completely closed system and in reality he self-destructed. From the moment he actually was elected Chancellor of Germany, he pushed the self-destruct button. He had his finger on the button all of his life and in many past lifetimes, but that was when he really started the spiral that was irreversible and that led to his own destruction.

You even have the old saying that: An idle mind is the devil's workshop and other sayings like that in many different countries. You can see that people who are totally focused on themselves (people who do not have a sense of purpose that reaches beyond themselves that they need to care about something beyond themselves), they will self-destruct psychologically. What you can then do is, you can scale this up.

Narcissism in modern democracies

You can say: "Well, what has happened to the modern democracies?" In a sense, you can see that the modern democracies in a psychological sense have become closed systems. If you think about the modern democracies as a person and look at that person's psychology, you can see that these modern democracies have actually started moving into displaying narcissistic personality disorder. The reason for this is that they have not let go of the old paradigms. This is both the Christian paradigm and the materialist paradigm.

You can even step back from this and you can see that when people are oppressed by a dictator, they are very focused on themselves and their own situation. The more people are oppressed (the more they face physical limitations and restrictions), the more focused they become on their own immediate situation. This is again Maslow's pyramid of needs. When you are hungry, all that matters, all you are focused on, is your stomach. You can see that your focus, the focus of your attention, becomes narrowed down, the world disappears, the rest of life disappears. It is just that growling stomach that eats up all of your attention. This is what happens in a dictatorship. People become very focused on their situation and on breaking free of these limitations that they cannot stand. What has happened in the democratic nations is: People have broken free of these limitations, but they have not broken free of the focus on self. They have not done that because they have not had a sense of purpose that reaches beyond themselves.

Now my beloved, if you look honestly at spiritual people, ascended master students, New Age people, anybody who has the concept of raising your consciousness, developing your consciousness, you can see that there are two types of people that are found almost everywhere. It is those who have a focus on self and those who have transcended that focus on self and are focusing on something bigger than themselves.

You will see that there are people who have used a spiritual teaching and spiritual tools to go into a mindset where they think that their goal in life is to evolve, to grow themselves personally in order to achieve some kind of goal—however they see it. It may be that they gain special powers, that they gain some kind of recognition, either from human beings or from spiritual beings, but they are focused on themselves and they are following the outer teaching and the outer path just in order to grow themselves.

Then, you also see that a majority of the people who are in spiritual movements, they do not have such a narrow focus on self. They are still pursuing a path of raising their consciousness, but they are doing it for a broader purpose. It may be (as we have given you teachings) that you are helping to raise the whole. Many spiritual movements have this concept that when you raise your own consciousness, you are raising the collective, you are raising the whole. Even though you are pursuing a path of raising yourself and developing your consciousness, you are not doing it with a narrow self-focus, you are doing it to raise something beyond yourself.

Many people also have the awareness that they need to have a spiritual teaching that reaches beyond themselves. That of course is the entire purpose for the ascended masters stepping forward and giving teachings that come from a level of consciousness that is beyond the human level so people have a frame of reference, so they do not become so self-focused.

Shifting from material to psychological welfare

You can see here that what ideally could have happened in the democratic nations, certainly in the 1960s, was that they had started making the shift of saying: "Now we have provided material welfare, now we need to focus on psychological well-being. That means we have to find a way to give people a sense of purpose." It can be both that you develop yourself and your own abilities, but you do not do it just to develop yourself, you do it because at some point, you can actually begin to help the whole.

What is a democratic nation? How is it functioning as opposed to a dictatorship? In a dictatorship, you have a top-down leadership structure, one person at the very top. There is a clear sense of hierarchy that the dictator appoints those people under him that he thinks he can trust and this then goes down. There is no upward mobility in a dictatorship, unless you happen to be born in the right family. For the people in general, there is no upward mobility. In a democratic nation there is complete freedom of upward mobility. You can be born of working class parents in a democratic nation and you can end up becoming Prime Minister.

What is it that you actually have the freedom to do in a democratic nation? You have the freedom physically to raise your consciousness to the point where you can begin to serve the whole in some capacity. Not necessarily going into politics, but there are so many ways where you can help other people. Of course, many people have done this. Doctors, nurses, teachers, many, many people in society who fill some kind of role where they are helping other people, and it is part of their job, but it is more than a job. It is a calling for many people.

You can see how this could be reinforced by having just some simple universal ideas about the fact that from childhood you can begin to see that you can plot your life of how you can raise your consciousness. You already have in these nations where people have the freedom that they can start at a young age thinking about what they want to do physically in life. You see how many children even at a young age, the parents or the adults in their families start asking them: "So, what do you want to be when you grow up?" Of course, for many people, it can be very difficult when you are 10 years old to know what you want to do for the rest of your life, especially in this day and age.

This goes back to again where people thought that now that we have freedom to plan our lives physically, we need to do it. We need to start early and plan how we are going to live our lives, what kind of job and career we are going to have. Then, we just need to do that for the next 40 years. This generation, they do not realize that young people coming into embodiment today, they cannot function that way, they cannot even bear to look at the rest of their lives as being on a track physically. What the younger generation needs is to be able to look at their lives and say:

"My life is not on a track, but I see that I have the opportunity to expand my consciousness, to develop my psyche, to heal my wounds." Therefore, instead of a physical career path, they can now begin to see a psychological path to higher states of consciousness. This is what can give the younger generation a sense of purpose. The sense of purpose they need in order to avoid going into substance abuse, mental illness or escapism. This is truly what can lead the democratic nations to make the transition from being focused on physical freedom to focusing on mental freedom.

The need to direct attention inwards

This is simply where most democratic nations are at today. If you could step back and look at the natural growth paths of nations, you would see that democratic nations are right there where they need to step up, they need to shift that focus. If they do not, tension will increase. There will be an external tension in the sense of terrorist threats, as there has been since 2001. There will also be the internal tension that is seen in many ways, including mental illness, but not just that. Also the fact of escapism where people have freedom but do not know what to do with it, simply do not know what to do with themselves. Because all of their lives, for the older generation, they have had their attention directed outwards.

If you take a person like that and put them in a jail cell, they will not know what to do with themselves, they will feel restricted, they will feel locked up. They will only be thinking about how to get out of there. There are actually people, both now and in the past, who have voluntarily gone into a cell. They call themselves monks and nuns. They voluntarily entered the cell because they were at a point where they were willing to focus internally, go within, meditate and therefore look at the psyche. This requires that you shift from an *external* to an *internal* focus.

You need to focus internally in order to develop your psyche. It cannot be done by outer means. It cannot be done by taking a pill. It cannot even be done by therapy or exercises. That is why we have said many times that even giving decrees and invocations does not guarantee that you grow psychologically because you need to look at yourself.

What is here now is not the highest

This is a shift that society can actually make. It is not impossible, at least for the top 10% of the people, to step back and look at history, look at historical development. There is a tendency in most societies where you think that what is here now is somehow the highest that ever could be.

That is why many people, because of their sense of security, want to maintain status quo. They want to maintain the society that is here now. This is what you see in this generation that is retiring now and who have pursued the materialistic lifestyle. They want to maintain a society that is focused on the material welfare. They do not want the society to shift because they feel threatened by this.

It is not impossible for people to look back at the past and see that 2,000 years ago in the Roman Empire, they thought they were at the pinnacle of civilization. They had the most sophisticated civilization ever seen on earth and they thought that nothing could be more sophisticated than what they had. Of course, today you look back at Roman civilization as being very primitive compared to modern civilization. You look back at medieval civilization where they also thought they had reached some pinnacle of development. It is not difficult for you to make that switch and see that many, many times in the past people have thought they had reached the highest stage of development. If we see this, how can we allow ourselves to think the same? How can we allow ourselves to believe that just because we have the modern democracies, we have reached some ultimate state? We should be able to step back, look at what has happened in the past, and then ask ourselves: "What is the next logical step for our civilization when we look at the future? What is the next logical step? Where are we going?" Once you start thinking like this, you can become open to seeing, as I have said, that the next logical step is to shift from material welfare to psychological well-being.

All societies have certain limitations

You can even go beyond this, because you can realize that if you look at the past, you will see that there has always been a tendency that at any given time, people have faced a certain set of limitations. In a sense you could say that the modern democracies are the most free societies that have so far been seen on earth, at least in recorded history. I would grant you that this is an accurate assessment, you have the greatest amount of freedom. You have the most free societies in the modern democracies, but if you look back at the past, you will see that every society that has preceded the modern democracies, they have all in a sense been part of the process that has led to the development of the society you have now. Therefore, you can go back and you can see how each of these societies, from the Roman Empire forward and even going back further if you want, they all faced certain limitations. They overcame those limitations and that was what brought society forward.

What you can then realize is that if you go back to, for example, medieval society, although that is a long period of time, but go back to the period when the Catholic church still reigned Europe and people believed that the earth was flat and was the center of the universe. They were facing a specific set of limitations. As we have said, what is the driving force behind progress? It is actually that you attain an increased understanding, a higher understanding, of some issue that allows you to see how you can move beyond that limitation. Either how you can remove the limitation or how you can circumvent it, but all of a sudden you see how to be free. You are limited by a certain condition but why are you limited? Because you have a limited understanding of the condition. When you acquire a higher understanding, then you can free yourself from the limitation.

You can see here that there is an ongoing process of humankind raising their understanding of certain issues of life. You can also see that in many past societies, they had thought that they had reached some ultimate understanding. You see, for example, in medieval society, they believed the earth was the center of the universe. They believed the earth was flat and that if you sailed West, across the Atlantic Ocean, you would not go across the Atlantic Ocean, you would come to the edge and fall off. What did that mean? It actually meant that European civilization was a closed system. They had nowhere to go. People had nowhere to go. They had to stay there as being subject to this feudal system that was very repressive. In their minds, there was nowhere else to go.

Now, do not underestimate the importance of Columbus's sailing West and discovering that he did not fall off the edge of the earth, he found new land. Suddenly, there was such a shift in Europe, which you can hardly fathom today, where people realized they could actually leave the feudal system, the feudal societies. They could leave. They could go somewhere else where there was opportunity for them. What was it in the feudal society? Everybody was born into a certain station. If you were born as a peasant, you were condemned to work the rest of your life as a peasant. You could not say: "I want to work harder. I want to start my own business. I want to have my own land. I'm willing to work and then I'll get a reward." You could not say that in the feudal system, but in America, you could. You could work hard and you would be rewarded for your efforts. This was such an incredible shift in awareness that you cannot even fathom it today.

What you can realize is that in every past society where they have had a limitation and overcome that limitation, there was that consciousness that I talked about where people are focused on the limitation that they are feeling restricted by right now. They think that if they can escape that limitation, then they have it made, then they have some ultimate society.

Modern democracies are stuck in limitations

This is what you have not understood in the modern democracies. You think the same way. You think because you have greater economic freedom, greater political freedom, than your parents or grandparents or great grandparents, you have reached some ultimate state here. Therefore, you do not know where to go. You do not know what to do with these democratic societies, which is why you are beginning to see the tension building from within and without. It could all be avoided if people would make that shift and say: "We have not reached an ultimate state. This is just the next step. What comes after that? Let's look to the future. Where are we meant to go here? Where do we have the opportunity to go with the freedom we have?" Of course, it is again mental well-being. The psychological well-being of all citizens is the next logical step for these modern democracies.

Once you make that shift, all of a sudden it can have so many ramifications for all levels of society. It can be parallel to what happened after Columbus where people realized: I have some place to go physically. But now you realize: I have some place to go psychologically.

What are people trapped by today? Nothing but their own psyches. What are the limitations people are facing today? It is not economic. It is not political. It is not physical. It is *psychological* limitations. They have been brought up in modern democracies to think there is no place to go. My psyche is the product of my brain activity or my genes or my upbringing.

It is locked on a track by the time I become an adult. Just like if I have a certain gene, I get cancer. Well, if I have another gene, I get depressed. Nothing I can do about it. There is no place to go in the modern worldview psychologically.

Materialism does not work on the psyche

You have the physical freedom that really frees you up to focus on psychological growth, but you do not know what to do with it because society has not been willing to provide people with a path. This, my beloved, is insanity. And what is fanaticism? *Fanaticism is a form of insanity.*

As we have said now, anytime you hold the belief that you think could not be replaced by a higher understanding, you are in the fanatical mindset. Just look at, as one clear example, you have a public health care system in a democratic nation. More and more people are coming to that system with psychological problems. What is this public health care system based on? It is based on a materialistic outlook on life. We have for generations had this materialistic approach to healing the physical body. We have almost uncritically transferred that to dealing with the human psyche.

If you are willing to look at it objectively, you can see that the materialistic approach is not working when it comes to psychological issues. It is not really working as well as it could with physical issues, but at least there is some effect, but it is not working with psychological issues. That demonstrates for anybody who is willing to look objectively and neutrally that we need to go beyond the materialistic paradigm in order to be able to help people with their psychological issues. Otherwise, we are simply admitting that we are not willing to help them, and that would not be in accordance with the democratic ideals that we claim to be based on.

You need to see here that the main characteristic, the main effect, of the fanatical mindset is what psychologists call cognitive dissonance. It is when you hold two viewpoints that are incompatible, but there is some mechanism that blocks you from seeing that they are incompatible.

The cognitive dissonance that you see in modern democracies is that on the one hand, you are holding a set of democratic ideals (all men are created equal, they are endowed by their creator with certain inalienable rights), but at the same time you are holding on to a materialistic paradigm that is limiting people's psychological welfare and growth. It is cognitive dissonance. The materialistic paradigm is incompatible with the democratic ideals. The Christian paradigm that you had before the democratic era (and still have to some degree) is also incompatible with democratic ideals. Somehow, society *cannot* recognize this, *will not* recognize this. It is because of the fanatical mindset where you go into a state of denial.

You have built a worldview that gives you a sense of security and you are saying: "I will not lose my sense of security and therefore I will not look at anything that threatens my worldview. I will not even consider that I have incompatible viewpoints, that I suffer from cognitive dissonance. I will not consider it. I'm right. I just need to continue to affirm this worldview and then I will get where I want to go (wherever that is)."

This is a tension that has been building since the 1960s. It has been reinforced by all of the people who have been into spiritual, New Age movements, all the people who have experimented with alternative healing, alternative psychology, alternative ways of living, alternative ways of looking at life. All of the people who have looked beyond the norm and looked beyond the materialistic approach to life and the Christian approach to life. All of these people have contributed to building this tension that is now there where the water in the glass is bulging over the edge. But there has not been that one little impulse, that one last drop, that punches the surface tension so the water spills over.

That is what you who are ascended master students can become. You can be that last drop that makes the glass overflow so everybody suddenly wakes up and realizes that they have had this cognitive dissonance and that we cannot continue to hold on to this worldview that we have had. Your calls can make a tremendous difference in this. A tremendous difference. You will not see it. They will not create some plaque in a public plaza somewhere that says the names of all the students that gave invocations and brought about the change. You will never get public recognition for this, but as Jesus said many years ago: "Do you want your reward on earth or do you want your reward in heaven?"

You will certainly gain recognition in the sense that *we* will recognize you, but also that you will make progress towards your ascension by doing this. Of course, by you raising your consciousness, healing your psychology and manifesting greater and greater degrees of mental freedom, you will pull up on the whole.

Modern democracies are not the ultimate stage

The main idea that I want to put out there (and that you have allowed me to use your chakras to radiate into the collective consciousness) is truly that the modern democracies are not the ultimate state, the ultimate stage for civilization. It is not the apex of civilization, there is a next step. We could have made that step a long time ago. Why have we not? Because of cognitive dissonance. We are frantically holding on to a paradigm that was useful for a time but that was never the final paradigm. Why are we doing this? Because it gives us this sense of security and we do not want to let go of this static sense of security and move into a dynamic sense of security where we realize that it truly comes from constantly refining, constantly expanding, our understanding of how the world works.

You still think in the modern democracies that the human psyche is flat and that if you sail out over the ocean of the psyche, you will fall off the edge. The human psyche is a sphere and it is time you realize that whereas space might be the *final* frontier in a physical sense, the *ultimate* frontier for human development is the human psyche. It is there that humanity will manifest its highest potential. I can assure you that humanity is very, very far from manifesting that highest potential.

That is why I can guarantee you with absolute certainty that in the not so distant future, people will look back at your time and they will think that the materialistic paradigm that you hold on to today is as primitive to them as when you think back to the people who believed the earth was flat. It will be just as primitive to future generations who will look back and say: "How could they be trapped in that paradigm for so long? Why couldn't they see what the next step was? Why couldn't they make that next step?"

Of course, they will look back at this with an entirely different consciousness than you have today. They will have long ago transcended the fanatical mindset, they will have embraced growth, they will be constantly looking for a higher understanding. That is why their society will have moved so much forward compared to where you are today that they look at you as primitive. Therefore, they will barely be able to understand the fanatical mindset and how people are trapped.

Just take a look and see how trapped people are in their current paradigm and worldview, and then ask yourself this: What is worse? A physical prison where you experience that you are in prison or a psychological prison where you do not even realize you are imprisoned. You might even think you are free and you have reached some ultimate state of development from which you can go no further. What is the most dangerous prison? Well, it certainly is the psychological prison that is not recognized as a prison because you think: "Oh, that's just the way it is. Nothing we can do about it."

My beloved, these were the remarks I wanted to give you and I want to express the gratitude that we all feel for your willingness to be here. It is very, very important to radiate this into the collective consciousness of Europe because Europe is the continent that has the greatest potential right now to make this transition out of the fanatical mindset and all of the subtle aspects of it that we will talk about in upcoming releases. With this, I seal you and I thank you for your attention and I wish you well in your journey towards mental freedom.

10 | INVOKING FREEDOM FROM MATERIALISTIC LIMITATIONS (PART 1)

In the name of the I AM THAT I AM, Jesus Christ, I use the authority that I have as a being in embodiment on earth to call upon Saint Germain to reinforce my calls and use my chakras to project the statements in this invocation into the collective consciousness and awaken people to the potential to overcome materialistic limitations. Awaken people to the reality that we are spiritual beings and that we can co-create a new future by working with the ascended masters. I especially call for ...

[Make your own calls here.]

Part 1

1. Saint Germain, shatter the energetic matrix that prevents people from seeing that in all of the modern democracies people believe they are free but are we truly free? Has our freedom gone as high as it can go, are people as free as they could be?

O Saint Germain, you do inspire,
my vision raised forever higher,
with you I form a figure-eight,
your Golden Age I co-create.

**O Saint Germain, what love you bring,
it truly makes all matter sing,
your violet flame does all restore,
with you we are becoming more.**

2. Saint Germain, shatter the energetic matrix that prevents people from seeing that this question is rarely asked because once a lower need has been fulfilled to a critical degree, we no longer think about it.

O Saint Germain, what Freedom Flame,
released when we recite your name,
acceleration is your gift,
our planet it will surely lift.

**O Saint Germain, what love you bring,
it truly makes all matter sing,
your violet flame does all restore,
with you we are becoming more.**

3. Saint Germain, shatter the energetic matrix that prevents people from seeing that when we are living in a dictatorship, most people will feel restricted. In the feudal societies of Europe, most of the population did not feel free because they could not improve their station in life.

O Saint Germain, in love we claim,
our right to bring your violet flame,
from you Above, to us below,
it is an all-transforming flow.

**O Saint Germain, what love you bring,
it truly makes all matter sing,
your violet flame does all restore,
with you we are becoming more.**

4. Saint Germain, shatter the energetic matrix that prevents people from seeing that there came a point where people started recognizing that they were being oppressed by the kings, by the noble class, by the power elite. There came that point where they took back their power and demanded freedom.

O Saint Germain, I love you so,
my aura filled with violet glow,
my chakras filled with violet fire,
I am your cosmic amplifier.

O Saint Germain, what love you bring,
it truly makes all matter sing,
your violet flame does all restore,
with you we are becoming more.

5. Saint Germain, shatter the energetic matrix that prevents people from seeing that throughout several centuries, there had been building this collective consciousness that: "We are oppressed, we want to be free." When we created democracies, that level of consciousness felt that it had gained freedom.

O Saint Germain, I am now free,
your violet flame is therapy,
transform all hang-ups in my mind,
as inner peace I surely find.

O Saint Germain, what love you bring,
it truly makes all matter sing,
your violet flame does all restore,
with you we are becoming more.

6. Saint Germain, shatter the energetic matrix that prevents people from seeing that in democracies there is still a power elite that are trying to set themselves up in a position where they have power and privilege beyond the general population.

O Saint Germain, my body pure,
your violet flame for all is cure,

consume the cause of all disease,
and therefore I am all at ease.

O Saint Germain, what love you bring,
it truly makes all matter sing,
your violet flame does all restore,
with you we are becoming more.

7. Saint Germain, shatter the energetic matrix that prevents people from seeing that the elite can only do this by taking freedom, privileges and abundance from the population. That is why we see this concentration of wealth in the hands of fewer and fewer people.

O Saint Germain, I'm karma-free,
the past no longer burdens me,
a brand new opportunity,
I am in Christic unity.

O Saint Germain, what love you bring,
it truly makes all matter sing,
your violet flame does all restore,
with you we are becoming more.

8. Saint Germain, shatter the energetic matrix that prevents people from seeing that this is a return towards a physical form of slavery where people are not enslaved by the threat of physical violence, but they are enslaved economically.

O Saint Germain, we are now one,
I am for you a violet sun,
as we transform this planet earth,
your Golden Age is given birth.

O Saint Germain, what love you bring,
it truly makes all matter sing,
your violet flame does all restore,
with you we are becoming more.

9. Saint Germain, shatter the energetic matrix that prevents people from seeing that even though we still have a high level of physical, political freedom, this is not enough. This level of freedom is not the highest potential for democratic nations.

O Saint Germain, the earth is free,
from burden of duality,
in oneness we bring what is best,
your Golden Age is manifest.

O Saint Germain, what love you bring,
it truly makes all matter sing,
your violet flame does all restore,
with you we are becoming more.

Part 2

1. Saint Germain, shatter the energetic matrix that prevents people from seeing that the need for a higher form of freedom is demonstrated by the rise in mental illness. A mental illness or depression is a state of non-freedom, of anti-freedom.

O Saint Germain, you do inspire,
my vision raised forever higher,
with you I form a figure-eight,
your Golden Age I co-create.

O Saint Germain, what love you bring,
it truly makes all matter sing,
your violet flame does all restore,
with you we are becoming more.

2. Saint Germain, shatter the energetic matrix that prevents a shift where people start realizing that physical freedom is just one side of the equation of freedom. We need to step higher in the democratic nations and realize that the only way to truly be free is to have freedom in the psyche. Mental freedom is true freedom.

O Saint Germain, what Freedom Flame,
released when we recite your name,
acceleration is your gift,
our planet it will surely lift.

**O Saint Germain, what love you bring,
it truly makes all matter sing,
your violet flame does all restore,
with you we are becoming more.**

3. Saint Germain, shatter the energetic matrix that prevents people from seeing that we can have political freedom, we can have economic freedom, but if we are still trapped in some limited psychology, we are not truly free.

O Saint Germain, in love we claim,
our right to bring your violet flame,
from you Above, to us below,
it is an all-transforming flow.

**O Saint Germain, what love you bring,
it truly makes all matter sing,
your violet flame does all restore,
with you we are becoming more.**

4. Saint Germain, shatter the energetic matrix that prevents people from seeing that the people who have used their political and physical freedom to gather more and more wealth are not free. Even though they have financial independence, they do not have psychological independence. They are not free in their minds.

O Saint Germain, I love you so,
my aura filled with violet glow,
my chakras filled with violet fire,
I am your cosmic amplifier.

**O Saint Germain, what love you bring,
it truly makes all matter sing,
your violet flame does all restore,
with you we are becoming more.**

5. Saint Germain, shatter the energetic matrix that prevents people from seeing that this applies not just to the elite, but also to the population. People are not free in their minds.

> O Saint Germain, I am now free,
> your violet flame is therapy,
> transform all hang-ups in my mind,
> as inner peace I surely find.

> **O Saint Germain, what love you bring,**
> **it truly makes all matter sing,**
> **your violet flame does all restore,**
> **with you we are becoming more.**

6. Saint Germain, shatter the energetic matrix that prevents people from seeing that physical, political freedom is just the first step in the process of becoming a free human being. We need to build on this and realize that political and economic freedom is the foundation for pursuing psychological freedom, mental freedom.

> O Saint Germain, my body pure,
> your violet flame for all is cure,
> consume the cause of all disease,
> and therefore I am all at ease.

> **O Saint Germain, what love you bring,**
> **it truly makes all matter sing,**
> **your violet flame does all restore,**
> **with you we are becoming more.**

7. Saint Germain, shatter the energetic matrix that prevents people from seeing that when people are oppressed, life is easy for them. They have very clearly defined outer parameters that they feel powerless to change. They do not have the options to choose from.

> O Saint Germain, I'm karma-free,
> the past no longer burdens me,
> a brand new opportunity,
> I am in Christic unity.

**O Saint Germain, what love you bring,
it truly makes all matter sing,
your violet flame does all restore,
with you we are becoming more.**

8. Saint Germain, shatter the energetic matrix that prevents people from seeing that in the affluent nations many people have lived a materialistic lifestyle, but when they retire, they do not know what to do with themselves. They do not know what to do with their freedom.

O Saint Germain, we are now one,
I am for you a violet sun,
as we transform this planet earth,
your Golden Age is given birth.

**O Saint Germain, what love you bring,
it truly makes all matter sing,
your violet flame does all restore,
with you we are becoming more.**

9. Saint Germain, shatter the energetic matrix that prevents people from seeing that freedom actually demands something. When you have physical freedom, political freedom, economic freedom this is not an easy state to be in.

O Saint Germain, the earth is free,
from burden of duality,
in oneness we bring what is best,
your Golden Age is manifest.

**O Saint Germain, what love you bring,
it truly makes all matter sing,
your violet flame does all restore,
with you we are becoming more.**

Part 3

1. Saint Germain, shatter the energetic matrix that prevents people from seeing that in the pre-democratic era, people assumed that: "If we just get free of the kings and the noble class, if we just have physical, political economic freedom, then we will have utopia, then we will have paradise then we will have the ideal society."

O Saint Germain, you do inspire,
my vision raised forever higher,
with you I form a figure-eight,
your Golden Age I co-create.

O Saint Germain, what love you bring,
it truly makes all matter sing,
your violet flame does all restore,
with you we are becoming more.

2. Saint Germain, shatter the energetic matrix that prevents people from seeing that when people are feeling oppressed, they look at what is oppressing them and they think that if we got rid of that, we would be free. This is a very limited understanding of what freedom means.

O Saint Germain, what Freedom Flame,
released when we recite your name,
acceleration is your gift,
our planet it will surely lift.

O Saint Germain, what love you bring,
it truly makes all matter sing,
your violet flame does all restore,
with you we are becoming more.

3. Saint Germain, shatter the energetic matrix that prevents people from seeing that after people gained political, economic freedom this has not been as easy as people thought. Many people have not been able to figure out what to do with their freedom.

O Saint Germain, in love we claim,
our right to bring your violet flame,
from you Above, to us below,
it is an all-transforming flow.

O Saint Germain, what love you bring,
it truly makes all matter sing,
your violet flame does all restore,
with you we are becoming more.

4. Saint Germain, shatter the energetic matrix that prevents people from seeing that many things that are happening in the modern democracies are an effect of the fact that people have not gained the psychological freedom to correspond with their physical freedom.

O Saint Germain, I love you so,
my aura filled with violet glow,
my chakras filled with violet fire,
I am your cosmic amplifier.

O Saint Germain, what love you bring,
it truly makes all matter sing,
your violet flame does all restore,
with you we are becoming more.

5. Saint Germain, shatter the energetic matrix that prevents people from seeing that the entire escapism industry serves to give people an excuse so that instead of making a choice of what they want to do with their freedom, they go into seeking some kind of escape, some kind of entertainment.

O Saint Germain, I am now free,
your violet flame is therapy,
transform all hang-ups in my mind,
as inner peace I surely find.

O Saint Germain, what love you bring,
it truly makes all matter sing,
your violet flame does all restore,
with you we are becoming more.

6. Saint Germain, shatter the energetic matrix that prevents people from seeing that in the democratic nations we now have free time. But if we are not free in our minds, we do not know what to do with our free time. There is an entire industry that only has one purpose, namely to help us pass our free time.

O Saint Germain, my body pure,
your violet flame for all is cure,
consume the cause of all disease,
and therefore I am all at ease.

O Saint Germain, what love you bring,
it truly makes all matter sing,
your violet flame does all restore,
with you we are becoming more.

7. Saint Germain, shatter the energetic matrix that prevents people from seeing that people cannot just sit around and do nothing. This is because the human psyche has a certain mechanism, it has a need to have a sense of purpose.

O Saint Germain, I'm karma-free,
the past no longer burdens me,
a brand new opportunity,
I am in Christic unity.

O Saint Germain, what love you bring,
it truly makes all matter sing,
your violet flame does all restore,
with you we are becoming more.

8. Saint Germain, shatter the energetic matrix that prevents people from seeing that we need to have a sense of purpose. Life must have some sense of purpose. As a human being, we cannot just live, we cannot just live in the moment, we cannot sit around and do nothing.

O Saint Germain, we are now one,
I am for you a violet sun,

as we transform this planet earth,
your Golden Age is given birth.

**O Saint Germain, what love you bring,
it truly makes all matter sing,
your violet flame does all restore,
with you we are becoming more.**

9. Saint Germain, shatter the energetic matrix that prevents people from seeing that human beings have a much more complex psyche than animals. Human beings cannot be happy by doing nothing. In order to function well psychologically, we need a sense of purpose.

O Saint Germain, the earth is free,
from burden of duality,
in oneness we bring what is best,
your Golden Age is manifest.

**O Saint Germain, what love you bring,
it truly makes all matter sing,
your violet flame does all restore,
with you we are becoming more.**

Part 4

1. Saint Germain, shatter the energetic matrix that prevents people from seeing that according to Maslow, if the lower needs are *not* fulfilled, we are not aware of the more subtle needs. When we have satisfied the lower needs, then the need for a sense of purpose begins to come to the foreground. The more free time we have, the more important becomes the need for purpose.

O Saint Germain, you do inspire,
my vision raised forever higher,
with you I form a figure-eight,
your Golden Age I co-create.

O Saint Germain, what love you bring,
it truly makes all matter sing,
your violet flame does all restore,
with you we are becoming more.

2. Saint Germain, shatter the energetic matrix that prevents people from seeing that if the democratic nations want to help people overcome their psychological problems, then we need to find a way to give people a sense of purpose.

O Saint Germain, what Freedom Flame,
released when we recite your name,
acceleration is your gift,
our planet it will surely lift.

O Saint Germain, what love you bring,
it truly makes all matter sing,
your violet flame does all restore,
with you we are becoming more.

3. Saint Germain, shatter the energetic matrix that prevents people from seeing that this is the only way to move to a point where the welfare system does not become overburdened by people with psychological illnesses because we can deal with them ourselves. We cannot deal with our psychology unless we have a sense of purpose.

O Saint Germain, in love we claim,
our right to bring your violet flame,
from you Above, to us below,
it is an all-transforming flow.

O Saint Germain, what love you bring,
it truly makes all matter sing,
your violet flame does all restore,
with you we are becoming more.

4. Saint Germain, shatter the energetic matrix that prevents people from seeing that a simple sense of purpose is to recognize that there is a path

whereby we can develop the psyche, we can grow, we can transcend our consciousness, we can reach higher levels of consciousness.

> O Saint Germain, I love you so,
> my aura filled with violet glow,
> my chakras filled with violet fire,
> I am your cosmic amplifier.

> **O Saint Germain, what love you bring,**
> **it truly makes all matter sing,**
> **your violet flame does all restore,**
> **with you we are becoming more.**

5. Saint Germain, shatter the energetic matrix that prevents people from seeing that another sense of purpose is to help other people, to use the free time we have, the abundance we have, to help other people. It can give us a sense of purpose that reaches beyond ourselves.

> O Saint Germain, I am now free,
> your violet flame is therapy,
> transform all hang-ups in my mind,
> as inner peace I surely find.

> **O Saint Germain, what love you bring,**
> **it truly makes all matter sing,**
> **your violet flame does all restore,**
> **with you we are becoming more.**

6. Saint Germain, shatter the energetic matrix that prevents people from seeing that what the human psyche needs is a sense of purpose that reaches beyond the psyche itself.

> O Saint Germain, my body pure,
> your violet flame for all is cure,
> consume the cause of all disease,
> and therefore I am all at ease.

> **O Saint Germain, what love you bring,**
> **it truly makes all matter sing,**

your violet flame does all restore,
with you we are becoming more.

7. Saint Germain, shatter the energetic matrix that prevents people from seeing that some people have become narcissists and narcissism is a problem in society. The essence of a narcissist is that this is a person who becomes, from a psychological perspective, a closed system.

O Saint Germain, I'm karma-free,
the past no longer burdens me,
a brand new opportunity,
I am in Christic unity.

O Saint Germain, what love you bring,
it truly makes all matter sing,
your violet flame does all restore,
with you we are becoming more.

8. Saint Germain, shatter the energetic matrix that prevents people from seeing that Adolph Hitler's psychology was a closed system. He did not believe that there was any God above him that he needed to listen to, he did not believe he needed to listen to his own advisors and generals, and certainly not the people.

O Saint Germain, we are now one,
I am for you a violet sun,
as we transform this planet earth,
your Golden Age is given birth.

O Saint Germain, what love you bring,
it truly makes all matter sing,
your violet flame does all restore,
with you we are becoming more.

9. Saint Germain, shatter the energetic matrix that prevents people from seeing that Hitler became a closed system and in reality he self-destructed. People who are totally focused on themselves will self-destruct psychologically.

O Saint Germain, the earth is free,
from burden of duality,
in oneness we bring what is best,
your Golden Age is manifest.

O Saint Germain, what love you bring,
it truly makes all matter sing,
your violet flame does all restore,
with you we are becoming more.

Part 5

1. Saint Germain, shatter the energetic matrix that prevents people from seeing that the modern democracies in a psychological sense have become closed systems. These modern democracies have actually started moving into displaying narcissistic personality disorder.

O Saint Germain, you do inspire,
my vision raised forever higher,
with you I form a figure-eight,
your Golden Age I co-create.

O Saint Germain, what love you bring,
it truly makes all matter sing,
your violet flame does all restore,
with you we are becoming more.

2. Saint Germain, shatter the energetic matrix that prevents people from seeing that the reason for this is that they have not let go of the old paradigms, both the Christian paradigm and the materialist paradigm.

O Saint Germain, what Freedom Flame,
released when we recite your name,
acceleration is your gift,
our planet it will surely lift.

**O Saint Germain, what love you bring,
it truly makes all matter sing,
your violet flame does all restore,
with you we are becoming more.**

3. Saint Germain, shatter the energetic matrix that prevents people from seeing that when people are oppressed by a dictator, they are very focused on themselves and their own situation. In the democratic nations we have broken free of these limitations, but we have not broken free of the focus on self. We have not done that because we have not had a sense of purpose that reaches beyond ourselves.

O Saint Germain, in love we claim,
our right to bring your violet flame,
from you Above, to us below,
it is an all-transforming flow.

**O Saint Germain, what love you bring,
it truly makes all matter sing,
your violet flame does all restore,
with you we are becoming more.**

4. Saint Germain, shatter the energetic matrix that prevents people from seeing that there are two types of people that are found almost everywhere. It is those who have a focus on self and those who have transcended that focus on self and are focusing on something bigger than themselves.

O Saint Germain, I love you so,
my aura filled with violet glow,
my chakras filled with violet fire,
I am your cosmic amplifier.

**O Saint Germain, what love you bring,
it truly makes all matter sing,
your violet flame does all restore,
with you we are becoming more.**

5. Saint Germain, shatter the energetic matrix that prevents people from seeing that it is possible to be pursuing a path of raising our consciousness, but we are doing it for a broader purpose, namely to raise the whole.

> O Saint Germain, I am now free,
> your violet flame is therapy,
> transform all hang-ups in my mind,
> as inner peace I surely find.

> **O Saint Germain, what love you bring,**
> **it truly makes all matter sing,**
> **your violet flame does all restore,**
> **with you we are becoming more.**

6. Saint Germain, shatter the energetic matrix that prevents people from seeing that when we raise our own consciousness, we are raising the collective, we are raising the whole. Even though we are pursuing a path of raising ourselves and developing our consciousness, we are not doing it with a narrow self-focus, we are doing it to raise something beyond ourselves.

> O Saint Germain, my body pure,
> your violet flame for all is cure,
> consume the cause of all disease,
> and therefore I am all at ease.

> **O Saint Germain, what love you bring,**
> **it truly makes all matter sing,**
> **your violet flame does all restore,**
> **with you we are becoming more.**

7. Saint Germain, shatter the energetic matrix that prevents people from seeing that the entire purpose for the ascended masters stepping forward and giving teachings from a level of consciousness that is beyond the human level, is to give us a frame of reference so we do not become so self-focused.

> O Saint Germain, I'm karma-free,
> the past no longer burdens me,

a brand new opportunity,
I am in Christic unity.

O Saint Germain, what love you bring,
it truly makes all matter sing,
your violet flame does all restore,
with you we are becoming more.

8. Saint Germain, shatter the energetic matrix that prevents people from seeing that what ideally could have happened in the democratic nations, certainly in the 1960s, was that we had started making the shift of saying: "Now we have provided material welfare, now we need to focus on psychological well-being."

O Saint Germain, we are now one,
I am for you a violet sun,
as we transform this planet earth,
your Golden Age is given birth.

O Saint Germain, what love you bring,
it truly makes all matter sing,
your violet flame does all restore,
with you we are becoming more.

9. Saint Germain, shatter the energetic matrix that prevents people from seeing that we have to find a way to give people a sense of purpose. It can be both that we develop ourselves and our own abilities, but we do not do it just to develop ourselves, we do it because at some point, we can actually begin to help the whole.

O Saint Germain, the earth is free,
from burden of duality,
in oneness we bring what is best,
your Golden Age is manifest.

O Saint Germain, what love you bring,
it truly makes all matter sing,
your violet flame does all restore,
with you we are becoming more.

Sealing

In the name of the I AM THAT I AM, I accept that Archangel Michael, Astrea and Shiva form an impenetrable shield around myself and all constructive people, sealing us from all fear-based energies in all four octaves. I accept that the Light of God is consuming and transforming all fear-based energies that make up the dark forces working against ending the era of fanaticism on earth!

11 | INVOKING FREEDOM FROM MATERIALISTIC LIMITATIONS (PART 2)

In the name of the I AM THAT I AM, Jesus Christ, I use the authority that I have as a being in embodiment on earth to call upon Saint Germain to reinforce my calls and use my chakras to project the statements in this invocation into the collective consciousness and awaken people to the potential to overcome materialistic limitations. Awaken people to the reality that we are spiritual beings and that we can co-create a new future by working with the ascended masters. I especially call for …

In the name of the I AM THAT I AM, Jesus Christ, I use the authority that I have as a being in embodiment on earth to call upon Saint Germain to reinforce my calls and use my chakras to project the statements in this invocation into the collective consciousness and awaken people to the need to leave Materialism behind. Awaken people to the reality that we are spiritual beings and that we can co-create a new future by working with the ascended masters. I especially call for …

[Make your own calls here.]

Part 1

1. Saint Germain, shatter the energetic matrix that prevents people from seeing that in a democratic nation there is freedom of upward mobility. You can be born of working class parents in a democratic nation and you can end up becoming Prime Minister.

O Saint Germain, you do inspire,
my vision raised forever higher,
with you I form a figure-eight,
your Golden Age I co-create.

O Saint Germain, what love you bring,
it truly makes all matter sing,
your violet flame does all restore,
with you we are becoming more.

2. Saint Germain, shatter the energetic matrix that prevents people from seeing that in a democratic nation we have the freedom to raise our consciousness to the point where we can begin to serve the whole in some capacity. Many people have done this.

O Saint Germain, what Freedom Flame,
released when we recite your name,
acceleration is your gift,
our planet it will surely lift.

O Saint Germain, what love you bring,
it truly makes all matter sing,
your violet flame does all restore,
with you we are becoming more.

3. Saint Germain, shatter the energetic matrix that prevents people from seeing that this could be reinforced by helping people from childhood plot how they can raise their consciousness.

O Saint Germain, in love we claim,
our right to bring your violet flame,

from you Above, to us below,
it is an all-transforming flow.

O Saint Germain, what love you bring,
it truly makes all matter sing,
your violet flame does all restore,
with you we are becoming more.

4. Saint Germain, shatter the energetic matrix that prevents people from seeing that people coming into embodiment today cannot look at the rest of their lives as being on a track physically. They need to see how to expand their consciousness, to develop their psyches, to heal their wounds.

O Saint Germain, I love you so,
my aura filled with violet glow,
my chakras filled with violet fire,
I am your cosmic amplifier.

O Saint Germain, what love you bring,
it truly makes all matter sing,
your violet flame does all restore,
with you we are becoming more.

5. Saint Germain, shatter the energetic matrix that prevents people from seeing that instead of a physical career path, they can see a psychological path to higher states of consciousness. This is what can give the younger generation a sense of purpose.

O Saint Germain, I am now free,
your violet flame is therapy,
transform all hang-ups in my mind,
as inner peace I surely find.

O Saint Germain, what love you bring,
it truly makes all matter sing,
your violet flame does all restore,
with you we are becoming more.

6. Saint Germain, shatter the energetic matrix that prevents people from seeing that this is what can lead the democratic nations to make the transition from being focused on physical freedom to focusing on mental freedom.

O Saint Germain, my body pure,
your violet flame for all is cure,
consume the cause of all disease,
and therefore I am all at ease.

O Saint Germain, what love you bring,
it truly makes all matter sing,
your violet flame does all restore,
with you we are becoming more.

7. Saint Germain, shatter the energetic matrix that prevents people from seeing that there is a natural growth paths of nations. Democratic nations need to shift the focus. If they do not, tension will increase.

O Saint Germain, I'm karma-free,
the past no longer burdens me,
a brand new opportunity,
I am in Christic unity.

O Saint Germain, what love you bring,
it truly makes all matter sing,
your violet flame does all restore,
with you we are becoming more.

8. Saint Germain, shatter the energetic matrix that prevents people from seeing that unless we shift, there will be an external tension in the form of terrorist threats, and there will be the internal tension, including mental illness, but also more escapism.

O Saint Germain, we are now one,
I am for you a violet sun,
as we transform this planet earth,
your Golden Age is given birth.

O Saint Germain, what love you bring,
it truly makes all matter sing,
your violet flame does all restore,
with you we are becoming more.

9. Saint Germain, shatter the energetic matrix that prevents the top 10% of the people from seeing that historically speaking most societies have thought that what is here now is somehow the highest that ever could be.

O Saint Germain, the earth is free,
from burden of duality,
in oneness we bring what is best,
your Golden Age is manifest.

O Saint Germain, what love you bring,
it truly makes all matter sing,
your violet flame does all restore,
with you we are becoming more.

Part 2

1. Saint Germain, shatter the energetic matrix that prevents people from seeing that because of their sense of security, many people want to maintain status quo. They want to maintain the society that is here now.

O Saint Germain, you do inspire,
my vision raised forever higher,
with you I form a figure-eight,
your Golden Age I co-create.

O Saint Germain, what love you bring,
it truly makes all matter sing,
your violet flame does all restore,
with you we are becoming more.

2. Saint Germain, shatter the energetic matrix that prevents people from seeing that the generation that is retiring now and who have pursued the

materialistic lifestyle, they want to maintain a society that is focused on material welfare. They do not want society to shift because they feel threatened by this.

O Saint Germain, what Freedom Flame,
released when we recite your name,
acceleration is your gift,
our planet it will surely lift.

**O Saint Germain, what love you bring,
it truly makes all matter sing,
your violet flame does all restore,
with you we are becoming more.**

3. Saint Germain, shatter the energetic matrix that prevents people from seeing that many times in the past people have thought they had reached the highest stage of development. How can we allow ourselves to think the same?

O Saint Germain, in love we claim,
our right to bring your violet flame,
from you Above, to us below,
it is an all-transforming flow.

**O Saint Germain, what love you bring,
it truly makes all matter sing,
your violet flame does all restore,
with you we are becoming more.**

4. Saint Germain, shatter the energetic matrix that prevents people from seeing that we need to step back, look at what has happened in the past, and then ask ourselves: "What is the next logical step for our civilization when we look at the future? Where are we going?"

O Saint Germain, I love you so,
my aura filled with violet glow,
my chakras filled with violet fire,
I am your cosmic amplifier.

O Saint Germain, what love you bring,
it truly makes all matter sing,
your violet flame does all restore,
with you we are becoming more.

5. Saint Germain, shatter the energetic matrix that prevents people from seeing that the next logical step is to shift from material welfare to psychological well-being.

O Saint Germain, I am now free,
your violet flame is therapy,
transform all hang-ups in my mind,
as inner peace I surely find.

O Saint Germain, what love you bring,
it truly makes all matter sing,
your violet flame does all restore,
with you we are becoming more.

6. Saint Germain, shatter the energetic matrix that prevents people from seeing that at any given time, people have faced a certain set of limitations. They overcame those limitations and that was what brought society forward.

O Saint Germain, my body pure,
your violet flame for all is cure,
consume the cause of all disease,
and therefore I am all at ease.

O Saint Germain, what love you bring,
it truly makes all matter sing,
your violet flame does all restore,
with you we are becoming more.

7. Saint Germain, shatter the energetic matrix that prevents people from seeing that the driving force behind progress is that we attain an increased understanding that allows us to see how we can move beyond our limitations.

O Saint Germain, I'm karma-free,
the past no longer burdens me,
a brand new opportunity,
I am in Christic unity.

**O Saint Germain, what love you bring,
it truly makes all matter sing,
your violet flame does all restore,
with you we are becoming more.**

8. Saint Germain, shatter the energetic matrix that prevents people from seeing that we are limited by a certain condition because we have a limited understanding of the condition. When we acquire a higher understanding, then we can free ourselves from the limitation.

O Saint Germain, we are now one,
I am for you a violet sun,
as we transform this planet earth,
your Golden Age is given birth.

**O Saint Germain, what love you bring,
it truly makes all matter sing,
your violet flame does all restore,
with you we are becoming more.**

9. Saint Germain, shatter the energetic matrix that prevents people from seeing that there is an ongoing process of humankind raising our understanding of certain issues of life. In many past societies, they thought they had reached some ultimate understanding.

O Saint Germain, the earth is free,
from burden of duality,
in oneness we bring what is best,
your Golden Age is manifest.

**O Saint Germain, what love you bring,
it truly makes all matter sing,
your violet flame does all restore,
with you we are becoming more.**

Part 3

1. Saint Germain, shatter the energetic matrix that prevents people from seeing that in every past society where they have had a limitation and overcome that limitation, people were focused on the limitation that they were feeling restricted by. They thought that if they could escape that limitation, then they would have some ultimate society.

> O Saint Germain, you do inspire,
> my vision raised forever higher,
> with you I form a figure-eight,
> your Golden Age I co-create.
>
> **O Saint Germain, what love you bring,**
> **it truly makes all matter sing,**
> **your violet flame does all restore,**
> **with you we are becoming more.**

2. Saint Germain, shatter the energetic matrix that prevents people from seeing that in the modern democracies we think the same way. We think that because we have greater economic and political freedom, we have reached some ultimate state. Therefore, we do not know where to go.

> O Saint Germain, what Freedom Flame,
> released when we recite your name,
> acceleration is your gift,
> our planet it will surely lift.
>
> **O Saint Germain, what love you bring,**
> **it truly makes all matter sing,**
> **your violet flame does all restore,**
> **with you we are becoming more.**

3. Saint Germain, shatter the energetic matrix that prevents people from seeing that we do not know what to do with these democratic societies, which is why we are beginning to see the tension building from within and without.

O Saint Germain, in love we claim,
our right to bring your violet flame,
from you Above, to us below,
it is an all-transforming flow.

O Saint Germain, what love you bring,
it truly makes all matter sing,
your violet flame does all restore,
with you we are becoming more.

4. Saint Germain, shatter the energetic matrix that prevents people from seeing that this could be avoided if we would make the shift and say: "We have not reached an ultimate state. This is just the next step. What comes after that? Let's look to the future. Where do we have the opportunity to go with the freedom we have?"

O Saint Germain, I love you so,
my aura filled with violet glow,
my chakras filled with violet fire,
I am your cosmic amplifier.

O Saint Germain, what love you bring,
it truly makes all matter sing,
your violet flame does all restore,
with you we are becoming more.

5. Saint Germain, shatter the energetic matrix that prevents people from seeing that the psychological well-being of all citizens is the next logical step for the modern democracies. This shift will help people realize: I have some place to go psychologically.

O Saint Germain, I am now free,
your violet flame is therapy,
transform all hang-ups in my mind,
as inner peace I surely find.

O Saint Germain, what love you bring,
it truly makes all matter sing,

your violet flame does all restore,
with you we are becoming more.

6. Saint Germain, shatter the energetic matrix that prevents people from seeing that we are trapped by nothing but our own psyches. The limitations we are facing today are psychological limitations.

O Saint Germain, my body pure,
your violet flame for all is cure,
consume the cause of all disease,
and therefore I am all at ease.

O Saint Germain, what love you bring,
it truly makes all matter sing,
your violet flame does all restore,
with you we are becoming more.

7. Saint Germain, shatter the energetic matrix that prevents people from seeing that in the modern democracies we have been brought up to think there is no place to go. The psyche is the product of brain activity or genes or upbringing. It is locked on a track by the time we become adults.

O Saint Germain, I'm karma-free,
the past no longer burdens me,
a brand new opportunity,
I am in Christic unity.

O Saint Germain, what love you bring,
it truly makes all matter sing,
your violet flame does all restore,
with you we are becoming more.

8. Saint Germain, shatter the energetic matrix that prevents people from seeing that we have the physical freedom that frees us up to focus on psychological growth, but we do not know what to do with it because society has not been willing to provide people with a path. This is insanity, and fanaticism is a form of insanity.

O Saint Germain, we are now one,
I am for you a violet sun,
as we transform this planet earth,
your Golden Age is given birth.

**O Saint Germain, what love you bring,
it truly makes all matter sing,
your violet flame does all restore,
with you we are becoming more.**

9. Saint Germain, shatter the energetic matrix that prevents people from seeing that anytime we hold a belief that we think could not be replaced by a higher understanding, we are in the fanatical mindset.

O Saint Germain, the earth is free,
from burden of duality,
in oneness we bring what is best,
your Golden Age is manifest.

**O Saint Germain, what love you bring,
it truly makes all matter sing,
your violet flame does all restore,
with you we are becoming more.**

Part 4

1. Saint Germain, shatter the energetic matrix that prevents people from seeing that our public health care systems are based on a materialistic outlook on life. We have for generations had a materialistic approach to healing the physical body. We have almost uncritically transferred that to dealing with the psyche.

O Saint Germain, you do inspire,
my vision raised forever higher,
with you I form a figure-eight,
your Golden Age I co-create.

**O Saint Germain, what love you bring,
it truly makes all matter sing,
your violet flame does all restore,
with you we are becoming more.**

2. Saint Germain, shatter the energetic matrix that prevents people from seeing that the materialistic approach is not working when it comes to psychological issues. We need to go beyond the materialistic paradigm in order to be able to help people with their psychological issues.

O Saint Germain, what Freedom Flame,
released when we recite your name,
acceleration is your gift,
our planet it will surely lift.

**O Saint Germain, what love you bring,
it truly makes all matter sing,
your violet flame does all restore,
with you we are becoming more.**

3. Saint Germain, shatter the energetic matrix that prevents people from seeing that otherwise, we are admitting that we are not willing to help them and that would not be in accordance with the democratic ideals that we claim to be based on.

O Saint Germain, in love we claim,
our right to bring your violet flame,
from you Above, to us below,
it is an all-transforming flow.

**O Saint Germain, what love you bring,
it truly makes all matter sing,
your violet flame does all restore,
with you we are becoming more.**

4. Saint Germain, shatter the energetic matrix that prevents people from seeing that the main characteristic of the fanatical mindset is cognitive dissonance. It is when we hold two viewpoints that are incompatible, but there is some mechanism that blocks us from seeing that they are incompatible.

O Saint Germain, I love you so,
my aura filled with violet glow,
my chakras filled with violet fire,
I am your cosmic amplifier.

O Saint Germain, what love you bring,
it truly makes all matter sing,
your violet flame does all restore,
with you we are becoming more.

5. Saint Germain, shatter the energetic matrix that prevents people from seeing that the cognitive dissonance in modern democracies is that on the one hand, we are holding a set of democratic ideals, but at the same time we are holding on to a materialistic paradigm that is limiting people's psychological welfare and growth. This is cognitive dissonance.

O Saint Germain, I am now free,
your violet flame is therapy,
transform all hang-ups in my mind,
as inner peace I surely find.

O Saint Germain, what love you bring,
it truly makes all matter sing,
your violet flame does all restore,
with you we are becoming more.

6. Saint Germain, shatter the energetic matrix that prevents people from seeing that the materialistic paradigm is incompatible with the democratic ideals. The Christian paradigm is also incompatible with democratic ideals.

O Saint Germain, my body pure,
your violet flame for all is cure,
consume the cause of all disease,
and therefore I am all at ease.

O Saint Germain, what love you bring,
it truly makes all matter sing,
your violet flame does all restore,
with you we are becoming more.

7. Saint Germain, shatter the energetic matrix that prevents people from seeing that society *cannot* recognize this, *will not* recognize this because of the fanatical mindset where we go into a state of denial.

> O Saint Germain, I'm karma-free,
> the past no longer burdens me,
> a brand new opportunity,
> I am in Christic unity.

> **O Saint Germain, what love you bring,**
> **it truly makes all matter sing,**
> **your violet flame does all restore,**
> **with you we are becoming more.**

8. Saint Germain, shatter the energetic matrix that prevents people from seeing that we have built a worldview that gives us a sense of security and we are saying: "I will not lose my sense of security and therefore I will not even consider that I have incompatible viewpoints, that I suffer from cognitive dissonance. I just need to continue to affirm this worldview and then I will get where I want to go."

> O Saint Germain, we are now one,
> I am for you a violet sun,
> as we transform this planet earth,
> your Golden Age is given birth.

> **O Saint Germain, what love you bring,**
> **it truly makes all matter sing,**
> **your violet flame does all restore,**
> **with you we are becoming more.**

9. Saint Germain, shatter the energetic matrix that prevents people from seeing that this tension has been building since the 1960s. It has been reinforced by all of the people who have experimented with alternative healing, alternative psychology, alternative ways of living, alternative ways of looking at life.

> O Saint Germain, the earth is free,
> from burden of duality,

in oneness we bring what is best,
your Golden Age is manifest.

**O Saint Germain, what love you bring,
it truly makes all matter sing,
your violet flame does all restore,
with you we are becoming more.**

Part 5

1. Saint Germain, shatter the energetic matrix that prevents people from seeing that all of the people who have looked beyond the norm, beyond the materialistic approach to life and the Christian approach to life, have contributed to building this tension.

O Saint Germain, you do inspire,
my vision raised forever higher,
with you I form a figure-eight,
your Golden Age I co-create.

**O Saint Germain, what love you bring,
it truly makes all matter sing,
your violet flame does all restore,
with you we are becoming more.**

2. Saint Germain, shatter the energetic matrix that prevents people from seeing that our societies have this cognitive dissonance. The modern democracies are not the ultimate stage for civilization. It is not the apex of civilization, there is a next step.

O Saint Germain, what Freedom Flame,
released when we recite your name,
acceleration is your gift,
our planet it will surely lift.

**O Saint Germain, what love you bring,
it truly makes all matter sing,**

**your violet flame does all restore,
with you we are becoming more.**

3. Saint Germain, shatter the energetic matrix that prevents people from seeing that we could have made that step a long time ago. Why have we not? Because of cognitive dissonance. We are frantically holding on to a paradigm that was useful for a time, but that was never the final paradigm.

O Saint Germain, in love we claim,
our right to bring your violet flame,
from you Above, to us below,
it is an all-transforming flow.

**O Saint Germain, what love you bring,
it truly makes all matter sing,
your violet flame does all restore,
with you we are becoming more.**

4. Saint Germain, shatter the energetic matrix that prevents people from seeing that we are doing this because it gives us this sense of security and we do not want to let go of this static sense of security and move into a dynamic sense of security where we realize that it truly comes from constantly refining our understanding of the world.

O Saint Germain, I love you so,
my aura filled with violet glow,
my chakras filled with violet fire,
I am your cosmic amplifier.

**O Saint Germain, what love you bring,
it truly makes all matter sing,
your violet flame does all restore,
with you we are becoming more.**

5. Saint Germain, shatter the energetic matrix that prevents people from seeing that in the modern democracies we think that the human psyche is flat and that if we sail out over the ocean of the psyche, we will fall off the edge.

O Saint Germain, I am now free,
your violet flame is therapy,
transform all hang-ups in my mind,
as inner peace I surely find.

**O Saint Germain, what love you bring,
it truly makes all matter sing,
your violet flame does all restore,
with you we are becoming more.**

6. Saint Germain, shatter the energetic matrix that prevents people from seeing that the human psyche is a sphere and whereas space might be the *final* frontier in a physical sense, the *ultimate* frontier for human development is the psyche. It is there that humanity will manifest our highest potential.

O Saint Germain, my body pure,
your violet flame for all is cure,
consume the cause of all disease,
and therefore I am all at ease.

**O Saint Germain, what love you bring,
it truly makes all matter sing,
your violet flame does all restore,
with you we are becoming more.**

7. Saint Germain, shatter the energetic matrix that prevents people from seeing that humanity is very far from manifesting our highest potential. In the future, people will look back at our time and they will think that the materialistic paradigm is as primitive as when we think back to the people who believed the earth was flat.

O Saint Germain, I'm karma-free,
the past no longer burdens me,
a brand new opportunity,
I am in Christic unity.

**O Saint Germain, what love you bring,
it truly makes all matter sing,**

your violet flame does all restore,
with you we are becoming more.

8. Saint Germain, shatter the energetic matrix that prevents people from seeing that future generations will look back and say: "How could they be trapped in that paradigm for so long? Why couldn't they see what the next step was? Why couldn't they make that next step?"

O Saint Germain, we are now one,
I am for you a violet sun,
as we transform this planet earth,
your Golden Age is given birth.

O Saint Germain, what love you bring,
it truly makes all matter sing,
your violet flame does all restore,
with you we are becoming more.

9. Saint Germain, shatter the energetic matrix that prevents people from asking: What is worse, a physical prison where we experience that we are in prison or a psychological prison, where we do not even realize we are imprisoned? The most dangerous prison is the psychological prison where we think: "Oh, that's just the way it is. Nothing we can do about it."

O Saint Germain, the earth is free,
from burden of duality,
in oneness we bring what is best,
your Golden Age is manifest.

O Saint Germain, what love you bring,
it truly makes all matter sing,
your violet flame does all restore,
with you we are becoming more.

Sealing

In the name of the I AM THAT I AM, I accept that Archangel Michael, Astrea and Shiva form an impenetrable shield around myself and all constructive people, sealing us from all fear-based energies in all four octaves. I accept that the Light of God is consuming and transforming all fear-based energies that make up the dark forces working against ending the era of fanaticism on earth!

12 | A BIOLOGICAL PERSPECTIVE ON FANATICISM

I AM the Ascended Master, Saint Germain. I wish to continue on what we had talked about earlier because I still have some remarks that I want to make to help set people free. Now, we have talked about various perspectives on fanaticism but what I would like to begin with here is to focus on fanaticism from a biological perspective.

You know very well that as ascended masters, we are not in any way saying that the theory of evolution in its current form is correct. However, we have never denied either that the biblical version of creation is not correct. There was not an instant creation where all of the species you see today on the planet were created in a matter of six days. Naturally, we have always said that the conditions you have on earth today are the products of a gradual, progressive and, therefore, evolutionary process. What we of course are saying is that this evolutionary process is not mechanical and unconscious. It is creative and conscious and the consciousness of human beings has had, and is having, an influence on the evolutionary process.

Before human beings, there were of course other conscious self-aware beings who had an influence on the evolutionary process, who started it and who at certain times have stepped in and caused it to accelerate very quickly to a higher level, such as you actually see when you look at the history of the evolution of species or the appearance of species. With this we can recognize that your physical bodies are the product of an evolutionary process. This process did start with more primitive life forms that gradually evolved to greater and greater complexity until this process was able to bring forth a physical body with the complex brain and nervous system that is necessary for a higher being to take embodiment in that body, for a higher being to come into that body and begin to express itself through that body.

The cognitive dissonance of unconscious evolution

What you realize as ascended master students is of course that animals do not have individual souls. Therefore, they are not self-aware beings. You are self-aware beings because you have a part of your being that came from outside of the body, that existed before the body, that will continue to exist after the body. Your being is so complex that you cannot take embodiment in a meaningful way through an animal. Therefore, there needed to be a gradual process that brought forth a human body that has the complex brain and nervous system that you need in order to express yourself and learn from that experience.

Your physical bodies were brought forth through a gradual evolutionary process that started with more primitive life forms. It is not exactly, as biological science portrays the theory of evolution, that it happened through an infinite variety of random events that gradually, through survival of the fittest, brought forth the current life forms. There was always a certain influence of consciousness so there was a certain ability to predict what physical qualities an organism needed in order to survive in a given environment.

This is incidentally one of the big explanation problems of the current theory of evolution. How did a species emerge that could live in an environment where none of the existing species could live? For example, the standard model says that life first evolved in the water with water organisms. Then, gradually these organisms became more and more complex, and they developed lungs and legs and migrated onto land. But you see, for evolution to work as an unconscious process, there is no ability to predict. That means that a trait, a new trait, that happens as a result of a random mutation can only survive if it gives the species an advantage for survival.

This means that there is a limit (and this is not recognized by human science currently) to the process of evolution. For example, a fish cannot survive in the air, a fish cannot reproduce on land. If you look at the ocean, you see that there are certain zones in the ocean where there is less oxygen. You can see that even in the very deep oceans, where there is very little oxygen and very little light, there are certain organisms that have survived and adapted. They have evolved so they can adapt to these conditions but there is no [complex] organism that can survive where there is no oxygen at all. They can survive on very little oxygen by having a lower metabolism, but if there is no oxygen they cannot survive.

Now, you look at a fish that is swimming right under the surface and you realize that this fish needs to breathe oxygen to survive. It does so through its gills, but the gills cannot extract oxygen from the air. You know that there is plenty of oxygen in the air above the surface of the water, but the fish cannot know this. There is no faculty in the unconscious process of evolution that can know that there is oxygen in the air. For a fish, there is no oxygen in the air because the fish cannot extract it. Therefore, the fish cannot survive above the water, it cannot reproduce above the water. And therefore, in current evolutionary theory there is no mechanism whereby a fish can gradually adapt to living above the water.

I know you have all been brought up with these images that first there were frogs that developed legs instead of fins, and then they developed outside lungs and the ability to breathe air. But this could not have happened through the gradual, random, *unconscious* process that you currently see science promoting. It could not have happened. To say that this could have happened is cognitive dissonance.

You cannot hold on to a strictly materialistic, unconscious, random process of evolution and at the same time explain how fish migrated to live on dry land. It cannot be the result of a gradual, random, unconscious process. There must have been some ability, some faculty, that could predict that there was an evolutionary advantage to developing an organ that could extract oxygen from the air instead of from water. Because there is no way in current evolutionary theory that you can say that the migration from fish to a frog happened as a result of just one random, genetic mutation. This means that in order for this process to happen, whereby a fish became a frog that could go on land, many mutations were necessary.

If mutations are completely random and not guided by any conscious ability to predict, then even two random mutations cannot build on each other. They cannot form a pattern. Random events cannot form a progressive pattern that leads to a result that could not be produced by one random event.

Listen to me. Two or more random events cannot produce a result that could not be the result of one random event. If every event is random, they cannot build upon each other. They might form a certain pattern, but it will not be a progressive pattern where one event leads to greater and greater complexity and suddenly you have an entirely new species emerge. *It cannot happen.* It is cognitive dissonance to believe this. There are already many biologists who have actually realized this. They have realized that biological science and physical science, the science of physics, has actually begun to challenge and invalidate the claim made in the early days of the evolutionary theory.

Loyalty to Darwin and his theory of evolution

Now again, we are not trying to blame anybody here. But we *are* trying to make the realistic assessment that Charles Darwin formulated the theory of evolution based on what was known at his time and based on where the collective consciousness was at at his time. Naturally, as progress moves on, as people know more and more and as the collective consciousness moves on, there comes these points where it is now necessary to look back at our paradigm and begin to question it. Is it consistent? Does it have contradictions? Are there things we cannot explain? Have we now, based on a higher understanding, become able to ask questions that Charles Darwin could not even imagine? Therefore, why should we be loyal to Darwin and the theory of evolution? Well, why indeed?

Why should an entire society be held back at a certain level of growth by one theory because some people are loyal to that theory? Well, what is the answer, my beloved? There is only one word that can answer this and it is: *fanaticism.* The people today in the western world, in the modern democracies, who are holding on to the theory of evolution as a purely materialistic, unconscious process—they are in the fanatical state of mind. They are fanatics. There is no other way to look at it.

You may have heard from previous times that I hold a certain flame of diplomacy, but there is no way I can express this in diplomatic terms. It is simply cognitive dissonance, and cognitive dissonance is one of the primary characteristics of fanaticism. Therefore, the people who will not see the dissonance, will not see the contradiction, are fanatics. They can only maintain their belief in evolution through a denial of the facts, the facts that have been proven, shown by science. They can only actually hold on to evolution by denying later discoveries, discoveries that came after Darwin. There are many biologists and other scientists and people outside the field of science who have begun to see this. There is a tension in the collective consciousness where your calls again can have a major impact in shattering this so that people can begin to question this entirely materialistic view of evolution.

Evolution is a process of conscious experimentation

Once that happens, you can then go a little bit further in looking at the connection between fanaticism and what you know about biological evolution. As I said: "What is the biological basis for, or the biological perspective on, fanaticism?" This is where you can acknowledge that you are human beings. You are not animals. You are not a gradual evolutionary step up from the animal level. The missing link is a quantum leap in consciousness. You are, in a qualitative way, different from animals. Your consciousness is qualitatively different. It is a quantum leap above animal species. Nevertheless, your bodies are based on a very long process of evolution that to some degree has something to do with survival. It is not necessarily the survival of the fittest in the way this has come to be seen today. Because current evolutionary theory based on Darwin's, or other people's, statement of "nature red in tooth and claw" is that it is only the most aggressive species that will survive. In reality, as we have said before, the dinosaurs proved that it is not the most aggressive or powerful species that survive, but the most adaptable, those who can adapt to changing circumstances.

Nevertheless, your bodies are a product of this very, very long process. It is actually a process that is very different from what can be accepted by both the religious people and the materialists. Because the evolutionary process is not a process that was created by God in some perfect state, nor is it entirely based on laws of nature. The evolutionary process is a process of *experimentation.* As we said, there were conscious beings directing the evolutionary process, but they were not all of them ascended beings. They were not all of them in the ascended state of consciousness. They (as we have explained about you) started out with a point-like sense of identity and they gradually grew from there. This means that they were not able to create a sustainable creation in the beginning. They had to experiment and by experimenting with bringing forth these biological life forms and seeing how they would survive, they learned. They learned what works, what does not work, what enables an organism to survive, what causes it to become extinct.

Killing your own is not survivable

When you look at this very, very long, gradual process, you see that the experiences on what is survivable and what is not, are built into your bodies today. The human body has what you often call instincts that are based on this very, very long (billions of years old) process of experimentation where the conscious beings behind this process have found out what works, what enables the species to survive. One of these instincts that you see, that is built in as a result of this long process is (and you see this most obviously in the animal kingdom) that if a species is to survive, it cannot kill members of its own species. You will see that in the vast majority of animal species, they do not kill members of their own species. Even the carnivores will rarely kill members of their own species. There can be certain special circumstances, but as a general rule they do not kill members of their own species because it is built in from this long process of experimentation that if a species starts killing its own members, it cannot survive.

What you are realizing here is that you come into a human body and it is almost like when you get into a car. The car is based on certain rules for how it works. If you want to go forward in your car, you have to put it in a forward gear. You cannot put it in reverse and go forward. You know that. It would be a complete idiot who would complain to the car manufacturer that he cannot drive forward while he has the gearshift in reverse. Makes no sense whatsoever.

You come into the human body, which is a vehicle, and it has certain rules that it is based upon. One of them is: You do not kill members of your own species. It is just that simple. This is a very, very strong instinct programmed into the human body and nervous system. Now, of course, you can say: "Oh, Saint Germain, are you ignoring history? Can't you see how people have been killing each other for a very long time?" Yes, of course I can. The conclusion we need to reach here is that from a biological perspective, people killing people is impossible. It is against the whole evolutionary process. It is endangering the survival of the species.

Therefore, you have to conclude that something has caused human beings to override this most basic instinct. This is, incidentally, a proof that human beings are not animals, are not entirely a product of the evolutionary process. Because if you were, you should not be able to override this instinct. You should function like an animal species and not kill members of your own species. Again, you can see there is a cognitive dissonance where you will not admit that even the current theory of evolution makes the conclusion that no animal species kill their own, but human beings do. How do you explain it? The reality is that it is not difficult for people in general to come to see that there must be something in the human mind that has caused people to be able to override this most basic instinct not to kill their own. Then, you can begin to wonder what that is and, of course, the answer is very simple. It is fanaticism.

Fanaticism overrides the instinct not to kill

When you go into a fanatical state of mind, you are able to override the instinct not to kill. How does this happen? This is the next question you can begin to ask yourself when you go through this process of reasoning. How has it happened that people have been able to override this instinct not to kill? This of course is a complex explanation, but fanaticism is a big part of it. It is not the only part of it. We have given you many other teachings. We do not expect the general public to be able to recognize these in the near future so what I will focus on here is the influence of fanaticism.

What happens is that when you go into a fanatical mindset, you are adopting an idealist view. You are adopting a certain idea of how human beings on earth think the world *should* work. You are adopting an idea of how human beings (based on their present level of consciousness, based on what they observe in the environment as it is currently on earth) decide that the universe *should* function. This is the one element of fanaticism. You formulate an idea, and then you elevate it to the status of somehow being absolute or infallible. This idea explains how the universe *should* work. This is one element.

First, you have the idea. You are not basing this on observation, at least not a complete or completely accurate observation. You are basing it on a partial understanding and a partial observation. Then, you say this is how the world *should* work. This is the first element.

Then, you go into a state of denial. This is the second element. There is denial because you are denying any evidence to the contrary. You are refusing to look at anything that contradicts your chosen belief. If you have the idea that the earth is the center of the universe, and that the sun and all the other stars in the heavens revolve around the earth, then you will not pick up a telescope and observe how the planets actually move and then say: "But the movements of the planets show that it cannot be true that the earth is the center because they clearly revolve around the sun. Maybe the earth also revolves around the sun and maybe the earth, therefore, isn't the center of the universe." The second element is denial of anything that contradicts your chosen theory.

Then, comes the third element of fanaticism, which, in essence, is the most crucial. It is that you somehow adopt the belief that the ends can justify the means. In other words, your fanatical theory creates a picture of how the world *should* work and then it defines a goal. In order to reach that goal, it is necessary and justified to take drastic measures. You will see that many of the theories that have been used by fanatics have defined a goal that was so important that it justified overriding the basic human instinct and therefore justified the killing of other human beings in order to reach this goal.

Evolution driven by cooperation

Now again, if you go back to biology, you can observe how species function. You have the common, traditional view of evolution that says it is all a matter of competition. Species are in constant competition for resources and those that are the most aggressive are the ones who will win the struggle for the survival of the fittest. Nature is one big struggle. As some modern biologists have observed by observing animal species, or even the cells of the human body, this is not a correct view. What drives the process of evolution is not actually *competition*. What drives the process of evolution is cooperation. What allows a certain species to survive is *cooperation*. Even cooperation with other species where you often see in what you call nature, in the ecosystem, that several species are interdependent on each other and they form a whole that allows all of them to survive.

Why are you alive right now? You are breathing oxygen. Where did that oxygen come from? Did it fall from the sky? No. It was produced by plants through photosynthesis. If there were no plants on earth who were capable of having the process of photosynthesis, there would be no oxygen and there would be no life on earth. Are the plants in competition with other species? How could they be? How would they have survived if they were in competition? You may say: "Well, there's grass on the field that produces oxygen and there's cows that eat the grass. Is there not competition?" But there is not. The cows eat the grass. They process it in their bodies. They produce manure, which fertilizes the grass. The grass produces oxygen that cows need. The cows need to eat, so they eat the grass. Where is the competition? There is no competition. In nature, as it functions "naturally," cooperation is the key to progress and survival and growth. Evolution has not been driven by competition. It has been driven by cooperation.

Survival of the fittest is anti-democratic

Human beings are the notable exception, but why is it that human beings are an exception? If you look at history, you see many, many examples of societies where there has been cooperation. What are the modern democracies based on? If they were based on the competitive mindset and survival of the fittest, you could not have a democracy. If you are only thinking about survival of the fittest, you would have only dictatorships because they are the most aggressive. Therefore, from an aggressive viewpoint, they are the most survivable. If there is one dictator at the top, who can command all of the people to support the army, he can build a bigger army than a democratic nation. Therefore, he can take over the world.

Again, the emergence of democracy is not a product of an aggressive, struggling process of evolution, it is the result of cooperation. You see many, many societies where they have had cooperation. You can see in the world today that the more you cooperate, the more you prosper. Why did the Soviet Union collapse? Because they isolated themselves from the rest of the world. Why have you seen the growth in material abundance over the last several decades in the West? Because they have cooperated. They have opened up. Instead of competing and fighting each other, they have joined forces and now they can accomplish more together than they could separately.

This is the same process you see in nature. You see it very clearly in your physical bodies. You do not think about this normally, but there are trillions of cells in your physical body. Now, according to a materialist view of evolution, if those cells were in competition with each other, how could so many trillions of cells ever have formed one organism that functions as a whole? How would it be possible? It could never, *ever* happen. Anybody who applies basic logic can see that this could not happen. They would have been in competition with each other and they would never have been able to form an organism with the complexity that you see in the human body. In fact, they would still have been single-celled organisms or very, very small, multiple-cell organisms. The reality here is that: Who will survive in the evolution of nations? It is not the nations that set themselves apart or attack other nations. It is the ones who survive by cooperating. They will cooperate and that is the key to survival.

Cooperation outcompetes competition

You can realize here that: What is it again that has gone wrong here in human life? You have, first of all, the very strong instinct to not kill your own species. But there is another instinct and it is the instinct to cooperate, to open up, to work with others. This is almost as strong as the do-not-kill-your-own instinct because it is, again, the result of this billion year long process of experimentation that has shown that cooperation works. Again, fanaticism is what allows people to override this and go into a state of mind where they see themselves as separated from other people. Again, how does this happen? Well, it happens because they adopt some kind of idea.

Now, you may go back to when people lived in more primitive societies, such as the hunter-gatherer societies that you saw here in Europe in the Stone Age. You may ask yourself: "Well, wasn't there competition back then between different tribes, between different groups of people? Wasn't there a certain competition for hunting grounds?" Yes, that is true. There came a point where the number of people in the hunter-gatherer culture had grown to such a level that they found it difficult to support themselves based on the natural resources that were available to a hunter-gatherer culture.

Like I said, for a fish there is no oxygen above the water's surface. For a hunter-gatherer there are only certain resources available: the animals that are there that can be hunted, the berries that can be picked up, the shellfish that you can get at the beach and so forth. This is the only resource you can see as a hunter-gatherer. There came a point where the number of people had grown to where they could not sustain themselves as hunter-gatherers. If they had all been in the competitive mindset, you would never have transcended the hunter-gatherer culture. You would have had constant competition where they had started to kill each other and then the human population would never have grown.

You see that the survival instinct or the instinct not to kill your own species can be overridden by the immediate need for survival. If somebody attacks you, you might kill that person instead of allowing him to kill you. If another tribe or group of hunter-gatherers come into your hunting territory and threaten your physical survival, then you might kill to ensure your own survival. This is one way that the not-to-kill instinct can be overridden. But this is not something that would lead to large scale warfare. How did society transcend the hunter-gatherer culture? Well, it was of course on an outer level that they received the technology or the knowledge of agriculture.

They started becoming agricultural societies and suddenly, by growing the land, by farming certain crops, there were resources available that the hunter-gatherers could not imagine and those resources could sustain a larger population. But my beloved, how did humanity make the transition from the hunter-gatherer culture to agricultural societies? It was not through competition. It was through cooperation. Hunter-gatherers can live (in the extreme) as single individuals. Of course, they cannot reproduce as single individuals so typically they live in small groups.

In order to manifest an agricultural society, there had to be much greater cooperation between people. You had to create a society with different functions, different specialties. There had to be a much greater level of cooperation, even in the first primitive agricultural societies. What you see is that ever since humanity made the shift to an agricultural society, cooperation has continued to increase and that is why you have seen the growth from small farming communities to larger communities, to larger and larger units, eventually nation states. Eventually leading to what you have now, an emerging global awareness. This has happened through cooperation, not through competition.

Ideas and fanaticism

Now, you look at again: You have these two very strong drives, not to kill your own and to cooperate in order to do more together than you can do alone. Obviously, war overrides this but how does that happen? Well, you can say that some wars have happened because one group of people attacked another group of people. The second group of people defended themselves and that is how they overrode their instinct not to kill. What caused the first group to attack? If you go far enough back, there may have been a certain primitive drive for plunder and conquest. As you move more and more into the modern world, you see that warfare has always been justified by an idea.

The closer you move to the modern world (but even in the ancient world), you see that warfare was justified by a certain idea. You can even go back in the Bible and you can see how the Jews believed that they had been given direction from an infallible god to seek the promised land. They went on a quest to find the promised land. They find what they think is the promised land. Unfortunately, there are these other people already living there. Now, they feel that their god has commanded them to go in and commit genocide against the people living in their promised land. An idea justified the killing, the wholesale slaughter and genocide, of other people. If the Jews had not had that idea, they could not have gone in there and conquered the promised land. They needed that justification. This is another proof that you are not further evolved animals. You are more complex beings because you need a justification.

In other words, what we see here is that human beings have certain basic instincts, not to kill, cooperate, but that they are able to override these instincts. Therefore, they can do something that goes against these basic principles that are defining what it takes to survive. You can actually create ideas whereby you endanger your own survival, but you refuse to see it, and *that* is another way to define fanaticism. You have created an idea that endangers your survival, but you are in denial about this. You refuse to see it. That is why you see that there can be sophisticated powerful civilizations that, in retrospect, you can see that they had certain beliefs that put them on a course towards disaster. They could not see it and that is why they continued to walk blindly towards the abyss and nobody could tell them that they were on the wrong course.

You see here so many civilizations that have had these beliefs, that have had these ideas, that have been out of touch with the basic principles of survivability. Therefore, they have collapsed, they have disappeared, they have gone the way of the dinosaurs. People are capable of looking at history and seeing that this has happened and then say: "But what about us? Are we as smart as we think we are, as sophisticated as we think we are? Are we doing the same thing? Are we holding on to certain ideas that are endangering our survival, our very survival?"

Ideas endanger the survival of modern society

Of course, you can see in the world today very clearly how in the Muslim world many, many people are in a fanatical state of mind. They clearly have cognitive dissonance. They clearly cannot see that even the pure statements in the Koran talk against killing other people and therefore, it is not justified what they are doing. You can clearly, from a western, modern, democratic perspective, see that they are endangering their own survival. They are going against these survival principles of do not kill your own and cooperate. Therefore, you can see that this cannot be sustained. Most people today in the western world can see that the Islamic culture is not sustainable—and it is not. There is no question about it. It will self-destruct. The question is how much suffering is produced before it does.

Can you then not turn around, look at your own societies and say: "What are we holding on to that is endangering our survival?" One of the things you are holding on to is precisely this: the theory of evolution as a completely materialistic process based on competition. You cannot have a truly functioning democracy if the people in that nation have that attitude of competition. Can you not see when you step back here (and again, when you make the calls, people will be able to see this) that most people in the democratic nations are in the cooperative mindset? They want to cooperate. How have the modern democracies grown to their current affluence? By cooperating, and therefore you see that this is the way forward. You also see that there is a small elite, even in the democratic nations, who are in the competitive mindset. They believe they are more fit than others. They believe they are fit to rule, that they should be allowed to rule, that they should be allowed to accumulate wealth beyond all reason. You can see that this is clearly against the principles of a democratic nation: All men are created equal, all people have the same inalienable rights. Therefore, you can see that this is clearly anti-democratic, that the democratic nations cannot survive if you uphold this state where a small elite are so in a competitive mindset that they feel they are more fit than others, more fit to rule.

Direct democracy and biology

That is why you need to make another leap in the democratic nations, and it is the leap, I have talked about before, of moving beyond representative democracy to a more direct form of democracy. Now, the messenger just read a book written by a biologist, who talks about how the cells in the body function and how they cooperate [*Spontaneous Evolution* by Bruce Lipton]. He makes the point in the book that all of the cells together, when they function in their natural state, they function in harmony. You can transfer this to a human community where you have the very old debate that the population at large cannot rule themselves because they will make the wrong decisions. What he points out is that scientific experiments and observations have been done that show that whereas one person can certainly make a wrong decision, if you take all of the people in a certain nation and let them all have influence on the decision, then collectively they will almost always make the best possible decision in any situation. The reality is that science has already pointed to what I am saying here. The true key to survival is cooperation.

Therefore, the modern democracies need to make that shift where they realize we do not need an elite that is in the competitive mindset, that feels they are more fit to rule than the population. This is a complete myth. Why are we dragging this along with us and have been doing so for centuries? Can we not see that this is a dinosaur left over from the age of dictatorships? There need not be a certain small group of people who somehow magically have been endowed by their creator, or by the laws of nature, with some magical ability to rule. If we are democracies, if we believe that all humans were created equal and that they all were endowed with the same rights, how can we uphold this elitist view that certain people are more fit to rule and that the population cannot rule itself?

The reality is, my beloved, as I have said before, if you look at the current state of affairs (that you have a ruling elite), do you think this is an ideal society? Look at all the warfare that the ruling elites, the power elites, the *competing* power elites have dragged the world into over the last hundred years. Do you really think the elite is capable of making good decisions? The reality is: "No, they cannot." The people themselves, all of them, will balance each other out, even though they have vastly different viewpoints. They will balance each other out and make the best possible decision. Why is that? Because of the biological principle that the key to survival is cooperation.

What is cooperation based on? It is based on a willingness to look beyond yourself and your own group and your own narrow interests. It is based on the concept that no man is an island, that you are not the only person in the world that matters. You are part of a whole, you are connected to a larger whole and because you are connected to a larger whole and part of that whole, what happens to the whole also affects you. Therefore, what is ultimately good for you is what is good for the whole and what is good for the whole is what is good for you. Therefore, you see that what, from a biological perspective, is the most survivable is the decision that is best for the greatest number of people.

Who can make a decision that is best for the greatest number of people? Can one dictator make that decision? Can a very small elite that sees themselves as apart from the population, as above and beyond the population, can they make that decision? Nay, my beloved, they cannot. But all of the people together *can*, when none of them see themselves as being better or higher than each other, but they see that they are all part of the whole. We are all in this together. We are in the same boat. When they have that awareness of the whole and do not set themselves apart as an elite, then together as an average they will make the best possible decision.

This means that when you have a democratic society where all of the people vote on an issue, then whatever they decide is what is the best for the nation at this particular stage. Why is it the best? Because whatever decision that people make, it is a reflection of their consciousness. They need to make that decision in order to have an opportunity to see their consciousness, see the limitations of it, and then grow beyond it.

Is there a specific goal that needs to happen on earth? Have we not so many times now over the last couple of years said that I, as the leader of the Golden Age, do not have a specific, clearly defined view of what *should* happen and what *should not* happen in the Golden Age. This is contrary to what many ascended master students in previous dispensations have interpreted. They have thought that I have a clear, exact plan of exactly what should happen and exactly what kind of society should be manifested. The reality is that as an ascended master, I am attuned to the very process instituted by the Creator, of growth through free will, growth in consciousness. The goal is growth in consciousness.

Fanaticism destroys natural experimentation

How can it happen? Through people exercising their will, experiencing the results and then evaluating their actions based on what they actually see. What is it that fanaticism does? It aborts this process, the natural process of experimentation. I have said that for billions of years there has been a natural process of experimentation that has led to certain principles that clearly define what is survivable and what is not. If human beings are in touch with this, if you constantly evaluate the result of your decisions, and change your decisions, change your view of life based on the results you see, then you will survive. What fanaticism has done, it has aborted the process by saying here is what society ideally *should* be like.

Again, Germany, 1930s, we have to create the Third Reich, the Aryan Nation. This is the overall goal and it is epically important to reach this goal. How can we reach it? Only by purifying the race from anyone who does not meet our standard. Therefore, it is justified to kill these people. What actually happened? You can look beyond all of the things you have been brought up to think about Hitler and the Nazi regime. Just look at it from a biological perspective. What happened in Nazi Germany? They violated the basic principle of biological survivability. They set themselves apart from the whole. They refused to cooperate. They went into a mind-set of being in competition with others who did not have their view. They started believing that it was justified that they kill their own species.

How can a society that violates the two basic principles of biological survival, how can such a society survive? It cannot and it did not. How hard is it to look at history and look at all of the civilizations that have gone down and then see that they have all had the same pattern. They had some kind of viewpoint, some kind of worldview, that was out of touch with the basic principles of survivability. Therefore, they self-destructed. How hard is it to then turn this around and see what is it in our democratic nations that threatens our survivability?

It is several things, as we have said, but certainly it is this entire phi-losophy that there is a natural process of selection that has selected the most fit among the human race and that they are the only ones who are capable of ruling. Whereas, the reality is that the only ones who are capable of truly ruling is all of the people working together. The average will always be better than the decisions of a small elite.

Of course, you can take this based on what you know. You can look at society. You can apply it in many different ways. You can begin to look at how society has in so many ways gotten into blind alleys where they have ideas that simply are not in alignment with reality. Anytime you have a society that is based on an idea that is out of touch with how the world actually works, you can see that this society cannot survive in the long run. It is threatening its own survival. Sometimes the death of that society will come in the form of an external enemy but who has external enemies? Only those who set themselves apart from the whole and think they are in competition with the others and that they should have certain advantages that the others should not have.

Cooperation leading to symbiosis

Do you not see, my beloved, that if you look at nature, you will see this symbiotic relationship where different species cooperate and they enhance each other. There are exceptions, of course. Nature is not in a completely balanced state because it is affected by human consciousness. Nevertheless, you see this symbiotic relationship where there is no competition and you can look at why that is. It is because there is some kind of awareness of the whole. Now naturally, you cannot go to the cows and the grass and say they have an awareness of each other and how they are cooperating. What I am saying is that there is some level of nature where there is a conscious being that is aware of the advantages of cooperation.

This is the basic principle. Whenever you set yourself apart from the whole and try to gain certain privileges, certain advantages that are above the rest, then you are going against the basic principles of nature. Therefore, you threaten your survivability. Of course, what you see in the fanatical mindset is that it is very much based on this idea that all men and women are not created equal by their creator, that it is possible to divide humanity into certain groups. Then, you apply a value judgment that says some are better than others, some are more right than others, some have more right to rule, some have more right to survive. Now, what are you doing? You are playing god. You are thinking that you know better than nature how nature should work. You have a situation where in the modern world you know there is a process of gradual evolution that goes back billions of years. That process has been able to bring life forward. Over that entire period of time life has been brought towards more and more complex life forms that can survive.

At the same time, you can look at human history in the last couple of thousand years. You can see how many societies there have been where they have had an idea that they thought was absolute but that idea was in violation of the experiences based on the long process of evolution. You can see that this society did not survive.

A long-term perspective on survivability

Is it that hard to make that leap and realize that human beings with a very short-sighted perspective cannot create ideas that can enable a society to survive in the long run? You need a longer perspective that reaches beyond the narrow self-interest of a particular group of people in a particular situation. If you want to create a society that can survive in the long run, you need to bring it into alignment with how the world actually works.

That is the very purpose of science, it *was* the very purpose of science. It was also the very purpose behind, not what you call religion, but spirituality or mysticism. It is using science, using observation of how the world works, and spirituality or mysticism, using intuition to tune in to a higher level of awareness than human beings have. If you have the alpha and the omega, the omega being observing the world around you and the alpha tuning in to a level of consciousness beyond yours, when you combine those two, you are able to tune in to how the world actually works. Then, you can build a society that is survivable, that is sustainable.

This does not mean that I am advocating that the modern democracies need to find or develop a new form of religion. Again, [messenger coughs] (apparently the messenger's voice has violated the principle of survivability) again, we are not in any way envisioning that the modern democracies will come to consciously recognize ascended masters and follow ascended master principles. We are not even envisioning a return to the time where you had oracles and that the leaders of nations would ask the oracles for a sign of what they should do. We are not envisioning that we would have messengers and that the leaders, the heads of state, would consult the messenger and call him up and say: "So what does Saint Germain say about this law we are considering? What should we do?" This is not what we are talking about.

We are talking about getting to a point where we have restored science to its original purity. We do not have a political overlay of scientific Materialism, but we are simply looking at how does the world work. We have restored a process whereby people can raise their consciousness on an individual basis. Thereby, they can increase their intuitive faculties so that they can tune in to a higher level of consciousness and get a perspective that is beyond the narrow self-interest. Through this alpha-omega action society can rise to an entirely different level where you overcome the fanatical mindset of thinking you can define how the world should work. Now, you are in tune with how the world actually works. You know that cooperation is the key to growth and you are pursuing that path of cooperating.

We will give you more teachings on why cooperation is so important and why it is the principle that has allowed life to survive. I am content to have given you what I have given you in this installment. I am grateful for your willingness to endure with us, to sit here. I know your minds sometimes wonder, I know your stomachs sometimes growl. I know that you can have all kinds of projections against you from the forces that do not want you to be where you are and to be the broadcast stations for this message being spread into the collective. Nevertheless, I am grateful for your willingness to be here and allow me to magnify this message by the consciousness of all of you.

The more people that are here, the more of a multiplication factor we can give and the more powerful is the wave that spreads through the collective consciousness. Therefore, it gradually awakens people where they suddenly see how obvious it is that we need to make a change in society. For this, my gratitude, and I seal you in the love of my heart.

13 | INVOKING A BIOLOGICAL VISION OF FANATICISM (PART 1)

In the name of the I AM THAT I AM, Jesus Christ, I use the authority that I have as a being in embodiment on earth to call upon Saint Germain to reinforce my calls and use my chakras to project the statements in this invocation into the collective consciousness and awaken people to the fact that fanaticism is against our biology. Awaken people to the reality that we are spiritual beings and that we can co-create a new future by working with the ascended masters. I especially call for …

[Make your own calls here.]

Part 1

1. Saint Germain, shatter the energetic matrix that prevents people from seeing that the conditions we have on earth today are the products of a gradual, progressive and, therefore, evolutionary process.

O Saint Germain, you do inspire,
my vision raised forever higher,

with you I form a figure-eight,
your Golden Age I co-create.

O Saint Germain, what love you bring,
it truly makes all matter sing,
your violet flame does all restore,
with you we are becoming more.

2. Saint Germain, shatter the energetic matrix that prevents people from seeing that this evolutionary process is not mechanical and unconscious. It is creative and the consciousness of human beings is having an influence on the evolutionary process.

O Saint Germain, what Freedom Flame,
released when we recite your name,
acceleration is your gift,
our planet it will surely lift.

O Saint Germain, what love you bring,
it truly makes all matter sing,
your violet flame does all restore,
with you we are becoming more.

3. Saint Germain, shatter the energetic matrix that prevents people from seeing that before human beings, other conscious self-aware beings had an influence on the evolutionary process.

O Saint Germain, in love we claim,
our right to bring your violet flame,
from you Above, to us below,
it is an all-transforming flow.

O Saint Germain, what love you bring,
it truly makes all matter sing,
your violet flame does all restore,
with you we are becoming more.

4. Saint Germain, shatter the energetic matrix that prevents people from seeing that the ascended masters started the process and at certain times

they stepped in and caused it to accelerate to a higher level, such as we see in the history of the appearance of species.

O Saint Germain, I love you so,
my aura filled with violet glow,
my chakras filled with violet fire,
I am your cosmic amplifier.

O Saint Germain, what love you bring,
it truly makes all matter sing,
your violet flame does all restore,
with you we are becoming more.

5. Saint Germain, shatter the energetic matrix that prevents people from seeing that our physical bodies are the product of an evolutionary process. This started with more primitive life forms that gradually evolved to greater and greater complexity.

O Saint Germain, I am now free,
your violet flame is therapy,
transform all hang-ups in my mind,
as inner peace I surely find.

O Saint Germain, what love you bring,
it truly makes all matter sing,
your violet flame does all restore,
with you we are becoming more.

6. Saint Germain, shatter the energetic matrix that prevents people from seeing that eventually this process was able to bring forth a physical body with the complex brain and nervous system that is necessary for a higher being to take embodiment in that body, for a higher being to come into that body and begin to express itself through that body.

O Saint Germain, my body pure,
your violet flame for all is cure,
consume the cause of all disease,
and therefore I am all at ease.

**O Saint Germain, what love you bring,
it truly makes all matter sing,
your violet flame does all restore,
with you we are becoming more.**

7. Saint Germain, shatter the energetic matrix that prevents people from seeing that animals do not have individual souls, they are not self-aware beings. We are self-aware beings because we have a part of our being that came from outside of the body, that existed before the body, that will continue to exist after the body.

O Saint Germain, I'm karma-free,
the past no longer burdens me,
a brand new opportunity,
I am in Christic unity.

**O Saint Germain, what love you bring,
it truly makes all matter sing,
your violet flame does all restore,
with you we are becoming more.**

8. Saint Germain, shatter the energetic matrix that prevents people from seeing that our being is so complex that we cannot take embodiment in a meaningful way through an animal. There needed to be a gradual process that brought forth a human body that has the complex brain and nervous system that we need in order to express ourselves and learn from that experience.

O Saint Germain, we are now one,
I am for you a violet sun,
as we transform this planet earth,
your Golden Age is given birth.

**O Saint Germain, what love you bring,
it truly makes all matter sing,
your violet flame does all restore,
with you we are becoming more.**

9. Saint Germain, shatter the energetic matrix that prevents people from seeing that our physical bodies were brought forth through a gradual evolutionary process that started with more primitive life forms.

O Saint Germain, the earth is free,
from burden of duality,
in oneness we bring what is best,
your Golden Age is manifest.

O Saint Germain, what love you bring,
it truly makes all matter sing,
your violet flame does all restore,
with you we are becoming more.

Part 2

1. Saint Germain, shatter the energetic matrix that prevents people from seeing that evolution did not happen through an infinite variety of random events that gradually, through survival of the fittest, brought forth the current life forms. There was always an influence of consciousness so there was a certain ability to predict what physical qualities an organism needed in order to survive in a given environment.

O Saint Germain, you do inspire,
my vision raised forever higher,
with you I form a figure-eight,
your Golden Age I co-create.

O Saint Germain, what love you bring,
it truly makes all matter sing,
your violet flame does all restore,
with you we are becoming more.

2. Saint Germain, shatter the energetic matrix that prevents people from seeing that one of the explanation problems of the current theory of evolution is how a species emerged that could live in an environment where none of the existing species could live.

O Saint Germain, what Freedom Flame,
released when we recite your name,
acceleration is your gift,
our planet it will surely lift.

O Saint Germain, what love you bring,
it truly makes all matter sing,
your violet flame does all restore,
with you we are becoming more.

3. Saint Germain, shatter the energetic matrix that prevents people from seeing that for evolution to work as an unconscious process, there is no ability to predict. This means that a new trait that happens as a result of a random mutation can only survive if it gives the species an advantage for survival.

O Saint Germain, in love we claim,
our right to bring your violet flame,
from you Above, to us below,
it is an all-transforming flow.

O Saint Germain, what love you bring,
it truly makes all matter sing,
your violet flame does all restore,
with you we are becoming more.

4. Saint Germain, shatter the energetic matrix that prevents people from seeing that there is a limit to the process of evolution. A fish cannot gradually adapt to breathing oxygen from the air because no mechanism can predict that there is oxygen in the air.

O Saint Germain, I love you so,
my aura filled with violet glow,
my chakras filled with violet fire,
I am your cosmic amplifier.

O Saint Germain, what love you bring,
it truly makes all matter sing,

**your violet flame does all restore,
with you we are becoming more.**

5. Saint Germain, shatter the energetic matrix that prevents people from seeing that fish evolving to live on land could not have happened through the gradual, random, unconscious process that science is promoting. To say that this could have happened is cognitive dissonance.

O Saint Germain, I am now free,
your violet flame is therapy,
transform all hang-ups in my mind,
as inner peace I surely find.

**O Saint Germain, what love you bring,
it truly makes all matter sing,
your violet flame does all restore,
with you we are becoming more.**

6. Saint Germain, shatter the energetic matrix that prevents people from seeing that we cannot hold on to a strictly materialistic, unconscious, random process of evolution and at the same time explain how fish migrated to live on dry land. It cannot be the result of a gradual, random, unconscious process.

O Saint Germain, my body pure,
your violet flame for all is cure,
consume the cause of all disease,
and therefore I am all at ease.

**O Saint Germain, what love you bring,
it truly makes all matter sing,
your violet flame does all restore,
with you we are becoming more.**

7. Saint Germain, shatter the energetic matrix that prevents people from seeing that there must have been some faculty that could predict that there was an evolutionary advantage to developing an organ that could extract oxygen from the air instead of from water.

O Saint Germain, I'm karma-free,
the past no longer burdens me,
a brand new opportunity,
I am in Christic unity.

**O Saint Germain, what love you bring,
it truly makes all matter sing,
your violet flame does all restore,
with you we are becoming more.**

8. Saint Germain, shatter the energetic matrix that prevents people from seeing that there is no way in current evolutionary theory to say that the migration from fish to a frog happened as a result of just one random mutation. In order for this process to happen, many mutations were necessary.

O Saint Germain, we are now one,
I am for you a violet sun,
as we transform this planet earth,
your Golden Age is given birth.

**O Saint Germain, what love you bring,
it truly makes all matter sing,
your violet flame does all restore,
with you we are becoming more.**

9. Saint Germain, shatter the energetic matrix that prevents people from seeing that if mutations are completely random and not guided by any conscious ability to predict, then even two random mutations cannot build on each other. They cannot form a pattern. Random events cannot form a progressive pattern that leads to a result that could not be produced by one random event.

O Saint Germain, the earth is free,
from burden of duality,
in oneness we bring what is best,
your Golden Age is manifest.

**O Saint Germain, what love you bring,
it truly makes all matter sing,**

**your violet flame does all restore,
with you we are becoming more.**

Part 3

1. Saint Germain, shatter the energetic matrix that prevents people from seeing that two or more random events cannot produce a result that could not be the result of one random event. If every event is random, they cannot build upon each other.

O Saint Germain, you do inspire,
my vision raised forever higher,
with you I form a figure-eight,
your Golden Age I co-create.

**O Saint Germain, what love you bring,
it truly makes all matter sing,
your violet flame does all restore,
with you we are becoming more.**

2. Saint Germain, shatter the energetic matrix that prevents people from seeing that random events might form a certain pattern, but it will not be a progressive pattern where one event leads to greater and greater complexity and suddenly an entirely new species emerges. It is cognitive dissonance to believe this.

O Saint Germain, what Freedom Flame,
released when we recite your name,
acceleration is your gift,
our planet it will surely lift.

**O Saint Germain, what love you bring,
it truly makes all matter sing,
your violet flame does all restore,
with you we are becoming more.**

3. Saint Germain, shatter the energetic matrix that prevents people from seeing that biological science and the science of physics has begun to challenge and invalidate the claim made in the early days of the evolutionary theory.

O Saint Germain, in love we claim,
our right to bring your violet flame,
from you Above, to us below,
it is an all-transforming flow.

O Saint Germain, what love you bring,
it truly makes all matter sing,
your violet flame does all restore,
with you we are becoming more.

4. Saint Germain, shatter the energetic matrix that prevents people from seeing that Charles Darwin formulated the theory of evolution based on what was known at his time and based on the collective consciousness at his time.

O Saint Germain, I love you so,
my aura filled with violet glow,
my chakras filled with violet fire,
I am your cosmic amplifier.

O Saint Germain, what love you bring,
it truly makes all matter sing,
your violet flame does all restore,
with you we are becoming more.

5. Saint Germain, shatter the energetic matrix that prevents people from seeing that as progress moves on, as people know more and more and as the collective consciousness moves on, there comes these points where it is necessary to look back at our paradigm and begin to question it.

O Saint Germain, I am now free,
your violet flame is therapy,
transform all hang-ups in my mind,
as inner peace I surely find.

**O Saint Germain, what love you bring,
it truly makes all matter sing,
your violet flame does all restore,
with you we are becoming more.**

6. Saint Germain, shatter the energetic matrix that prevents people from seeing that we need to ask if the theory of evolution is consistent or has contradictions? Are there things we cannot explain? Have we now, based on a higher understanding, become able to ask questions that Charles Darwin could not even imagine?

O Saint Germain, my body pure,
your violet flame for all is cure,
consume the cause of all disease,
and therefore I am all at ease.

**O Saint Germain, what love you bring,
it truly makes all matter sing,
your violet flame does all restore,
with you we are becoming more.**

7. Saint Germain, shatter the energetic matrix that prevents people from seeing that we need to ask why we should be loyal to Darwin and the theory of evolution? Why should an entire society be held back at a certain level of growth by one theory because some people are loyal to that theory?

O Saint Germain, I'm karma-free,
the past no longer burdens me,
a brand new opportunity,
I am in Christic unity.

**O Saint Germain, what love you bring,
it truly makes all matter sing,
your violet flame does all restore,
with you we are becoming more.**

8. Saint Germain, shatter the energetic matrix that prevents people from seeing that the only word that can explain such loyalty is: *fanaticism*. The

people in the modern democracies who are holding on to the theory of evolution as a purely materialistic, unconscious process—they are in the fanatical state of mind. They are fanatics.

> O Saint Germain, we are now one,
> I am for you a violet sun,
> as we transform this planet earth,
> your Golden Age is given birth.

> **O Saint Germain, what love you bring,**
> **it truly makes all matter sing,**
> **your violet flame does all restore,**
> **with you we are becoming more.**

9. Saint Germain, shatter the energetic matrix that prevents people from seeing that Materialism is cognitive dissonance, and cognitive dissonance is one of the primary characteristics of fanaticism. Therefore, the people who will not see the dissonance, will not see the contradiction, are fanatics.

> O Saint Germain, the earth is free,
> from burden of duality,
> in oneness we bring what is best,
> your Golden Age is manifest.

> **O Saint Germain, what love you bring,**
> **it truly makes all matter sing,**
> **your violet flame does all restore,**
> **with you we are becoming more.**

Part 4

1. Saint Germain, shatter the energetic matrix that prevents people from seeing that we can only maintain a belief in evolution through a denial of the facts, the facts that have been proven by science. We can only hold on to evolution by denying discoveries that came after Darwin.

O Saint Germain, you do inspire,
my vision raised forever higher,
with you I form a figure-eight,
your Golden Age I co-create.

O Saint Germain, what love you bring,
it truly makes all matter sing,
your violet flame does all restore,
with you we are becoming more.

2. Saint Germain, shatter the energetic matrix that prevents biologists, other scientists and people outside the field of science from questioning the entirely materialistic view of evolution.

O Saint Germain, what Freedom Flame,
released when we recite your name,
acceleration is your gift,
our planet it will surely lift.

O Saint Germain, what love you bring,
it truly makes all matter sing,
your violet flame does all restore,
with you we are becoming more.

3. Saint Germain, shatter the energetic matrix that prevents people from seeing that we are human beings. We are not animals. We are not a gradual evolutionary step up from the animal level. The missing link is a quantum leap in consciousness.

O Saint Germain, in love we claim,
our right to bring your violet flame,
from you Above, to us below,
it is an all-transforming flow.

O Saint Germain, what love you bring,
it truly makes all matter sing,
your violet flame does all restore,
with you we are becoming more.

4. Saint Germain, shatter the energetic matrix that prevents people from seeing that we are, in a qualitative way, different from animals. Our consciousness is qualitatively different. It is a quantum leap above animal species.

O Saint Germain, I love you so,
my aura filled with violet glow,
my chakras filled with violet fire,
I am your cosmic amplifier.

**O Saint Germain, what love you bring,
it truly makes all matter sing,
your violet flame does all restore,
with you we are becoming more.**

5. Saint Germain, shatter the energetic matrix that prevents people from seeing that our bodies are based on a very long process of evolution that to some degree has to do with survival. It is not the survival of the fittest in the way portrayed by evolutionary theory.

O Saint Germain, I am now free,
your violet flame is therapy,
transform all hang-ups in my mind,
as inner peace I surely find.

**O Saint Germain, what love you bring,
it truly makes all matter sing,
your violet flame does all restore,
with you we are becoming more.**

6. Saint Germain, shatter the energetic matrix that prevents people from seeing that the dinosaurs proved that it is not the most aggressive or powerful species that survive, but the most adaptable, those who can adapt to changing circumstances.

O Saint Germain, my body pure,
your violet flame for all is cure,
consume the cause of all disease,
and therefore I am all at ease.

**O Saint Germain, what love you bring,
it truly makes all matter sing,
your violet flame does all restore,
with you we are becoming more.**

7. Saint Germain, shatter the energetic matrix that prevents people from seeing that our bodies are a product of this very long process that is different from what can be accepted by both the religious people and the materialists.

O Saint Germain, I'm karma-free,
the past no longer burdens me,
a brand new opportunity,
I am in Christic unity.

**O Saint Germain, what love you bring,
it truly makes all matter sing,
your violet flame does all restore,
with you we are becoming more.**

8. Saint Germain, shatter the energetic matrix that prevents people from seeing that the evolutionary process was not created by God in some perfect state, nor is it entirely based on laws of nature. The evolutionary process is a process of experimentation.

O Saint Germain, we are now one,
I am for you a violet sun,
as we transform this planet earth,
your Golden Age is given birth.

**O Saint Germain, what love you bring,
it truly makes all matter sing,
your violet flame does all restore,
with you we are becoming more.**

9. Saint Germain, shatter the energetic matrix that prevents people from seeing that there were conscious beings directing the evolutionary process, but they were not all of them ascended beings. They were not all of them in the ascended state of consciousness.

O Saint Germain, the earth is free,
from burden of duality,
in oneness we bring what is best,
your Golden Age is manifest.

O Saint Germain, what love you bring,
it truly makes all matter sing,
your violet flame does all restore,
with you we are becoming more.

Sealing

In the name of the I AM THAT I AM, I accept that Archangel Michael, Astrea and Shiva form an impenetrable shield around myself and all constructive people, sealing us from all fear-based energies in all four octaves. I accept that the Light of God is consuming and transforming all fear-based energies that make up the dark forces working against ending the era of fanaticism on earth!

14 | INVOKING A BIOLOGICAL VISION OF FANATICISM (PART 2)

In the name of the I AM THAT I AM, Jesus Christ, I use the authority that I have as a being in embodiment on earth to call upon Saint Germain to reinforce my calls and use my chakras to project the statements in this invocation into the collective consciousness and awaken people to the fact that fanaticism is against our biology. Awaken people to the reality that we are spiritual beings and that we can co-create a new future by working with the ascended masters. I especially call for …

[Make your own calls here.]

Part 1

1. Saint Germain, shatter the energetic matrix that prevents people from seeing that some of these beings started out with a point-like sense of identity and they gradually grew from there. This means that they were not able to create a sustainable creation in the beginning.

O Saint Germain, you do inspire,
my vision raised forever higher,
with you I form a figure-eight,
your Golden Age I co-create.

O Saint Germain, what love you bring,
it truly makes all matter sing,
your violet flame does all restore,
with you we are becoming more.

2. Saint Germain, shatter the energetic matrix that prevents people from seeing that the beings influencing evolution had to experiment. By experimenting with bringing forth these biological life forms, they learned what enables an organism to survive, what causes it to become extinct.

O Saint Germain, what Freedom Flame,
released when we recite your name,
acceleration is your gift,
our planet it will surely lift.

O Saint Germain, what love you bring,
it truly makes all matter sing,
your violet flame does all restore,
with you we are becoming more.

3. Saint Germain, shatter the energetic matrix that prevents people from seeing that the experiences gleaned from this very long, gradual process are built into our bodies today. The human body has instincts that are based on the conscious beings learning what enables a species to survive.

O Saint Germain, in love we claim,
our right to bring your violet flame,
from you Above, to us below,
it is an all-transforming flow.

O Saint Germain, what love you bring,
it truly makes all matter sing,
your violet flame does all restore,
with you we are becoming more.

4. Saint Germain, shatter the energetic matrix that prevents people from seeing that one of the instincts that is built in as a result of this long process is that if a species is to survive, it cannot kill members of its own species. The vast majority of animal species do not kill members of their own species.

O Saint Germain, I love you so,
my aura filled with violet glow,
my chakras filled with violet fire,
I am your cosmic amplifier.

**O Saint Germain, what love you bring,
it truly makes all matter sing,
your violet flame does all restore,
with you we are becoming more.**

5. Saint Germain, shatter the energetic matrix that prevents people from seeing that coming into a human body is almost like when we get into a car. The car is based on certain rules for how it works. If we want to go forward in a car, we have to put it in a forward gear. We cannot put it in reverse and go forward.

O Saint Germain, I am now free,
your violet flame is therapy,
transform all hang-ups in my mind,
as inner peace I surely find.

**O Saint Germain, what love you bring,
it truly makes all matter sing,
your violet flame does all restore,
with you we are becoming more.**

6. Saint Germain, shatter the energetic matrix that prevents people from seeing that we come into the human body, which is a vehicle, and it has certain rules that it is based upon. One of them is: You do not kill members of your own species. This is a very strong instinct programmed into the human body and nervous system.

O Saint Germain, my body pure,
your violet flame for all is cure,
consume the cause of all disease,
and therefore I am all at ease.

**O Saint Germain, what love you bring,
it truly makes all matter sing,
your violet flame does all restore,
with you we are becoming more.**

7. Saint Germain, shatter the energetic matrix that prevents people from seeing that from a biological perspective, people killing people is impossible. It is against the whole evolutionary process. It is endangering the survival of the species.

O Saint Germain, I'm karma-free,
the past no longer burdens me,
a brand new opportunity,
I am in Christic unity.

**O Saint Germain, what love you bring,
it truly makes all matter sing,
your violet flame does all restore,
with you we are becoming more.**

8. Saint Germain, shatter the energetic matrix that prevents people from seeing that something has caused human beings to override this most basic instinct. This is proof that we are not animals, we are not entirely a product of the evolutionary process.

O Saint Germain, we are now one,
I am for you a violet sun,
as we transform this planet earth,
your Golden Age is given birth.

**O Saint Germain, what love you bring,
it truly makes all matter sing,
your violet flame does all restore,
with you we are becoming more.**

9. Saint Germain, shatter the energetic matrix that prevents people from seeing that it is cognitive dissonance that the current theory of evolution makes the conclusion that no animal species kill their own, but human beings do.

O Saint Germain, the earth is free,
from burden of duality,
in oneness we bring what is best,
your Golden Age is manifest.

O Saint Germain, what love you bring,
it truly makes all matter sing,
your violet flame does all restore,
with you we are becoming more.

Part 2

1. Saint Germain, shatter the energetic matrix that prevents people from seeing that there must be something in the human mind that has caused people to be able to override this most basic instinct not to kill their own. The answer is very simple: fanaticism.

O Saint Germain, you do inspire,
my vision raised forever higher,
with you I form a figure-eight,
your Golden Age I co-create.

O Saint Germain, what love you bring,
it truly makes all matter sing,
your violet flame does all restore,
with you we are becoming more.

2. Saint Germain, shatter the energetic matrix that prevents people from seeing that when we go into a fanatical state of mind, we are able to override the instinct not to kill.

O Saint Germain, what Freedom Flame,
released when we recite your name,
acceleration is your gift,
our planet it will surely lift.

**O Saint Germain, what love you bring,
it truly makes all matter sing,
your violet flame does all restore,
with you we are becoming more.**

3. Saint Germain, shatter the energetic matrix that prevents people from seeing that when we go into a fanatical mindset, we are adopting an idealist view. We are adopting a certain idea of how human beings on earth think the world *should* work.

O Saint Germain, in love we claim,
our right to bring your violet flame,
from you Above, to us below,
it is an all-transforming flow.

**O Saint Germain, what love you bring,
it truly makes all matter sing,
your violet flame does all restore,
with you we are becoming more.**

4. Saint Germain, shatter the energetic matrix that prevents people from seeing that one element of fanaticism is that we formulate an idea, and then we elevate it to the status of being absolute or infallible. This idea explains how the universe *should* work.

O Saint Germain, I love you so,
my aura filled with violet glow,
my chakras filled with violet fire,
I am your cosmic amplifier.

**O Saint Germain, what love you bring,
it truly makes all matter sing,
your violet flame does all restore,
with you we are becoming more.**

5. Saint Germain, shatter the energetic matrix that prevents people from seeing that first, we have the idea. We are not basing this on observation, at least not a complete or completely accurate observation. We are basing it on a partial understanding and a partial observation. Then, we say this is how the world *should* work. This is the first element of fanaticism.

O Saint Germain, I am now free,
your violet flame is therapy,
transform all hang-ups in my mind,
as inner peace I surely find.

O Saint Germain, what love you bring,
it truly makes all matter sing,
your violet flame does all restore,
with you we are becoming more.

6. Saint Germain, shatter the energetic matrix that prevents people from seeing that then, we go into a state of denial. We are denying any evidence to the contrary. We are refusing to look at anything that contradicts our chosen belief. The second element is denial of anything that contradicts our chosen theory.

O Saint Germain, my body pure,
your violet flame for all is cure,
consume the cause of all disease,
and therefore I am all at ease.

O Saint Germain, what love you bring,
it truly makes all matter sing,
your violet flame does all restore,
with you we are becoming more.

7. Saint Germain, shatter the energetic matrix that prevents people from seeing that we now adopt the belief that the ends can justify the means. Our fanatical theory creates a picture of how the world *should* work and then it defines a goal. In order to reach that goal, it is necessary and justified to take drastic measures.

O Saint Germain, I'm karma-free,
the past no longer burdens me,
a brand new opportunity,
I am in Christic unity.

**O Saint Germain, what love you bring,
it truly makes all matter sing,
your violet flame does all restore,
with you we are becoming more.**

8. Saint Germain, shatter the energetic matrix that prevents people from seeing that many of the theories that have been used by fanatics have defined a goal that was so important that it justified overriding the basic human instinct and therefore justified the killing of other human beings in order to reach this goal. This is the third element of fanaticism.

O Saint Germain, we are now one,
I am for you a violet sun,
as we transform this planet earth,
your Golden Age is given birth.

**O Saint Germain, what love you bring,
it truly makes all matter sing,
your violet flame does all restore,
with you we are becoming more.**

9. Saint Germain, shatter the energetic matrix that prevents people from seeing that the traditional view of evolution says it is all a matter of competition. Species are in constant competition for resources and those that are the most aggressive are the ones who will win the struggle for the survival of the fittest. Nature is one big struggle.

O Saint Germain, the earth is free,
from burden of duality,
in oneness we bring what is best,
your Golden Age is manifest.

**O Saint Germain, what love you bring,
it truly makes all matter sing,**

**your violet flame does all restore,
with you we are becoming more.**

Part 3

1. Saint Germain, shatter the energetic matrix that prevents people from seeing that what drives the process of evolution is not actually *competition*. What drives the process of evolution is cooperation. What allows a certain species to survive is *cooperation*.

O Saint Germain, you do inspire,
my vision raised forever higher,
with you I form a figure-eight,
your Golden Age I co-create.

**O Saint Germain, what love you bring,
it truly makes all matter sing,
your violet flame does all restore,
with you we are becoming more.**

2. Saint Germain, shatter the energetic matrix that prevents people from seeing that survival is based on cooperation with other species where several species are interdependent on each other and they form a whole that allows all of them to survive.

O Saint Germain, what Freedom Flame,
released when we recite your name,
acceleration is your gift,
our planet it will surely lift.

**O Saint Germain, what love you bring,
it truly makes all matter sing,
your violet flame does all restore,
with you we are becoming more.**

3. Saint Germain, shatter the energetic matrix that prevents people from seeing that in nature, as it functions "naturally," cooperation is the key to

progress, survival and growth. Evolution has not been driven by competition. It has been driven by cooperation.

> O Saint Germain, in love we claim,
> our right to bring your violet flame,
> from you Above, to us below,
> it is an all-transforming flow.

> **O Saint Germain, what love you bring,**
> **it truly makes all matter sing,**
> **your violet flame does all restore,**
> **with you we are becoming more.**

4. Saint Germain, shatter the energetic matrix that prevents people from seeing that history has many examples of societies with cooperation. If the modern democracies had been based on the competitive mindset and survival of the fittest, we could not have a democracy.

> O Saint Germain, I love you so,
> my aura filled with violet glow,
> my chakras filled with violet fire,
> I am your cosmic amplifier.

> **O Saint Germain, what love you bring,**
> **it truly makes all matter sing,**
> **your violet flame does all restore,**
> **with you we are becoming more.**

5. Saint Germain, shatter the energetic matrix that prevents people from seeing that if we are only thinking about survival of the fittest, we would have only dictatorships because they are the most aggressive. From an aggressive viewpoint, they are the most survivable.

> O Saint Germain, I am now free,
> your violet flame is therapy,
> transform all hang-ups in my mind,
> as inner peace I surely find.

O Saint Germain, what love you bring,
it truly makes all matter sing,
your violet flame does all restore,
with you we are becoming more.

6. Saint Germain, shatter the energetic matrix that prevents people from seeing that the emergence of democracy is not a product of an aggressive, struggling process of evolution, it is the result of cooperation.

O Saint Germain, my body pure,
your violet flame for all is cure,
consume the cause of all disease,
and therefore I am all at ease.

O Saint Germain, what love you bring,
it truly makes all matter sing,
your violet flame does all restore,
with you we are becoming more.

7. Saint Germain, shatter the energetic matrix that prevents people from seeing that the more we cooperate, the more we prosper. The growth in material abundance over the last several decades is based on cooperation. Instead of competing, we have joined forces and now we can accomplish more together than we could separately.

O Saint Germain, I'm karma-free,
the past no longer burdens me,
a brand new opportunity,
I am in Christic unity.

O Saint Germain, what love you bring,
it truly makes all matter sing,
your violet flame does all restore,
with you we are becoming more.

8. Saint Germain, shatter the energetic matrix that prevents people from seeing that there are trillions of cells in a human body. According to a materialist view of evolution, if those cells were in competition with each other, how could they have formed one organism that functions as a whole?

O Saint Germain, we are now one,
I am for you a violet sun,
as we transform this planet earth,
your Golden Age is given birth.

O Saint Germain, what love you bring,
it truly makes all matter sing,
your violet flame does all restore,
with you we are becoming more.

9. Saint Germain, shatter the energetic matrix that prevents people from seeing that the nations that will survive in the evolution of nations are not the nations that set themselves apart or attack other nations. It is the ones who are cooperating. The will to cooperate is the key to survival.

O Saint Germain, the earth is free,
from burden of duality,
in oneness we bring what is best,
your Golden Age is manifest.

O Saint Germain, what love you bring,
it truly makes all matter sing,
your violet flame does all restore,
with you we are becoming more.

Part 4

1. Saint Germain, shatter the energetic matrix that prevents people from seeing that we humans have a strong instinct to not kill your own species. We also have an instinct to cooperate, to open up, to work with others. This is also the result of this billion year long process of experimentation that has shown that cooperation works.

O Saint Germain, you do inspire,
my vision raised forever higher,
with you I form a figure-eight,
your Golden Age I co-create.

**O Saint Germain, what love you bring,
it truly makes all matter sing,
your violet flame does all restore,
with you we are becoming more.**

2. Saint Germain, shatter the energetic matrix that prevents people from seeing that fanaticism is what allows people to override this and go into a state of mind where they see themselves as separated from other people. This happens because they adopt some kind of idea.

O Saint Germain, what Freedom Flame,
released when we recite your name,
acceleration is your gift,
our planet it will surely lift.

**O Saint Germain, what love you bring,
it truly makes all matter sing,
your violet flame does all restore,
with you we are becoming more.**

3. Saint Germain, shatter the energetic matrix that prevents people from seeing that if our forefathers had been in the competitive mindset, we would never have transcended the hunter-gatherer culture. We would have had constant competition where they had started to kill each other and then the human population would never have grown.

O Saint Germain, in love we claim,
our right to bring your violet flame,
from you Above, to us below,
it is an all-transforming flow.

**O Saint Germain, what love you bring,
it truly makes all matter sing,
your violet flame does all restore,
with you we are becoming more.**

4. Saint Germain, shatter the energetic matrix that prevents people from seeing that humanity made the transition from the hunter-gatherer culture

to agricultural societies through cooperation. In order to manifest an agricultural society, there had to be greater cooperation between people.

> O Saint Germain, I love you so,
> my aura filled with violet glow,
> my chakras filled with violet fire,
> I am your cosmic amplifier.

> **O Saint Germain, what love you bring,**
> **it truly makes all matter sing,**
> **your violet flame does all restore,**
> **with you we are becoming more.**

5. Saint Germain, shatter the energetic matrix that prevents people from seeing that ever since humanity made the shift to an agricultural society, cooperation has continued to increase and that is why we have seen the growth leading to an emerging global awareness. This has happened through cooperation, not through competition.

> O Saint Germain, I am now free,
> your violet flame is therapy,
> transform all hang-ups in my mind,
> as inner peace I surely find.

> **O Saint Germain, what love you bring,**
> **it truly makes all matter sing,**
> **your violet flame does all restore,**
> **with you we are becoming more.**

6. Saint Germain, shatter the energetic matrix that prevents people from seeing that in the modern world, warfare has always been justified by an idea. Human beings have certain basic instincts, not to kill and to cooperate, but we are able to override these instincts.

> O Saint Germain, my body pure,
> your violet flame for all is cure,
> consume the cause of all disease,
> and therefore I am all at ease.

**O Saint Germain, what love you bring,
it truly makes all matter sing,
your violet flame does all restore,
with you we are becoming more.**

7. Saint Germain, shatter the energetic matrix that prevents people from seeing that we can do something that goes against these basic principles that are defining what it takes to survive. We can create ideas whereby we endanger our own survival, but we refuse to see it, and *that* is another way to define fanaticism.

O Saint Germain, I'm karma-free,
the past no longer burdens me,
a brand new opportunity,
I am in Christic unity.

**O Saint Germain, what love you bring,
it truly makes all matter sing,
your violet flame does all restore,
with you we are becoming more.**

8. Saint Germain, shatter the energetic matrix that prevents people from seeing that fanaticism is when we have created an idea that endangers our survival, but we are in denial about this. We refuse to see it.

O Saint Germain, we are now one,
I am for you a violet sun,
as we transform this planet earth,
your Golden Age is given birth.

**O Saint Germain, what love you bring,
it truly makes all matter sing,
your violet flame does all restore,
with you we are becoming more.**

9. Saint Germain, shatter the energetic matrix that prevents people from seeing that there can be sophisticated powerful civilizations that, in retrospect, had certain beliefs that put them on a course towards disaster. They

could not see it and that is why they continued to walk blindly towards the abyss and nobody could tell them that they were on the wrong course.

> O Saint Germain, the earth is free,
> from burden of duality,
> in oneness we bring what is best,
> your Golden Age is manifest.

> **O Saint Germain, what love you bring,**
> **it truly makes all matter sing,**
> **your violet flame does all restore,**
> **with you we are becoming more.**

Sealing

In the name of the I AM THAT I AM, I accept that Archangel Michael, Astrea and Shiva form an impenetrable shield around myself and all constructive people, sealing us from all fear-based energies in all four octaves. I accept that the Light of God is consuming and transforming all fear-based energies that make up the dark forces working against ending the era of fanaticism on earth!

15 | INVOKING A BIOLOGICAL VISION OF FANATICISM (PART 3)

In the name of the I AM THAT I AM, Jesus Christ, I use the authority that I have as a being in embodiment on earth to call upon Saint Germain to reinforce my calls and use my chakras to project the statements in this invocation into the collective consciousness and awaken people to the fact that fanaticism is against our biology. Awaken people to the reality that we are spiritual beings and that we can co-create a new future by working with the ascended masters. I especially call for …

[Make your own calls here.]

Part 1

1. Saint Germain, shatter the energetic matrix that prevents people from seeing that many civilizations have had ideas that were out of touch with the basic principles of survivability. Therefore, they have gone the way of the dinosaurs.

O Saint Germain, you do inspire,
my vision raised forever higher,
with you I form a figure-eight,
your Golden Age I co-create.

**O Saint Germain, what love you bring,
it truly makes all matter sing,
your violet flame does all restore,
with you we are becoming more.**

2. Saint Germain, shatter the energetic matrix that prevents people from saying: "But what about us? Are we as smart as we think we are, as sophisticated as we think we are? Are we doing the same thing? Are we holding on to certain ideas that are endangering our survival?"

O Saint Germain, what Freedom Flame,
released when we recite your name,
acceleration is your gift,
our planet it will surely lift.

**O Saint Germain, what love you bring,
it truly makes all matter sing,
your violet flame does all restore,
with you we are becoming more.**

3. Saint Germain, shatter the energetic matrix that prevents people from seeing that in the Muslim world many people are in a fanatical state of mind. They have cognitive dissonance and cannot see that the pure statements in the Koran talk against killing other people and therefore, it is not justified what they are doing.

O Saint Germain, in love we claim,
our right to bring your violet flame,
from you Above, to us below,
it is an all-transforming flow.

**O Saint Germain, what love you bring,
it truly makes all matter sing,**

your violet flame does all restore,
with you we are becoming more.

4. Saint Germain, shatter the energetic matrix that prevents people from seeing that from a western democratic perspective, we see that they are endangering their own survival. Most people today in the western world can see that the Islamic culture is not sustainable.

O Saint Germain, I love you so,
my aura filled with violet glow,
my chakras filled with violet fire,
I am your cosmic amplifier.

O Saint Germain, what love you bring,
it truly makes all matter sing,
your violet flame does all restore,
with you we are becoming more.

5. Saint Germain, shatter the energetic matrix that prevents people from turning around, looking at your own societies and saying: "What are we holding on to that is endangering our survival?"

O Saint Germain, I am now free,
your violet flame is therapy,
transform all hang-ups in my mind,
as inner peace I surely find.

O Saint Germain, what love you bring,
it truly makes all matter sing,
your violet flame does all restore,
with you we are becoming more.

6. Saint Germain, shatter the energetic matrix that prevents people from seeing that one of the things we are holding on to is the theory of evolution as a completely materialistic process based on competition. We cannot have a truly functioning democracy if the people in that nation have that attitude of competition.

O Saint Germain, my body pure,
your violet flame for all is cure,
consume the cause of all disease,
and therefore I am all at ease.

**O Saint Germain, what love you bring,
it truly makes all matter sing,
your violet flame does all restore,
with you we are becoming more.**

7. Saint Germain, shatter the energetic matrix that prevents people from seeing that most people in the democratic nations are in the cooperative mindset. They want to cooperate. How have the modern democracies grown to their current affluence? By cooperating, and therefore we see that this is the way forward.

O Saint Germain, I'm karma-free,
the past no longer burdens me,
a brand new opportunity,
I am in Christic unity.

**O Saint Germain, what love you bring,
it truly makes all matter sing,
your violet flame does all restore,
with you we are becoming more.**

8. Saint Germain, shatter the energetic matrix that prevents people from seeing that there is a small elite, even in the democratic nations, who are in the competitive mindset. They believe they are more fit than others. They believe they are fit to rule, that they should be allowed to rule, that they should be allowed to accumulate wealth beyond all reason.

O Saint Germain, we are now one,
I am for you a violet sun,
as we transform this planet earth,
your Golden Age is given birth.

**O Saint Germain, what love you bring,
it truly makes all matter sing,**

your violet flame does all restore,
with you we are becoming more.

9. Saint Germain, shatter the energetic matrix that prevents people from seeing that elitism is clearly against the principles of a democratic nation: All men are created equal, all people have the same inalienable rights. Elitism is clearly anti-democratic, and the democratic nations cannot survive if we uphold this state where a small elite feel they are more fit to rule.

O Saint Germain, the earth is free,
from burden of duality,
in oneness we bring what is best,
your Golden Age is manifest.

O Saint Germain, what love you bring,
it truly makes all matter sing,
your violet flame does all restore,
with you we are becoming more.

Part 2

1. Saint Germain, shatter the energetic matrix that prevents people from seeing that we need to make another leap in the democratic nations of moving beyond representative democracy to a more direct form of democracy.

O Saint Germain, you do inspire,
my vision raised forever higher,
with you I form a figure-eight,
your Golden Age I co-create.

O Saint Germain, what love you bring,
it truly makes all matter sing,
your violet flame does all restore,
with you we are becoming more.

2. Saint Germain, shatter the energetic matrix that prevents people from seeing that all of the cells together, when they function in their natural state, function in harmony.

> O Saint Germain, what Freedom Flame,
> released when we recite your name,
> acceleration is your gift,
> our planet it will surely lift.

> **O Saint Germain, what love you bring,**
> **it truly makes all matter sing,**
> **your violet flame does all restore,**
> **with you we are becoming more.**

3. Saint Germain, shatter the energetic matrix that prevents people from seeing that we can transfer this to a human community where we have the old debate that the population cannot rule themselves because they will make the wrong decisions.

> O Saint Germain, in love we claim,
> our right to bring your violet flame,
> from you Above, to us below,
> it is an all-transforming flow.

> **O Saint Germain, what love you bring,**
> **it truly makes all matter sing,**
> **your violet flame does all restore,**
> **with you we are becoming more.**

4. Saint Germain, shatter the energetic matrix that prevents people from seeing that scientific experiments and observations have shown that whereas one person can make a wrong decision, all of the people in a certain nation will almost always make the best possible decision in any situation. The true key to survival is cooperation.

> O Saint Germain, I love you so,
> my aura filled with violet glow,
> my chakras filled with violet fire,
> I am your cosmic amplifier.

> **O Saint Germain, what love you bring,**
> **it truly makes all matter sing,**
> **your violet flame does all restore,**
> **with you we are becoming more.**

5. Saint Germain, shatter the energetic matrix that prevents people from seeing that the modern democracies need to make a shift where we realize we do not need an elite that is in the competitive mindset, that feel they are more fit to rule than the population. This is a complete myth.

> O Saint Germain, I am now free,
> your violet flame is therapy,
> transform all hang-ups in my mind,
> as inner peace I surely find.

> **O Saint Germain, what love you bring,**
> **it truly makes all matter sing,**
> **your violet flame does all restore,**
> **with you we are becoming more.**

6. Saint Germain, shatter the energetic matrix that prevents people from seeing that elitism is a dinosaur left over from the age of dictatorships. There need not be a small group of people who magically have been endowed by their creator, or by the laws of nature, with some magical ability to rule.

> O Saint Germain, my body pure,
> your violet flame for all is cure,
> consume the cause of all disease,
> and therefore I am all at ease.

> **O Saint Germain, what love you bring,**
> **it truly makes all matter sing,**
> **your violet flame does all restore,**
> **with you we are becoming more.**

7. Saint Germain, shatter the energetic matrix that prevents people from seeing that if we are democracies, if we believe that all humans were created equal, and that they all were endowed with the same rights, how can

we uphold this elitist view that certain people are more fit to rule and that the population cannot rule itself?

> O Saint Germain, I'm karma-free,
> the past no longer burdens me,
> a brand new opportunity,
> I am in Christic unity.

> **O Saint Germain, what love you bring,**
> **it truly makes all matter sing,**
> **your violet flame does all restore,**
> **with you we are becoming more.**

8. Saint Germain, shatter the energetic matrix that prevents people from seeing that in the current state of affairs, where we have a ruling elite, this is *not* an ideal society. The competing power elites have dragged the world into countless wars over the last hundred years.

> O Saint Germain, we are now one,
> I am for you a violet sun,
> as we transform this planet earth,
> your Golden Age is given birth.

> **O Saint Germain, what love you bring,**
> **it truly makes all matter sing,**
> **your violet flame does all restore,**
> **with you we are becoming more.**

9. Saint Germain, shatter the energetic matrix that prevents people from seeing that the elite is not capable of making good decisions. The people themselves, all of us, will balance each other out, even though we have vastly different viewpoints. We will make the best possible decision because of the biological principle that the key to survival is cooperation.

> O Saint Germain, the earth is free,
> from burden of duality,
> in oneness we bring what is best,
> your Golden Age is manifest.

**O Saint Germain, what love you bring,
it truly makes all matter sing,
your violet flame does all restore,
with you we are becoming more.**

Part 3

1. Saint Germain, shatter the energetic matrix that prevents people from seeing that cooperation is based on a willingness to look beyond ourselves and our own group and our narrow interests.

O Saint Germain, you do inspire,
my vision raised forever higher,
with you I form a figure-eight,
your Golden Age I co-create.

**O Saint Germain, what love you bring,
it truly makes all matter sing,
your violet flame does all restore,
with you we are becoming more.**

2. Saint Germain, shatter the energetic matrix that prevents people from seeing that cooperation is based on the concept that no man is an island, that we are not the only persons in the world that matter.

O Saint Germain, what Freedom Flame,
released when we recite your name,
acceleration is your gift,
our planet it will surely lift.

**O Saint Germain, what love you bring,
it truly makes all matter sing,
your violet flame does all restore,
with you we are becoming more.**

3. Saint Germain, shatter the energetic matrix that prevents people from seeing that we are part of a whole, we are connected to a larger whole and

because we are connected to a larger whole and part of that whole, what happens to the whole also affects us.

> O Saint Germain, in love we claim,
> our right to bring your violet flame,
> from you Above, to us below,
> it is an all-transforming flow.

> **O Saint Germain, what love you bring,**
> **it truly makes all matter sing,**
> **your violet flame does all restore,**
> **with you we are becoming more.**

4. Saint Germain, shatter the energetic matrix that prevents people from seeing that what is ultimately good for us is what is good for the whole and what is good for the whole is what is good for us. From a biological perspective, the most survivable is the decision that is best for the greatest number of people.

> O Saint Germain, I love you so,
> my aura filled with violet glow,
> my chakras filled with violet fire,
> I am your cosmic amplifier.

> **O Saint Germain, what love you bring,**
> **it truly makes all matter sing,**
> **your violet flame does all restore,**
> **with you we are becoming more.**

5. Saint Germain, shatter the energetic matrix that prevents people from seeing that a dictator cannot make a decision that is best for the greatest number of people. A very small elite that sees themselves as apart from the population, as above and beyond the population, cannot make that decision.

> O Saint Germain, I am now free,
> your violet flame is therapy,
> transform all hang-ups in my mind,
> as inner peace I surely find.

O Saint Germain, what love you bring,
it truly makes all matter sing,
your violet flame does all restore,
with you we are becoming more.

6. Saint Germain, shatter the energetic matrix that prevents people from seeing that when none of us see ourselves as being better or higher than each other, then together as an average we will make the best possible decision.

O Saint Germain, my body pure,
your violet flame for all is cure,
consume the cause of all disease,
and therefore I am all at ease.

O Saint Germain, what love you bring,
it truly makes all matter sing,
your violet flame does all restore,
with you we are becoming more.

7. Saint Germain, shatter the energetic matrix that prevents people from seeing that when we have a democratic society where all of the people vote on an issue, then whatever we decide is what is the best for the nation at this particular stage.

O Saint Germain, I'm karma-free,
the past no longer burdens me,
a brand new opportunity,
I am in Christic unity.

O Saint Germain, what love you bring,
it truly makes all matter sing,
your violet flame does all restore,
with you we are becoming more.

8. Saint Germain, shatter the energetic matrix that prevents people from seeing that whatever decision the people make, it is a reflection of our consciousness. We need to make that decision in order to have an opportunity to see our consciousness, see the limitations of it, and then grow beyond it.

O Saint Germain, we are now one,
I am for you a violet sun,
as we transform this planet earth,
your Golden Age is given birth.

**O Saint Germain, what love you bring,
it truly makes all matter sing,
your violet flame does all restore,
with you we are becoming more.**

9. Saint Germain, shatter the energetic matrix that prevents people from seeing that there is not a specific goal that needs to happen on earth. The basic process on earth is growth through free will, growth in consciousness. The goal is growth in consciousness.

O Saint Germain, the earth is free,
from burden of duality,
in oneness we bring what is best,
your Golden Age is manifest.

**O Saint Germain, what love you bring,
it truly makes all matter sing,
your violet flame does all restore,
with you we are becoming more.**

Part 4

1. Saint Germain, shatter the energetic matrix that prevents people from seeing that growth happens through us exercising our will, experiencing the results and then evaluating our actions based on what we see.

O Saint Germain, you do inspire,
my vision raised forever higher,
with you I form a figure-eight,
your Golden Age I co-create.

O Saint Germain, what love you bring,
it truly makes all matter sing,
your violet flame does all restore,
with you we are becoming more.

2. Saint Germain, shatter the energetic matrix that prevents people from seeing that fanaticism aborts the natural process of experimentation. For billions of years there has been a natural process of experimentation and if we are in touch with this, we can constantly evaluate the result of our decisions, and change our consciousness so we will survive.

O Saint Germain, what Freedom Flame,
released when we recite your name,
acceleration is your gift,
our planet it will surely lift.

O Saint Germain, what love you bring,
it truly makes all matter sing,
your violet flame does all restore,
with you we are becoming more.

3. Saint Germain, shatter the energetic matrix that prevents people from seeing that fanaticism has aborted this process by saying here is what society ideally *should* be like.

O Saint Germain, in love we claim,
our right to bring your violet flame,
from you Above, to us below,
it is an all-transforming flow.

O Saint Germain, what love you bring,
it truly makes all matter sing,
your violet flame does all restore,
with you we are becoming more.

4. Saint Germain, shatter the energetic matrix that prevents people from seeing that Nazi Germany violated the basic principle of biological survivability. They set themselves apart from the whole. They refused to cooperate. They went into a mindset of being in competition with others who did

not have their view. They started believing that it was justified that they kill
their own species.

O Saint Germain, I love you so,
my aura filled with violet glow,
my chakras filled with violet fire,
I am your cosmic amplifier.

O Saint Germain, what love you bring,
it truly makes all matter sing,
your violet flame does all restore,
with you we are becoming more.

5. Saint Germain, shatter the energetic matrix that prevents people from
seeing that a society that violates the two basic principles of biological
survival cannot survive. All of the civilizations that have gone down have
had the same pattern.

O Saint Germain, I am now free,
your violet flame is therapy,
transform all hang-ups in my mind,
as inner peace I surely find.

O Saint Germain, what love you bring,
it truly makes all matter sing,
your violet flame does all restore,
with you we are becoming more.

6. Saint Germain, shatter the energetic matrix that prevents people from
seeing that these dead civilizations had a worldview that was out of touch
with the basic principles of survivability. Therefore, they self-destructed.

O Saint Germain, my body pure,
your violet flame for all is cure,
consume the cause of all disease,
and therefore I am all at ease.

O Saint Germain, what love you bring,
it truly makes all matter sing,

your violet flame does all restore,
with you we are becoming more.

7. Saint Germain, shatter the energetic matrix that prevents people from asking: "What is it in our democratic nations that threatens our survivability?" One is the philosophy that there is a natural process of selection that has selected the most fit among the human race and that they are the only ones who are capable of ruling.

O Saint Germain, I'm karma-free,
the past no longer burdens me,
a brand new opportunity,
I am in Christic unity.

O Saint Germain, what love you bring,
it truly makes all matter sing,
your violet flame does all restore,
with you we are becoming more.

8. Saint Germain, shatter the energetic matrix that prevents people from seeing that the reality is that the only ones who are capable of truly ruling is all of the people working together. The average will always be better than the decisions of a small elite.

O Saint Germain, we are now one,
I am for you a violet sun,
as we transform this planet earth,
your Golden Age is given birth.

O Saint Germain, what love you bring,
it truly makes all matter sing,
your violet flame does all restore,
with you we are becoming more.

9. Saint Germain, shatter the energetic matrix that prevents people from seeing that anytime we have a society that is based on an idea that is out of touch with how the world actually works, that society cannot survive in the long run. It is threatening its own survival.

O Saint Germain, the earth is free,
from burden of duality,
in oneness we bring what is best,
your Golden Age is manifest.

**O Saint Germain, what love you bring,
it truly makes all matter sing,
your violet flame does all restore,
with you we are becoming more.**

Part 5

1. Saint Germain, shatter the energetic matrix that prevents people from seeing that sometimes the death of a society will come in the form of an external enemy. Only those who set themselves apart from the whole and think they are in competition with others have external enemies.

O Saint Germain, you do inspire,
my vision raised forever higher,
with you I form a figure-eight,
your Golden Age I co-create.

**O Saint Germain, what love you bring,
it truly makes all matter sing,
your violet flame does all restore,
with you we are becoming more.**

2. Saint Germain, shatter the energetic matrix that prevents people from seeing that in nature we see symbiotic relationships where different species cooperate and they enhance each other. The reason is that there is some kind of awareness of the whole.

O Saint Germain, what Freedom Flame,
released when we recite your name,
acceleration is your gift,
our planet it will surely lift.

**O Saint Germain, what love you bring,
it truly makes all matter sing,
your violet flame does all restore,
with you we are becoming more.**

3. Saint Germain, shatter the energetic matrix that prevents people from seeing that whenever we set ourselves apart from the whole and try to gain certain privileges, then we are going against the basic principles of nature and we threaten our survivability.

O Saint Germain, in love we claim,
our right to bring your violet flame,
from you Above, to us below,
it is an all-transforming flow.

**O Saint Germain, what love you bring,
it truly makes all matter sing,
your violet flame does all restore,
with you we are becoming more.**

4. Saint Germain, shatter the energetic matrix that prevents people from seeing that in the fanatical mindset all men and women are not created equal by their creator. It is possible to divide humanity into certain groups and apply a value judgment that says some are better than others, some have more right to rule, some have more right to survive.

O Saint Germain, I love you so,
my aura filled with violet glow,
my chakras filled with violet fire,
I am your cosmic amplifier.

**O Saint Germain, what love you bring,
it truly makes all matter sing,
your violet flame does all restore,
with you we are becoming more.**

5. Saint Germain, shatter the energetic matrix that prevents people from seeing that this is playing god. We are thinking that we know better than nature how nature should work.

O Saint Germain, I am now free,
your violet flame is therapy,
transform all hang-ups in my mind,
as inner peace I surely find.

O Saint Germain, what love you bring,
it truly makes all matter sing,
your violet flame does all restore,
with you we are becoming more.

6. Saint Germain, shatter the energetic matrix that prevents people from seeing that in the modern world we know there is a process of gradual evolution that goes back billions of years. At the same time, many societies have had an idea that they thought was absolute but that idea was in violation of the experiences based on the long process of evolution. Those societies did not survive.

O Saint Germain, my body pure,
your violet flame for all is cure,
consume the cause of all disease,
and therefore I am all at ease.

O Saint Germain, what love you bring,
it truly makes all matter sing,
your violet flame does all restore,
with you we are becoming more.

7. Saint Germain, shatter the energetic matrix that prevents people from seeing that human beings with a very short-sighted perspective cannot create ideas that can enable a society to survive in the long run. We need a longer perspective that is in alignment with how the world actually works.

O Saint Germain, I'm karma-free,
the past no longer burdens me,
a brand new opportunity,
I am in Christic unity.

O Saint Germain, what love you bring,
it truly makes all matter sing,

your violet flame does all restore,
with you we are becoming more.

8. Saint Germain, shatter the energetic matrix that prevents people from seeing that only by using science to observe the world and mysticism to tune in to a level of consciousness beyond ours, will we be able to build a society that is survivable, that is sustainable.

O Saint Germain, we are now one,
I am for you a violet sun,
as we transform this planet earth,
your Golden Age is given birth.

O Saint Germain, what love you bring,
it truly makes all matter sing,
your violet flame does all restore,
with you we are becoming more.

9. Saint Germain, shatter the energetic matrix that prevents people from seeing that through this alpha-omega action, society can rise to an entirely different level where we overcome the fanatical mindset of thinking we can define how the world should work. We are in tune with how the world actually works and we know that cooperation is the key to growth and we are pursuing that path of cooperating.

O Saint Germain, the earth is free,
from burden of duality,
in oneness we bring what is best,
your Golden Age is manifest.

O Saint Germain, what love you bring,
it truly makes all matter sing,
your violet flame does all restore,
with you we are becoming more.

Sealing

In the name of the I AM THAT I AM, I accept that Archangel Michael, Astrea and Shiva form an impenetrable shield around myself and all constructive people, sealing us from all fear-based energies in all four octaves. I accept that the Light of God is consuming and transforming all fear-based energies that make up the dark forces working against ending the era of fanaticism on earth!

16 | AN ENERGETIC PERSPECTIVE ON FANATICISM

I AM the Ascended Master Saint Germain. I have decided to monopolize this day because I want to give you certain teachings that I feel are necessary in order to give a foundation for people in the future who want to understand fanaticism from a deeper perspective. I have given you the biological perspective, now I want to give you the energetic perspective.

Science often prides itself on having created tremendous progress in human society. They often look at the scientific era being ushered in a few hundred years ago; they see how little progress there was before the advent of science and how much progress there has been since. This is of course correct from a certain perspective. Given that I was one, as an ascended master (and even in some of my embodiments), who set the foundation for modern science. I can assure you that there are certain areas where I feel that science is a very, very slow process and that scientists, after they developed the materialistic paradigm, have actually become the greatest hindrance to progress. This is no more clearly demonstrated than in the understanding of energy.

Matter cannot explain everything

You have certain of the ancient Greek philosophers, called the atomists, who wanted to explain everything in the world as the result of these small physical particles that they called atoms, and everything in the world could be explained as the interactions between these unseen, invisible billiard balls. They did not have billiard balls back then in ancient Greece, but you get my point. There were also other Greek philosophers who wanted to explain everything as being created from water; everything was created out of water. Of course, scientists today can look back at this and say this was a primitive view.

There came a point where scientists began to realize that not everything can be explained in terms of particles because there is also something called energy. Energy, they realized after Newton, cannot be explained as a particle, it is not even a stream of particles. It is a phenomenon that you can best describe with the physical process of a wave, such as what you see on the water. There is a physical substance of water but there is a wave of energy that can move through that water and create an effect, such as ripples on the surface. They developed this view of the world as being made up of two substances, particles and waves.

In the Newtonian worldview, these two substances are separate, they are not interchangeable and one cannot be turned into the other. There was a time in the late 1800's where physicists believed that they had discovered all the major processes needed to explain how the world works. What was left was just a few decimal places in their equations. There were even physicists who talked about "the end of physics" or the end of science, because surely, everything had been discovered. Then, a young impertinent physicist in Switzerland has an intuitive vision that matter and energy are not separate substances, that they are interchangeable. One can be exchanged into the other. His name was of course Albert Einstein and he published the theory of relativity in 1905, my beloved. You are talking way over a century here and yet to this day, the materialistic scientists are ignoring or denying the logical consequence of Einstein's discovery.

What Einstein proved was very, very simple. The world is not made up of two separate substances. The world is made up of one substance, namely energy. The underlying reality in the world is energy. What Newtonian scientists called particles, was actually a form of energy that had been captured into a more stationary matrix where it was no longer moving, as you traditionally see a wave moving. It had become more like a standing wave that was not moving in space, yet still vibrating. Einstein's equation puts an equal sign between mass and energy, making scientists realize that by splitting the atom (as they say), they could free the energy that had been captured into a more stationary matrix in the atom. It proves beyond any doubt that everything is made from energy, or as Gautama would say: "Everything is the Buddha nature."

The end of Materialism

This discovery was made in 1905, my beloved. Still, over a century later, scientists are ignoring the meaning of it. They are denying, they are not even ignoring, and they are actively *denying* the consequences of this theory because if we realize that everything is energy, then suddenly Materialism falls apart at the very foundation. Materialism is built on a model of the world that says we can create a box, that inside the box is all material phenomena and outside the box is nothing. This is the essence of Materialism. What have we said is the foundation of fanaticism? You adopt a certain view of how you want the world to work, how you think the world works, and then you elevate it to the status of being absolute and infallible.

This is exactly what Materialism has done. It has said: "Here is a box – the material world – what we can see with our senses, what we can measure with our scientific instruments. *That* is real, *that* exists, there is nothing outside the box."

The reason why this is such a limiting paradigm is that now you have all of these phenomena that you can observe here in the material universe and you have to explain them all as the effect of causes in the material universe. This is limiting in itself. What is worse is of course this absolute denial that if a phenomenon cannot be explained by a material cause, then either the phenomenon is not real or we just have not yet found the cause because one day we will see a material cause for this phenomenon.

The reality is that if we had not had this limited materialistic paradigm, then the modern democracies over a hundred years ago could have started shifting into a worldview based on Einstein's discovery that everything is energy. Once you realize that everything is energy, you realize that energy is vibration but there is no limit to how high vibration can go. Suddenly, you can see that this idea that you can create a box that contains all material phenomena is unrealistic. Yes, in a certain sense, if you are only looking at it in terms of matter and particles and waves, then you can say here is a box and inside is the material universe. When you realize that everything is really energy, this no longer has any meaning because what you realize is that all the material phenomena you see are made up of energies that vibrate within a certain spectrum. There is certainly no theoretical limit to how high beyond the material frequency spectrum energies can vibrate. This of course opens up the possibility that there could be other energetic spectra beyond the material spectrum. Just like the octaves on the tonal scale, it can be the physical octave and there could be other octaves.

Energetic psychology

If society had accepted this in 1905 and started changing the paradigm based on this, then it would have had fundamental ramifications for the science of psychology and the entire approach to psychology. Therefore, the modern democracies would not have been in the situation they are in today where they have this increase in mental illness that materialistic science cannot deal with, and now they are at a loss to find a way to deal with it.

If you had had a century to build on the realization that everything is energy, you could have had a fundamentally different approach to psychology developed today. Even developed in the 1960's so that societies could have made use of that opportunity we have talked about, made that transition from material welfare to psychological well-being because you have an entirely different approach to how life functions.

One of the simply logical consequences of Einstein's theory is that if everything is energy, then there is no separation between mind and matter. One of the cornerstones of Materialism is that there is a fundamental difference between mind and matter. Matter came first, then, when the brain evolved to a certain level of complexity, consciousness came into being because consciousness is an epiphenomenon, it is a result of the material processes in the brain. This is one of the cornerstones of Materialism but it cannot stand the light of logic, when you acknowledge that everything is energy.

Now, you realize that: What is mind? What is an emotion? What is a thought? It is not a physical substance, right? Nevertheless you experience that it is real. As Descartes said: "I think therefore I am." So you must say: "We experience that we are conscious, we cannot deny that we are conscious. Our thoughts, what gives us consciousness is not a material phenomenon, we cannot see it, we cannot measure it, therefore it must be an energy, a form of energy. Our thoughts, even our state of consciousness must be a form of energy."

What Einstein says is that energy came first and matter came later. Because everything is actually energy, matter is just energy that has taken on another form. Meaning, in the beginning was energy. When you acknowledge this, you realize that it makes no sense to say that consciousness could only have come into being when matter had developed the complexity of the physical brain. This means that if we are to help people solve their psychological issues, we need to look at the psyche as an energetic phenomenon, not as a material phenomenon.

It is completely backwards to think that the way to cure mental illness is to affect the chemical processes in the physical brain. I am not saying it cannot have some effect because the brain is so complex that it does have almost a mind of its own. Nevertheless, as has been demonstrated for anyone who is willing to look at facts, you cannot cure all mental illness, you cannot in fact cure *any* mental illness (you can mask the symptoms but you cannot cure it) by tinkering with the brain.

You need to then develop a different approach to psychology, an energetic form of psychology. In a sense, this is what we have given you in our teachings where we say that there is something beyond the material realm. You have three "higher bodies," the emotional, mental and identity level. If societies had been willing to look at this, they could long ago have received the ideas from us where they could have developed an energetic approach to healing psychological problems. This would have had widespread ramifications in society. Many more than I can even list to you in one dictation. I have no intention of listing them all but just simply giving you a few examples of this.

Objectivity requires a study of consciousness

What really is the essence of it all, the deepest level of it all, is to recognize that there is a fundamental connection between mind and matter, between consciousness and what you call the physical reality but which I prefer to call the macroscopic reality, the macroscopic level of energy, what you recognize with the senses. There is a connection and this connection has been proven by physics since the 1920s. In quantum physics they have proven that the old dream of the materialists – of the neutral, objective observer – is an illusion. It is fantasy. Materialists thought that the religious superstition of the middle ages was the product of the lack of reliability of the human psyche where people went into superstitions. In order to avoid this, science had to eliminate all influence of consciousness on their experiments. They created this idea that a scientist could become an objective, neutral observer who was standing outside the phenomenon, looking at this separate phenomenon and not influencing it in any way with his or her consciousness. This was the dream of the materialists. That dream was shattered in the 1920s with quantum physics where they discovered that when a quantum physicist is trying to observe the level of subatomic particles, as they called it, he cannot be a neutral observer that is standing outside because his consciousness becomes part of the entire measurement situation. He is not observing something that is happening separate from himself. He is actually co-creating the phenomenon that is being observed.

Now, this was of course shocking to physicists but it did not stop them from doing science. They did not say: "Well, that means we can never make any valid observations." They still tried to find a way to make valid observations about the quantum level.

Of course, you can see by the fact that they have not really moved on since the 1920s, that they have not fully accepted, or they have not even started to accept, the consequences of this discovery. They have not started to research with scientific instruments, the influence of consciousness.

Ideally, what really should have happened is that in 1905, and certainly in the 1920s, scientists should have realized the materialist paradigm was valuable for a time but it has outlived its usefulness because we can no longer ignore the influence of consciousness. If we really want to understand how the universe works, we have to use scientific methods to research consciousness because we have now proven that at the most fundamental level of matter, consciousness is an integral part of the process. We cannot explain the subatomic level without incorporating consciousness. We cannot incorporate consciousness if we do not understand it and we cannot understand it, if we do not study it. They should have started applying the scientific method to the study of consciousness and the connection between consciousness and energy, and energy and matter.

If that had happened over a century ago, tremendous progress could have been made. I would of course, and other masters would, have been ready to inspire the scientists who were open to this line of inquiry with all kinds of ideas that could bring humanity forward.

Energy and fanaticism

If we take this energetic view of the human psyche and apply it to fanaticism, we need to recognize that there is an energetic component to fanaticism. We cannot actually understand fanaticism unless we understand that one way to define fanaticism is to say that fanaticism is a specific form of energy. You would actually be able to take the scientific instruments that are already developed and measure the energy waves in people's consciousness. You would be able to measure a person who was in a neutral state of mind and the brain activity of that person. Then, you can measure a person who is in a fanatical state of mind and you would be able to see a difference.

There is a difference in the brain activity that people have, based on their level of fanaticism. You would be able to identify a specific vibrational signature of the fanatical state of mind. This could then open you up for a deeper understanding of why some people become so extreme in their fanaticism that they feel justified in killing other human beings. It is simply because these people's minds are filled up with this specific type of energy that forms a magnetic pull on their minds. When you understand the mind from an energetic perspective, you understand of course that energy waves can exert a certain pull on each other based on their intensity and their concentration. There are many examples of this in physics and chemistry.

You recognize here that what actually happens to a person is that the person might start out being more moderate. You can name any number of examples, you can take a young Muslim that becomes influenced by some radical fundamentalist ideas, you can take a Christian and go back to the Crusades or the Inquisition, you can take a person in the Soviet Union or even in the western world who became a convinced Marxist. You can see, if you measured that person's energy field, how there could be a certain type of energy that started appearing in the energy field. Then, it would gradually build in intensity and when it reached a certain level of intensity, it would start pulling on the person's conscious mind. It would, by doing this, gain more and more attention from the person and the attention would actually intensify the energy.

There could come a point where there was a dramatic shift, what scientists call a "phase transition." You see sometimes in a gas where at first the molecules are all random, but then a few molecules start being aligned in a certain direction, more molecules start being aligned and then all of a sudden there is that shift where now all of the molecules in that gas are aligned in the same direction. The same thing can happen in a person's mind. When there is a certain concentration of energy in the person's energy field, when it reaches a certain intensity, suddenly the person's conscious mind shifts and now the person is fully taken over by this fanatical mindset.

It is something you can see if you look at the rallies of Adolph Hitler. You can see that people would go into them in a somewhat neutral state of mind (somewhat normal state of mind, you might say, as was normal back then) but when they had listened to Hitler for a while, when they had listened to his rhetoric of how he whipped up a certain hatred, suddenly you could see that there was a shift, even in people's physical expressions. You could even see a shift in their eyes where suddenly their eyes were glazed over. Now, there was not a person there that you could reach and communicate with because they were taken over by this common mob mind. Now, as with one mind, they would cry out, "Heil Hitler, Sieg Heil!" and all of this nonsense.

You would actually have been able to measure this with scientific instruments, even decades ago. This would then allow people to understand that fanaticism starts out, as we have said, with a more innocent, seemingly benign state of mind. People have a certain viewpoint, they have this sense of security, they think their viewpoint is absolute and they do not want to let go of it.

Then, gradually the intensity can build, people feel more and more threatened. They feel their viewpoint is more and more threatened. They become more and more aggressive in denying or refuting any threats, even to the point where now they have come to that phase shift where they are no longer content at trying to convince other people that they are wrong. They accept that some people will not be convinced and therefore it is acceptable that you kill those who will not be converted to your beliefs.

You would actually be able to measure in a person's energy field when that shift happens. You would be able to see this on these scientific instruments that have already been developed, how there is a shift in that person's energy field. Now suddenly, the mind is completely focused on this "the ends can justify the means," and it is acceptable to kill those who oppose our epically important idea. You could actually measure this at an energy level. You could even, with today's technology, make it visible on a computer screen. If people had developed this, it would have been easier to understand fanaticism. It would have opened up for some perspectives that we will talk about in coming dictations where you go even deeper and go beyond what most people can accept today. But if there had been that energetic awareness for over a century, then people might in fact have been ready to accept what you are now accepting and what we have told you.

Tremendous growth in psychological healing

First of all, if that had happened, if this new science had been developed, then 9/11 would not have happened. The entire phenomenon of Muslim fundamentalism and Muslim terror against the west would not have happened, it would not have occurred. The western democracies would have moved beyond that point where they needed to see this extreme outplaying of their own state of consciousness, their fanaticism in defending Materialism. They could not see this so they needed to see the extreme outplaying of fanaticism in the Muslims. That would not have been necessary if they had made that transition a long time ago.

You see here that what has been building for a long time now is a tension in the collective consciousness. More and more people are ready to simply go through the process that I have outlined here, of realizing the consequences of Einstein's discoveries of quantum physics and starting to apply them to other areas of life than just physics. Therefore, more and more people are ready for an energetic approach to physical healing but also an energetic approach to psychological healing. *That is*, my beloved, when you make the calls and when this begins to break through, at least in the top 10%, as I know it has happened already for many people. When it reaches a more critical mass, then you will start to see a real shift.

You will start to see how all kinds of new technologies will be developed for helping people with mental illness. You cannot even fathom today, the technology that could have been developed by now, that could be developed very, very quickly. I should even say it cannot be *developed* but it can be *released*. Whenever there is the openness in the mind to receive the technology, it *will* be released. I have already released these ideas from the spiritual realm into the identity, mental and emotional realm. They are just ready to drop into the physical. All it takes is open minds who are willing to receive them, who *can* receive them because they are not fixated on the materialistic paradigm.

Measuring fanaticism

If you had these techniques for measuring the energy in the mind, you could study the minds of scientific materialists, those who are the so-called militant atheists, who are attacking religion and trying to defend Materialism. If you measured the brainwaves or the brain activity of some of these people and compared them to a Muslim terrorist, you would see a very, very similar pattern. You could of course take a Christian fundamentalist and also see a very similar pattern. You could take a Catholic cardinal, who is covering over and denying paedophilia in order to avoid damaging the image of the church, and you would see a very similar pattern of fanaticism, of the belief that the ends can justify the means.

You could actually measure that if a person believes that the ends can justify the means, there are certain energy vibrations in that person's energy field. They have reached that level of intensity where they are pulling on, even taking over, the person's conscious mind. The person is not actually, at that point, able to make a free, conscious choice.

The person's conscious mind is overwhelmed by this energy and the magnetic pull pulls the conscious mind into a state of denial where it is not able to see reality. It is only able to see this particular image of reality that it has come to accept and it denies or ignores anything that contradicts it.

You would actually be able to see that there are of course various ways to help people shift out of this. You would be able to take a person who was in the fanatical state of mind, measure that person's energy field and then give that person the tools (if the person was willing to do this) to overcome the fanatical mindset—or at least deal with the energy behind it, dissipate the energy behind it. You would be able to measure that when the energy goes down to a certain level, suddenly the conscious mind of that person shifts and he now sees the limitations of the fanatical mindset. You could actually have developed technology, not exactly material technology but certainly the technology of certain techniques, that could help people go out of the fanatical mindset. They could of course only work if they were willing to get out of it.

At least if you could see this demonstrated, you would realize that you cannot actually understand a phenomenon like fanaticism unless you understand the energy component behind it. Therefore, you cannot actually hope to cure mental illness unless you understand the energy component and deal with that energy, find ways to help people through various techniques, dissipate certain energies in their energy fields, the energies that pull them into these unhealthy patterns.

Energy and depression

Why is a person depressed? You could take a person with depression and create an energetic signature of their energy field, their subconscious mind. You would be able to identify a certain quantity, a certain cloud (you might say) of energy of a certain vibration. This is the energy that pulls that persons' conscious mind into a state of hopelessness, a sense that nothing matters, that life has no purpose, that it is not worth living and nothing you do will make a difference and all of these things. It is all created by the energy pulling on the conscious mind. You would be able to see that when you dissipate that energy, suddenly the person snaps out of depression just like that.

This is a phenomenon, and there is almost no limit to how much scientific research could be done here. It would have to be scientific research that incorporated consciousness and was therefore willing to acknowledge that we cannot weigh and measure everything with material instruments. There are certain phenomena in consciousness that cannot be detected by material instruments.

Those of you who know about the history of scientific instruments will know that there was a time where they only had what they called optical microscopes. This is a microscope where you are looking through the microscope with your physical eye and you are seeing visible light, you are using visible light to see this microscopic object. You have lenses that magnify the object but they are working with physical light. What scientists discovered was that physical light has a certain wavelength. This meant that any objects smaller than the wavelength of physical light could not be detected by an optical microscope. Then, they developed what they call electron microscopes that can see atoms and even some other particles as they called it. It is exactly the same thing. There are certain aspects of consciousness, there are certain forms of energies that are beyond the material frequency spectrum. They cannot be detected by instruments that are made out of energy within the material spectrum.

Does that mean that humankind has no way to ever investigate, research and detect such energies? No, because humanity has been given an instrument that can detect energy waves beyond the material spectrum. That instrument is called the mind but what scientists decided with the advent of Materialism, was that they should ignore the mind, they should exclude the mind, they should look at the mind as if it could only be subjective, it could never give reliable observations.

The elite behind Materialism

My beloved, again go back to what we have said about elitism and the whole idea that there is only a small elite that is able to rule society. In reality, they create far more disasters than the population would do, if you could have all people vote on a certain issue. The "common people" so to speak, would make better, less aggressive, less disastrous decisions than the power elite. In a sense, scientific Materialism is based on this elitist mindset. Only certain scientists are able to define what science should be, how science should function and how to interpret scientific observations. Their minds are supposedly objective and neutral but the mind of the general population could never be objective and neutral.

You will see here that there is a cognitive dissonance in Materialism, in the sense that they think that the mind in general is not reliable. They are convinced that their minds are giving them a neutral, objective observation and proof that there is nothing beyond the material universe. They are not willing to recognize that materialistic science has not, cannot, will never prove that there is nothing beyond the material universe. Science has not proven that God does not exist because you cannot prove that something does not exist, especially when you have limited your observation to instruments that cannot detect anything beyond the material universe.

How could you take instruments that can only detect the material spectrum of energy and use those instruments to prove that there is something beyond that spectrum? It cannot be done, my beloved! Have you proven that there is nothing beyond the material world? No! You have only proven that you cannot detect what you are not looking for. You cannot detect something if you are not using the proper instrument.

Measuring the objectivity of the mind

If a hundred years ago (or for that matter even before) science and society had been willing to investigate consciousness and use scientific instruments (as imperfect as they were) for that purpose a hundred years ago, they could have made progress. They could have come to the point where they could actually realize that the human mind *can* make accurate observations. It is possible for a human being to attain a state of consciousness where that person is neutral, in the sense that the person is open to seeing something new. The person does not do what the fanatical mindset causes people to do, namely formulate an image in the mind of how the world *should* work and then seeking to project that image onto the universe.

You can again create an energetic signature and you can see that here is a person who has the particular energies that lead to the fanatical mindset. That person has a mental image and in order to hold on to the sense of security, that person is not open to seeing anything beyond that mental image. It is clear that when you see this energetic signature, it is almost like a lie detector, my beloved, where you see a certain movement on the screen and you know that the person is lying. When you see a certain energetic signature, you know that the person is not in a neutral state of mind. Yes, that person is not objective, that person can only make subjective observations that very likely confirm the persons' superstition. It is actually possible to move out of that state of mind, to attain a neutral state of mind where you are not projecting a mental image onto the world, you are just observing the world.

This means that the person can make a neutral, objective observation. In fact, such a person could make a much more objective observation than a materialistic scientist who has an overarching intent of proving the validity of Materialism and disproving anything beyond it. Materialists are not objective. It is simply that way. It is one of these shifts that can happen (when you make the calls) where just as people see that the Emperor has nothing on, they see that "the materialists are not objective." They want the world to function a certain way. They want to uphold the materialist paradigm, even when science itself has pointed beyond it. They are as fanatical about this as medieval Catholics were about the infallibility of the Pope and Catholic doctrine. When people make this shift, they can start realizing that if you train people to go into a neutral state of mind, they can make accurate observations with the mind of energies that cannot be detected by material instruments. It is not a matter of having one person do this and everybody else believes it. It is a matter of having a great number of people being trained to do this. Then, when you have people who use the mind to investigate what is beyond the material universe, you can start looking at how much are they in agreement? When you see that a large majority of the people who investigate this all make the same observations, then you must say that these observations made through the instrument of the mind are as reliable as the observations made through physical instruments.

This shift could have happened decades ago if people had been willing to look at the consequences of Einstein and quantum physics. It is a tension that has been building ever since, it is a shift that is ready to happen and break through in the physical. It only needs some impetus of a critical mass of people making the calls and suddenly there can be that shift where more and more people begin to see the limitations of the materialist paradigm and just wake up and say: "But it's so obvious, we have to look at consciousness. After all, what kind of beings are we? What determines whether we are happy or unhappy in life? Is it our genes? Is it our astrology? Is it the chemicals in our brain? No—it's the psyche. It's our consciousness. If we want to be happy, if we want to overcome this problem of mental illness, we have to start seriously investigating consciousness. We cannot have a science that is publicly funded but that ignores consciousness because of some outdated paradigm. We cannot accept this anymore. It is nonsense, and we will not stand for it. We will not see our taxpayer money go to finance these people in the scientific establishment, who are as fanatical as the people in the Catholic church and other churches that we are not financing with public money. Why should we have these Cardinals or Popes of science that are financed by public money, when all they are doing is spreading a paradigm that is as fanatical as most religious paradigms?"

The separation of Materialism and state

You realize here that one of the fundamental principles of democracy is the separation of church and state. The state must be independent of any particular religion. What is scientific Materialism? *It is a religion.* It is a religion that denies God but it is still a religion because the denial of God is not based on fact, not based on observation. It is based on *belief.* If we are true to the democratic principles, we must say: "Yes society can fund science but it cannot fund scientific Materialism because that is a religion and we need to free science from the influence of this religion, just as we have freed society from the influence of Catholicism or other forms of Christianity."

This is a shift that is realistic for you to call into the physical with your decrees and invocations and your willingness to shift your own consciousness. So with this, I am grateful for your patience, again your willingness to let your chakras be the broadcast stations for this to go into the collective consciousness where it has already started to awaken the people who were close to awakening. You will see how this can spread like rings in the water and have a decisive impact. My gratitude and my great joy for being able to deliver this address in the physical octave, where it clearly has a greater effect than if I just spoke it from the identity realm or the spiritual realm.

17 | INVOKING FREEDOM FROM THE MATERIALISTIC LIE (PART 1)

In the name of the I AM THAT I AM, Jesus Christ, I use the authority that I have as a being in embodiment on earth to call upon Saint Germain to reinforce my calls and use my chakras to project the statements in this invocation into the collective consciousness and awaken people to the need to leave behind the materialistic lie. Awaken people to the reality that we are spiritual beings and that we can co-create a new future by working with the ascended masters. I especially call for …

[Make your own calls here.]

Part 1

1. Saint Germain, shatter the energetic matrix that prevents people from seeing that in certain areas science is a very slow process and the materialistic paradigm is the greatest hindrance to progress.

O Saint Germain, you do inspire,
my vision raised forever higher,

with you I form a figure-eight,
your Golden Age I co-create.

O Saint Germain, what love you bring,
it truly makes all matter sing,
your violet flame does all restore,
with you we are becoming more.

2. Saint Germain, shatter the energetic matrix that prevents people from seeing that Einstein proved that matter and energy are interchangeable in 1905, yet materialistic scientists are ignoring or denying the logical consequence of Einstein's discovery.   .

O Saint Germain, what Freedom Flame,
released when we recite your name,
acceleration is your gift,
our planet it will surely lift.

O Saint Germain, what love you bring,
it truly makes all matter sing,
your violet flame does all restore,
with you we are becoming more.

3. Saint Germain, shatter the energetic matrix that prevents people from seeing that Einstein proved that the world is not made up of two separate substances. The world is made up of one substance, namely energy. The underlying reality in the world is energy.

O Saint Germain, in love we claim,
our right to bring your violet flame,
from you Above, to us below,
it is an all-transforming flow.

O Saint Germain, what love you bring,
it truly makes all matter sing,
your violet flame does all restore,
with you we are becoming more.

4. Saint Germain, shatter the energetic matrix that prevents people from seeing that Einstein's equation puts an equal sign between mass and energy. It proves that everything is made from energy.

O Saint Germain, I love you so,
my aura filled with violet glow,
my chakras filled with violet fire,
I am your cosmic amplifier.

**O Saint Germain, what love you bring,
it truly makes all matter sing,
your violet flame does all restore,
with you we are becoming more.**

5. Saint Germain, shatter the energetic matrix that prevents people from seeing that materialists are actively denying the consequences of Einstein's theory because if we acknowledge that everything is energy, then Materialism falls apart at the very foundation.

O Saint Germain, I am now free,
your violet flame is therapy,
transform all hang-ups in my mind,
as inner peace I surely find.

**O Saint Germain, what love you bring,
it truly makes all matter sing,
your violet flame does all restore,
with you we are becoming more.**

6. Saint Germain, shatter the energetic matrix that prevents people from seeing that Materialism is built on a model of the world that says we can create a box, and inside the box is all material phenomena and outside the box is nothing. This is the essence of Materialism.

O Saint Germain, my body pure,
your violet flame for all is cure,
consume the cause of all disease,
and therefore I am all at ease.

O Saint Germain, what love you bring,
it truly makes all matter sing,
your violet flame does all restore,
with you we are becoming more.

7. Saint Germain, shatter the energetic matrix that prevents people from seeing that the foundation of fanaticism is that we adopt a certain view of how we want the world to work, how we think the world works, and then we elevate it to the status of being absolute and infallible. This is exactly what Materialism has done.

O Saint Germain, I'm karma-free,
the past no longer burdens me,
a brand new opportunity,
I am in Christic unity.

O Saint Germain, what love you bring,
it truly makes all matter sing,
your violet flame does all restore,
with you we are becoming more.

8. Saint Germain, shatter the energetic matrix that prevents people from seeing that Materialism has said: "Here is a box – the material world – what we can see with our senses, what we can measure with our scientific instruments. *That* is real, *that* exists, there is nothing outside the box."

O Saint Germain, we are now one,
I am for you a violet sun,
as we transform this planet earth,
your Golden Age is given birth.

O Saint Germain, what love you bring,
it truly makes all matter sing,
your violet flame does all restore,
with you we are becoming more.

9. Saint Germain, shatter the energetic matrix that prevents people from seeing that this is a very limiting paradigm because it seeks to explain all

phenomena in the material universe as the effect of causes in the material universe.

> O Saint Germain, the earth is free,
> from burden of duality,
> in oneness we bring what is best,
> your Golden Age is manifest.

> **O Saint Germain, what love you bring,**
> **it truly makes all matter sing,**
> **your violet flame does all restore,**
> **with you we are becoming more.**

Part 2

1. Saint Germain, shatter the energetic matrix that prevents people from seeing that Materialism also defines an absolute denial that if a phenomenon cannot be explained by a material cause, then either the phenomenon is not real or we have not yet found the cause.

> O Saint Germain, you do inspire,
> my vision raised forever higher,
> with you I form a figure-eight,
> your Golden Age I co-create.

> **O Saint Germain, what love you bring,**
> **it truly makes all matter sing,**
> **your violet flame does all restore,**
> **with you we are becoming more.**

2. Saint Germain, shatter the energetic matrix that prevents people from seeing that if we had not had this limited materialistic paradigm, then the modern democracies over a hundred years ago could have started shifting into a worldview based on Einstein's discovery that everything is energy.

> O Saint Germain, what Freedom Flame,
> released when we recite your name,

acceleration is your gift,
our planet it will surely lift.

**O Saint Germain, what love you bring,
it truly makes all matter sing,
your violet flame does all restore,
with you we are becoming more.**

3. Saint Germain, shatter the energetic matrix that prevents people from seeing that once we realize that everything is energy, we realize that energy is vibration but there is no limit to how high vibration can go. The idea that we can create a box that contains all material phenomena is unrealistic.

O Saint Germain, in love we claim,
our right to bring your violet flame,
from you Above, to us below,
it is an all-transforming flow.

**O Saint Germain, what love you bring,
it truly makes all matter sing,
your violet flame does all restore,
with you we are becoming more.**

4. Saint Germain, shatter the energetic matrix that prevents people from seeing that all the material phenomena are made up of energies that vibrate within a certain spectrum. There is no theoretical limit to how high beyond the material frequency spectrum energies can vibrate.

O Saint Germain, I love you so,
my aura filled with violet glow,
my chakras filled with violet fire,
I am your cosmic amplifier.

**O Saint Germain, what love you bring,
it truly makes all matter sing,
your violet flame does all restore,
with you we are becoming more.**

5. Saint Germain, shatter the energetic matrix that prevents people from seeing that this opens up the possibility that there could be other energetic spectra beyond the material spectrum. Just like the octaves on the tonal scale, it can be the physical octave and there could be other octaves.

O Saint Germain, I am now free,
your violet flame is therapy,
transform all hang-ups in my mind,
as inner peace I surely find.

O Saint Germain, what love you bring,
it truly makes all matter sing,
your violet flame does all restore,
with you we are becoming more.

6. Saint Germain, shatter the energetic matrix that prevents people from seeing that if society had accepted this in 1905, then it would have had fundamental ramifications for the science of psychology and the entire approach to psychology.

O Saint Germain, my body pure,
your violet flame for all is cure,
consume the cause of all disease,
and therefore I am all at ease.

O Saint Germain, what love you bring,
it truly makes all matter sing,
your violet flame does all restore,
with you we are becoming more.

7. Saint Germain, shatter the energetic matrix that prevents people from seeing that the modern democracies would not have been in a situation where we have an increase in mental illness that materialistic science cannot deal with, and now we are at a loss to find a way to deal with it.

O Saint Germain, I'm karma-free,
the past no longer burdens me,
a brand new opportunity,
I am in Christic unity.

**O Saint Germain, what love you bring,
it truly makes all matter sing,
your violet flame does all restore,
with you we are becoming more.**

8. Saint Germain, shatter the energetic matrix that prevents people from seeing that if we had built on the realization that everything is energy, we could have had a fundamentally different approach to psychology.

O Saint Germain, we are now one,
I am for you a violet sun,
as we transform this planet earth,
your Golden Age is given birth.

**O Saint Germain, what love you bring,
it truly makes all matter sing,
your violet flame does all restore,
with you we are becoming more.**

9. Saint Germain, shatter the energetic matrix that prevents people from seeing that a new psychology could have been developed in the 1960's so that societies could have made the transition from material welfare to psychological well-being because we have an entirely different approach to how life functions.

O Saint Germain, the earth is free,
from burden of duality,
in oneness we bring what is best,
your Golden Age is manifest.

**O Saint Germain, what love you bring,
it truly makes all matter sing,
your violet flame does all restore,
with you we are becoming more.**

Part 3

1. Saint Germain, shatter the energetic matrix that prevents people from seeing that since everything is energy, there is no separation between mind and matter.

> O Saint Germain, you do inspire,
> my vision raised forever higher,
> with you I form a figure-eight,
> your Golden Age I co-create.

> **O Saint Germain, what love you bring,**
> **it truly makes all matter sing,**
> **your violet flame does all restore,**
> **with you we are becoming more.**

2. Saint Germain, shatter the energetic matrix that prevents people from seeing that one of the cornerstones of Materialism is that there is a fundamental difference between mind and matter. This cannot stand the light of logic, when we acknowledge that everything is energy.

> O Saint Germain, what Freedom Flame,
> released when we recite your name,
> acceleration is your gift,
> our planet it will surely lift.

> **O Saint Germain, what love you bring,**
> **it truly makes all matter sing,**
> **your violet flame does all restore,**
> **with you we are becoming more.**

3. Saint Germain, shatter the energetic matrix that prevents people from seeing that we experience that we are conscious, we cannot deny that we are conscious.

> O Saint Germain, in love we claim,
> our right to bring your violet flame,

from you Above, to us below,
it is an all-transforming flow.

**O Saint Germain, what love you bring,
it truly makes all matter sing,
your violet flame does all restore,
with you we are becoming more.**

4. Saint Germain, shatter the energetic matrix that prevents people from seeing that our thoughts, what gives us consciousness, is not a material phenomenon. We cannot see it, we cannot measure it, therefore it must be a form of energy. Our thoughts, even our state of consciousness must be a form of energy.

O Saint Germain, I love you so,
my aura filled with violet glow,
my chakras filled with violet fire,
I am your cosmic amplifier.

**O Saint Germain, what love you bring,
it truly makes all matter sing,
your violet flame does all restore,
with you we are becoming more.**

5. Saint Germain, shatter the energetic matrix that prevents people from seeing that Einstein says that energy came first and matter came later. Because everything is actually energy, matter is energy that has taken on another form.

O Saint Germain, I am now free,
your violet flame is therapy,
transform all hang-ups in my mind,
as inner peace I surely find.

**O Saint Germain, what love you bring,
it truly makes all matter sing,
your violet flame does all restore,
with you we are becoming more.**

6. Saint Germain, shatter the energetic matrix that prevents people from seeing that in the beginning was energy. It makes no sense to say that consciousness could only have come into being when matter had developed the complexity of the physical brain.

O Saint Germain, my body pure,
your violet flame for all is cure,
consume the cause of all disease,
and therefore I am all at ease.

O Saint Germain, what love you bring,
it truly makes all matter sing,
your violet flame does all restore,
with you we are becoming more.

7. Saint Germain, shatter the energetic matrix that prevents people from seeing that if we are to help people solve their psychological issues, we need to look at the psyche as an energetic phenomenon, not as a material phenomenon.

O Saint Germain, I'm karma-free,
the past no longer burdens me,
a brand new opportunity,
I am in Christic unity.

O Saint Germain, what love you bring,
it truly makes all matter sing,
your violet flame does all restore,
with you we are becoming more.

8. Saint Germain, shatter the energetic matrix that prevents people from seeing that it is completely backwards to think that the way to cure mental illness is to affect the chemical processes in the physical brain. We cannot cure mental illness by tinkering with the brain.

O Saint Germain, we are now one,
I am for you a violet sun,
as we transform this planet earth,
your Golden Age is given birth.

**O Saint Germain, what love you bring,
it truly makes all matter sing,
your violet flame does all restore,
with you we are becoming more.**

9. Saint Germain, shatter the energetic matrix that prevents people from seeing that we need to develop a different approach to psychology, an energetic form of psychology. Society could long ago have developed an energetic approach to healing psychological problems. This would have had widespread ramifications.

O Saint Germain, the earth is free,
from burden of duality,
in oneness we bring what is best,
your Golden Age is manifest.

**O Saint Germain, what love you bring,
it truly makes all matter sing,
your violet flame does all restore,
with you we are becoming more.**

Part 4

1. Saint Germain, shatter the energetic matrix that prevents people from seeing that there is a fundamental connection between mind and matter, between consciousness and the physical reality we recognize with the senses.

O Saint Germain, you do inspire,
my vision raised forever higher,
with you I form a figure-eight,
your Golden Age I co-create.

**O Saint Germain, what love you bring,
it truly makes all matter sing,
your violet flame does all restore,
with you we are becoming more.**

2. Saint Germain, shatter the energetic matrix that prevents people from seeing that this connection has been proven by physics since the 1920s. In quantum physics they have proven that the old dream of the materialists – of the neutral, objective observer – is an illusion.

> O Saint Germain, what Freedom Flame,
> released when we recite your name,
> acceleration is your gift,
> our planet it will surely lift.

> **O Saint Germain, what love you bring,**
> **it truly makes all matter sing,**
> **your violet flame does all restore,**
> **with you we are becoming more.**

3. Saint Germain, shatter the energetic matrix that prevents people from seeing that materialists thought that the religious superstition of the middle ages was the product of the lack of reliability of the human psyche where people went into superstitions.

> O Saint Germain, in love we claim,
> our right to bring your violet flame,
> from you Above, to us below,
> it is an all-transforming flow.

> **O Saint Germain, what love you bring,**
> **it truly makes all matter sing,**
> **your violet flame does all restore,**
> **with you we are becoming more.**

4. Saint Germain, shatter the energetic matrix that prevents people from seeing that in order to avoid superstition, science had to eliminate all influence of consciousness on their experiments. They created the idea that a scientist could become an objective, neutral observer who was standing outside the phenomenon.

> O Saint Germain, I love you so,
> my aura filled with violet glow,

my chakras filled with violet fire,
I am your cosmic amplifier.

**O Saint Germain, what love you bring,
it truly makes all matter sing,
your violet flame does all restore,
with you we are becoming more.**

5. Saint Germain, shatter the energetic matrix that prevents people from seeing that the dream of the materialists was shattered in the 1920s with quantum physics where they discovered that a quantum physicist becomes part of the entire measurement situation. He is actually co-creating the phenomenon that is being observed.

O Saint Germain, I am now free,
your violet flame is therapy,
transform all hang-ups in my mind,
as inner peace I surely find.

**O Saint Germain, what love you bring,
it truly makes all matter sing,
your violet flame does all restore,
with you we are becoming more.**

6. Saint Germain, shatter the energetic matrix that prevents people from seeing that scientists have not accepted the consequences of this discovery. They have not started to research with scientific instruments, the influence of consciousness.

O Saint Germain, my body pure,
your violet flame for all is cure,
consume the cause of all disease,
and therefore I am all at ease.

**O Saint Germain, what love you bring,
it truly makes all matter sing,
your violet flame does all restore,
with you we are becoming more.**

7. Saint Germain, shatter the energetic matrix that prevents people from seeing that in the 1920s, scientists should have realized the materialist paradigm was valuable for a time but it had outlived its usefulness because they could no longer ignore the influence of consciousness.

O Saint Germain, I'm karma-free,
the past no longer burdens me,
a brand new opportunity,
I am in Christic unity.

O Saint Germain, what love you bring,
it truly makes all matter sing,
your violet flame does all restore,
with you we are becoming more.

8. Saint Germain, shatter the energetic matrix that prevents people from seeing that if we really want to understand how the universe works, we have to use scientific methods to research consciousness because we have now proven that at the most fundamental level of matter, consciousness is an integral part of the process.

O Saint Germain, we are now one,
I am for you a violet sun,
as we transform this planet earth,
your Golden Age is given birth.

O Saint Germain, what love you bring,
it truly makes all matter sing,
your violet flame does all restore,
with you we are becoming more.

9. Saint Germain, shatter the energetic matrix that prevents people from seeing that we cannot explain the subatomic level without incorporating consciousness. We cannot incorporate consciousness if we do not understand it and we cannot understand it, if we do not study it.

O Saint Germain, the earth is free,
from burden of duality,

in oneness we bring what is best,
your Golden Age is manifest.

**O Saint Germain, what love you bring,
it truly makes all matter sing,
your violet flame does all restore,
with you we are becoming more.**

Part 5

1. Saint Germain, shatter the energetic matrix that prevents people from seeing that if we take the energetic view of the human psyche and apply it to fanaticism, we need to recognize that there is an energetic component to fanaticism.

O Saint Germain, you do inspire,
my vision raised forever higher,
with you I form a figure-eight,
your Golden Age I co-create.

**O Saint Germain, what love you bring,
it truly makes all matter sing,
your violet flame does all restore,
with you we are becoming more.**

2. Saint Germain, shatter the energetic matrix that prevents people from seeing that we cannot understand fanaticism unless we realize it is a specific form of energy. There is a specific vibrational signature of the fanatical state of mind.

O Saint Germain, what Freedom Flame,
released when we recite your name,
acceleration is your gift,
our planet it will surely lift.

**O Saint Germain, what love you bring,
it truly makes all matter sing,**

**your violet flame does all restore,
with you we are becoming more.**

3. Saint Germain, shatter the energetic matrix that prevents people from seeing that this explains why some people become so extreme in their fanaticism that they feel justified in killing other human beings. These people's subconscious minds are filled with a specific type of energy that forms a magnetic pull on their conscious minds.

O Saint Germain, in love we claim,
our right to bring your violet flame,
from you Above, to us below,
it is an all-transforming flow.

**O Saint Germain, what love you bring,
it truly makes all matter sing,
your violet flame does all restore,
with you we are becoming more.**

4. Saint Germain, shatter the energetic matrix that prevents people from seeing that when we understand the mind from an energetic perspective, we see that energy waves can exert a pull on each other based on their intensity and concentration.

O Saint Germain, I love you so,
my aura filled with violet glow,
my chakras filled with violet fire,
I am your cosmic amplifier.

**O Saint Germain, what love you bring,
it truly makes all matter sing,
your violet flame does all restore,
with you we are becoming more.**

5. Saint Germain, shatter the energetic matrix that prevents people from seeing that a certain type of energy starts building in a person's energy field. As it reaches a certain level of intensity, it starts pulling on the person's conscious mind.

O Saint Germain, I am now free,
your violet flame is therapy,
transform all hang-ups in my mind,
as inner peace I surely find.

O Saint Germain, what love you bring,
it truly makes all matter sing,
your violet flame does all restore,
with you we are becoming more.

6. Saint Germain, shatter the energetic matrix that prevents people from seeing that the energy gains more and more attention from the person and the attention intensifies the energy. When the energy reaches a certain intensity, the person's conscious mind shifts and is taken over by the fanatical mindset.

O Saint Germain, my body pure,
your violet flame for all is cure,
consume the cause of all disease,
and therefore I am all at ease.

O Saint Germain, what love you bring,
it truly makes all matter sing,
your violet flame does all restore,
with you we are becoming more.

7. Saint Germain, shatter the energetic matrix that prevents people from seeing that fanaticism starts out with a more innocent, seemingly benign state of mind. People have a certain viewpoint, they have this sense of security, they think their viewpoint is absolute and they do not want to let go of it.

O Saint Germain, I'm karma-free,
the past no longer burdens me,
a brand new opportunity,
I am in Christic unity.

O Saint Germain, what love you bring,
it truly makes all matter sing,

your violet flame does all restore,
with you we are becoming more.

8. Saint Germain, shatter the energetic matrix that prevents people from seeing that gradually the intensity can build, people feel more and more threatened. They feel their viewpoint is more and more threatened. They become more and more aggressive in denying or refuting any threats.

O Saint Germain, we are now one,
I am for you a violet sun,
as we transform this planet earth,
your Golden Age is given birth.

O Saint Germain, what love you bring,
it truly makes all matter sing,
your violet flame does all restore,
with you we are becoming more.

9. Saint Germain, shatter the energetic matrix that prevents people from seeing that there comes a phase shift where they are no longer content with trying to convince other people that they are wrong. They accept that some people will not be convinced and therefore it is acceptable to kill those who will not be converted to their beliefs.

O Saint Germain, the earth is free,
from burden of duality,
in oneness we bring what is best,
your Golden Age is manifest.

O Saint Germain, what love you bring,
it truly makes all matter sing,
your violet flame does all restore,
with you we are becoming more.

Sealing

In the name of the I AM THAT I AM, I accept that Archangel Michael, Astrea and Shiva form an impenetrable shield around myself and all constructive people, sealing us from all fear-based energies in all four octaves. I accept that the Light of God is consuming and transforming all fear-based energies that make up the dark forces working against ending the era of fanaticism on earth!

18 | INVOKING FREEDOM FROM THE MATERIALISTIC LIE (PART 2)

In the name of the I AM THAT I AM, Jesus Christ, I use the authority that I have as a being in embodiment on earth to call upon Saint Germain to reinforce my calls and use my chakras to project the statements in this invocation into the collective consciousness and awaken people to the need to leave behind the materialistic lie. Awaken people to the reality that we are spiritual beings and that we can co-create a new future by working with the ascended masters. I especially call for …

[Make your own calls here.]

Part 1

1. Saint Germain, shatter the energetic matrix that prevents people from seeing that we could measure in a person's energy field when that shift happens. Suddenly, the mind is focused on "the ends can justify the means," and it is acceptable to kill those who oppose our epically important idea.

O Saint Germain, you do inspire,
my vision raised forever higher,
with you I form a figure-eight,
your Golden Age I co-create.

O Saint Germain, what love you bring,
it truly makes all matter sing,
your violet flame does all restore,
with you we are becoming more.

2. Saint Germain, shatter the energetic matrix that prevents people from seeing that if we had used existing technology to measure people's energy fields, it would have been easier to understand fanaticism.

O Saint Germain, what Freedom Flame,
released when we recite your name,
acceleration is your gift,
our planet it will surely lift.

O Saint Germain, what love you bring,
it truly makes all matter sing,
your violet flame does all restore,
with you we are becoming more.

3. Saint Germain, shatter the energetic matrix that prevents people from seeing that if there had been an energetic awareness for over a century, then 9/11 would not have happened. The phenomenon of Muslim fundamentalism and Muslim terror against the West would not have occurred.

O Saint Germain, in love we claim,
our right to bring your violet flame,
from you Above, to us below,
it is an all-transforming flow.

O Saint Germain, what love you bring,
it truly makes all matter sing,
your violet flame does all restore,
with you we are becoming more.

4. Saint Germain, shatter the energetic matrix that prevents people from seeing that the western democracies would have moved beyond the point where they needed to see this extreme outplaying of their own state of consciousness, their fanaticism in defending Materialism.

> O Saint Germain, I love you so,
> my aura filled with violet glow,
> my chakras filled with violet fire,
> I am your cosmic amplifier.

> **O Saint Germain, what love you bring,**
> **it truly makes all matter sing,**
> **your violet flame does all restore,**
> **with you we are becoming more.**

5. Saint Germain, shatter the energetic matrix that prevents people from realizing the consequences of Einstein's discoveries, of quantum physics and starting to apply them to other areas of life than just physics.

> O Saint Germain, I am now free,
> your violet flame is therapy,
> transform all hang-ups in my mind,
> as inner peace I surely find.

> **O Saint Germain, what love you bring,**
> **it truly makes all matter sing,**
> **your violet flame does all restore,**
> **with you we are becoming more.**

6. Saint Germain, shatter the energetic matrix that prevents people from seeing that we are ready for an energetic approach to physical healing but also an energetic approach to psychological healing. I call forth a shift so a critical mass of people will see this.

> O Saint Germain, my body pure,
> your violet flame for all is cure,
> consume the cause of all disease,
> and therefore I am all at ease.

O Saint Germain, what love you bring,
it truly makes all matter sing,
your violet flame does all restore,
with you we are becoming more.

7. Saint Germain, shatter the energetic matrix that prevents the development of new technologies for helping people with mental illness. I call forth the openness in the mind to receive this technology.

O Saint Germain, I'm karma-free,
the past no longer burdens me,
a brand new opportunity,
I am in Christic unity.

O Saint Germain, what love you bring,
it truly makes all matter sing,
your violet flame does all restore,
with you we are becoming more.

8. Saint Germain, shatter the energetic matrix that prevents people from opening their minds so they are not fixated on the materialistic paradigm, thereby enabling them to receive new ideas from Saint Germain.

O Saint Germain, we are now one,
I am for you a violet sun,
as we transform this planet earth,
your Golden Age is given birth.

O Saint Germain, what love you bring,
it truly makes all matter sing,
your violet flame does all restore,
with you we are becoming more.

9. Saint Germain, shatter the energetic matrix that prevents people from seeing that if we measured the brain waves of scientific materialists, the militant atheists, and compared them to a Muslim terrorist, we would see a similar pattern.

O Saint Germain, the earth is free,
from burden of duality,
in oneness we bring what is best,
your Golden Age is manifest.

O Saint Germain, what love you bring,
it truly makes all matter sing,
your violet flame does all restore,
with you we are becoming more.

Part 2

1. Saint Germain, shatter the energetic matrix that prevents people from seeing that we could measure that if a person believes that the ends can justify the means, there are certain energy vibrations in that person's energy field. They have reached that level of intensity where they are taking over the person's conscious mind.

O Saint Germain, you do inspire,
my vision raised forever higher,
with you I form a figure-eight,
your Golden Age I co-create.

O Saint Germain, what love you bring,
it truly makes all matter sing,
your violet flame does all restore,
with you we are becoming more.

2. Saint Germain, shatter the energetic matrix that prevents people from seeing that at this point a person is not able to make a free, conscious choice. The person's conscious mind is overwhelmed by this energy and it pulls the conscious mind into a state of denial where it is not able to see reality.

O Saint Germain, what Freedom Flame,
released when we recite your name,

acceleration is your gift,
our planet it will surely lift.

O Saint Germain, what love you bring,
it truly makes all matter sing,
your violet flame does all restore,
with you we are becoming more.

3. Saint Germain, shatter the energetic matrix that prevents people from seeing that there are various ways to help people shift out of this. We could give people the tools to overcome the fanatical mindset and dissipate the energy behind it.

O Saint Germain, in love we claim,
our right to bring your violet flame,
from you Above, to us below,
it is an all-transforming flow.

O Saint Germain, what love you bring,
it truly makes all matter sing,
your violet flame does all restore,
with you we are becoming more.

4. Saint Germain, shatter the energetic matrix that prevents people from seeing that when the energy goes down to a certain level, the conscious mind of that person shifts and he now sees the limitations of the fanatical mindset.

O Saint Germain, I love you so,
my aura filled with violet glow,
my chakras filled with violet fire,
I am your cosmic amplifier.

O Saint Germain, what love you bring,
it truly makes all matter sing,
your violet flame does all restore,
with you we are becoming more.

5. Saint Germain, shatter the energetic matrix that prevents people from seeing that we can develop certain techniques that could help people go out of the fanatical mindset.

O Saint Germain, I am now free,
your violet flame is therapy,
transform all hang-ups in my mind,
as inner peace I surely find.

**O Saint Germain, what love you bring,
it truly makes all matter sing,
your violet flame does all restore,
with you we are becoming more.**

6. Saint Germain, shatter the energetic matrix that prevents people from seeing that we cannot hope to cure mental illness unless we understand the energy component and deal with the energy that pulls people into these unhealthy patterns.

O Saint Germain, my body pure,
your violet flame for all is cure,
consume the cause of all disease,
and therefore I am all at ease.

**O Saint Germain, what love you bring,
it truly makes all matter sing,
your violet flame does all restore,
with you we are becoming more.**

7. Saint Germain, shatter the energetic matrix that prevents people from seeing that we could take a person with depression and create an energetic signature of their energy field, their subconscious mind. We would be able to identify a certain quantity of energy of a certain vibration.

O Saint Germain, I'm karma-free,
the past no longer burdens me,
a brand new opportunity,
I am in Christic unity.

**O Saint Germain, what love you bring,
it truly makes all matter sing,
your violet flame does all restore,
with you we are becoming more.**

8. Saint Germain, shatter the energetic matrix that prevents people from seeing that it is the energy that pulls a persons' conscious mind into a state of hopelessness. It is created by the energy pulling on the conscious mind. When we dissipate that energy, the person snaps out of depression.

O Saint Germain, we are now one,
I am for you a violet sun,
as we transform this planet earth,
your Golden Age is given birth.

**O Saint Germain, what love you bring,
it truly makes all matter sing,
your violet flame does all restore,
with you we are becoming more.**

9. Saint Germain, shatter the energetic matrix that prevents people from seeing that there is almost no limit to how much scientific research could be done by studying consciousness.

O Saint Germain, the earth is free,
from burden of duality,
in oneness we bring what is best,
your Golden Age is manifest.

**O Saint Germain, what love you bring,
it truly makes all matter sing,
your violet flame does all restore,
with you we are becoming more.**

Part 3

1. Saint Germain, shatter the energetic matrix that prevents people from seeing that there are certain aspects of consciousness, there are certain forms of energies, that are beyond the material frequency spectrum. They cannot be detected by instruments that are made out of energy within the material spectrum.

O Saint Germain, you do inspire,
my vision raised forever higher,
with you I form a figure-eight,
your Golden Age I co-create.

O Saint Germain, what love you bring,
it truly makes all matter sing,
your violet flame does all restore,
with you we are becoming more.

2. Saint Germain, shatter the energetic matrix that prevents people from seeing that we have been given an instrument that can detect energy waves beyond the material spectrum. That instrument is the mind but what scientists decided with the advent of Materialism, was that they should ignore the mind.

O Saint Germain, what Freedom Flame,
released when we recite your name,
acceleration is your gift,
our planet it will surely lift.

O Saint Germain, what love you bring,
it truly makes all matter sing,
your violet flame does all restore,
with you we are becoming more.

3. Saint Germain, shatter the energetic matrix that prevents people from seeing that scientific Materialism is based on the elitist mindset. Only certain scientists are able to define how science should function and how to

interpret scientific observations. Their minds are supposedly objective and neutral but the mind of the general population could never be objective.

> O Saint Germain, in love we claim,
> our right to bring your violet flame,
> from you Above, to us below,
> it is an all-transforming flow.

> **O Saint Germain, what love you bring,**
> **it truly makes all matter sing,**
> **your violet flame does all restore,**
> **with you we are becoming more.**

4. Saint Germain, shatter the energetic matrix that prevents people from seeing that there is a cognitive dissonance in Materialism, in the sense that they think that the mind in general is not reliable. They are convinced that their minds are giving them a neutral, objective observation and proof that there is nothing beyond the material universe.

> O Saint Germain, I love you so,
> my aura filled with violet glow,
> my chakras filled with violet fire,
> I am your cosmic amplifier.

> **O Saint Germain, what love you bring,**
> **it truly makes all matter sing,**
> **your violet flame does all restore,**
> **with you we are becoming more.**

5. Saint Germain, shatter the energetic matrix that prevents people from seeing that materialistic science will never prove that there is nothing beyond the material universe. Science has not proven that God does not exist because we cannot prove that something does not exist, especially when we have limited our observation to instruments that cannot detect anything beyond the material universe.

> O Saint Germain, I am now free,
> your violet flame is therapy,

transform all hang-ups in my mind,
as inner peace I surely find.

**O Saint Germain, what love you bring,
it truly makes all matter sing,
your violet flame does all restore,
with you we are becoming more.**

6. Saint Germain, shatter the energetic matrix that prevents people from seeing that we cannot take instruments that can only detect the material spectrum of energy and use those instruments to prove that there is something beyond that spectrum.

O Saint Germain, my body pure,
your violet flame for all is cure,
consume the cause of all disease,
and therefore I am all at ease.

**O Saint Germain, what love you bring,
it truly makes all matter sing,
your violet flame does all restore,
with you we are becoming more.**

7. Saint Germain, shatter the energetic matrix that prevents people from seeing that science has not proven that there is nothing beyond the material world. It has only proven that we cannot detect what we are not looking for. We cannot detect something if we are not using the proper instrument.

O Saint Germain, I'm karma-free,
the past no longer burdens me,
a brand new opportunity,
I am in Christic unity.

**O Saint Germain, what love you bring,
it truly makes all matter sing,
your violet flame does all restore,
with you we are becoming more.**

8. Saint Germain, shatter the energetic matrix that prevents people from seeing that the human mind can make accurate observations. It is possible for a human being to attain a state of consciousness where that person is neutral.

> O Saint Germain, we are now one,
> I am for you a violet sun,
> as we transform this planet earth,
> your Golden Age is given birth.

> **O Saint Germain, what love you bring,**
> **it truly makes all matter sing,**
> **your violet flame does all restore,**
> **with you we are becoming more.**

9. Saint Germain, shatter the energetic matrix that prevents people from seeing that when we are open to seeing something new, we do not do what the fanatical mindset causes people to do, namely formulate an image in the mind of how the world *should* work and then seeking to project that image onto the universe.

> O Saint Germain, the earth is free,
> from burden of duality,
> in oneness we bring what is best,
> your Golden Age is manifest.

> **O Saint Germain, what love you bring,**
> **it truly makes all matter sing,**
> **your violet flame does all restore,**
> **with you we are becoming more.**

Part 4

1. Saint Germain, shatter the energetic matrix that prevents people from seeing that we can create an energetic signature and we can see that a person has the particular energies that lead to the fanatical mindset. That

person has a mental image and in order to hold on to the sense of security, that person is not open to seeing anything beyond that mental image.

O Saint Germain, you do inspire,
my vision raised forever higher,
with you I form a figure-eight,
your Golden Age I co-create.

O Saint Germain, what love you bring,
it truly makes all matter sing,
your violet flame does all restore,
with you we are becoming more.

2. Saint Germain, shatter the energetic matrix that prevents people from seeing that this energetic signature is almost like a lie detector. When we see a certain energetic signature, we know that a person is not in a neutral state of mind.

O Saint Germain, what Freedom Flame,
released when we recite your name,
acceleration is your gift,
our planet it will surely lift.

O Saint Germain, what love you bring,
it truly makes all matter sing,
your violet flame does all restore,
with you we are becoming more.

3. Saint Germain, shatter the energetic matrix that prevents people from seeing that it is possible to move out of that state of mind, to attain a neutral state of mind where we are not projecting a mental image onto the world, we are just observing the world.

O Saint Germain, in love we claim,
our right to bring your violet flame,
from you Above, to us below,
it is an all-transforming flow.

**O Saint Germain, what love you bring,
it truly makes all matter sing,
your violet flame does all restore,
with you we are becoming more.**

4. Saint Germain, shatter the energetic matrix that prevents people from seeing that such a person can make a neutral objective observation. Such a person could make a much more objective observation than a materialistic scientist who has an intent of proving the validity of Materialism and disproving anything beyond it.

O Saint Germain, I love you so,
my aura filled with violet glow,
my chakras filled with violet fire,
I am your cosmic amplifier.

**O Saint Germain, what love you bring,
it truly makes all matter sing,
your violet flame does all restore,
with you we are becoming more.**

5. Saint Germain, shatter the energetic matrix that prevents people from seeing that materialists are not objective. They want the world to function a certain way. They want to uphold the materialist paradigm, even when science itself has pointed beyond it. They are as fanatical about this as medieval Catholics were about the infallibility of the Pope and Catholic doctrine.

O Saint Germain, I am now free,
your violet flame is therapy,
transform all hang-ups in my mind,
as inner peace I surely find.

**O Saint Germain, what love you bring,
it truly makes all matter sing,
your violet flame does all restore,
with you we are becoming more.**

6. Saint Germain, shatter the energetic matrix that prevents people from seeing that if we train people to go into a neutral state of mind, they can make accurate observations with the mind of energies that cannot be detected by material instruments.

O Saint Germain, my body pure,
your violet flame for all is cure,
consume the cause of all disease,
and therefore I am all at ease.

**O Saint Germain, what love you bring,
it truly makes all matter sing,
your violet flame does all restore,
with you we are becoming more.**

7. Saint Germain, shatter the energetic matrix that prevents people from seeing that when a great number of people have been trained to do this, they can use the mind to investigate what is beyond the material universe.

O Saint Germain, I'm karma-free,
the past no longer burdens me,
a brand new opportunity,
I am in Christic unity.

**O Saint Germain, what love you bring,
it truly makes all matter sing,
your violet flame does all restore,
with you we are becoming more.**

8. Saint Germain, shatter the energetic matrix that prevents people from seeing that when a large majority of people make the same observations, then we must say that these observations made through the instrument of the mind are as reliable as the observations made through physical instruments.

O Saint Germain, we are now one,
I am for you a violet sun,
as we transform this planet earth,
your Golden Age is given birth.

**O Saint Germain, what love you bring,
it truly makes all matter sing,
your violet flame does all restore,
with you we are becoming more.**

9. Saint Germain, shatter the energetic matrix that prevents people from seeing the limitations of the materialist paradigm and saying: "But it's so obvious, we have to look at consciousness. After all, what kind of beings are we? What determines whether we are happy or unhappy in life? It's our consciousness.

O Saint Germain, the earth is free,
from burden of duality,
in oneness we bring what is best,
your Golden Age is manifest.

**O Saint Germain, what love you bring,
it truly makes all matter sing,
your violet flame does all restore,
with you we are becoming more.**

Part 5

1. Saint Germain, shatter the energetic matrix that prevents people from seeing that if we want to be happy, if we want to overcome the problem of mental illness, we have to start seriously investigating consciousness.

O Saint Germain, you do inspire,
my vision raised forever higher,
with you I form a figure-eight,
your Golden Age I co-create.

**O Saint Germain, what love you bring,
it truly makes all matter sing,
your violet flame does all restore,
with you we are becoming more.**

2. Saint Germain, shatter the energetic matrix that prevents people from seeing that we cannot have a science that is publicly funded but that ignores consciousness because of some outdated paradigm. We cannot accept this anymore. It is nonsense, and we will not stand for it.

> O Saint Germain, what Freedom Flame,
> released when we recite your name,
> acceleration is your gift,
> our planet it will surely lift.

> **O Saint Germain, what love you bring,**
> **it truly makes all matter sing,**
> **your violet flame does all restore,**
> **with you we are becoming more.**

3. Saint Germain, shatter the energetic matrix that prevents people from seeing that we will not see our taxpayer money go to finance these people in the scientific establishment, who are as fanatical as the people in the Catholic church and other churches that we are not financing with public money.

> O Saint Germain, in love we claim,
> our right to bring your violet flame,
> from you Above, to us below,
> it is an all-transforming flow.

> **O Saint Germain, what love you bring,**
> **it truly makes all matter sing,**
> **your violet flame does all restore,**
> **with you we are becoming more.**

4. Saint Germain, shatter the energetic matrix that prevents people from seeing that why should we have these Cardinals or Popes of science that are financed by public money, when all they are doing is spreading a paradigm that is as fanatical as most religious paradigms?

> O Saint Germain, I love you so,
> my aura filled with violet glow,

my chakras filled with violet fire,
I am your cosmic amplifier.

O Saint Germain, what love you bring,
it truly makes all matter sing,
your violet flame does all restore,
with you we are becoming more.

5. Saint Germain, shatter the energetic matrix that prevents people from seeing that one of the fundamental principles of democracy is the separation of church and state. The state must be independent of any particular religion.

O Saint Germain, I am now free,
your violet flame is therapy,
transform all hang-ups in my mind,
as inner peace I surely find.

O Saint Germain, what love you bring,
it truly makes all matter sing,
your violet flame does all restore,
with you we are becoming more.

6. Saint Germain, shatter the energetic matrix that prevents people from seeing that scientific Materialism is a religion. It is a religion that denies God but it is still a religion because the denial of God is not based on fact, not based on observation. It is based on *belief.*

O Saint Germain, my body pure,
your violet flame for all is cure,
consume the cause of all disease,
and therefore I am all at ease.

O Saint Germain, what love you bring,
it truly makes all matter sing,
your violet flame does all restore,
with you we are becoming more.

7. Saint Germain, shatter the energetic matrix that prevents people from seeing that if we are true to the democratic principles, we must say: "Yes, society can fund science but it cannot fund scientific Materialism."

O Saint Germain, I'm karma-free,
the past no longer burdens me,
a brand new opportunity,
I am in Christic unity.

O Saint Germain, what love you bring,
it truly makes all matter sing,
your violet flame does all restore,
with you we are becoming more.

8. Saint Germain, shatter the energetic matrix that prevents people from seeing that Materialism is a religion and we need to free science from the influence of this religion, just as we have freed society from the influence of Catholicism or other forms of Christianity.

O Saint Germain, we are now one,
I am for you a violet sun,
as we transform this planet earth,
your Golden Age is given birth.

O Saint Germain, what love you bring,
it truly makes all matter sing,
your violet flame does all restore,
with you we are becoming more.

9. Saint Germain, shatter the energetic matrix that prevents people from seeing that we will no longer accept that our society is based on the doctrines of Materialism. We want our democracies to be based on neutral observations of how the world actually functions, not on a fanatical dream of how it should function.

O Saint Germain, the earth is free,
from burden of duality,
in oneness we bring what is best,
your Golden Age is manifest.

**O Saint Germain, what love you bring,
it truly makes all matter sing,
your violet flame does all restore,
with you we are becoming more.**

Sealing

In the name of the I AM THAT I AM, I accept that Archangel Michael, Astrea and Shiva form an impenetrable shield around myself and all constructive people, sealing us from all fear-based energies in all four octaves. I accept that the Light of God is consuming and transforming all fear-based energies that make up the dark forces working against ending the era of fanaticism on earth!

19 | FANATICISM IS AN ADDICTION

I AM the Ascended Master the Elohim Astrea. What I would like to do, in the beginning of this discourse at least, is build upon what Saint Germain gave you in his last installment where you talked about the development of technology or the use of technology to detect vibration, therefore developing an energetic, or an energy psychology. Now, if you take this a little bit further, you could see that one of the unexplained phenomena that you see in psychology is addictions.

What exactly is an addiction? Why do some people become addicted and other people do not? Why is it so difficult for people to break an addiction once they have crossed a certain threshold? If there had been developed an energetic approach to psychology, you would already have had technology that could show what happens in the energy field of an addicted person. This would have allowed you to see that when a person becomes addicted, this is not an internal process. You can actually measure, or even make visible, what happens and these instruments can be developed in the relatively near future because the technology is already there. You can actually measure and make visible that the phenomenon of addiction cannot be explained by only looking at a person's energy field.

You have to realize that a person becomes addicted only because there is an influx of energy from outside its own energy field. Of course, once you see this, it makes you realize that you then need to explain, well, where does the energy come from? We do not expect that science will begin to accept the ideas that we have given you or the concepts we have given you about the astral plane and demons. But it would very much be possible for scientists to realize that beyond the material frequency spectrum that is associated with matter and matter particles, there are other realms of energy. It would be possible to detect that there is a certain realm that is linked to people's emotional bodies and that when people become addicted, it is because their energy fields have become open to this larger collective energy field. Therefore, an addict has an influx of energy coming into the emotional body that overwhelms that person. They actually are pulled into the addiction and they do not have the conscious willpower to resist it because the magnetic pull on the emotional body is too strong.

This could be taken further where you will begin to investigate where this energy comes from, what produces it and what directs it. It could very quickly become clear that this is not simply some passive energy that is floating around. It is a very directed energy, it is a very aggressive energy. It clearly seeks to gain something, there is some kind of intent behind it. It is not just a matter of invading a person's energy field because you could also measure that there is energy going out through the addictive behavior. There is energy going out of a person's energy field into this larger field that is associated with the emotional body.

You then can begin to ask yourself: Well, why is there this exchange of energy? Why would there be a need for energy to flow from people's emotional bodies into some larger energy field? Why does there seem to be an aggressive intent coming from this larger field to invade and take over people's emotional bodies and extract energy from them? What is it that exists in this larger emotional field that needs energy from people? This is where it could actually be, not necessarily with current technology, proven by science, but certainly it could be intuited by people who would study the phenomenon in an objective systematic manner, that there must be some kind of somewhat conscious being existing in this, what we might call the collective emotional body. There are certain, we might call them in a neutral tone, energy beings in this emotional realm that seem to need energy from human beings. They have somehow developed a way to invade people's energy fields and extract energy from them. This could then be used to make further studies of what happens, for example, in a war situation, what happens at the energetic level on a battlefield. If you could do this, you would be able to see that when people are killed on a battlefield, there is a very, very strong influence from this collective emotional realm. The people who are killed or wounded, there is energy extracted from their energy fields through this trauma.

Fanaticism is an addiction

You could then begin to study all kinds of people who experienced trauma and you will see that in many cases a trauma opens up a person's emotional body to an influence from the collective emotional body. Therefore, scientists could begin to realize that there are these energy beings existing in the collective emotional body who are actually extracting energy from people through various processes, primarily through trauma and addiction. This would mean you could now use this to take a look at fanaticism and come up with another definition, or another layer of definition, and say that fanaticism is actually an addiction.

You would be able to take a person in the fanatical mindset, and you could see that the person in his or her emotional body has an opening that is very similar to what an addict has. There is an opening whereby there is an influx of emotional energy, and energy is being extracted from the person's energy field, going to these energy beings in the collective emotional body.

This is something that already would have happened if the scenario Saint Germain painted (the ideal scenario) would have taken place. It is something that could be developed within one to two decades if there were scientists who were open-minded, neutral and objective enough to use current technology and develop some of it a little bit further. We are not talking about some Utopian fantasy that is far into the future. We are talking about something that is very realistic, based on the technology you already have. It simply needs to be applied in a different way with a quite frankly more objective awareness and intent.

Clearly, fanaticism is an addiction. You could now begin to study this based on what psychologists know about addictions, you could begin to find ways to help people out of it. You could have a "Fanatics Anonymous" 12-step program, or many other programs that could actually help people overcome this mindset. Again, of course there are people in the western world who would say: "Well, but what does that help when the most fanatical people are in the Middle East and they will not listen to anything coming from western science or western democracies. They think it's all decadent nonsense that's contrary to Islam so they will ignore it completely" But you see, this is where you can use what I have just said to make people realize that there is a collective emotional body, a planetary emotional body, and all people are tied to it.

Fanatics cannot help mankind overcome fanaticism

Once you begin to recognize that everything is energy, you see that energy does not know physical boundaries. As Saint Germain said, quantum physics has already proven that particles separated by a great distance can be connected. Truly, when you look at the energetic approach, you realize that the whole idea that people are separated, that there is a separation in space, is just an illusion that comes from a certain perspective, a certain level of consciousness. In reality, everything is interconnected and one of the ways that all people are interconnected is through this collective emotional body. The simple fact is that when people in the democratic nations begin to raise themselves above this fanatical mindset, and for that matter other kinds of addictions, then you will actually stop giving energy, stop feeding energy, to these energetic beings in the collective emotional body. As you feed them less energy, they have less power to take over the emotional bodies of other people. This means that when the people in the democratic nations raise their awareness, you will also raise up the people in Muslim countries or other areas around the world.

The emotional body of the planet is like a piece of cloth. You can pull up one corner and for a while it seems like you are only raising a small corner. As you keep pulling it up, you eventually raise the entire cloth. It is quite frankly possible for people in the western nations to remove that emotional, aggressive force, those aggressive beings in the emotional body that are the cause behind fanaticism, at least the emotional cause behind fanaticism. It is possible that when that emotional pull is less, then the people who are now totally immersed in the fanatical mindset will be able to wake up and start coming out of it.

The energetic history of fanaticism

Now, you can even look at history again and say that, clearly if you look at the western democracies, you can go back in time and see that people were much more into the fanatical mindset in previous ages. You go back to medieval times when the Catholic church had a dominant position and you see that most people who were believing Catholics were truly in the fanatical mindset about the Christian faith and especially the Catholic church. Many believing Catholics are still in the fanatical mindset. Actually, if you would compare the mindset of most Catholics today to the mindset of Catholics 500 years ago, you would see that there has been a very clear shift, so people are not as fanatical as they were. You can see the same thing in other areas.

Therefore, you can see that the very fact that democracies could emerge shows you that people had begun a collective process of raising themselves above this lower state of consciousness that they were in during the feudal societies. These people did not have the power to break free. In a sense, you could say that poverty is a form of addiction, that feeling suppressed by an external force that you cannot stand up against also becomes a form of addiction. If you could study the energy fields of medieval peasants, you would see that they also had an opening to the astral plane and they were overwhelmed by these feelings of hopelessness, feeling powerless, not thinking they could do anything.

People can even, by becoming more conscious, becoming more aware, raise themselves above this. You see that there is a way that people can raise themselves above this influence from the collective emotional realm by raising their awareness, by using conscious willpower. You can also see that it is a slow process. You can see that even in the western democracies, many people still have addictions, which demonstrates that they have a tie to the collective emotional body.

Clearly, again the more conscious you become of an issue, of a problem, the more power you have to do something about it. I can assure you that there will come a point in the not too distant future where this whole shift to an energetic worldview will have happened. It will become self-evident to most people that energy is the underlying reality.

You go back a few hundred years, and you see how they were dealing with certain diseases back then. They had certain ways to deal with disease that had a certain effectiveness. But because they had not discovered bacteria, there were very strict limits to what they could do. There were many diseases that seemed incurable, simply because they did not know about the real cause. Once knowledge had expanded and bacteria were discovered, there was a whole new world of possibilities that opened up for fighting certain diseases.

Why Materialism cannot cure addictions

You can see again that materialistic psychology has not been very effective in dealing with addictions. Why is that? Well, it can only be because they do not have the knowledge of what really causes the addictions. If you could make the shift that I have outlined (realizing that an addiction is very much tied to this openness to the collective emotional body that overwhelms people and these energetic beings that need to steal energy from human beings), then you have a whole new world of possibilities that opens up for helping people overcome this.

Of course, we have given you some tools but other tools can be developed where they could help people close their emotional bodies to this influence. This would have to deal with also going deeper into the psychology of looking at the mental level and even the identity level, which is beyond what I want to do right now.

As I said, there will come a point where they will look back at your time and simply be stunned over the fact that you knew Einstein's theory of relativity that says everything is energy, but nobody was really willing to apply it and realize that this opens up so many possibilities for improving life when you look at the energetic level. In the future, it will be obvious that people's emotional bodies can be vulnerable to an influence from the outside. Therefore, in order to treat addiction and many other mental conditions, mental illnesses, you need to deal with the emotional body and you need to teach people how to seal their emotional bodies from this influence of these fear-based beings who need to steal energy from people. In a sense, you could say that it will be obvious to people in the future that the real currency in the world is energy. It is not about money. It is really about energy, who has the most energy.

Why fanatical leaders must steal people's energy

We have said before that Adolph Hitler during the 1930s, why did he create these mass rallies where he had people going into this fanatical, hypnotic state and scream at the top of their lungs at the top of their voices, these slogans? What was the purpose behind it? Well, when you realize what energy is and what energy does, then you saw that Hitler was simply creating a reservoir of emotional energy that he could use to drive his war effort. I am not saying Hitler was conscious of this, but that was really the purpose of these mass rallies: to extract energy from the German people and to pool it together in the emotional body, the collective emotional body.

You saw that when Hitler started the war, in the beginning, the German army seemed almost like it could conquer anything. It seemed unstoppable and why was it? It was because they were riding that wave of this emotional energy that had been built up. Then there came a point where the tide started turning and the Germans started losing and why was that? Because the energy had now been dissipated. They did not have the energy anymore.

You could look at the Soviet Union and see that, why did Stalin have to kill 21 million people? Was it just so he could personally stay in power, because most of these people obviously were not a threat to Stalin? No, it was because by killing them and by all the torture and imprisonment, again you force people's emotional bodies open and energy was extracted from them and it created a certain reservoir that kept the Soviet Union going for a time. Then, of course you saw that the Soviet Union came to a point where it started stagnating because there simply was not any currency left to drive their expansion. There was not enough energy, there was not enough energy being extracted.

You can go to China and see how the great Chairman Mao killed so many millions of Chinese. Again, this created this pool of energy, this reservoir of energy in the collective emotional body that drove Chinese communism for a while. There is still some of that energy that is left that drives the personality cult around Chairman Mao and that is also being fed by that personality cult. This is an energy that is still to a large degree hypnotizing the Chinese people and the Chinese leaders, keeping at least some of them believing in the communist philosophy. You will see that there will come a point where the energy will have been dissipated and suddenly people will wake up and say: "Why are we even bothering, trying to uphold the illusion that we are communist when in reality, we are more capitalist than the decadent West."

Why people cannot see contradictory viewpoints

This again ties in with what we have said about cognitive dissonance. People are holding viewpoints that are mutually exclusive or incompatible, but they cannot see it. Why can they not see it? Well, because they have an opening in their emotional body that is creating an influx of a certain fear-based emotional energy and this pulls on their conscious minds, it pulls them into certain emotions. This prevents them from having the clarity in the mental body to see the incompatibility of their beliefs.

If you look at many Muslims today, you will see that the more radical they become, the more their minds are taken over by hatred. You could take one of these warriors from ISIS or a suicide bomber and you could examine their energy field and you could see that their energy fields have an influx of hatred energy from the collective emotional body, from certain aggressive energy beings in the emotional body. The conscious attention of these people is pulled into this hatred, they are so focused on this hatred that they cannot simply rise up to the mental body. They cannot connect to their normal intelligence and see that some of these beliefs they hold are incompatible.

Naturally, we can say that the belief that the ends can justify the means resides in the mental body. The more immediate problem for people who are in the fanatical mindset is that their emotional bodies are so chaotic, they are so taken over by this influx of energy from the collective emotional body, that they cannot think clearly. They cannot see what they are really believing, they cannot see the contradictions and incompatibilities. They cannot see that the ends can never justify the means, or at least they cannot see that neither the Koran nor the New Testament can actually justify a philosophy that the ends can justify the means. They cannot see that there are certain very, very clear statements that have come through all religions: "Do unto others, what you want them to do onto you" and they cannot see that this can never be compatible with killing other people. They cannot see that there is a biological imperative not to kill your own species, there is a biological imperative to cooperate instead of opposing others. They cannot see that the philosophy that the ends can justify the means, and therefore it is justified to kill other people, is in complete contradiction to this.

Why is it that they cannot see it? It is not because they are not intelligent enough to see it, but because their attention, their conscious minds, are simply pulled away from the mental body and into the emotional body focused on this hatred—this sense of urgency, this sense that something needs to be done now to these terrible people who are threatening God's plan for the universe.

It really is an addiction. It is just as much an addiction as a person who can only worry about how to get the next bottle of alcohol and will do anything to get that alcohol, including steal. You see that these people are not rational, you cannot reason with them. You actually could reason with them, if their emotional bodies were not in such turmoil. Therefore, you would say that the first step towards changing the situation is to change the equation at the emotional level and then, once you have done that, then you have other options. As long as people are in this hypnotized state of mind, you cannot do anything with them. You look at the mass rallies of Hitler where they are screaming, "Sieg Heil!" and you look how their eyes are glazed over and you say: "Well, how can we reason with that?" You cannot even have a conversation with these people. You cannot communicate with them and therefore, you need to change the equation at the emotional level.

As we have said before, once you have knowledge, you are empowered, you no longer need to feel disempowered. If the people in the West, at least a critical mass of them (the more mature, advanced beings), would make the shift, they would see that there is something that the modern democracies can do about fanaticism, but it must start at home. It must start by removing the fanaticism in your own societies.

All people are connected

Quite frankly, everything is interconnected. This is what really should have been realized after Einstein. Because at the level of matter, where you have matter particles, the macroscopic level where you see with your senses, you can maintain the illusion that things can be separate. You can say, to a certain degree (at least from a certain viewpoint) that planet earth is separated by a vast distance from Venus or Mars, and by an even greater distance from distant solar systems and galaxies. Therefore, you can believe that earth is just an independent self-contained unit floating around in space. You can think that a person living in Sweden and a person living in Arabia, that they are separated by vast distances in space and therefore, they are not connected. But at the energetic level, there is no separation. Space at the energetic level does not mean separation because everything is connected.

Now, in fact if you really understand space at the physical level, you will see that space also is interconnected. Did not Einstein talk about the space-time continuum? He saw that everything was connected, and even space and time were connected so that you cannot even say that the past is separated from the present or the present from the future. This is because everything is connected in a greater unity, a greater whole. When you realize this, you realize that all people are connected and that everything interacts and that everything influences everything else.

Therefore, you can see that if the western democracies really wanted to make an effort to combat fanaticism or remove fanaticism, you would have to start at home and you would say: What are the elements in our societies that are actually reinforcing that collective pool of energy, the reservoir of energy and these energetic beings in the emotional body that are causing fanaticism? Well, any kind of addiction reinforces that whole dynamic so you would have to help people in the modern democracies overcome addictions. Now, you could look at some of the people who are standing there at the mass rallies and screaming and you could take pictures of young people at a rock concert, and you would see that their eyes look very similar. They are hypnotized by something. They are screaming at the top of their voices and releasing tremendous energy. Just like Hitler was taking that energy, many rock musicians can only exist in the physical because they are getting energy from their fans. You have many, many elements of western culture that reinforce that very fanatical, addictive energy dynamic.

Think about the concept of a "fan?" Do you not see the connection to the word, *fan*aticism. When you are fanatic, you are a fan of some kind of ism, it could be communism, humanism, Materialism, Christianism, Judaism, religionism, any kind of idea—any kind of idea where you say, this is how the world *should* work. Then, you refuse to test your theory against reality by using both neutral scientific observation and neutral intuitive observation, to see if your theory actually fits reality. Does the world work the way your theory says it should work? If it does not, then you change the theory because it is better for you that you come closer to basing your worldview on how the world actually works.

You have the concept of Plato's cave where the people are tied in the cave and cannot see what is going on outside the cave, they can only see the shadows on the wall. You have a concept of shadowboxing where you are boxing against your own shadow and this is essentially what humankind has been doing now for all of known history. You have been looking at the shadows and based on observing the shadows, you have formulated elaborate theories and isms about what goes on outside the shadow world that you can see with your senses or even the scientific instruments that extend the senses.

The philosophical cause of fanaticism

This, my beloved, could actually be seen, not with scientific instruments, I give you, but it could certainly be seen intuitively that this very mindset (that we can formulate an accurate theory of how the world works based on our present perception, our present state of consciousness) this is an addiction and it is actually the underlying cause of fanaticism. You think that the world should work a certain way and all you are looking at is confirmation that it does work that way. You filter out anything that goes against that. Therefore, you can never overcome the illusion. You become a self-fulfilling prophecy because you only see what your theory allows you to see. You think that by having this very inaccurate, very limited view of the world, you can deduce how the world actually works.

It would be comparable to if you were at the Grand Canyon in America, and you had this binocular that had a very high zoom factor so it would show, on the opposite side of the canyon, just one little area, one little rock the size of a human head. Then, you would have a person who is standing there, they cannot move their binocular, they cannot zoom in and out, they can only look through this and they are inside a tent so they cannot see anything else. Then, outside of the tent, you have people standing, and they are asking the person inside the tent: "So, what does the Grand Canyon look like?" He says: "Well, it looks like this oval shaped round rock, it's probably the size of a football. I don't know why they call that the 'Grand' Canyon, it doesn't look very grand to me." All of the people outside are standing there, taking in the entire breathtaking view and they can of course see how limited is the view or the person in the tent.

Now, imagine that the person from inside the tent starts making up a theory, based on his observation of that one rock, of what the Grand Canyon is like and he then wants the people outside the tent to believe him and accept his theory. The theory is completely contradictory to what these people are seeing so who is going to believe him? Now imagine that you had another situation where the tent was bigger. There were not any people outside the tent, they were all inside the tent, but there was only one person looking through the binocular and he still, based on what he sees through the binocular, comes up with a theory about what the Grand Canyon is and how it works. Now, the people who cannot even see through the binocular, they might actually believe him.

Well, throughout the history of humankind, you have had certain religious people who have claimed that they had the binocular that could allow them to see into the universe and then some scientific people claimed that no, they had the binocular and they could see into the universe. But all of them have had a very, very limited perspective. It is not necessarily totally inaccurate in some cases. The observations made by science are not inaccurate. It is just that they are not the whole story. They are still showing one little rock and ignoring the totality of the Grand Canyon.

Humankind's limited view of reality

You can see how incredibly limited is the approach that humankind has had. How incredibly limited it is and therefore how completely unrealistic it is to think that you can start out with such a limited perspective and deduce how the vastness of the universe (which you are now only beginning to glimpse) functions. It is so "far out" compared to reality, to use the popular expression, that from the level of an ascended being who sees the totality of the grand creation, it is unfathomable that people can be stuck in this for century after century.

It is sometimes so that from the ascended level, we want to go down there and shake people awake and say: Come out of the tent, pull your eyes away from that binocular and see the whole view. Of course, we respect free will. The fact that we respect free will does not prevent us from once in a while saying: "How long O Lord? How long can this go on? How long can they stick to this limited view and not want something more?"

The explanation for this is of course what I have given you, people's emotional bodies are so overwhelmed that they are literally hypnotized, they are in a state of addiction. They cannot pull themselves away from this belief that their theory gives them an accurate view of how the world functions, and the only real way to get out of this is to somehow break that hypnotic spell.

Of course, this is what can be done through the School of Hard Knocks, as has happened to some degree during history. Why has history progressed to the point where it is at now? Well, through the School of Hard Knocks. People have had some very, very hard knocks—an incredible amount of suffering that finally brought them to a point where they challenged their worldview.

What we offer from the ascended realm is of course the alternative where you do not have to go through all of this suffering. You just have to tune your mind to the ascended realm and receive the ideas that will set you free from this limited view. What I have left to do here is simply to offer a dispensation where I will anchor my Presence in the emotional realm of this planet and anyone who makes the calls, the invocation, based on this dictation and the other dictations for this conference, I will multiply their calls by a very significant factor for the clearing out of the astral plane, for the breaking of this emotional, hypnotic spell that keeps people trapped in the addiction of fanaticism.

20 | INVOKING FREEDOM FROM THE ADDICTION OF FANATICISM (PART 1)

In the name of the I AM THAT I AM, Jesus Christ, I use the authority that I have as a being in embodiment on earth to call upon Elohim Astrea to reinforce my calls and use my chakras to project the statements in this invocation into the collective consciousness and set people free from the addiction of fanaticism. Awaken people to the reality that we are spiritual beings and that we can co-create a new future by working with the ascended masters. I especially call for ...

[Make your own calls here.]

Part 1

1. Astrea, shatter the energetic matrix that prevents people from seeing that when a person becomes addicted, this is not an internal process.

> Beloved Astrea, your heart is so true,
> your Circle and Sword of white and blue,

cut all life free from dramas unwise,
on wings of Purity our planet will rise.

**Beloved Astrea, in oneness with you,
your circle and sword of electric blue,
with Purity's Light cutting right through,
raising the earth into all that is true.**

2. Astrea, shatter the energetic matrix that prevents people from seeing that instruments can be developed that can measure and make visible that the phenomenon of addiction cannot be explained by only looking at a person's energy field.

Beloved Astrea, in God Purity,
accelerate all of our life energy,
we're rising beyond every impurity,
as Purity's Light forever we see.

**Beloved Astrea, in oneness with you,
your circle and sword of electric blue,
with Purity's Light cutting right through,
raising the earth into all that is true.**

3. Astrea, shatter the energetic matrix that prevents people from seeing that a person becomes addicted only because there is an influx of energy from outside its own energy field.

Beloved Astrea, from Purity's Ray,
send forth deliverance to all life today,
acceleration to Purity, we are now free
from all that is less than love's Purity.

**Beloved Astrea, in oneness with you,
your circle and sword of electric blue,
with Purity's Light cutting right through,
raising the earth into all that is true.**

4. Astrea, shatter the energetic matrix that prevents people from seeing that beyond the material frequency spectrum, there are other realms of energy.

> Beloved Astrea, accelerate us all,
> as for your deliverance we fervently call,
> set all life free from vision impure
> beyond fear and doubt, we're rising for sure.

> **Beloved Astrea, in oneness with you,**
> **your circle and sword of electric blue,**
> **with Purity's Light cutting right through,**
> **raising the earth into all that is true.**

5. Astrea, shatter the energetic matrix that prevents people from seeing that there is a realm that is linked to people's emotional bodies and when people become addicted, it is because their energy fields have become open to this larger collective energy field.

> Beloved Astrea, we're willing to see,
> all of the lies that keep us unfree,
> we surrender all lies causing the fall,
> forever affirming the oneness of All.

> **Beloved Astrea, in oneness with you,**
> **your circle and sword of electric blue,**
> **with Purity's Light cutting right through,**
> **raising the earth into all that is true.**

6. Astrea, shatter the energetic matrix that prevents people from seeing that an addict has an influx of energy coming into the emotional body that overwhelms that person. People actually are pulled into the addiction and they do not have the conscious willpower to resist it because the magnetic pull on the emotional body is too strong.

> Beloved Astrea, accelerate life
> beyond all duality's struggle and strife,
> consume all division between God and man,
> accelerate fulfillment of God's perfect plan.

Beloved Astrea, in oneness with you,
your circle and sword of electric blue,
with Purity's Light cutting right through,
raising the earth into all that is true.

7. Astrea, shatter the energetic matrix that prevents people from seeing that this is not simply some passive energy that is floating around. It is a very directed energy, it is a very aggressive energy. It clearly seeks to gain something, there is some kind of intent behind it.

Beloved Astrea, we lovingly call,
break down separation's invisible wall,
raising our minds into true unity
with the Masters of love in Infinity.

Beloved Astrea, in oneness with you,
your circle and sword of electric blue,
with Purity's Light cutting right through,
raising the earth into all that is true.

8. Astrea, shatter the energetic matrix that prevents people from seeing that there is energy going out through the addictive behavior. There is energy going out of a person's energy field into this larger field that is associated with the emotional body.

Beloved Astrea, help all of us find,
the secret that we create with the mind,
and thus what in ignorance we decreate,
in knowledge we easily can recreate.

Beloved Astrea, in oneness with you,
your circle and sword of electric blue,
with Purity's Light cutting right through,
raising the earth into all that is true.

9. Astrea, shatter the energetic matrix that prevents people from seeing that there are conscious beings in this the collective emotional body. These energy beings in the emotional realm need energy from human beings.

Beloved Astrea, we all do aspire,
to learning to use your purity's fire,
to raise every form in infamy sown,
as Saint Germain makes this planet his own.

Beloved Astrea, in oneness with you,
your circle and sword of electric blue,
with Purity's Light cutting right through,
raising the earth into all that is true.

Part 2

1. Astrea, shatter the energetic matrix that prevents people from seeing that these energy beings have developed a way to invade people's energy fields and extract energy from them.

Beloved Astrea, your heart is so true,
your Circle and Sword of white and blue,
cut all life free from dramas unwise,
on wings of Purity our planet will rise.

Beloved Astrea, in oneness with you,
your circle and sword of electric blue,
with Purity's Light cutting right through,
raising the earth into all that is true.

2. Astrea, shatter the energetic matrix that prevents people from seeing that when people are killed on a battlefield, there is a strong influence from the collective emotional realm. The people who are killed or wounded, there is energy extracted from their energy fields through this trauma.

Beloved Astrea, in God Purity,
accelerate all of our life energy,
we're rising beyond every impurity,
as Purity's Light forever we see.

Beloved Astrea, in oneness with you,
your circle and sword of electric blue,
with Purity's Light cutting right through,
raising the earth into all that is true.

3. Astrea, shatter the energetic matrix that prevents people from seeing that in many cases a trauma opens up a person's emotional body to an influence from the collective emotional body.

Beloved Astrea, from Purity's Ray,
send forth deliverance to all life today,
acceleration to Purity, we are now free
from all that is less than love's Purity.

Beloved Astrea, in oneness with you,
your circle and sword of electric blue,
with Purity's Light cutting right through,
raising the earth into all that is true.

4. Astrea, shatter the energetic matrix that prevents people from seeing that there are energy beings in the collective emotional body who are actually extracting energy from people through various processes, primarily through trauma and addiction.

Beloved Astrea, accelerate us all,
as for your deliverance we fervently call,
set all life free from vision impure
beyond fear and doubt, we're rising for sure.

Beloved Astrea, in oneness with you,
your circle and sword of electric blue,
with Purity's Light cutting right through,
raising the earth into all that is true.

5. Astrea, shatter the energetic matrix that prevents people from seeing that fanaticism is actually an addiction. A person in the fanatical mindset has in his or her emotional body an opening that is very similar to that of an addict.

Beloved Astrea, we're willing to see,
all of the lies that keep us unfree,
we surrender all lies causing the fall,
forever affirming the oneness of All.

**Beloved Astrea, in oneness with you,
your circle and sword of electric blue,
with Purity's Light cutting right through,
raising the earth into all that is true.**

6. Astrea, shatter the energetic matrix that prevents people from seeing that there is an opening whereby there is an influx of emotional energy and energy is being extracted from the person's energy field, going to these energy beings in the collective emotional body.

Beloved Astrea, accelerate life
beyond all duality's struggle and strife,
consume all division between God and man,
accelerate fulfillment of God's perfect plan.

**Beloved Astrea, in oneness with you,
your circle and sword of electric blue,
with Purity's Light cutting right through,
raising the earth into all that is true.**

7. Astrea, shatter the energetic matrix that prevents open-minded scientists from using current technology and developing it to detect the individual and collective energy fields. Cut free the scientists to apply current technology with a more objective awareness and intent.

Beloved Astrea, we lovingly call,
break down separation's invisible wall,
raising our minds into true unity
with the Masters of love in Infinity.

**Beloved Astrea, in oneness with you,
your circle and sword of electric blue,
with Purity's Light cutting right through,
raising the earth into all that is true.**

8. Astrea, shatter the energetic matrix that prevents people from seeing that because fanaticism is an addiction, it must be studied based on what psychologists know about addictions, and how to help people get out of it.

Beloved Astrea, help all of us find,
the secret that we create with the mind,
and thus what in ignorance we decreate,
in knowledge we easily can recreate.

**Beloved Astrea, in oneness with you,
your circle and sword of electric blue,
with Purity's Light cutting right through,
raising the earth into all that is true.**

9. Astrea, shatter the energetic matrix that prevents people from seeing that we need to develop programs that could help people overcome the fanatical mindset.

Beloved Astrea, we all do aspire,
to learning to use your purity's fire,
to raise every form in infamy sown,
as Saint Germain makes this planet his own.

**Beloved Astrea, in oneness with you,
your circle and sword of electric blue,
with Purity's Light cutting right through,
raising the earth into all that is true.**

Part 3

1. Astrea, shatter the energetic matrix that prevents people from seeing that there is a collective emotional body, a planetary emotional body, and all people are tied to it.

Beloved Astrea, your heart is so true,
your Circle and Sword of white and blue,

cut all life free from dramas unwise,
on wings of Purity our planet will rise.

Beloved Astrea, in oneness with you,
your circle and sword of electric blue,
with Purity's Light cutting right through,
raising the earth into all that is true.

2. Astrea, shatter the energetic matrix that prevents people from seeing that the idea that people are separated, that there is a separation in space, is an illusion that comes from a certain perspective, a certain level of consciousness.

Beloved Astrea, in God Purity,
accelerate all of our life energy,
we're rising beyond every impurity,
as Purity's Light forever we see.

Beloved Astrea, in oneness with you,
your circle and sword of electric blue,
with Purity's Light cutting right through,
raising the earth into all that is true.

3. Astrea, shatter the energetic matrix that prevents people from seeing that everything is interconnected and one of the ways that all people are interconnected is through the collective emotional body.

Beloved Astrea, from Purity's Ray,
send forth deliverance to all life today,
acceleration to Purity, we are now free
from all that is less than love's Purity.

Beloved Astrea, in oneness with you,
your circle and sword of electric blue,
with Purity's Light cutting right through,
raising the earth into all that is true.

4. Astrea, shatter the energetic matrix that prevents people from seeing that when we in the democratic nations begin to raise ourselves above the

fanatical mindset, then we will stop giving energy to the energetic beings in the collective emotional body.

> Beloved Astrea, accelerate us all,
> as for your deliverance we fervently call,
> set all life free from vision impure
> beyond fear and doubt, we're rising for sure.

> **Beloved Astrea, in oneness with you,**
> **your circle and sword of electric blue,**
> **with Purity's Light cutting right through,**
> **raising the earth into all that is true.**

5. Astrea, shatter the energetic matrix that prevents people from seeing that as we feed them less energy, they have less power to take over the emotional bodies of other people. When we in the democratic nations raise our awareness, we will also raise up the people in Muslim countries or other areas around the world.

> Beloved Astrea, we're willing to see,
> all of the lies that keep us unfree,
> we surrender all lies causing the fall,
> forever affirming the oneness of All.

> **Beloved Astrea, in oneness with you,**
> **your circle and sword of electric blue,**
> **with Purity's Light cutting right through,**
> **raising the earth into all that is true.**

6. Astrea, shatter the energetic matrix that prevents people from seeing that the emotional body of the planet is like a piece of cloth. We can pull up one corner, and eventually raise the entire cloth.

> Beloved Astrea, accelerate life
> beyond all duality's struggle and strife,
> consume all division between God and man,
> accelerate fulfillment of God's perfect plan.

Beloved Astrea, in oneness with you,
your circle and sword of electric blue,
with Purity's Light cutting right through,
raising the earth into all that is true.

7. Astrea, shatter the energetic matrix that prevents people from seeing that it is possible for people in the western nations to remove the emotional, aggressive force, those aggressive beings in the emotional body that are the emotional cause behind fanaticism.

Beloved Astrea, we lovingly call,
break down separation's invisible wall,
raising our minds into true unity
with the Masters of love in Infinity.

Beloved Astrea, in oneness with you,
your circle and sword of electric blue,
with Purity's Light cutting right through,
raising the earth into all that is true.

8. Astrea, shatter the energetic matrix that prevents people from seeing that when the emotional pull is reduced, then the people who are now totally immersed in the fanatical mindset will be able to wake up and start coming out of it.

Beloved Astrea, help all of us find,
the secret that we create with the mind,
and thus what in ignorance we decreate,
in knowledge we easily can recreate.

Beloved Astrea, in oneness with you,
your circle and sword of electric blue,
with Purity's Light cutting right through,
raising the earth into all that is true.

9. Astrea, shatter the energetic matrix that prevents people from seeing that the very fact that democracies could emerge shows that people had begun a collective process of raising themselves above this lower state of consciousness that they were in during the Middle Ages.

Beloved Astrea, we all do aspire,
to learning to use your purity's fire,
to raise every form in infamy sown,
as Saint Germain makes this planet his own.

Beloved Astrea, in oneness with you,
your circle and sword of electric blue,
with Purity's Light cutting right through,
raising the earth into all that is true.

Part 4

1. Astrea, shatter the energetic matrix that prevents people from seeing that we can raise ourselves above the influence from the collective emotional realm by raising our awareness, by using conscious willpower.

Beloved Astrea, your heart is so true,
your Circle and Sword of white and blue,
cut all life free from dramas unwise,
on wings of Purity our planet will rise.

Beloved Astrea, in oneness with you,
your circle and sword of electric blue,
with Purity's Light cutting right through,
raising the earth into all that is true.

2. Astrea, shatter the energetic matrix that prevents people from seeing that this is a slow process. Even in the western democracies, many people still have addictions, which demonstrates that they have a tie to the collective emotional body.

Beloved Astrea, in God Purity,
accelerate all of our life energy,
we're rising beyond every impurity,
as Purity's Light forever we see.

Beloved Astrea, in oneness with you,
your circle and sword of electric blue,
with Purity's Light cutting right through,
raising the earth into all that is true.

3. Astrea, shatter the energetic matrix that prevents people from seeing that the more conscious we become of a problem, the more power we have to do something about it. I call forth the shift to an energetic worldview so it becomes self-evident to most people that energy is the underlying reality.

Beloved Astrea, from Purity's Ray,
send forth deliverance to all life today,
acceleration to Purity, we are now free
from all that is less than love's Purity.

Beloved Astrea, in oneness with you,
your circle and sword of electric blue,
with Purity's Light cutting right through,
raising the earth into all that is true.

4. Astrea, shatter the energetic matrix that prevents people from seeing that materialistic psychology has not been very effective in dealing with addictions. They do not have the knowledge that an addiction is tied to an openness to the collective emotional body.

Beloved Astrea, accelerate us all,
as for your deliverance we fervently call,
set all life free from vision impure
beyond fear and doubt, we're rising for sure.

Beloved Astrea, in oneness with you,
your circle and sword of electric blue,
with Purity's Light cutting right through,
raising the earth into all that is true.

5. Astrea, shatter the energetic matrix that prevents people from seeing that it is contradictory that Einstein's theory of relativity says everything is energy, but nobody is willing to apply it and realize that this opens up many possibilities for improving life at the energetic level.

Beloved Astrea, we're willing to see,
all of the lies that keep us unfree,
we surrender all lies causing the fall,
forever affirming the oneness of All.

Beloved Astrea, in oneness with you,
your circle and sword of electric blue,
with Purity's Light cutting right through,
raising the earth into all that is true.

6. Astrea, shatter the energetic matrix that prevents people from seeing that people's emotional bodies can be vulnerable to an influence from the outside. Therefore, in order to treat addiction and many other mental illnesses, we need to deal with the emotional body.

Beloved Astrea, accelerate life
beyond all duality's struggle and strife,
consume all division between God and man,
accelerate fulfillment of God's perfect plan.

Beloved Astrea, in oneness with you,
your circle and sword of electric blue,
with Purity's Light cutting right through,
raising the earth into all that is true.

7. Astrea, shatter the energetic matrix that prevents people from seeing that we need to teach people how to seal their emotional bodies from the influence of these fear-based beings who need to steal energy from people.

Beloved Astrea, we lovingly call,
break down separation's invisible wall,
raising our minds into true unity
with the Masters of love in Infinity.

Beloved Astrea, in oneness with you,
your circle and sword of electric blue,
with Purity's Light cutting right through,
raising the earth into all that is true.

8. Astrea, shatter the energetic matrix that prevents people from seeing that the real currency in the world is energy. It is not about money. It is really about who has the most energy.

> Beloved Astrea, help all of us find,
> the secret that we create with the mind,
> and thus what in ignorance we decreate,
> in knowledge we easily can recreate.

> **Beloved Astrea, in oneness with you,**
> **your circle and sword of electric blue,**
> **with Purity's Light cutting right through,**
> **raising the earth into all that is true.**

9. Astrea, shatter the energetic matrix that prevents people from seeing that dictatorial leaders must also steal people's energy in order to expand and maintain their power.

> Beloved Astrea, we all do aspire,
> to learning to use your purity's fire,
> to raise every form in infamy sown,
> as Saint Germain makes this planet his own.

> **Beloved Astrea, in oneness with you,**
> **your circle and sword of electric blue,**
> **with Purity's Light cutting right through,**
> **raising the earth into all that is true.**

Sealing

In the name of the I AM THAT I AM, I accept that Archangel Michael, Astrea and Shiva form an impenetrable shield around myself and all constructive people, sealing us from all fear-based energies in all four octaves. I accept that the Light of God is consuming and transforming all fear-based energies that make up the dark forces working against ending the era of fanaticism on earth!

21 | INVOKING FREEDOM FROM THE ADDICTION OF FANATICISM (PART 2)

In the name of the I AM THAT I AM, Jesus Christ, I use the authority that I have as a being in embodiment on earth to call upon Elohim Astrea to reinforce my calls and use my chakras to project the statements in this invocation into the collective consciousness and set people free from the addiction of fanaticism. Awaken people to the reality that we are spiritual beings and that we can co-create a new future by working with the ascended masters. I especially call for ...

[Make your own calls here.]

Part 1

1. Astrea, shatter the energetic matrix that prevents people from seeing that by killing, torturing and imprisoning people, their emotional bodies are forced open and energy is extracted from them.

Beloved Astrea, your heart is so true,
your Circle and Sword of white and blue,

cut all life free from dramas unwise,
on wings of Purity our planet will rise.

**Beloved Astrea, in oneness with you,
your circle and sword of electric blue,
with Purity's Light cutting right through,
raising the earth into all that is true.**

2. Astrea, shatter the energetic matrix that prevents people from seeing that Hitler, Stalin and Mao all created a pool of energy that expanded their power and kept them in power until it ran out.

Beloved Astrea, in God Purity,
accelerate all of our life energy,
we're rising beyond every impurity,
as Purity's Light forever we see.

**Beloved Astrea, in oneness with you,
your circle and sword of electric blue,
with Purity's Light cutting right through,
raising the earth into all that is true.**

3. Astrea, shatter the energetic matrix that prevents people from seeing that a dictator can use this energy to create a personality cult and hypnotizing the people to follow him.

Beloved Astrea, from Purity's Ray,
send forth deliverance to all life today,
acceleration to Purity, we are now free
from all that is less than love's Purity.

**Beloved Astrea, in oneness with you,
your circle and sword of electric blue,
with Purity's Light cutting right through,
raising the earth into all that is true.**

4. Astrea, shatter the energetic matrix that prevents the Chinese people from saying: "Why are we even bothering, trying to uphold the illusion

that we are communist when in reality, we are more capitalist than the decadent West."

Beloved Astrea, accelerate us all,
as for your deliverance we fervently call,
set all life free from vision impure
beyond fear and doubt, we're rising for sure.

**Beloved Astrea, in oneness with you,
your circle and sword of electric blue,
with Purity's Light cutting right through,
raising the earth into all that is true.**

5. Astrea, shatter the energetic matrix that prevents people from seeing that when we are trapped in cognitive dissonance, holding viewpoints that are mutually exclusive or incompatible, it is because there is an opening in the emotional body.

Beloved Astrea, we're willing to see,
all of the lies that keep us unfree,
we surrender all lies causing the fall,
forever affirming the oneness of All.

**Beloved Astrea, in oneness with you,
your circle and sword of electric blue,
with Purity's Light cutting right through,
raising the earth into all that is true.**

6. Astrea, shatter the energetic matrix that prevents people from seeing that there is an influx of a certain fear-based emotional energy and this pulls on our conscious minds, pulling us into certain emotions. This prevents us from having the clarity in the mental body to see the incompatibility of our beliefs.

Beloved Astrea, accelerate life
beyond all duality's struggle and strife,
consume all division between God and man,
accelerate fulfillment of God's perfect plan.

**Beloved Astrea, in oneness with you,
your circle and sword of electric blue,
with Purity's Light cutting right through,
raising the earth into all that is true.**

7. Astrea, shatter the energetic matrix that prevents people from seeing that the more radical people become, the more their minds are taken over by hatred. Their energy fields have an influx of hatred energy from beings in the collective emotional body.

Beloved Astrea, we lovingly call,
break down separation's invisible wall,
raising our minds into true unity
with the Masters of love in Infinity.

**Beloved Astrea, in oneness with you,
your circle and sword of electric blue,
with Purity's Light cutting right through,
raising the earth into all that is true.**

8. Astrea, shatter the energetic matrix that prevents people from seeing that when the conscious attention of people is pulled into hatred, they are so focused on this hatred that they cannot rise up to the mental body. They cannot connect to their normal intelligence and see that some of the beliefs they hold are incompatible.

Beloved Astrea, help all of us find,
the secret that we create with the mind,
and thus what in ignorance we decreate,
in knowledge we easily can recreate.

**Beloved Astrea, in oneness with you,
your circle and sword of electric blue,
with Purity's Light cutting right through,
raising the earth into all that is true.**

9. Astrea, shatter the energetic matrix that prevents people from seeing that when people are in the fanatical mindset, their emotional bodies are so

chaotic, they are so taken over by this influx of energy from the collective emotional body, that they cannot think clearly.

> Beloved Astrea, we all do aspire,
> to learning to use your purity's fire,
> to raise every form in infamy sown,
> as Saint Germain makes this planet his own.

> **Beloved Astrea, in oneness with you,**
> **your circle and sword of electric blue,**
> **with Purity's Light cutting right through,**
> **raising the earth into all that is true.**

Part 2

1. Astrea, shatter the energetic matrix that prevents people from seeing that fanatics cannot see what they are really believing, they cannot see the contradictions and incompatibilities.

> Beloved Astrea, your heart is so true,
> your Circle and Sword of white and blue,
> cut all life free from dramas unwise,
> on wings of Purity our planet will rise.

> **Beloved Astrea, in oneness with you,**
> **your circle and sword of electric blue,**
> **with Purity's Light cutting right through,**
> **raising the earth into all that is true.**

2. Astrea, shatter the energetic matrix that prevents people from seeing that fanatics cannot see that the ends can never justify the means, or at least they cannot see that neither the Koran nor the New Testament can justify a philosophy that the ends can justify the means.

> Beloved Astrea, in God Purity,
> accelerate all of our life energy,

we're rising beyond every impurity,
as Purity's Light forever we see.

**Beloved Astrea, in oneness with you,
your circle and sword of electric blue,
with Purity's Light cutting right through,
raising the earth into all that is true.**

3. Astrea, shatter the energetic matrix that prevents people from seeing that it is not because they are not intelligent enough to see it, but because their conscious minds are pulled away from the mental body and into the emotional body, focused on hatred, the sense of urgency, the sense that something needs to be done now to these terrible people who are threatening God's plan for the universe.

Beloved Astrea, from Purity's Ray,
send forth deliverance to all life today,
acceleration to Purity, we are now free
from all that is less than love's Purity.

**Beloved Astrea, in oneness with you,
your circle and sword of electric blue,
with Purity's Light cutting right through,
raising the earth into all that is true.**

4. Astrea, shatter the energetic matrix that prevents people from seeing that this is as much an addiction as a person who can only worry about how to get the next bottle of alcohol and will do anything to get it.

Beloved Astrea, accelerate us all,
as for your deliverance we fervently call,
set all life free from vision impure
beyond fear and doubt, we're rising for sure.

**Beloved Astrea, in oneness with you,
your circle and sword of electric blue,
with Purity's Light cutting right through,
raising the earth into all that is true.**

5. Astrea, shatter the energetic matrix that prevents people from seeing that fanatics are not rational, we cannot reason with them. We could reason with them if their emotional bodies were not in such turmoil.

> Beloved Astrea, we're willing to see,
> all of the lies that keep us unfree,
> we surrender all lies causing the fall,
> forever affirming the oneness of All.

> **Beloved Astrea, in oneness with you,**
> **your circle and sword of electric blue,**
> **with Purity's Light cutting right through,**
> **raising the earth into all that is true.**

6. Astrea, shatter the energetic matrix that prevents people from seeing that the first step towards changing the situation is to change the equation at the emotional level and then we have other options.

> Beloved Astrea, accelerate life
> beyond all duality's struggle and strife,
> consume all division between God and man,
> accelerate fulfillment of God's perfect plan.

> **Beloved Astrea, in oneness with you,**
> **your circle and sword of electric blue,**
> **with Purity's Light cutting right through,**
> **raising the earth into all that is true.**

7. Astrea, shatter the energetic matrix that prevents people from seeing that as long as people are in this hypnotized state of mind, we cannot do anything with them. We cannot even have a conversation with these people, and therefore, we need to change the equation at the emotional level.

> Beloved Astrea, we lovingly call,
> break down separation's invisible wall,
> raising our minds into true unity
> with the Masters of love in Infinity.

Beloved Astrea, in oneness with you,
your circle and sword of electric blue,
with Purity's Light cutting right through,
raising the earth into all that is true.

8. Astrea, shatter the energetic matrix that prevents people from seeing that once we have knowledge, we are empowered. By making a shift, we see that there is something that the modern democracies can do about fanaticism, but it must start at home. It must start by removing the fanaticism in our own societies.

Beloved Astrea, help all of us find,
the secret that we create with the mind,
and thus what in ignorance we decreate,
in knowledge we easily can recreate.

Beloved Astrea, in oneness with you,
your circle and sword of electric blue,
with Purity's Light cutting right through,
raising the earth into all that is true.

9. Astrea, shatter the energetic matrix that prevents people from seeing that everything is interconnected. At the energetic level, there is no separation. Space at the energetic level does not mean separation because everything is connected.

Beloved Astrea, we all do aspire,
to learning to use your purity's fire,
to raise every form in infamy sown,
as Saint Germain makes this planet his own.

Beloved Astrea, in oneness with you,
your circle and sword of electric blue,
with Purity's Light cutting right through,
raising the earth into all that is true.

Part 3

1. Astrea, shatter the energetic matrix that prevents people from seeing that all people are connected and that everything interacts and that everything influences everything else.

> Beloved Astrea, your heart is so true,
> your Circle and Sword of white and blue,
> cut all life free from dramas unwise,
> on wings of Purity our planet will rise.

> **Beloved Astrea, in oneness with you,**
> **your circle and sword of electric blue,**
> **with Purity's Light cutting right through,**
> **raising the earth into all that is true.**

2. Astrea, shatter the energetic matrix that prevents people from seeing that if the western democracies really wanted to make an effort to remove fanaticism, we would have to start at home and say: What are the elements in our societies that are reinforcing the collective pool of energy and these energetic beings in the emotional body that are causing fanaticism?

> Beloved Astrea, in God Purity,
> accelerate all of our life energy,
> we're rising beyond every impurity,
> as Purity's Light forever we see.

> **Beloved Astrea, in oneness with you,**
> **your circle and sword of electric blue,**
> **with Purity's Light cutting right through,**
> **raising the earth into all that is true.**

3. Astrea, shatter the energetic matrix that prevents people from seeing that any kind of addiction reinforces that whole dynamic so we would have to help people in the modern democracies overcome addictions.

> Beloved Astrea, from Purity's Ray,
> send forth deliverance to all life today,

acceleration to Purity, we are now free
from all that is less than love's Purity.

Beloved Astrea, in oneness with you,
your circle and sword of electric blue,
with Purity's Light cutting right through,
raising the earth into all that is true.

4. Astrea, shatter the energetic matrix that prevents people from seeing that many people are hypnotized by something. Many elements of western culture reinforce the fanatical, addictive energy dynamic.

Beloved Astrea, accelerate us all,
as for your deliverance we fervently call,
set all life free from vision impure
beyond fear and doubt, we're rising for sure.

Beloved Astrea, in oneness with you,
your circle and sword of electric blue,
with Purity's Light cutting right through,
raising the earth into all that is true.

5. Astrea, shatter the energetic matrix that prevents people from seeing that a fanatic is a fan of some kind of ism, any kind of idea where we say, this is how the world *should* work.

Beloved Astrea, we're willing to see,
all of the lies that keep us unfree,
we surrender all lies causing the fall,
forever affirming the oneness of All.

Beloved Astrea, in oneness with you,
your circle and sword of electric blue,
with Purity's Light cutting right through,
raising the earth into all that is true.

6. Astrea, shatter the energetic matrix that prevents people from seeing that fanatics refuse to test their theory against reality by using both neutral

scientific observation and neutral intuitive observation, seeing if the theory actually fits reality.

> Beloved Astrea, accelerate life
> beyond all duality's struggle and strife,
> consume all division between God and man,
> accelerate fulfillment of God's perfect plan.

> **Beloved Astrea, in oneness with you,**
> **your circle and sword of electric blue,**
> **with Purity's Light cutting right through,**
> **raising the earth into all that is true.**

7. Astrea, shatter the energetic matrix that prevents people from seeing that if the world does not work the way our theory says it should work, then we change the theory because it is better for us that we come closer to basing our worldview on how the world actually works.

> Beloved Astrea, we lovingly call,
> break down separation's invisible wall,
> raising our minds into true unity
> with the Masters of love in Infinity.

> **Beloved Astrea, in oneness with you,**
> **your circle and sword of electric blue,**
> **with Purity's Light cutting right through,**
> **raising the earth into all that is true.**

8. Astrea, shatter the energetic matrix that prevents people from seeing that humankind has been working with shadows for all of known history. We have been looking at the shadows and based on observing the shadows, we have formulated elaborate theories and isms about what goes on outside the shadow world that we can see with our senses or scientific instruments.

> Beloved Astrea, help all of us find,
> the secret that we create with the mind,
> and thus what in ignorance we decreate,
> in knowledge we easily can recreate.

**Beloved Astrea, in oneness with you,
your circle and sword of electric blue,
with Purity's Light cutting right through,
raising the earth into all that is true.**

9. Astrea, shatter the energetic matrix that prevents people from seeing that the mindset that we can formulate an accurate theory of how the world works based on our present perception is an addiction and it is the underlying cause of fanaticism.

Beloved Astrea, we all do aspire,
to learning to use your purity's fire,
to raise every form in infamy sown,
as Saint Germain makes this planet his own.

**Beloved Astrea, in oneness with you,
your circle and sword of electric blue,
with Purity's Light cutting right through,
raising the earth into all that is true.**

Part 4

1. Astrea, shatter the energetic matrix that prevents people from seeing that we think the world should work a certain way and all we are looking for is confirmation that it does work that way. We filter out anything that goes against that.

Beloved Astrea, your heart is so true,
your Circle and Sword of white and blue,
cut all life free from dramas unwise,
on wings of Purity our planet will rise.

**Beloved Astrea, in oneness with you,
your circle and sword of electric blue,
with Purity's Light cutting right through,
raising the earth into all that is true.**

2. Astrea, shatter the energetic matrix that prevents people from see-ing that we can never overcome the illusion. We become a self-fulfilling prophecy because we only see what our theory allows us to see. We think that by having this limited view of the world, we can deduce how the world actually works.

> Beloved Astrea, in God Purity,
> accelerate all of our life energy,
> we're rising beyond every impurity,
> as Purity's Light forever we see.

> **Beloved Astrea, in oneness with you,**
> **your circle and sword of electric blue,**
> **with Purity's Light cutting right through,**
> **raising the earth into all that is true.**

3. Astrea, shatter the energetic matrix that prevents people from seeing that throughout the history of humankind, certain people have claimed that they knew the universe, but all of them have had a very limited perspective.

> Beloved Astrea, from Purity's Ray,
> send forth deliverance to all life today,
> acceleration to Purity, we are now free
> from all that is less than love's Purity.

> **Beloved Astrea, in oneness with you,**
> **your circle and sword of electric blue,**
> **with Purity's Light cutting right through,**
> **raising the earth into all that is true.**

4. Astrea, shatter the energetic matrix that prevents people from seeing that the observations are not necessarily inaccurate, but they are not the whole story.

> Beloved Astrea, accelerate us all,
> as for your deliverance we fervently call,
> set all life free from vision impure
> beyond fear and doubt, we're rising for sure.

Beloved Astrea, in oneness with you,
your circle and sword of electric blue,
with Purity's Light cutting right through,
raising the earth into all that is true.

5. Astrea, shatter the energetic matrix that prevents people from seeing that we have had an incredibly limited approach, and therefore it is unrealistic to think that we can start with such a limited perspective and deduce how the vastness of the universe functions.

Beloved Astrea, we're willing to see,
all of the lies that keep us unfree,
we surrender all lies causing the fall,
forever affirming the oneness of All.

Beloved Astrea, in oneness with you,
your circle and sword of electric blue,
with Purity's Light cutting right through,
raising the earth into all that is true.

6. Astrea, shatter the energetic matrix that prevents people from seeing that it is unfathomable that we can be stuck in this, century after century.

Beloved Astrea, accelerate life
beyond all duality's struggle and strife,
consume all division between God and man,
accelerate fulfillment of God's perfect plan.

Beloved Astrea, in oneness with you,
your circle and sword of electric blue,
with Purity's Light cutting right through,
raising the earth into all that is true.

7. Astrea, shatter the energetic matrix that prevents people from seeing that people's emotional bodies are so overwhelmed that they are literally hypnotized, they are in a state of addiction.

Beloved Astrea, we lovingly call,
break down separation's invisible wall,

raising our minds into true unity
with the Masters of love in Infinity.

Beloved Astrea, in oneness with you,
your circle and sword of electric blue,
with Purity's Light cutting right through,
raising the earth into all that is true.

8. Astrea, shatter the energetic matrix that prevents people from seeing that we are blinded by this belief that our theory gives us an accurate view of how the world functions. The only real way out is to break that hypnotic spell.

Beloved Astrea, help all of us find,
the secret that we create with the mind,
and thus what in ignorance we decreate,
in knowledge we easily can recreate.

Beloved Astrea, in oneness with you,
your circle and sword of electric blue,
with Purity's Light cutting right through,
raising the earth into all that is true.

9. Astrea, I invoke your Presence in the emotional realm, and I call for you to multiply my calls for the clearing out of the astral plane, for the breaking of this emotional, hypnotic spell that keeps people trapped in the addiction of fanaticism.

Beloved Astrea, we all do aspire,
to learning to use your purity's fire,
to raise every form in infamy sown,
as Saint Germain makes this planet his own.

Beloved Astrea, in oneness with you,
your circle and sword of electric blue,
with Purity's Light cutting right through,
raising the earth into all that is true.

Sealing

In the name of the I AM THAT I AM, I accept that Archangel Michael, Astrea and Shiva form an impenetrable shield around myself and all constructive people, sealing us from all fear-based energies in all four octaves. I accept that the Light of God is consuming and transforming all fear-based energies that make up the dark forces working against ending the era of fanaticism on earth!

22 | FANATICISM GOES AGAINST NATURE'S QUEST FOR DIVERSITY

I AM the Ascended Master Jesus Christ. My contribution to this conference is to continue on the idea of energy psychology, looking at the energy field with scientific instruments that could be developed. Now, you have an explanation problem in terms of fanaticism because if you look at history, you can see that in previous ages they had certain beliefs, such as the earth is flat and the center of the universe. At the time, they thought these beliefs were infallible, could never be expanded upon by a higher understanding. Therefore, they were fanatical, according to the basic definition of fanaticism we have given you.

You can also see from medieval Catholics that the way they conducted themselves, a very aggressive attempt to put down the first scientists, the Inquisition, the witch hunts, were clearly very, very fanatical acts. There is no way to look at these actions perpetrated by the Catholic church without admitting that this was an expression of fanaticism and the fanatical mindset. If you see that Muslim terrorists today are fanatics, then certainly you must say that medieval Catholics were fanatics, the Crusaders were fanatics, the Muslims who fought the Crusaders were fanatics, the Inquisitors were fanatics, those who rounded up witches and burned them at the stake were clearly fanatics. There is no way around this.

When you look at all of these fanatical beliefs that have been held in the past, when you look at them today, you can clearly see the inherent contradictions that are always there in fanatical beliefs. We have talked about cognitive dissonance, which is that you hold two viewpoints at the same time that are incompatible or contradictory, but you cannot see it. When you look back at these previous beliefs, you can clearly see that they had cognitive dissonance. You can clearly see that these viewpoints were incompatible or contradictory. Therefore, the question becomes: "Why couldn't people see it at the time?" You may look today at Muslim fanatics and some of the viewpoints that they hold, and you, from your perspective, can see that they have certain viewpoints that are clearly contradictory. Therefore, you must ask yourself: "Why can't they see it?"

The cause of cognitive dissonance

What you need to recognize here is that the human mind has, as we have said, a mental level, a mental aspect. This is not difficult for people in the world to recognize. You already know about the intellectual mind, intellectual thinking, logical, rational thinking, and therefore you know that the mind has a mental aspect. You need to realize here that this mental mind, this analytical mind, is actually very, very good at comparing things. Therefore, the analytical mind is very good at looking at different viewpoints, comparing them either to each other or to some kind of standard set up, and therefore the mind is very good at seeing that here are two viewpoints that are contradictory.

You have to acknowledge here that when people have this cognitive dissonance, when they hold two incompatible viewpoints, it is not because their minds are incapable of seeing the contradiction. Their analytical minds are perfectly capable of seeing the contradiction. You can look back at medieval Catholics, and you can think, as many modern people think, that they must have been less intelligent back then. But they were not, at least not in the sense that they were incapable of seeing contradictions. They *were* capable. Their minds *were* capable of seeing them. The same thing with Muslim fundamentalists today, or Christian fundamentalists, or materialist fundamentalists, or Marxist fundamentalists, or whatever you have. Their minds are fully capable of seeing the contradictions of their beliefs or the contradiction between what they claim to believe and their actions.

The reality is here that an aspect of fanaticism is the belief that the ends can justify the means. You have people who claim to believe in, for example, some religion, and let me just use the obvious example of the Christian religion where you must ask yourself: "How is it possible that Christians, on the one hand, proclaim to believe in a spiritual teacher who said: 'Do unto others. Forgive your enemies. Love your enemies. Turn the other cheek;' how is it possible for people to claim to be followers of such a spiritual leader and, at the same time, feel fully justified by God in killing other human beings? How is that possible?"

Is that not the essential cognitive dissonance you could possibly come up with on this planet: Those who claim to be following Jesus Christ but even think they are killing people in my name and thinking that I approve of this? Is there a greater example, a more drastic example, of cognitive dissonance? So how is it possible that people could do this? Surely, you cannot say that their minds were incapable of comparing the statements I made to their actions and seeing that there is no way that the example and the teachings I gave could be used to justify killing other people. Surely, their minds *could* do this. Then, you have the undeniable fact that this *did* happen, people *did* do this, and you must ask yourself why. Why was it that they had minds that were capable of seeing the contradiction, but they did not see it?

This is where you will go back to energy psychology. Surely, it is correct, as Astrea said, that in many cases people were pulled into these strong emotions of anger and hatred so that their conscious minds could not even really connect to the intellectual level. There is more to it than that, because what Astrea also said was that people's emotional bodies were overwhelmed by an influx of energy, aggressive energy, from the collective emotional body. You could actually develop scientific instruments that would allow you to see, even in a graphic way (and illustrate in a graphic way) that there is also a collective mental body. You would be able to measure and see that people who are in the fanatical mindset, they have openings in their mental bodies to this collective mental body, and there is an influx of a very, very aggressive energy into these people's mental bodies.

It is this energy that creates, not the turmoil you see in the emotional body, but it creates almost a veil, a fog, a wall, in the mind that people cannot see through, cannot see beyond. If you could see this, as of course *we* can see it and as of course intuitive people will be able to see it, then you would realize that this is actually the only explanation for this phenomenon of cognitive dissonance. People's mental bodies, on an individual level, have been invaded by a very aggressive energy that creates a veil. In the simplest form you could say you have one belief on the right, you have another belief on the left, and there is a veil in between so that the person's intellectual mind cannot see both beliefs at the same time.

The veil in the mental mind

It is almost like you could have the illustration that you had a curtain in the middle of this room, and you could not see out both sides of the windows at the same time. In order to see out one side, you would have to go around the curtain, and then you could not see the other side. That is what happens in people's mental bodies. There is a veil that prevents them from seeing both viewpoints at the same time. Therefore, they cannot use the analytical mind to compare them and see the incompatibility. What people end up doing is that they switch back and forth. At some point, they can be on the one side of the veil, and now they see that: "Oh, Jesus was such a loving teacher, and he told us to love our neighbor as ourselves." Then, very quickly some people can switch, go on the other side of the veil, and now they believe Jesus wants them to go out and kill all non-believers. This is what you actually saw in some of the Inquisitors, some of the Crusaders. You saw this kind of switch, and they did not realize that they were switching. They did not realize the incompatibility of their beliefs. This is what you will see in all fanatics around the world, especially when you have people that come to the point where they are willing to kill other human beings in order to further what they see as an epically important cause. They simply cannot see it.

This brings up a topic that is another explanation problem that society has. What you see that psychologists and philosophers are grappling with is that when you look at human history, and you look at some of these manifestations of wars and atrocities, you are wondering: "How is it possible that something like this could happen? How could people do these kind of things?" You have the statement that the road to hell is paved with good intentions because people have seen that the people who are committing atrocities, in most cases they feel justified in doing this, and they feel they are doing it for some greater cause.

Now, *I* would say that the road to hell is not paved with *good* intentions. It is paved with *fanatical* intentions. Because people have gone into this fanatical mindset where they cannot see that their intentions are not actually good, or they cannot see that perhaps their intentions are good, but their actions are not. They cannot see that maybe they actually have a correct view of *what* should ideally happen, but they do not have the correct view of *how* to accomplish it without killing other people.

Evil is not part of human nature

What this leads to is that many psychologists and philosophers have drawn the conclusion: We see throughout history how human beings have committed atrocities against each other. This means that this kind of evil and aggression is just part of human nature. It is simply human nature. Evil is a potential that lies latent in all people. Now, we run into the limitations of the materialist worldview because they cannot come any further in an explanation of this phenomenon. They can only claim that this is human nature.

This leads to other explanation problems. Because do you see in the animal kingdom this kind of evil, this kind of atrocity? Obviously, you do not. If this is human nature, and if humans are evolved from animals, where did evil come from in the human? It is obviously not a gradual evolution of something you see in animals so how did it suddenly pop up in human beings when it has never been there in any animal species? This is where so far we have attempted to give you explanations of fanaticism that we evaluate that people in the mainstream could actually come to accept within a relatively short period of time.

Now, we have sort of reached the limitations of that approach because, as I said, there is no way that people with the common worldview they have today can come to understand this. That is where, if you want to understand it, you need to go beyond and realize that evil as such is not part of human nature. It is something that people can be pulled into doing through the fanatical mindset and the cognitive dissonance where they do not see the incompatibility between their beliefs and their actions.

Therefore, we must make a very important conclusion here. You can see throughout history how many, many people have been pulled into fanatical actions, committing atrocities based on a fanatical mindset, but the vast majority of these people have not been evil. You may look at the Holocaust, and you may see it as the quintessential example of human evil. You may look at some of the German soldiers and even the leaders who committed these actions, and you may think, as many people have done, that these people must have been evil, but the reality is these people were not evil.

They had been pulled into the fanatical mindset. They could not see what they were doing. The commandant of Auschwitz lived close to the camp with his family. During the day, he would oversee this massive factory of death that killed thousands of children, but after a hard day of work, he would go home to his family and be the ideal family father, playing with his children. He could not see the incompatibility in killing children during the day and playing with his own children at night. He could not see that children are children, and that the ones in the camp were just as much children and just as much humans as his own.

He was not an evil man. You cannot come up with any standard or definition that made this man evil. He was simply blinded by fanaticism, blinded to an almost unbelievable degree, but nevertheless blinded by fanaticism. If you could just see the soul of many of these Nazi leaders, you would see that they are not evil. Today, many of them are full of regret of what they did and seeking to compensate for it or to raise themselves above it. They are not evil lifestreams.

The origin of evil

This then leads us to the question: Where does evil come from? There is no explanation in the materialist mindset, in a materialist worldview. Now, you could say that in some religions, including Christianity, they could have what approaches an explanation because they do talk about the devil and dark forces and demons that can take over people. Many Christians have of course seen this as an explanation for human evil. But it is not the *full* explanation.

We have attempted to give you a much fuller explanation by talking about fallen beings that are in a fundamental way different from what you normally consider human beings. Therefore, we can say that Hitler was a fundamentally different being from many of the leaders of the Nazi regime. Not all of them because certain of the others were fallen beings as well. This of course we do not expect that the general public will begin to recognize in the near future, but it is necessary to have the perspective for yourselves that evil is not part of human nature.

There are many, many people throughout the ages who have felt, as even Mother Teresa used to say, that we all have a little Hitler inside of us, but it just is not true. *It just is not true.* It is not correct to say that Hitler was a more extreme version of what all human beings could become. You cannot go out and take any person off the street and put that person through some kind of program and turn them into a Hitler. You can do that with *some* people in the sense that you can put them in the fanatical mindset. The German Nazi regime certainly proved very effective in doing this, taking ordinary people and putting them through this machine, putting them through a certain discipline, a certain propaganda machine, putting a uniform on them, and putting them in a situation where they either had to follow orders or be shot as traitors. You could see a few of the guards in Auschwitz who displayed certain sadistic tendencies and ended up enjoying what they were doing, and they did not need to be forced to do it. But many others just did it because they did not want to get shot for treason, or they did not want to go to the Eastern Front and get shot there.

What you realize here is that you can *force* people to commit evil acts, but you cannot force them to envision, to plan, to plot those evil acts like Hitler did. There were people who followed Hitler, but they could never, *ever* have risen to the point of plotting the evil that he plotted. It simply is impossible. He was a fundamentally different being than most of the human beings on earth.

Most people are not evil

It is important for you as spiritual people to recognize that in yourself. You will actually see that last year, as this messenger was driving to the conference here in Holland, he was in conversation, found himself saying: "With all the psychological work I've done on myself, I've never seen anything evil in my being." He was surprised by this because he was also brought up with this idea that all human beings had the potential to become evil and commit evil acts. He realized that in his long history on this planet he had not crossed that line, and you need to all realize the same. You have not in past lives, despite what you might have been pulled into, you have not crossed that line of becoming evil and doing something evil.

It is important for you to be willing to recognize this so that you can see that your mental body has also been invaded, or you have had it projected into you from the collective mental body, this very subtle doubt about whether you could be evil and you could do some of these terrible things, or have done some of these terrible things in past lives. You need to recognize that this projection has caused the formation of a separate self. You need to be willing to look at this, see it as a separate self, come to the point of view where you have separated yourself from it, and you can then let it die. There is no constructive reason why a spiritual student should hold on to this doubt about yourself—absolutely none.

Nature proves diversity is the key to survival

Now, let me step back and take a slightly different approach. Saint Germain talked about the biological perspective on fanaticism so let me build on that. Let us take the concept of evolution. There is a gradual evolutionary process in nature that has been going on for a very, very long time. It has brought forth more and more species, more and more complex species, supposedly culminating in human beings.

If you step back and look at this neutrally, you can see something that materialists have not been able to see. The reason they have not been able to see it is of course that their approach to evolution and studying the phenomenon of evolution has been to disprove religion. Since Darwin came out with his theory of evolution, materialists have jumped on it because they saw it as their primary weapon against religion. This has blinded them because again if you could look at these materialists, these very intellectual people, you would see that they have a veil in their mental bodies. Their mental bodies have been invaded by this aggressive energy from the collective mental realm, and they simply cannot see certain things.

Let us look at this gradual evolutionary process. What does it show us? Well, first of all, it shows us that life has a tremendous force that moves through all obstacles, moves around all obstacles. Somehow, life finds a way to adapt to all kinds of extreme conditions. How does it do this? By creating life forms that are more and more adaptable. We have said it before: If you look at animal species, the vast majority of animal species are specifically adapted to a particular environment, but the supposedly most advanced animal species on the planet, Homo Sapiens, can live in almost any environment on the planet. That shows you what? It does not show you that human beings are the most fit, meaning the most aggressive. It shows you that human beings are the most fit because they are the most adaptable. They can adapt to all kinds of conditions. What is adaptability based on? It is based on diversity, the ability to adapt to diverse conditions. What makes the human race survivable from an evolutionary, biological viewpoint? It is *diversity*. Not only in a physical sense, but in a psychological sense. There are people who can adapt psychologically so they can live under some very specific conditions that other people could not handle living in, from a psychological perspective. You can look at some of the native peoples, from the Eskimos in Greenland to the Aborigines in Australia, and you can see how they have psychologically adapted to living in this very harsh environment that forces them into a very specific lifestyle. Then, you could take the typical Westerner in the western democracies and put him in an igloo on the inland ice on Greenland, and the first thing he would say is: "What—no Internet?" Just because of that, he or she would not be able to adapt.

Even having people from the modern democracies considering living that kind of a lifestyle, they would not be able to handle it psychologically. You see here that what actually, from a biological viewpoint, makes the human species so successful is this adaptability, the diversity you see in the human race. Not *only* physical, but you see also some physical adaptability where some people have darker skin so they can handle living in an area with more sun and other conditions like that. First of all, what makes the human race successful from an evolutionary survivability standpoint is the psychological diversity that you see.

Fanaticism is not a survival strategy

Now, take this and look at fanaticism. What is it that fanaticism attempts to do? It attempts to suppress diversity. There is one group of people who believe they have some absolute view of how the universe should work, how a society should function. They believe that if only everybody would accept their view and live accordingly, then you would have paradise on earth. As we have explained to you, this is not the case. We have explained about previous civilizations that had attempted to create harmony through squashing diversity, suppressing diversity, creating sameness and conformity.

You can even look at this from a purely biological standpoint, and you can see that it is only diversity that creates success. Why is that? Well, because as we have said, the process of evolution is actually a process of experimentation. Does it work? Can a species survive? If it does not, then evolution goes in another direction but often building on the previous. Do you not see that the whole idea of evolution is that you start out with certain life forms that gradually evolve into other life forms and still other life forms, so you are not starting from ground zero every time? This is the whole idea of evolution.

The primary weapon they used against the biblical version of instant creation is that things have evolved gradually, building on each other. You could say that once you recognize that there must be a conscious evaluation behind evolution, you could say that the experiences gained from developing amoeba led to multi-celled organisms, that then led to the first species in the ocean, that eventually led to fish, that eventually led to mammals, and so forth. There is a clear progression. If you think that evolution is a completely unconscious process that is driven by these random genetic mutations, there is no way to explain that evolution does not start from ground zero with every species. It builds upon the previous species. How are you going to explain this from a materialist viewpoint? *You cannot.* The materialists of course will not see this, and why will they not? Because they have cognitive dissonance. They have a veil in their mental bodies. They cannot see that this is incompatible. This is a contradiction in Darwin's view of evolution.

What you realize here is that the very key to the survivability of the human race and any society is diversification. The very idea that you could create a thousand-year kingdom that was based on a particular philosophy that did not change for a thousand years, this very idea is completely out of touch with reality, as you can see by observing biological evolution. Nothing can last forever. Conditions will constantly change on earth. If there is one constant on earth, the only constant is constant change.

The idea that you could formulate a religion, such as Christianity, and that you could base a society on this, and this society could survive without changing its basic paradigm, is cognitive dissonance. Why cannot people see it? Again, the veil, but it is very possible that with your calls more and more people can come to see this. They can come to see that part of the intellectual appeal of many fanatical ideas (ideas that you clearly today see as fanatical) is precisely this dream that one day we will have the ideal society where everybody can agree because they all believe the same.

Diversity is the keystone of democracy

This is a very old dream that goes very far back in history, much further than known history. You can come to see that this is just an illusion, and it is an illusion that throughout the ages has, more than any other, encouraged fanaticism. Because now you think it becomes so important to either force people to accept your beliefs or to kill those people.

As we have said, killing people, killing your own species, clearly goes against the basic principle of nature and the principle of survivability. You do not kill your own species if you want your species to survive. Therefore, from nature you are programmed *not* to kill other human beings. Your bodies, your instincts, are programmed. This goes against it.

What also goes against nature is this idea of suppressing diversity because nature clearly demonstrates that diversity or diversification is the key to survival and adaptability. You could also look at it another way and say: When you have conformity and lack of diversity, what are you? You are rigid, you are inflexible, you are standing still. When you have the willingness to adapt, you are not rigid, you are not standing still, you are flowing. You are willing to flow and change with changing conditions, adapting to them, making the best of them, and therefore you can survive.

This is what you see in human societies. The Roman Empire came to a point where it could not transcend itself so it collapsed. The Catholic empire of the Middle Ages came to a point where it could not transcend itself and adapt so it lost most of its influence. The Soviet Union, Japan, ancient China, ancient Egypt, many of these ancient civilizations that you look at and consider great civilizations. You look at the temples and the pyramids they have built around the world, and you see that it must have been a great and greatly organized civilization to build such incredible monuments with the primitive tools they had. Nevertheless, they are gone, they have disappeared. Why? Because they could not adapt. They could not transcend themselves.

Now, some of them have disappeared because they did transcend themselves and the civilization morphed into something else. Many of them have simply collapsed and disappeared because they were so rigid that they could not adapt to certain changes. Therefore, you can look at your modern democracies and say: "Well, if we want to survive, what do we need to do? We need to diversify. We need to make sure we are not rigid." That means: (1) You need to question the materialistic paradigm. (2) You need to move towards the direct democracy where you diversify the decision process. Instead of having a small elite make the decisions, even if it is elected by the people, you are having all of the people, with all of the diversity there is in your population, make the important decisions. You need to realize that the more diversity you have in your population, the better decisions that population will be able to make. Diversity is not a threat. This is what the modern democracies are very close to recognizing, and it is very, very logical. How did you ever come to have democracies? Well, it was because you overcame the lack of diversity that was there in the feudal societies where a small elite made all of the decisions. You diversify the decision-making process by creating a democracy. What we are saying here is not that you need to change democracy in a fundamental way. You just need to take the next logical step in the democratization process where there is another level of diversification of the decision-making process.

The original intent behind Christianity

Now, I could of course go on for an indefinite period of time here because there are so many things to say. What I would like to focus a little bit on is Christianity as a religion. What did I attempt to do 2,000 years ago? I attempted to create a spiritual movement that would be different from the dominant religion that was there in Israel, the mainstream Jewish church of the time. What was that church based on? Exactly the same: squashing diversity. Look at the entire Jewish culture, the entire Jewish mindset, going back to the first records in the Old Testament. The Jewish people are very, very rigid, very, very focused on outer rituals where everything is ritualized, and I can assure you it was 2,000 years ago as well. This was simply a lack of diversity.

The reason why I chose to embody in that region of the world was not that it was a holy land, but that it had such a low tolerance for diversity. Now, if you look at my teachings based on this perspective, you can see: What did I attempt to do? I attempted to create a shift in the Jewish population, but also to set an example that went beyond the Jews, of the need to diversify. Look at some of my parables, the parable of the Good Samaritan. The Jews would not help the man, but the Samaritan would. The Samaritan was an outcast in Jewish society, and the Jews looked down upon the Samaritans. It was only through diversity that this man received help. If everybody that came by had been Jews, he would have died on the road, but because there was diversity, instead of sameness, somebody was willing to do what others were not willing to do.

I also showed that, on a greater scale, the real problem on earth is that most people are stuck in a certain mindset where they cannot see beyond a certain veil. I came to give an example and a teaching that could jolt people out of their traditional way of thinking and reach a more diverse level of thinking, which is what we today call Christ discernment, or the vision of Christ, where they could see that there was a higher perspective. You see so many of my statements: "He who is without sin amongst you, let him cast the first stone," "The kingdom of God is within you," many of my statements are meant to jolt people out of their conformist way of thinking into seeing that there are other ways to look at things than the way we have been brought up to look at them.

Therefore, you could say that in its essence Christianity was meant to be a movement that encouraged the diversification of thought. The mental aspect of Christianity was to encourage the diversification of thought so that people could come to see what they could not see now. They could see different perspectives, different possibilities. They could see, for example, that it was in their own best interest to do unto others what you want them to do to you because all people are connected. If you are doing something to others, sooner or later that will come back to you because the cosmic mirror will reflect back to you what you are doing to others.

By transcending this willingness to look at what is your short-term interests and needs, and looking at a greater perspective, you can see it is enlightened self-interest to treat other people well. Many other aspects of this, but my entire purpose was to create a movement that would bring more diversity of thought. What did instead happen? From the moment of the formation of the Roman Catholic church, Christianity became turned into a movement that did everything it could to suppress the diversification of thought and create uniformity of thought and belief among all people. Those that would not conform to the Christian doctrines, well, they should be either killed by the Crusaders or burned at the stake or tortured in the Inquisition's torture chambers. It was suddenly of epic importance to create uniformity of thought, in complete contradiction to what I actually intended. You see again that this is clearly fanaticism. You see it is not survivable in the long run because it goes against one of the basic principles of nature: diversification.

With this, I have completed what I wanted to give you in this installment. I am grateful for your attention, for your willingness to be here and wrestle with this, quite frankly, very difficult topic of fanaticism that many, many people are reluctant to even look at. You can look at the western democracies and you can see how, after these nations were confronted with the outburst of fanaticism in 9/11 and forward, how many, many people have simply refused to even consider this. They have refused to even look at it, look at the deeper cause, look at: "Do we have elements of it, and is there something we could do to change the equation by changing ourselves?"

Why is it that they do not want to look at it? Well, it is because they feel powerless to do something about it. Why do they feel powerless? Because in their mental bodies, mental minds, there is a veil that prevents them from seeing the incompatibility of their own viewpoints. You feel powerless when you have these incompatible beliefs where, on the one hand, you realize you are not violent people anymore and therefore you cannot just go and kill all the Muslim terrorists. On the other hand, you cannot see what you can then do about it because you are not willing to look at the fact that if you change *your* consciousness, you will also change the collective consciousness.

With this, I seal you in my love and my gratitude for your willingness to diversify your thoughts on the topic of fanaticism.

23 | INVOKING APPRECIATION FOR DIVERSITY (PART 1)

In the name of the I AM THAT I AM, Jesus Christ, I use the authority that I have as a being in embodiment on earth to call upon Jesus to reinforce my calls and use my chakras to project the statements in this invocation into the collective consciousness and awaken people to the fact that diversity is the key to survival and that fanaticism seeks to limit diversity. Awaken people to the reality that we are spiritual beings and that we can co-create a new future by working with the ascended masters. I especially call for …

[Make your own calls here.]

Part 1

1. Jesus, shatter the energetic matrix that prevents people from seeing that in previous ages they had beliefs that they thought were infallible. Therefore, they were fanatical, according to the basic definition of fanaticism.

O Jesus, blessed brother mine,
I walk the path that you outline,
a great example to us all,
I follow now your inner call.

O Jesus, let the Fire of Joy,
consume the devil's subtle ploy,
transfigured is our planet earth,
the golden age is given birth.

2. Jesus, shatter the energetic matrix that prevents people from seeing that medieval Catholics and their attempt to put down the first scientists, the Inquisition, the witch hunts, these were fanatical acts.

O Jesus, open inner sight,
the ego wants to prove it's right,
but this I will no longer do,
I want to be all one with you.

O Jesus, let the Fire of Joy,
consume the devil's subtle ploy,
transfigured is our planet earth,
the golden age is given birth.

3. Jesus, shatter the energetic matrix that prevents people from seeing that there is no way to look at the actions perpetrated by the Catholic church without admitting that this was an expression of fanaticism and the fanatical mindset.

O Jesus, I now clearly see,
the Key of Knowledge given me,
my Christ self I hereby embrace,
as you fill up my inner space.

O Jesus, let the Fire of Joy,
consume the devil's subtle ploy,
transfigured is our planet earth,
the golden age is given birth.

4. Jesus, shatter the energetic matrix that prevents people from seeing that if we say that Muslim terrorists today are fanatics, then we must say that medieval Catholics were fanatics, the Crusaders were fanatics, the Muslims were fanatics, the Inquisitors were fanatics, those who burned witches were fanatics.

O Jesus, show me serpent's lie,
expose the beam in my own eye,
as Christ discernment you me give,
in oneness I forever live.

**O Jesus, let the Fire of Joy,
consume the devil's subtle ploy,
transfigured is our planet earth,
the golden age is given birth.**

5. Jesus, shatter the energetic matrix that prevents people from seeing that there are always inherent contradictions in fanatical beliefs. There is a cognitive dissonance, which is that we hold two viewpoints at the same time that are incompatible or contradictory, but we cannot see it.

O Jesus, I am truly meek,
and thus I turn the other cheek,
when the accuser attacks me,
I go within and merge with thee.

**O Jesus, let the Fire of Joy,
consume the devil's subtle ploy,
transfigured is our planet earth,
the golden age is given birth.**

6. Jesus, shatter the energetic matrix that prevents people from seeing that we need to understand why fanatics cannot see that they have cognitive dissonance.

O Jesus, ego I let die,
surrender ev'ry earthly tie,
the dead can bury what is dead,
I choose to walk with you instead.

O Jesus, let the Fire of Joy,
consume the devil's subtle ploy,
transfigured is our planet earth,
the golden age is given birth.

7. Jesus, shatter the energetic matrix that prevents people from seeing that the human mind has a mental level, a mental aspect. This analytical mind is very good at comparing things, looking at different viewpoints, comparing them and seeing if they are contradictory.

O Jesus, help me rise above,
the devil's test through higher love,
show me separate self unreal,
my formless self you do reveal.

O Jesus, let the Fire of Joy,
consume the devil's subtle ploy,
transfigured is our planet earth,
the golden age is given birth.

8. Jesus, shatter the energetic matrix that prevents people from seeing that when people have cognitive dissonance, when they hold two incompatible viewpoints, it is not because their minds are incapable of seeing the contradiction. Their analytical minds are perfectly capable of seeing the contradiction.

O Jesus, what is that to me,
I just let go and follow thee,
with this I do pass ev'ry test,
to find with you eternal rest.

O Jesus, let the Fire of Joy,
consume the devil's subtle ploy,
transfigured is our planet earth,
the golden age is given birth.

9. Jesus, shatter the energetic matrix that prevents people from seeing that an aspect of fanaticism is the belief that the ends can justify the means. The essential cognitive dissonance we could possibly come up with is those

who claim to be following Jesus Christ but think they are killing people in his name and that he approves of this.

> O Jesus, fiery master mine,
> my heart now melting into thine,
> I love with heart and mind and soul,
> the God who is my highest goal.

> **O Jesus, let the Fire of Joy,**
> **consume the devil's subtle ploy,**
> **transfigured is our planet earth,**
> **the golden age is given birth.**

Part 2

1. Jesus, shatter the energetic matrix that prevents people from seeing that in many cases people were pulled into these strong emotions of anger and hatred so that their conscious minds could not connect to the intellectual level.

> O Jesus, blessed brother mine,
> I walk the path that you outline,
> a great example to us all,
> I follow now your inner call.

> **O Jesus, let the Fire of Joy,**
> **consume the devil's subtle ploy,**
> **transfigured is our planet earth,**
> **the golden age is given birth.**

2. Jesus, shatter the energetic matrix that prevents people from seeing that we could develop scientific instruments that would allow us to see that there is a collective mental body.

> O Jesus, open inner sight,
> the ego wants to prove it's right,

but this I will no longer do,
I want to be all one with you.

**O Jesus, let the Fire of Joy,
consume the devil's subtle ploy,
transfigured is our planet earth,
the golden age is given birth.**

3. Jesus, shatter the energetic matrix that prevents people from seeing that it is possible to measure and see that people who are in the fanatical mind-set have openings in their mental bodies to this collective mental body, and there is an influx of aggressive energy into these people's mental bodies.

O Jesus, I now clearly see,
the Key of Knowledge given me,
my Christ self I hereby embrace,
as you fill up my inner space.

**O Jesus, let the Fire of Joy,
consume the devil's subtle ploy,
transfigured is our planet earth,
the golden age is given birth.**

4. Jesus, shatter the energetic matrix that prevents people from seeing that this energy creates a veil in the mind that people cannot see through, cannot see beyond. This is the only explanation for the phenomenon of cognitive dissonance.

O Jesus, show me serpent's lie,
expose the beam in my own eye,
as Christ discernment you me give,
in oneness I forever live.

**O Jesus, let the Fire of Joy,
consume the devil's subtle ploy,
transfigured is our planet earth,
the golden age is given birth.**

5. Jesus, shatter the energetic matrix that prevents people from seeing that people's mental bodies, on an individual level, have been invaded by a very aggressive energy that creates a veil. They have one belief on the right, another belief on the left, and there is a veil between so that the person's intellectual mind cannot see both beliefs at the same time.

> O Jesus, I am truly meek,
> and thus I turn the other cheek,
> when the accuser attacks me,
> I go within and merge with thee.

> **O Jesus, let the Fire of Joy,**
> **consume the devil's subtle ploy,**
> **transfigured is our planet earth,**
> **the golden age is given birth.**

6. Jesus, shatter the energetic matrix that prevents people from seeing that the veil means we cannot use the analytical mind to compare views and see the incompatibility. We switch back and forth, from one view to the other.

> O Jesus, ego I let die,
> surrender ev'ry earthly tie,
> the dead can bury what is dead,
> I choose to walk with you instead.

> **O Jesus, let the Fire of Joy,**
> **consume the devil's subtle ploy,**
> **transfigured is our planet earth,**
> **the golden age is given birth.**

7. Jesus, shatter the energetic matrix that prevents people from seeing that on one side of the veil, people see Jesus as a loving teacher. On the other side of the veil they believe Jesus wants them to go out and kill all non-believers.

> O Jesus, help me rise above,
> the devil's test through higher love,
> show me separate self unreal,
> my formless self you do reveal.

O Jesus, let the Fire of Joy,
consume the devil's subtle ploy,
transfigured is our planet earth,
the golden age is given birth.

8. Jesus, shatter the energetic matrix that prevents people from seeing that fanatics do not realize the incompatibility of their beliefs. This is especially the case when people are willing to kill other human beings in order to further what they see as an epically important cause.

O Jesus, what is that to me,
I just let go and follow thee,
with this I do pass ev'ry test,
to find with you eternal rest.

O Jesus, let the Fire of Joy,
consume the devil's subtle ploy,
transfigured is our planet earth,
the golden age is given birth.

9. Jesus, shatter the energetic matrix that prevents people from seeing that the road to hell is not paved with *good* intentions. It is paved with *fanatical* intentions. People have gone into this fanatical mindset where they cannot see that their intentions are not good, or that their intentions are good, but their actions are not.

O Jesus, fiery master mine,
my heart now melting into thine,
I love with heart and mind and soul,
the God who is my highest goal.

O Jesus, let the Fire of Joy,
consume the devil's subtle ploy,
transfigured is our planet earth,
the golden age is given birth.

Part 3

1. Jesus, shatter the energetic matrix that prevents people from seeing that fanatics cannot see that maybe they have a correct view of *what* should ideally happen, but they do not have the correct view of *how* to accomplish it without killing other people.

> O Jesus, blessed brother mine,
> I walk the path that you outline,
> a great example to us all,
> I follow now your inner call.
>
> **O Jesus, let the Fire of Joy,**
> **consume the devil's subtle ploy,**
> **transfigured is our planet earth,**
> **the golden age is given birth.**

2. Jesus, shatter the energetic matrix that prevents people from seeing that many psychologists and philosophers have drawn the conclusion that evil and aggression is part of human nature. Evil is a potential that lies latent in all people.

> O Jesus, open inner sight,
> the ego wants to prove it's right,
> but this I will no longer do,
> I want to be all one with you.
>
> **O Jesus, let the Fire of Joy,**
> **consume the devil's subtle ploy,**
> **transfigured is our planet earth,**
> **the golden age is given birth.**

3. Jesus, shatter the energetic matrix that prevents people from seeing that we do not see in the animal kingdom this kind of evil, this kind of atrocity. If this is human nature, and if humans are evolved from animals, where did evil come from in the human?

O Jesus, I now clearly see,
the Key of Knowledge given me,
my Christ self I hereby embrace,
as you fill up my inner space.

**O Jesus, let the Fire of Joy,
consume the devil's subtle ploy,
transfigured is our planet earth,
the golden age is given birth.**

4. Jesus, shatter the energetic matrix that prevents people from seeing that evil is not a gradual evolution of something we see in animals so how did it suddenly occur in human beings when it has never been there in any animal species?

O Jesus, show me serpent's lie,
expose the beam in my own eye,
as Christ discernment you me give,
in oneness I forever live.

**O Jesus, let the Fire of Joy,
consume the devil's subtle ploy,
transfigured is our planet earth,
the golden age is given birth.**

5. Jesus, shatter the energetic matrix that prevents people from seeing that there is no way that we can understand evil with the common worldview. If we want to understand evil, we need to go beyond and realize that evil is not part of human nature.

O Jesus, I am truly meek,
and thus I turn the other cheek,
when the accuser attacks me,
I go within and merge with thee.

**O Jesus, let the Fire of Joy,
consume the devil's subtle ploy,
transfigured is our planet earth,
the golden age is given birth.**

6. Jesus, shatter the energetic matrix that prevents people from seeing that evil is something that people can be pulled into doing through the fanatical mindset and the cognitive dissonance where they do not see the incompatibility between their beliefs and their actions.

O Jesus, ego I let die,
surrender ev'ry earthly tie,
the dead can bury what is dead,
I choose to walk with you instead.

**O Jesus, let the Fire of Joy,
consume the devil's subtle ploy,
transfigured is our planet earth,
the golden age is given birth.**

7. Jesus, shatter the energetic matrix that prevents people from seeing that throughout history many people have been pulled into fanatical actions, committing atrocities based on the fanatical mindset, but the vast majority of these people have not been evil.

O Jesus, help me rise above,
the devil's test through higher love,
show me separate self unreal,
my formless self you do reveal.

**O Jesus, let the Fire of Joy,
consume the devil's subtle ploy,
transfigured is our planet earth,
the golden age is given birth.**

8. Jesus, shatter the energetic matrix that prevents people from seeing that many of the people involved with the Holocaust were not evil men, they were blinded by fanaticism, blinded to an almost unbelievable degree, but nevertheless blinded by fanaticism.

O Jesus, what is that to me,
I just let go and follow thee,
with this I do pass ev'ry test,
to find with you eternal rest.

O Jesus, let the Fire of Joy,
consume the devil's subtle ploy,
transfigured is our planet earth,
the golden age is given birth.

9. Jesus, shatter the energetic matrix that prevents people from seeing that there is no explanation for evil in the materialist mindset, in the materialist worldview. Even religions do not have a full explanation of evil.

O Jesus, fiery master mine,
my heart now melting into thine,
I love with heart and mind and soul,
the God who is my highest goal.

O Jesus, let the Fire of Joy,
consume the devil's subtle ploy,
transfigured is our planet earth,
the golden age is given birth.

Part 4

1. Jesus, shatter the energetic matrix that prevents people from seeing that some beings are in a fundamental way different from what we normally consider human beings. Evil is not part of human nature.

O Jesus, blessed brother mine,
I walk the path that you outline,
a great example to us all,
I follow now your inner call.

O Jesus, let the Fire of Joy,
consume the devil's subtle ploy,
transfigured is our planet earth,
the golden age is given birth.

2. Jesus, shatter the energetic matrix that prevents people from seeing that it is not correct to say that Hitler was a more extreme version of what all human beings could become.

> O Jesus, open inner sight,
> the ego wants to prove it's right,
> but this I will no longer do,
> I want to be all one with you.

> **O Jesus, let the Fire of Joy,**
> **consume the devil's subtle ploy,**
> **transfigured is our planet earth,**
> **the golden age is given birth.**

3. Jesus, shatter the energetic matrix that prevents people from seeing that we cannot take people off the street and put them through a program and turn them into a Hitler. We can do that with *some* people in the sense that we can put them in the fanatical mindset.

> O Jesus, I now clearly see,
> the Key of Knowledge given me,
> my Christ self I hereby embrace,
> as you fill up my inner space.

> **O Jesus, let the Fire of Joy,**
> **consume the devil's subtle ploy,**
> **transfigured is our planet earth,**
> **the golden age is given birth.**

4. Jesus, shatter the energetic matrix that prevents people from seeing that we can *force* people to commit evil acts, but we cannot force them to envision, to plan, to plot those evil acts like Hitler did.

> O Jesus, show me serpent's lie,
> expose the beam in my own eye,
> as Christ discernment you me give,
> in oneness I forever live.

O Jesus, let the Fire of Joy,
consume the devil's subtle ploy,
transfigured is our planet earth,
the golden age is given birth.

5. Jesus, shatter the energetic matrix that prevents people from seeing that there were people who followed Hitler, but they could never have risen to the point of plotting the evil that he plotted. Hitler was a fundamentally different being than most of the human beings on earth.

O Jesus, I am truly meek,
and thus I turn the other cheek,
when the accuser attacks me,
I go within and merge with thee.

O Jesus, let the Fire of Joy,
consume the devil's subtle ploy,
transfigured is our planet earth,
the golden age is given birth.

6. Jesus, shatter the energetic matrix that prevents people from seeing that we need to recognize in ourselves that despite what we might have been pulled into in the past, we have not crossed that line of becoming evil and doing something evil.

O Jesus, ego I let die,
surrender ev'ry earthly tie,
the dead can bury what is dead,
I choose to walk with you instead.

O Jesus, let the Fire of Joy,
consume the devil's subtle ploy,
transfigured is our planet earth,
the golden age is given birth.

7. Jesus, shatter the energetic matrix that prevents people from seeing that our mental bodies have been invaded with the subtle doubt about whether we could be evil and we could do some of these terrible things, or have done some of these terrible things in past lives.

O Jesus, help me rise above,
the devil's test through higher love,
show me separate self unreal,
my formless self you do reveal.

**O Jesus, let the Fire of Joy,
consume the devil's subtle ploy,
transfigured is our planet earth,
the golden age is given birth.**

8. Jesus, shatter the energetic matrix that prevents people from seeing that this projection has caused the formation of a separate self and we need to let it die. There is no constructive reason why a spiritual student should hold on to this doubt.

O Jesus, what is that to me,
I just let go and follow thee,
with this I do pass ev'ry test,
to find with you eternal rest.

**O Jesus, let the Fire of Joy,
consume the devil's subtle ploy,
transfigured is our planet earth,
the golden age is given birth.**

9. Jesus, shatter the energetic matrix that prevents people from seeing that there is a gradual evolutionary process in nature that has been going on for a very long time. It has brought forth more and more species, more and more complex species, supposedly culminating in human beings.

O Jesus, fiery master mine,
my heart now melting into thine,
I love with heart and mind and soul,
the God who is my highest goal.

**O Jesus, let the Fire of Joy,
consume the devil's subtle ploy,
transfigured is our planet earth,
the golden age is given birth.**

Sealing

In the name of the I AM THAT I AM, I accept that Archangel Michael, Astrea and Shiva form an impenetrable shield around myself and all constructive people, sealing us from all fear-based energies in all four octaves. I accept that the Light of God is consuming and transforming all fear-based energies that make up the dark forces working against ending the era of fanaticism on earth!

24 | INVOKING APPRECIATION FOR DIVERSITY (PART 2)

In the name of the I AM THAT I AM, Jesus Christ, I use the authority that I have as a being in embodiment on earth to call upon Jesus to reinforce my calls and use my chakras to project the statements in this invocation into the collective consciousness and awaken people to the fact that diversity is the key to survival and that fanaticism seeks to limit diversity. Awaken people to the reality that we are spiritual beings and that we can co-create a new future by working with the ascended masters. I especially call for ...

[Make your own calls here.]

Part 1

1. Jesus, shatter the energetic matrix that prevents people from seeing that the evolutionary process shows us that life has a tremendous force that moves through all obstacles, moves around all obstacles.

O Jesus, blessed brother mine,
I walk the path that you outline,
a great example to us all,
I follow now your inner call.

O Jesus, let the Fire of Joy,
consume the devil's subtle ploy,
transfigured is our planet earth,
the golden age is given birth.

2. Jesus, shatter the energetic matrix that prevents people from seeing that life finds a way to adapt to all kinds of extreme conditions. It does so by creating life forms that are more and more adaptable.

O Jesus, open inner sight,
the ego wants to prove it's right,
but this I will no longer do,
I want to be all one with you.

O Jesus, let the Fire of Joy,
consume the devil's subtle ploy,
transfigured is our planet earth,
the golden age is given birth.

3. Jesus, shatter the energetic matrix that prevents people from seeing that the supposedly most advanced animal species on the planet, Homo Sapiens, can live in almost any environment. Human beings are the most fit, not because we are the most aggressive but because we are the most adaptable.

O Jesus, I now clearly see,
the Key of Knowledge given me,
my Christ self I hereby embrace,
as you fill up my inner space.

O Jesus, let the Fire of Joy,
consume the devil's subtle ploy,
transfigured is our planet earth,
the golden age is given birth.

4. Jesus, shatter the energetic matrix that prevents people from seeing that adaptability is based on diversity, the ability to adapt to diverse conditions. What makes the human race survivable from an evolutionary, biological viewpoint is *diversity*.

O Jesus, show me serpent's lie,
expose the beam in my own eye,
as Christ discernment you me give,
in oneness I forever live.

O Jesus, let the Fire of Joy,
consume the devil's subtle ploy,
transfigured is our planet earth,
the golden age is given birth.

5. Jesus, shatter the energetic matrix that prevents people from seeing that adaptability is not only physical, but also psychological. There are people who can adapt psychologically so they can live under conditions that other people could not handle.

O Jesus, I am truly meek,
and thus I turn the other cheek,
when the accuser attacks me,
I go within and merge with thee.

O Jesus, let the Fire of Joy,
consume the devil's subtle ploy,
transfigured is our planet earth,
the golden age is given birth.

6. Jesus, shatter the energetic matrix that prevents people from seeing that from a biological viewpoint, what makes the human species so successful is adaptability, the diversity we see in the human race.

O Jesus, ego I let die,
surrender ev'ry earthly tie,
the dead can bury what is dead,
I choose to walk with you instead.

O Jesus, let the Fire of Joy,
consume the devil's subtle ploy,
transfigured is our planet earth,
the golden age is given birth.

7. Jesus, shatter the energetic matrix that prevents people from seeing that diversity is not *only* physical. What makes the human race successful from an evolutionary survivability standpoint is psychological diversity.

O Jesus, help me rise above,
the devil's test through higher love,
show me separate self unreal,
my formless self you do reveal.

O Jesus, let the Fire of Joy,
consume the devil's subtle ploy,
transfigured is our planet earth,
the golden age is given birth.

8. Jesus, shatter the energetic matrix that prevents people from seeing that fanaticism attempts to suppress diversity. One group of people believe they have the absolute view of how the universe should work. If only everybody would accept their view, then we would have paradise on earth.

O Jesus, what is that to me,
I just let go and follow thee,
with this I do pass ev'ry test,
to find with you eternal rest.

O Jesus, let the Fire of Joy,
consume the devil's subtle ploy,
transfigured is our planet earth,
the golden age is given birth.

9. Jesus, shatter the energetic matrix that prevents people from seeing that from a purely biological standpoint, it is only diversity that creates success. The process of evolution is actually a process of experimentation.

O Jesus, fiery master mine,
my heart now melting into thine,
I love with heart and mind and soul,
the God who is my highest goal.

O Jesus, let the Fire of Joy,
consume the devil's subtle ploy,
transfigured is our planet earth,
the golden age is given birth.

Part 2

1. Jesus, shatter the energetic matrix that prevents people from seeing that the whole idea of evolution is that it starts with certain life forms that gradually evolve into other life forms and still other life forms, so we are not starting from ground zero every time.

O Jesus, blessed brother mine,
I walk the path that you outline,
a great example to us all,
I follow now your inner call.

O Jesus, let the Fire of Joy,
consume the devil's subtle ploy,
transfigured is our planet earth,
the golden age is given birth.

2. Jesus, shatter the energetic matrix that prevents people from seeing that the experiences gained from developing amoeba led to multi-celled organisms, that then led to the first species in the ocean, that eventually led to fish, that eventually led to mammals, and so forth. There is a clear progression.

O Jesus, open inner sight,
the ego wants to prove it's right,
but this I will no longer do,
I want to be all one with you.

O Jesus, let the Fire of Joy,
consume the devil's subtle ploy,
transfigured is our planet earth,
the golden age is given birth.

3. Jesus, shatter the energetic matrix that prevents people from seeing that if evolution is a completely unconscious process that is driven by random genetic mutations, there is no way to explain that evolution does not start from ground zero with every species. It builds upon the previous species.

O Jesus, I now clearly see,
the Key of Knowledge given me,
my Christ self I hereby embrace,
as you fill up my inner space.

O Jesus, let the Fire of Joy,
consume the devil's subtle ploy,
transfigured is our planet earth,
the golden age is given birth.

4. Jesus, shatter the energetic matrix that prevents people from seeing that we cannot explain this from a materialist viewpoint. Materialists will not see this, and the reason is cognitive dissonance. They have a veil in their mental bodies. They cannot see that this is a contradiction in Darwin's view of evolution.

O Jesus, show me serpent's lie,
expose the beam in my own eye,
as Christ discernment you me give,
in oneness I forever live.

O Jesus, let the Fire of Joy,
consume the devil's subtle ploy,
transfigured is our planet earth,
the golden age is given birth.

5. Jesus, shatter the energetic matrix that prevents people from seeing that the very key to the survivability of the human race and any society is diversification.

O Jesus, I am truly meek,
and thus I turn the other cheek,
when the accuser attacks me,
I go within and merge with thee.

**O Jesus, let the Fire of Joy,
consume the devil's subtle ploy,
transfigured is our planet earth,
the golden age is given birth.**

6. Jesus, shatter the energetic matrix that prevents people from seeing that the very idea that we could create a thousand-year kingdom based on a particular philosophy that did not change for a thousand years, is completely out of touch with the reality of biological evolution.

O Jesus, ego I let die,
surrender ev'ry earthly tie,
the dead can bury what is dead,
I choose to walk with you instead.

**O Jesus, let the Fire of Joy,
consume the devil's subtle ploy,
transfigured is our planet earth,
the golden age is given birth.**

7. Jesus, shatter the energetic matrix that prevents people from seeing that nothing can last forever. Conditions will constantly change on earth. If there is one constant on earth, the only constant is constant change.

O Jesus, help me rise above,
the devil's test through higher love,
show me separate self unreal,
my formless self you do reveal.

**O Jesus, let the Fire of Joy,
consume the devil's subtle ploy,
transfigured is our planet earth,
the golden age is given birth.**

8. Jesus, shatter the energetic matrix that prevents people from seeing that the idea that we could formulate a religion and that we could base a society on this, and this society could survive without changing its basic paradigm, is cognitive dissonance.

> O Jesus, what is that to me,
> I just let go and follow thee,
> with this I do pass ev'ry test,
> to find with you eternal rest.

> **O Jesus, let the Fire of Joy,**
> **consume the devil's subtle ploy,**
> **transfigured is our planet earth,**
> **the golden age is given birth.**

9. Jesus, shatter the energetic matrix that prevents people from seeing that the intellectual appeal of many fanatical ideas is precisely this dream that one day we will have the ideal society where everybody can agree because they all believe the same.

> O Jesus, fiery master mine,
> my heart now melting into thine,
> I love with heart and mind and soul,
> the God who is my highest goal.

> **O Jesus, let the Fire of Joy,**
> **consume the devil's subtle ploy,**
> **transfigured is our planet earth,**
> **the golden age is given birth.**

Part 3

1. Jesus, shatter the energetic matrix that prevents people from seeing that this is a very old dream that goes very far back in history. It is an illusion that throughout the ages has encouraged fanaticism.

O Jesus, blessed brother mine,
I walk the path that you outline,
a great example to us all,
I follow now your inner call.

O Jesus, let the Fire of Joy,
consume the devil's subtle ploy,
transfigured is our planet earth,
the golden age is given birth.

2. Jesus, shatter the energetic matrix that prevents people from seeing that fanaticism makes people think it is so important to either force people to accept their beliefs or to kill those people.

O Jesus, open inner sight,
the ego wants to prove it's right,
but this I will no longer do,
I want to be all one with you.

O Jesus, let the Fire of Joy,
consume the devil's subtle ploy,
transfigured is our planet earth,
the golden age is given birth.

3. Jesus, shatter the energetic matrix that prevents people from seeing that killing people, killing our own species, goes against the basic principle of nature and the principle of survivability.

O Jesus, I now clearly see,
the Key of Knowledge given me,
my Christ self I hereby embrace,
as you fill up my inner space.

O Jesus, let the Fire of Joy,
consume the devil's subtle ploy,
transfigured is our planet earth,
the golden age is given birth.

4. Jesus, shatter the energetic matrix that prevents people from seeing that you do not kill your own species if you want your species to survive. Therefore, from nature we are programmed not to kill other human beings. Our bodies, our instincts, are programmed not to kill.

O Jesus, show me serpent's lie,
expose the beam in my own eye,
as Christ discernment you me give,
in oneness I forever live.

**O Jesus, let the Fire of Joy,
consume the devil's subtle ploy,
transfigured is our planet earth,
the golden age is given birth.**

5. Jesus, shatter the energetic matrix that prevents people from seeing that what also goes against nature is the idea of suppressing diversity because nature clearly demonstrates that diversification is the key to survival and adaptability.

O Jesus, I am truly meek,
and thus I turn the other cheek,
when the accuser attacks me,
I go within and merge with thee.

**O Jesus, let the Fire of Joy,
consume the devil's subtle ploy,
transfigured is our planet earth,
the golden age is given birth.**

6. Jesus, shatter the energetic matrix that prevents people from seeing that when we have conformity and lack of diversity, we are rigid, we are inflexible, we are standing still.

O Jesus, ego I let die,
surrender ev'ry earthly tie,
the dead can bury what is dead,
I choose to walk with you instead.

**O Jesus, let the Fire of Joy,
consume the devil's subtle ploy,
transfigured is our planet earth,
the golden age is given birth.**

7. Jesus, shatter the energetic matrix that prevents people from seeing that when we have the willingness to adapt, we are not rigid, we are not standing still. We are willing to flow and change with changing conditions, adapting to them, making the best of them, and therefore we can survive.

O Jesus, help me rise above,
the devil's test through higher love,
show me separate self unreal,
my formless self you do reveal.

**O Jesus, let the Fire of Joy,
consume the devil's subtle ploy,
transfigured is our planet earth,
the golden age is given birth.**

8. Jesus, shatter the energetic matrix that prevents people from seeing that the Roman Empire came to a point where it could not transcend itself so it collapsed. The Catholic empire of the Middle Ages came to a point where it could not transcend itself and adapt so it lost most of its influence.

O Jesus, what is that to me,
I just let go and follow thee,
with this I do pass ev'ry test,
to find with you eternal rest.

**O Jesus, let the Fire of Joy,
consume the devil's subtle ploy,
transfigured is our planet earth,
the golden age is given birth.**

9. Jesus, shatter the energetic matrix that prevents people from seeing that the Soviet Union, Japan, ancient China, ancient Egypt, many of these civilizations disappeared because they could not adapt, they could not transcend themselves.

O Jesus, fiery master mine,
my heart now melting into thine,
I love with heart and mind and soul,
the God who is my highest goal.

**O Jesus, let the Fire of Joy,
consume the devil's subtle ploy,
transfigured is our planet earth,
the golden age is given birth.**

Part 4

1. Jesus, shatter the energetic matrix that prevents people from seeing that we can look at modern democracies and say: "Well, if we want to survive, what do we need to do? We need to diversify. We need to make sure we are not rigid."

O Jesus, blessed brother mine,
I walk the path that you outline,
a great example to us all,
I follow now your inner call.

**O Jesus, let the Fire of Joy,
consume the devil's subtle ploy,
transfigured is our planet earth,
the golden age is given birth.**

2. Jesus, shatter the energetic matrix that prevents people from seeing that this means we need to question the materialistic paradigm.

O Jesus, open inner sight,
the ego wants to prove it's right,
but this I will no longer do,
I want to be all one with you.

**O Jesus, let the Fire of Joy,
consume the devil's subtle ploy,**

**transfigured is our planet earth,
the golden age is given birth.**

3. Jesus, shatter the energetic matrix that prevents people from seeing that we need to move towards direct democracy where we diversify the decision process. Instead of having a small elite make the decisions, we are having all of the people, with all of the diversity there is in our population, make the important decisions.

O Jesus, I now clearly see,
the Key of Knowledge given me,
my Christ self I hereby embrace,
as you fill up my inner space.

**O Jesus, let the Fire of Joy,
consume the devil's subtle ploy,
transfigured is our planet earth,
the golden age is given birth.**

4. Jesus, shatter the energetic matrix that prevents people from seeing that the more diversity we have in our population, the better decisions that population will be able to make. Diversity is not a threat.

O Jesus, show me serpent's lie,
expose the beam in my own eye,
as Christ discernment you me give,
in oneness I forever live.

**O Jesus, let the Fire of Joy,
consume the devil's subtle ploy,
transfigured is our planet earth,
the golden age is given birth.**

5. Jesus, shatter the energetic matrix that prevents people from seeing that we came to have democracies because we overcame the lack of diversity that was there in the feudal societies where a small elite made all of the decisions.

O Jesus, I am truly meek,
and thus I turn the other cheek,
when the accuser attacks me,
I go within and merge with thee.

O Jesus, let the Fire of Joy,
consume the devil's subtle ploy,
transfigured is our planet earth,
the golden age is given birth.

6. Jesus, shatter the energetic matrix that prevents people from seeing that we diversify the decision-making process by creating a democracy. The next logical step in the democratization process is another level of diversification of the decision-making process.

O Jesus, ego I let die,
surrender ev'ry earthly tie,
the dead can bury what is dead,
I choose to walk with you instead.

O Jesus, let the Fire of Joy,
consume the devil's subtle ploy,
transfigured is our planet earth,
the golden age is given birth.

7. Jesus, shatter the energetic matrix that prevents people from seeing that Jesus attempted to create a spiritual movement that would be different from the religions that are based on squashing diversity.

O Jesus, help me rise above,
the devil's test through higher love,
show me separate self unreal,
my formless self you do reveal.

O Jesus, let the Fire of Joy,
consume the devil's subtle ploy,
transfigured is our planet earth,
the golden age is given birth.

8. Jesus, shatter the energetic matrix that prevents people from seeing that Jesus attempted to set an example of the need to diversify.

O Jesus, what is that to me,
I just let go and follow thee,
with this I do pass ev'ry test,
to find with you eternal rest.

O Jesus, let the Fire of Joy,
consume the devil's subtle ploy,
transfigured is our planet earth,
the golden age is given birth.

9. Jesus, shatter the energetic matrix that prevents people from seeing that Jesus also showed that the real problem on earth is that most people are stuck in a mindset where they cannot see beyond a certain veil.

O Jesus, fiery master mine,
my heart now melting into thine,
I love with heart and mind and soul,
the God who is my highest goal.

O Jesus, let the Fire of Joy,
consume the devil's subtle ploy,
transfigured is our planet earth,
the golden age is given birth.

Part 5

1. Jesus, shatter the energetic matrix that prevents people from seeing that Jesus came to give an example and a teaching that could jolt people out of their traditional way of thinking and reach a more diverse level of thinking where they could see that there is a higher perspective.

O Jesus, blessed brother mine,
I walk the path that you outline,

a great example to us all,
I follow now your inner call.

**O Jesus, let the Fire of Joy,
consume the devil's subtle ploy,
transfigured is our planet earth,
the golden age is given birth.**

2. Jesus, shatter the energetic matrix that prevents people from seeing that so many of your statements are meant to jolt people out of their conformist way of thinking into seeing that there are other ways to look at things than the way we have been brought up to look at them.

O Jesus, open inner sight,
the ego wants to prove it's right,
but this I will no longer do,
I want to be all one with you.

**O Jesus, let the Fire of Joy,
consume the devil's subtle ploy,
transfigured is our planet earth,
the golden age is given birth.**

3. Jesus, shatter the energetic matrix that prevents people from seeing that in its essence Christianity was meant to be a movement that encouraged the diversification of thought. The mental aspect of Christianity was to encourage the diversification of thought so that people could come to see what they could not see.

O Jesus, I now clearly see,
the Key of Knowledge given me,
my Christ self I hereby embrace,
as you fill up my inner space.

**O Jesus, let the Fire of Joy,
consume the devil's subtle ploy,
transfigured is our planet earth,
the golden age is given birth.**

4. Jesus, shatter the energetic matrix that prevents people from seeing that you wanted us to see that it is in our own best interest to do unto others what we want them to do to us because all people are connected. If we are doing something to others, sooner or later that will come back to us because the cosmic mirror will reflect back to us what we are doing to others.

O Jesus, show me serpent's lie,
expose the beam in my own eye,
as Christ discernment you me give,
in oneness I forever live.

O Jesus, let the Fire of Joy,
consume the devil's subtle ploy,
transfigured is our planet earth,
the golden age is given birth.

5. Jesus, shatter the energetic matrix that prevents people from seeing that your entire purpose was to create a movement that would bring more diversity of thought. Instead, from the moment of the formation of the Roman Catholic church, Christianity became turned into a movement that did everything it could to suppress the diversification of thought.

O Jesus, I am truly meek,
and thus I turn the other cheek,
when the accuser attacks me,
I go within and merge with thee.

O Jesus, let the Fire of Joy,
consume the devil's subtle ploy,
transfigured is our planet earth,
the golden age is given birth.

6. Jesus, shatter the energetic matrix that prevents people from seeing that it was suddenly of epic importance to create uniformity of thought, in complete contradiction to what you actually intended. This is clearly fanaticism. It is not survivable in the long run because it goes against one of the basic principles of nature: diversification.

O Jesus, ego I let die,
surrender ev'ry earthly tie,
the dead can bury what is dead,
I choose to walk with you instead.

**O Jesus, let the Fire of Joy,
consume the devil's subtle ploy,
transfigured is our planet earth,
the golden age is given birth.**

7. Jesus, shatter the energetic matrix that prevents people from seeing that after the western democracies were confronted with the outburst of fanaticism in 9/11, we have refused to consider: "Do we have elements of fanaticism? Is there something we could do to change the equation by changing ourselves?"

O Jesus, help me rise above,
the devil's test through higher love,
show me separate self unreal,
my formless self you do reveal.

**O Jesus, let the Fire of Joy,
consume the devil's subtle ploy,
transfigured is our planet earth,
the golden age is given birth.**

8. Jesus, shatter the energetic matrix that prevents people from seeing that we feel powerless when there is a veil in the mental body that prevents us from seeing the incompatibility of our own viewpoints.

O Jesus, what is that to me,
I just let go and follow thee,
with this I do pass ev'ry test,
to find with you eternal rest.

**O Jesus, let the Fire of Joy,
consume the devil's subtle ploy,
transfigured is our planet earth,
the golden age is given birth.**

9. Jesus, shatter the energetic matrix that prevents people from seeing that we feel powerless when, on the one hand, we realize we cannot kill all the Muslim terrorists. On the other hand, we cannot see what to do about it because we are not willing to look at the fact that if we change our consciousness, we will also change the collective consciousness.

O Jesus, fiery master mine,
my heart now melting into thine,
I love with heart and mind and soul,
the God who is my highest goal.

**O Jesus, let the Fire of Joy,
consume the devil's subtle ploy,
transfigured is our planet earth,
the golden age is given birth.**

Sealing

In the name of the I AM THAT I AM, I accept that Archangel Michael, Astrea and Shiva form an impenetrable shield around myself and all constructive people, sealing us from all fear-based energies in all four octaves. I accept that the Light of God is consuming and transforming all fear-based energies that make up the dark forces working against ending the era of fanaticism on earth!

25 | FANATICS DIVIDE PEOPLE INTO SUB- AND SUPER-HUMANS

I AM the Ascended Master the Great Divine Director, and I come to give you the identity-level perspective on the topic of fanaticism. The essence of the fanatical mindset is that it divides humanity into at least two groups, those who are the fanatics (who of course do not see themselves as the fanatics) and then those who are the scapegoats. There might be three groups: the fanatics, the scapegoats and all the others. Nevertheless, the foundation for this division, or the foundation for fanaticism, is the division of humanity into separate groups.

Now, we have talked about the fact that you have a biological programming not to kill your own species. If you look at many of the acts that have been committed throughout history by people in the fanatical mindset, you would see that in a certain way they actually think they have not killed members of their own species, or at least their own group. What always happens is that when people go into the fanatical mindset, they dehumanize the group that is their scapegoat. They almost do not see them as human beings, which is why, as we talked about, the commandant of Auschwitz could during his working day orchestrate the killing of children and then go home and play with his own children. He did not see the ones in the camp as real human children.

This is what you see in many of these fanatical groups that you have seen throughout history. They had a scapegoat that they did not consider human, at least not human in the same way as themselves. This has many potential perspectives and ramifications. You can say from a purely biological standpoint that there is no animal species who divides its own members up into separate groups where some are good and some are bad. You cannot explain this from a purely biological, materialistic perspective. There is no precedent, there is no parallel in the animal kingdom.

The psychological basis for division

Again, where could this have come from? It could not have come from your biology. If it does not come from your biology, it must come from somewhere else. Of course, if it does not come from the *biology,* it must come from the *psychology.* That is logic. You realize that there must be something in the human psyche that makes it possible for people to divide human beings into at least two separate groups, to dehumanize the other group, those who are seen as the *others* versus *us* who are the good group. They dehumanize that scapegoat group to the point where they do not really think they are killing human beings by killing the scapegoats.

How does this happen? Well, you who are ascended master students are familiar with the concepts we have that you have the four lower bodies, the physical, the emotional, the mental and the identity body. You know that in the identity body is of course where your sense of identity is defined. You realize that the division of humankind into separate groups starts at the identity level. You can see, when you trace what you know about history, how this goes back quite far in human history. You can see, for example, when you look at the Old Testament how there came a point a very long time ago where the Jewish people started developing a certain identity that set them apart from all who were not Jews. Then, came the idea that whereas all of the other tribes in the area were worshiping idols, the Jews were worshiping the superior god, the one god of the universe. Then, came the idea that they were the chosen people of that god.

Therefore, when they went into the land that was promised them by their superior god, they did not think that the people who occupied that land were human beings like themselves. They saw themselves as being in a category that was superior to the inhabitants of the promised land. Therefore, they did not think they were killing their own species or at least their own race. You can see that there is an element of the human psyche that enables people to create these divisions that are clearly not based on biology. Therefore again, what are they based on? Well, you could say in a certain way that they are based on some kind of "ism," some kind of religion, some kind of theory, political theory. Even scientific Materialism has created the concept that some are more fit than others. This has immediately been interpreted to mean that some are fit to rule and should be the elite that rules society and the rest of the population should just be the slaves that support the elite.

You could say that there are these outer theories, these images that people create of how they think the world *should* work. Throughout history, certain groups of people had developed these theories that set themselves apart from others, but also defined that they had a superior position to others. This is something that many people in the modern democracies are ready to grasp, to understand, to see and to realize. There has always been this tendency and this is something of course that we need to look at.

A superficial understanding of democracy

We need to again recognize that there is a certain cognitive dissonance here. In other words, you could take another view and step back and say: "What do people actually understand about democracy?" You could realize that most people in the democratic nations have a very superficial understanding of what democracy means. They tend to think that democracy is a very easy form of society. Once you have a democracy, you are free and you will remain free for the indefinite future, at least unless you are attacked by some outer enemy. Democracy is an easy form of government because all you have to do as a citizen is that every four years or so you go and vote, then you have fulfilled your obligation. Then, the ruling elite are somehow supposed to take care of everything else and you can focus on enjoying your daily life.

The reality is that the easiest form of government is a dictatorship where the people do not need to make any choices because the system chooses for them. At least that is the easiest for people at a certain level of consciousness. Why then did democracies emerge and dictatorships retreat? Because humankind has been raised to a certain level where there are many, many people in embodiment on earth who cannot be satisfied by living the easy life of a dictatorship where they never have to make decisions, they never have to take responsibility for themselves. When you step back and look at this, you realize that there is a very, very clear connection between the growth in humankind's consciousness and the emergence of democracies.

What you actually see is that the only reason democracies could emerge was that many, many people had reached that level of spiritual maturity where they were ready to start taking responsibility for themselves and their lives, ready to start making decisions, learning from the consequences of those decisions. That is essentially what it means to take responsibility for your own growth. You are willing to make decisions based on what you know now, and you look at the results of your decisions. If you do not like the results, then you expand your understanding so you can make better decisions in the future. That is the process of growth in its essential form. When you look at this from a broader perspective than scientific Materialism or orthodox Christianity, you can see that the history of humankind has actually been a growth process and it has primarily been a growth in consciousness.

Historians still tend to look at the outer events, the increase in knowledge, the increase in inventions and technology. What actually drives the progress you have seen in history is a raising of the collective consciousness, which is driven by individuals raising their individual consciousness. This is not something that is too difficult to grasp for many people in the democratic nations.

You need to recognize that democracy is the direct result of people starting to take responsibility for themselves. Then, you also need to recognize that people have not, at least not a critical mass of them, continued that process of taking more and more responsibility for themselves. They have sort of come to a plateau, they have stagnated, they have been lulled to sleep by thinking: "Now that we live in a democracy, we are free." What needs to happen is that people need to start a new cycle, a new awakening, of starting to take responsibility for their lives.

This is again something that is being partly driven by the increase in mental illness because, as we have said, there are advanced souls embodying in the democratic nations. They want to use the opportunity to work on themselves, work on their psychology, but because they have not been given a teaching about how to raise their consciousness, how to deal with their psychology, how to heal their wounds, how to evolve to a higher level of consciousness, they then manifest various forms of depression or mental illness. This forces them to start looking at themselves and many of them have come to a point where they have decided to start to take more responsibility for themselves than what they were brought up to do.

Democracies cannot function with division

You can see here that democracy can really only survive if people are in this process of taking more and more responsibility for themselves, for their lives, for their situation, for their nation, even for the world. They develop a more and more global awareness. What makes a democracy function? A democracy is by definition not a form of government where a small elite rules the majority of the population. It is, at least in theory, a society where all people are involved in the decision making process.

How can a democratic nation function in the best possible way? Well, it can only function in the best possible way if all of the people in that nation have some sense of connection with each other. They must feel that we are in the same boat, we are all being affected by the decisions made. We need to therefore look at each other, seek to raise up the whole instead of raising up just one small portion of the whole. We cannot have an elitist society where there is one rich and privileged elite and the majority of the population living in limited conditions. That is not the idea behind democracy.

Democracies require that the people develop some kind of connection between them. What is that connection? It is what we have in later dictations called your basic or your essential humanity. All men and women are created equal, all of them are endowed from a higher authority with certain rights. All people have those rights. That is an expression in words of the basic humanity. Do unto others what you want others to do to you, is an expression in words of the basic humanity. When people feel compassion for others and want to do something to relieve the suffering of others, that is because they have that sense of the basic humanity. What then works against this basic humanity? Well, precisely the fanatical mindset that divides humanity into separate groups that are not just separated by degree, but are separated in a fundamental way that makes it possible to dehumanize one group.

You can see that when democracies emerged, there was a tremendous shift in the collective awareness. If you could actually look at this from our perspective, you could see that when democracies started to emerge and become more common, there were shock waves radiating through the emotional body of the planet, the collective emotional body, the collective mental body and the collective identity body. There were literally riptides, currents, shock waves going through those bodies because it was such a new and, compared to the old, very radical idea.

People saw tremendous hope and opportunity in not having to live their entire lives in a fixed station determined by their birth, but where they could actually do something to improve their lives, improve their station in life. Consider people who had grown up in the feudal societies of Europe in a peasant family, thinking, the rest of their lives they would be working for next to nothing for the landlord as peasants, working 12-14 hours a day in the field, just getting enough to survive. Now, suddenly they see across the ocean is a new nation called America that has democracy. They will even give you a piece of land to farm where you get everything that you produce, you can keep it yourself. It was a revolutionary idea for the peasants of Europe. It sent shock waves through the collective consciousness. It sent shock waves into the dictatorial nations that were still there both in Europe and elsewhere. The dictators started feeling threatened by this.

The basis for democracy is equality

It was a tremendous growth for a time in the collective consciousness. What was the basis of it? What was it that was so special about America? It was an opportunity for everyone. It was: The effort you make determines your reward, not your station in society. Not your birth, not your family background but your own effort. Then, when democracy started spreading in Europe, the same thing—the process was reinforced and more shock waves. The whole basis for it was the equal opportunity based on your own efforts. There was suddenly a new sense of equality.

Now, there were people who were very disturbed by this because there were certain people in those feudal societies in Europe who were content with living this life as peasants. They always knew what they had, they could not get any less, they would always be given a place to live and food to eat and clothes to wear, and they were satisfied with this. There were actually people who regretted the disappearance of the feudal societies. They did not know what to do, they were not ready to take responsibility for themselves, they were used to that they could put in a minimal work effort and they would still be given what they needed to survive. They were afraid to go to America where suddenly, if they did not put in enough of an effort, they would not get anything and they might actually starve to death. What you saw here was that those people who were ready to take responsibility for themselves immigrated to America, or they embodied in America, and those who were not willing, they stayed in Europe. Then, later they embodied in communist countries where again they had a certain minimum standard of living, but they knew they could not do any worse, they would always have enough to meet their basic needs.

You see here that the basis for democracy is this sense of equality, based on the basic humanity. All people share in this essential humanity, therefore all people have rights, all people have a right to be here. More importantly, all people are just people, human beings. You cannot divide humanity into separate groups, say one is superior, one is inferior, one is right, the other group is bad and they can be killed. If we kill them, we are not even really killing human beings because the Jews are not really human beings in the eyes of the Nazis.

You see here that at the identity level, it is the division of human beings into separate groups that starts fanaticism. You may say that there is a certain aspect of fanaticism that is based on hatred and anger in the emotional body, or driven by it at least. There is a certain aspect of fanaticism that is driven by these "isms," these beliefs in the mental body. The bottom level, the most fundamental aspect of fanaticism, is the division in the identity body between those who are really humans and those who are sub-humans. Super-humans and sub-humans and maybe there are some that are just humans. The Nazis had a division like that: There were the Aryan super-humans, there were those who were just humans and then there were the sub-humans: the Jews (and those who were in other ways inferior, for example having mental illnesses or mental handicaps).

Growing division in democracies

This is where it all starts. Many people in the democratic nations are ready to see this, and see that we need to recognize this mechanism whereby people divide humanity up. We need to look at the democracies and see that we had a period where there was more of a sense of equality. Now, in later decades, we have actually gone in the opposite direction and there is a growing inequality.

It happens at different levels. You have a very, very clear tendency that there is the emergence of a very, very rich and privileged elite. They have become an elite through money and how they are using money, how they are making money, creating all of these financial instruments. Therefore, creating a very clear division of the population of democratic nations between the very rich and the majority of the population who are not really poor, but who certainly are nowhere near the rich elite.

This is a division that is a danger sign for democracy. It is a potential threat to democracy because it moves back towards the feudal societies where instead of a few people owning the land, a few people own all of the financial system. This ensures that the majority of the population can only stay at the level of what we might call the working people, those who have to do actual work to make a living, whereas the elite make their money off of their money. The money makes more money, and this keeps going indefinitely.

You also see other tendencies for divisions where you see that, especially after 9/11 in 2001 and the attack by Muslim fundamentalists, you have seen the emergence of a new type of anti-Muslim fundamentalists in the West. Those who are against terrorists, those who are the extreme right wing, from the Neo-Nazis to the more conservative people who want to shut out immigrants, close the borders, close the societies.

Again, what have we said is the key to survival: diversification. This works directly against diversification. You have seen how the modern democracies have become more open, more tolerant in a certain way, but there are certain people that cannot accept this so they have become more polarized against it. This is another danger sign where you see that these people are actually going into the same fanatical mindset as the Muslim extremists that they are so afraid of—without of course being willing to see this because of cognitive dissonance. The general population need to be able to see this and they *are* able to see it, and to see that this is a danger sign in democracy. It is a sign that the modern democracies have started losing some of that sense of the basic connection that we are all equal, that we all have the same basic humanity, and therefore have the same rights and deserve the same opportunity.

Of course, this just points out a mechanism. It is valuable to know the mechanism and understand how it works, but it does not point to the cause. What is the cause of this? Of course, this we do not expect the broad population to be able to accept, but you need to realize this as ascended master students because you can make the calls for the judgment and the binding of those beings who are behind it. Of course, the beings who are behind this is what we have called the fallen beings.

The origin of division

We have explained that in a previous sphere, a creation before your creation, these beings were not willing to grow, they were not willing to use their free will to transcend themselves, they wanted to hold on to something, and therefore they fell into the next sphere that was created.

Now, in that very process of them going into this state of consciousness, this lower state of consciousness, they developed a sense of identity as being set apart from all other beings. They saw themselves before they fell as being superior to other beings in their sphere based on their accomplishments, and based on their beliefs, which were quite frankly illusions. You need to recognize here that there are certain beings, some of them in physical embodiment on earth, some of them in the emotional realm, some are in the mental and some in the identity realm. These beings see themselves as being fundamentally different from all other beings on earth. They believe they are in a fundamental way superior to human beings. They do not consider themselves human beings.

You can see this most clearly in those who have embodied physically, such as again, the perennial example: Hitler and the dream of the Aryan race, the super race. They simply did not consider themselves to be human beings as others. Therefore, they thought it was their right to look at human beings as chess pieces that could be moved around or knocked over at will. They thought that humanity is just a playground for them to outplay their desire for power.

Beings without empathy

There are beings who have that same attitude in the identity realm and think that humanity is just like chess pieces that they can move around in their overall agenda. We have given you teachings on various aspects of that agenda, including their desire to prove God wrong. Nevertheless, the important point here is that you cannot actually explain fanaticism, the cause of fanaticism, unless you recognize that there is a certain group of beings (some in embodiment, some in the three higher realms) who see themselves as being fundamentally different from human beings. They see human beings as being lower than themselves. They have absolutely no empathy, no sense of connection. They have no sense of essential humanity. They have no pity, no mercy upon human beings.

They have absolutely no compunctions about starting a war that kills millions of human beings. If they had been able to do so, they would have started the Third World War, fought with nuclear weapons, and might have killed hundreds of millions of people. They would have had absolutely no pity, no empathy with the suffering of human beings. You cannot explain fanaticism, you cannot explain the presence of evil, as we talked about earlier, without recognizing this.

The subtle challenge posed by fallen beings

When you come to this recognition, you are presented with quite a challenge. The presence of these fallen beings on earth presents humanity with a very subtle challenge. What have I just said is the very essence of fanaticism? You divide humanity into separate categories. What are we now telling you? There are human beings and there are fallen beings. Well, if you are in the fanatical mindset, you could take these teachings expressed in words and you could use them to try to go around and identify fallen beings in embodiment and then create some death squad that would hunt them down and kill them so that we could get them off the planet. This of course would mean that you would use our teachings to reinforce the fanatical mindset.

Take note of how I have used words. I have not at all said that the fallen beings *are* in a fundamentally different category, I have only said that *they see themselves* as being in a fundamentally different category.

What is the challenge that is presented to you who are in embodiment, you who are ascended master students? It is to recognize the presence of fallen beings, recognize how they are working, what they are doing, without going into the fanatical mindset of judging them as being fundamentally different and because they are evil, it is justified to kill them. It is the same that faces humanity in general. It is necessary to know that there is a certain group of beings who do not have any empathy for the suffering of humanity in general, who are willing to inflict suffering for their own ends. It is necessary to see this so that you can avoid becoming tools for them. It is not constructive at all to go into the fanatical mindset where you now think that because these people are evil, it is justified to kill them.

You might think, as some have thought: "Oh, could not Hitler have been run over by a car when he was five years old and playing in the street. Look at all the suffering we would have been spared for." You see my beloved, if Hitler had been run over, somebody else would have played that role. It was necessary to out-picture this extreme evil as the only way people could learn the lessons in the School of *very* Hard Knocks. Somehow humanity, given the state of the planet, had to see this out-pictured.

Of course, this does not mean that humanity needs to be in the School of Hard Knocks for all eternity. It is possible to transcend the School of Hard Knocks. Who are the people who can do this? The people in the modern democracies who have risen to a higher level of spiritual development, spiritual maturity. As a result of rising to a higher level of spiritual maturity, they have also gained a sense of the basic humanity. At least those who have not been trapped in a certain form of spirituality that sets them apart as being superior because they are members of that religion or following this or that guru.

Calling forth the judgment of Christ

You realize here that you yourselves are facing this delicate challenge of realizing the fallen beings exist, but you avoid going into any kind of negative, angry, judgmental state of mind about them. You leave judgment unto us. You call for the judgment of Christ upon these fallen beings. We asked you to call for the judgment of Christ because it says that you are willing to suspend your outer awareness, your outer mind, your outer sense of judgment and let the action you are calling for be done according to the higher vision of the Christ mind. Some of you have the vision of the Christ mind but nevertheless it is a safety mechanism. You call forth the judgment of Christ and we are the ones who decide, based on our vision from the ascended realm, how to execute that judgment.

Of course, you could say: "What if there were no ascended master students and nobody made the calls for the judgment of the fallen beings who are behind fanaticism?" Well, then humanity would continue in the School of Hard Knocks. Then, you could say: "Well, isn't that the only way people can learn their lessons?" No, it is not. It is legitimate that there is a small group of people who are making the calls for the removal of these dark forces so that the rest of humanity can become free from the blinding influence of these dark forces. Therefore, they can make better choices. They can naturally make better choices because, as we have said, evil is not in human nature. This is why we have said previously: "If people knew better, they would do better."

When they truly *know,* the vast majority of people *will* make better choices. What actually prevents them from making better choices is when their minds are distorted by the fallen beings who pull them into supporting these "isms," these epic causes that cause people to be blinded by the mechanism we have described in the mental body where there is a veil that prevents them from seeing their cognitive dissonance.

People are fooled into supporting evil

People have throughout the ages been tricked by these fallen beings time and time again. This is again something that people actually can come to understand, without even knowing about fallen beings. People can come to see that there must be certain types of human beings who have a particular agenda, an agenda that always leads to conflict, warfare and suffering. There are not enough of these people that they themselves can create the atrocities, can execute the atrocities, can create the mayhem that we have seen in history.

Again, you can use the concept of narcissists or psychopaths that have no empathy for the suffering of others. How can a few of these beings have created so much suffering in history? Well, only because they managed to take what we might call normal human beings and pull them into doing the dirty work for them, pull them into serving their epic causes. Then, you can begin to see how, throughout history, people have been seduced by these epic causes. Such as medieval Christians who thought it was epically important to make all human beings members of the Catholic religion. If they would not be converted, it was better to kill them so that their souls would not burn forever in hell because they were not baptized in a Christian church.

Clearly you could look back at this and see that this was a complete illusion, a complete deception that pulled people into going on these crusades. You can actually make the calls that there will be a certain awareness, a certain awakening, where people realize that there has been a tendency throughout history for the emergence of a small elite. A small power elite have had this mindset of defining certain epic causes and then pulling people into supporting a very aggressive militant action to promote this cause by killing all those people who stand in the way, all those people who will not come into conformity, all those people who are different. You can see, people can come to see, how they have accomplished this. Many times it starts right there by dividing humanity into at least two groups. There are us, we are the superior, we are those who are right, then there are the scapegoats, they are inferior. They are not even really human. We are not really killing our own species by killing them because they are subhuman.

Then, at the mental level there is the definition of an epic cause. We must spread Christianity around the world or there will be hell to pay. We must spread communism around the world because it is a historical necessity. We must do this, we must do that. We must spread freedom and democracy around the world, courtesy of the US army, or there will be no future for humanity. All of these epic causes that have been defined have pulled people in at the mental level to becoming *fan*s of an *ism,* thereby going into *fan*-atic-*ism.*

The emotional component of anger

Then you can see at the emotional level how this elite have been so absolutely experts in whipping up certain emotions in an entire population of anger and hatred that causes them to direct the frustrations they have against another group of people. If you look at the German population in the 1930s, you can see that after the Treaty of Versailles after the First World War there was a great frustration. Then, you had all of the economic problems with hyperinflation and many other problems. There was an enormous frustration in the German people because they felt they should have been able to do better. Hitler simply used this frustration.

Now, the frustration could have been channeled productively into the German people saying: "Well, how can we improve ourselves? What do we need to do to improve ourselves?" What Hitler did was he misdirected the frustration into saying: "All of your problems are caused by the Jews. So if you take your anger and frustration and direct it towards eradicating the Jews, you will solve all your problems and get a better future."

Naturally, everybody knows today that this did not happen. The German people to their credit were then able, after the war, to start looking at: "How do we need to change ourselves in order to improve our situation?" That is why you have seen the tremendous progress you have seen in the German nation after the Second World War. If they could have done that in the 1930s, Hitler would not have been necessary, at least not for them. He might have been necessary for other people learning a certain lesson. Again, we are not lamenting what did happen, we are just trying to help people see the dynamics. There was always that emotional component, directing anger at the scapegoat. Therefore, when you are angry enough, you do not even stop to think: "Wait a minute, is it logical what we are doing? Is it rational what we are doing? Is it actually against our professed beliefs, our deeper principles? Is it against our sense of humanity? Why are we doing this? What are we doing?" Nobody asks that question when they are so taken over by anger and they have an outlet for their anger: Kill the Jews. Kill the scapegoats.

How to use these teachings

These are mechanisms that you of course can understand. You can raise your awareness of it, thereby pulling up on the collective. You can make the calls for this. You can of course use these teachings to write all kinds of things, as you might desire where you do not need to say where your ideas come from at all. Just put the ideas out there and let people do whatever they do with them. There is a tremendous potential.

As we have said: The tension has been built so that the water in the glass is already bulging over the edge but the surface tension has not been punctured. Therefore, it is all held in and people have not seen the new understanding. You can, a relatively small number of people can, actually puncture that surface tension and suddenly people wake up and see: "This is obvious. If we really are who we profess to be in the democratic nations, this is what we need to do."

The potential there is tremendous. We are not telling you this to try to put some kind of pressure on you. You need to be very, very clear here that you do not use our teachings to build some sense of frustration, some sense that: "Oh, I *should* be doing more. I *should* be out on the barricades saving the world."

My beloved, you do what you *can* do. You all have a personal spiritual path to follow. You all have a practical outer situation where there are certain things you need to take care of. We are not asking you to take our teachings and build some kind of frustration. We are certainly not asking you to go into a fanatical mindset where you feel this obsessive-compulsive need to save the world by 12 o'clock tomorrow. We are asking you to do what you *can*, raise your consciousness, make the calls, do whatever else you can and be content about this. My beloved, we want to make one thing very, very clear, not just based on the teaching we have given at this conference but at all previous conferences. You realize that when you are given a teaching, it is an opportunity. *We* also realize, and *you* need to realize as well, that just through this messenger alone in these past 15, 16 years, we have given so many teachings that there is not a single one of you who can act on all of them. Most of you can barely even find time to study them all so we are not expecting, we are not demanding, that you should act on all of them.

Perhaps you could consider that there is a certain area of life that you feel a particular attraction to? You study those teachings. You make the calls for that particular area to change. Between all of you, you will cover the whole spectrum that we are giving you. We want to make it clear that you have an opportunity here to, in the old-fashioned way, make good karma, but really to raise your consciousness and free yourself from what holds you back from ascending. It is not so, my beloved, that once you go out of embodiment after this lifetime, there is some ascended master who is going to be standing up there and saying: "How did you apply the teaching?" That is not going to happen.

We are grateful for your willingness to put your attention on this, to change yourselves, to walk the path. We are, and we have said this now many times, not like the fallen beings. We are not like the judgmental, angry god in the sky portrayed by so many religions. We accept you for who you are. We know that it is difficult to be in embodiment on a planet like earth. We are grateful for everything you do.

There was a point where this messenger was young and had found an ascended master teaching that also had a lot of teachings and a lot of ideas about how many hours a day you should be giving decrees, and how early you should get up to give those decrees. He came to a point where he realized that if he was supposed to do everything that was recommended, 24 hours simply was not enough. Since he only had 24 hours, he realized he had to make peace with the fact that he could not do all of it.

Therefore, he simply decided that the normal human tendency is all or nothing. You get so fired up, so anxious to do something, that you try to do everything and after a while you burn out and now you do nothing. He simply decided: "What is the point in repeating that pattern? Because anything I do is better than doing nothing." This could be your motto as well. Anything you do is better than doing nothing. Anything you do will have a positive effect, both on your own growth and on the collective and on the situation of raising the earth. I can assure you, my beloved, that calling forth the judgment of Christ upon the fallen beings who have used fanaticism to create all of these atrocities, will have a tremendous impact on the planet and the future of this planet. Therefore again, you have our acceptance of who you are, what you can do. You have our gratitude for everything you do. And you have simply our love for each and every one of you.

We are in the Aquarian Age, my beloved. In the Age of Pisces the dynamic was different. That is why you saw so many religions that created these strict outer rules, even ascended master organizations with so many rules that people could not follow them. You saw so many, both religious and other organizations, that developed this very judgmental mindset of those who are following the rules and those who are not, those who are living up to the standard and those who are not.

All of this is obsolete in the Age of Aquarius. We want you to do what you do out of love, not out of fear, not out of the sense of being forced, not out of some obsessive compulsion. Just do it out of love. That is all we ask: Is it too much to ask my beloved? Is it? (Audience answers: "No"). Then, remember this and do not ask more of yourselves than we are asking of you. And with this, my love and my gratitude.

26 | INVOKING APPRECIATION FOR TRUE EQUALITY (PART 1)

In the name of the I AM THAT I AM, Jesus Christ, I use the authority that I have as a being in embodiment on earth to call upon the Divine Director to reinforce my calls and use my chakras to project the statements in this invocation into the collective consciousness and awaken people to the fact that fanatics divide human beings into two groups and that this will always create conflict. Awaken people to the reality that we are spiritual beings and that we can co-create a new future by working with the ascended masters. I especially call for …

[Make your own calls here.]

Part 1

1. Divine Director, shatter the energetic matrix that prevents people from seeing that the essence of the fanatical mindset is that it divides humanity into at least two groups, those who are the fanatics and those who are the scapegoats.

Divine Director, I now see,
the world is unreality,
in my heart I now truly feel,
the Spirit is all that is real.

**Divine Director, send the light,
from blindness clear my inner sight,
my vision free, my vision clear,
your guidance is forever here.**

2. Divine Director, shatter the energetic matrix that prevents people from seeing that many of the acts that have been committed throughout history by people in the fanatical mindset, these people think they have not killed members of their own species, or at least their own group.

Divine Director, vision give,
in clarity I want to live,
I now behold my plan Divine,
the plan that is uniquely mine.

**Divine Director, send the light,
from blindness clear my inner sight,
my vision free, my vision clear,
your guidance is forever here.**

3. Divine Director, shatter the energetic matrix that prevents people from seeing that when people go into the fanatical mindset, they dehumanize the group that is their scapegoat. They almost do not see them as human beings.

Divine Director, show in me,
the ego games, and set me free,
help me escape the ego's cage,
to help bring in the golden age.

**Divine Director, send the light,
from blindness clear my inner sight,
my vision free, my vision clear,
your guidance is forever here.**

4. Divine Director, shatter the energetic matrix that prevents people from seeing that many fanatical groups have had a scapegoat that they did not consider human, at least not human in the same way as themselves.

Divine Director, I'm with you,
my vision one, no longer two,
as karma's veil you do disperse,
I see a whole new universe.

Divine Director, send the light,
from blindness clear my inner sight,
my vision free, my vision clear,
your guidance is forever here.

5. Divine Director, shatter the energetic matrix that prevents people from seeing that from a purely biological standpoint, there is no animal species who divides its own members up into separate groups where some are good and some are bad.

Divine Director, I go up,
electric light now fills my cup,
consume in me all shadows old,
bestow on me a vision bold.

Divine Director, send the light,
from blindness clear my inner sight,
my vision free, my vision clear,
your guidance is forever here.

6. Divine Director, shatter the energetic matrix that prevents people from seeing that we cannot explain this from a purely biological, materialistic perspective. There is no precedent in the animal kingdom.

Divine Director, heart of gold,
my sacred labor I unfold,
o blessed Guru, I now see,
where my own plan is taking me.

Divine Director, send the light,
from blindness clear my inner sight,
my vision free, my vision clear,
your guidance is forever here.

7. Divine Director, shatter the energetic matrix that prevents people from seeing that since this could not come from our *biology,* it must come from our *psychology.*

Divine Director, by your grace,
in grander scheme I find my place,
my individual flame I see,
uniqueness God has given me.

Divine Director, send the light,
from blindness clear my inner sight,
my vision free, my vision clear,
your guidance is forever here.

8. Divine Director, shatter the energetic matrix that prevents people from seeing that there must be something in the human psyche that makes it possible for people to divide human beings into at least two separate groups.

Divine Director, vision one,
I see that I AM God's own Sun,
with your direction so Divine,
I am now letting my light shine.

Divine Director, send the light,
from blindness clear my inner sight,
my vision free, my vision clear,
your guidance is forever here.

9. Divine Director, shatter the energetic matrix that prevents people from seeing that we can dehumanize the scapegoat group to the point where we do not really think we are killing human beings by killing the scapegoats.

Divine Director, what a gift,
to be a part of Spirit's lift,

to raise mankind out of the night,
to bask in Spirit's loving sight.

Divine Director, send the light,
from blindness clear my inner sight,
my vision free, my vision clear,
your guidance is forever here.

Part 2

1. Divine Director, shatter the energetic matrix that prevents people from seeing that the division of humankind into separate groups starts at the identity level.

Divine Director, I now see,
the world is unreality,
in my heart I now truly feel,
the Spirit is all that is real.

Divine Director, send the light,
from blindness clear my inner sight,
my vision free, my vision clear,
your guidance is forever here.

2. Divine Director, shatter the energetic matrix that prevents people from seeing that there is an element of the human psyche that enables people to create these divisions that are clearly not based on biology.

Divine Director, vision give,
in clarity I want to live,
I now behold my plan Divine,
the plan that is uniquely mine.

Divine Director, send the light,
from blindness clear my inner sight,
my vision free, my vision clear,
your guidance is forever here.

3. Divine Director, shatter the energetic matrix that prevents people from seeing that the divisions are based on some kind of "ism," some kind of religion, some kind of political theory.

> Divine Director, show in me,
> the ego games, and set me free,
> help me escape the ego's cage,
> to help bring in the golden age.

> **Divine Director, send the light,**
> **from blindness clear my inner sight,**
> **my vision free, my vision clear,**
> **your guidance is forever here.**

4. Divine Director, shatter the energetic matrix that prevents people from seeing that even scientific Materialism has created the concept that some are more fit than others. This has been interpreted to mean that some are fit to rule and should be the elite that rules society and the rest of the population should just be the slaves that support the elite.

> Divine Director, I'm with you,
> my vision one, no longer two,
> as karma's veil you do disperse,
> I see a whole new universe.

> **Divine Director, send the light,**
> **from blindness clear my inner sight,**
> **my vision free, my vision clear,**
> **your guidance is forever here.**

5. Divine Director, shatter the energetic matrix that prevents people from seeing that there are these outer theories, these images that people create of how they think the world *should* work.

> Divine Director, I go up,
> electric light now fills my cup,
> consume in me all shadows old,
> bestow on me a vision bold.

**Divine Director, send the light,
from blindness clear my inner sight,
my vision free, my vision clear,
your guidance is forever here.**

6. Divine Director, shatter the energetic matrix that prevents people from seeing that throughout history, certain groups of people developed these theories that set themselves apart from others, but also defined that they had a superior position to others.

Divine Director, heart of gold,
my sacred labor I unfold,
o blessed Guru, I now see,
where my own plan is taking me.

**Divine Director, send the light,
from blindness clear my inner sight,
my vision free, my vision clear,
your guidance is forever here.**

7. Divine Director, shatter the energetic matrix that prevents people from seeing that most people in the democratic nations have a very superficial understanding of what democracy means.

Divine Director, by your grace,
in grander scheme I find my place,
my individual flame I see,
uniqueness God has given me.

**Divine Director, send the light,
from blindness clear my inner sight,
my vision free, my vision clear,
your guidance is forever here.**

8. Divine Director, shatter the energetic matrix that prevents people from seeing that we tend to think that democracy is a very easy form of society. Once we have a democracy, we are free and we will remain free for the indefinite future.

Divine Director, vision one,
I see that I AM God's own Sun,
with your direction so Divine,
I am now letting my light shine.

**Divine Director, send the light,
from blindness clear my inner sight,
my vision free, my vision clear,
your guidance is forever here.**

9. Divine Director, shatter the energetic matrix that prevents people from seeing that democracy seems like an easy form of government because all we have to do as a citizen is to vote, then the ruling elite are supposed to take care of everything else and we can focus on enjoying our daily lives.

Divine Director, what a gift,
to be a part of Spirit's lift,
to raise mankind out of the night,
to bask in Spirit's loving sight.

**Divine Director, send the light,
from blindness clear my inner sight,
my vision free, my vision clear,
your guidance is forever here.**

Part 3

1. Divine Director, shatter the energetic matrix that prevents people from seeing that in reality the easiest form of government is a dictatorship where the people do not need to make any choices because the system chooses for them.

Divine Director, I now see,
the world is unreality,
in my heart I now truly feel,
the Spirit is all that is real.

Divine Director, send the light,
from blindness clear my inner sight,
my vision free, my vision clear,
your guidance is forever here.

2. Divine Director, shatter the energetic matrix that prevents people from seeing that democracies emerged and dictatorships retreated because humankind has been raised to a level where many people cannot be satisfied by living the easy life of a dictatorship where they never have to make decisions.

Divine Director, vision give,
in clarity I want to live,
I now behold my plan Divine,
the plan that is uniquely mine.

Divine Director, send the light,
from blindness clear my inner sight,
my vision free, my vision clear,
your guidance is forever here.

3. Divine Director, shatter the energetic matrix that prevents people from seeing that we need to take responsibility for ourselves. There is a clear connection between the growth in humankind's consciousness and the emergence of democracies.

Divine Director, show in me,
the ego games, and set me free,
help me escape the ego's cage,
to help bring in the golden age.

Divine Director, send the light,
from blindness clear my inner sight,
my vision free, my vision clear,
your guidance is forever here.

4. Divine Director, shatter the energetic matrix that prevents people from seeing that the only reason democracies could emerge was that many people had reached that level of spiritual maturity where they were ready to

start taking responsibility for themselves and their lives, ready to start making decisions, learning from the consequences of those decisions.

Divine Director, I'm with you,
my vision one, no longer two,
as karma's veil you do disperse,
I see a whole new universe.

**Divine Director, send the light,
from blindness clear my inner sight,
my vision free, my vision clear,
your guidance is forever here.**

5. Divine Director, shatter the energetic matrix that prevents people from seeing that taking responsibility for our own growth means being willing to make decisions based on what we know now, and then look at the results of our decisions. If we do not like the results, then we expand your understanding so we can make better decisions in the future.

Divine Director, I go up,
electric light now fills my cup,
consume in me all shadows old,
bestow on me a vision bold.

**Divine Director, send the light,
from blindness clear my inner sight,
my vision free, my vision clear,
your guidance is forever here.**

6. Divine Director, shatter the energetic matrix that prevents people from seeing that the history of humankind has been a growth process and it has primarily been a growth in consciousness.

Divine Director, heart of gold,
my sacred labor I unfold,
o blessed Guru, I now see,
where my own plan is taking me.

Divine Director, send the light,
from blindness clear my inner sight,
my vision free, my vision clear,
your guidance is forever here.

7. Divine Director, shatter the energetic matrix that prevents people from seeing that what drives the progress seen in history is a raising of the collective consciousness, which is driven by individuals raising their individual consciousness.

Divine Director, by your grace,
in grander scheme I find my place,
my individual flame I see,
uniqueness God has given me.

Divine Director, send the light,
from blindness clear my inner sight,
my vision free, my vision clear,
your guidance is forever here.

8. Divine Director, shatter the energetic matrix that prevents people from seeing that democracy is the direct result of people starting to take responsibility for themselves. We have not continued the process of taking more and more responsibility for ourselves.

Divine Director, vision one,
I see that I AM God's own Sun,
with your direction so Divine,
I am now letting my light shine.

Divine Director, send the light,
from blindness clear my inner sight,
my vision free, my vision clear,
your guidance is forever here.

9. Divine Director, shatter the energetic matrix that prevents people from seeing that we have come to a plateau, we have stagnated, we have been lulled to sleep by thinking: "Now that we live in a democracy, we are free."

We need to start a new cycle, a new awakening, of taking more responsibility for our lives.

> Divine Director, what a gift,
> to be a part of Spirit's lift,
> to raise mankind out of the night,
> to bask in Spirit's loving sight.

> **Divine Director, send the light,**
> **from blindness clear my inner sight,**
> **my vision free, my vision clear,**
> **your guidance is forever here.**

Part 4

1. Divine Director, shatter the energetic matrix that prevents people from seeing that there are advanced souls embodying in the democratic nations. They want to use the opportunity to work on themselves, work on their psychology.

> Divine Director, I now see,
> the world is unreality,
> in my heart I now truly feel,
> the Spirit is all that is real.

> **Divine Director, send the light,**
> **from blindness clear my inner sight,**
> **my vision free, my vision clear,**
> **your guidance is forever here.**

2. Divine Director, shatter the energetic matrix that prevents people from seeing that because they have not been given a teaching about how to raise their consciousness, how to deal with their psychology, they manifest various forms of depression or mental illness.

> Divine Director, vision give,
> in clarity I want to live,

I now behold my plan Divine,
the plan that is uniquely mine.

Divine Director, send the light,
from blindness clear my inner sight,
my vision free, my vision clear,
your guidance is forever here.

3. Divine Director, shatter the energetic matrix that prevents people from seeing that this forces us to start looking at ourselves, and many of us have come to a point where we have decided to start to take more responsibility for ourselves than what we were brought up to do.

Divine Director, show in me,
the ego games, and set me free,
help me escape the ego's cage,
to help bring in the golden age.

Divine Director, send the light,
from blindness clear my inner sight,
my vision free, my vision clear,
your guidance is forever here.

4. Divine Director, shatter the energetic matrix that prevents people from seeing that democracy can only survive if people are in this process of taking more and more responsibility for ourselves, even for the world. We develop a more and more global awareness.

Divine Director, I'm with you,
my vision one, no longer two,
as karma's veil you do disperse,
I see a whole new universe.

Divine Director, send the light,
from blindness clear my inner sight,
my vision free, my vision clear,
your guidance is forever here.

5. Divine Director, shatter the energetic matrix that prevents people from seeing that a democracy is by definition not a form of government where a small elite rules the majority of the population. It is, at least in theory, a society where all people are involved in the decision making process.

Divine Director, I go up,
electric light now fills my cup,
consume in me all shadows old,
bestow on me a vision bold.

Divine Director, send the light,
from blindness clear my inner sight,
my vision free, my vision clear,
your guidance is forever here.

6. Divine Director, shatter the energetic matrix that prevents people from seeing that a democratic nation can only function in the best possible way if all of the people in that nation have some sense of connection with each other. They must feel that we are in the same boat, we are all being affected by the decisions made.

Divine Director, heart of gold,
my sacred labor I unfold,
o blessed Guru, I now see,
where my own plan is taking me.

Divine Director, send the light,
from blindness clear my inner sight,
my vision free, my vision clear,
your guidance is forever here.

7. Divine Director, shatter the energetic matrix that prevents people from seeing that we need to raise up the whole instead of one small portion of the whole. We cannot have an elitist society where there is one rich and privileged elite and the majority of the population living in limited conditions. That is not the idea behind democracy.

Divine Director, by your grace,
in grander scheme I find my place,

my individual flame I see,
uniqueness God has given me.

**Divine Director, send the light,
from blindness clear my inner sight,
my vision free, my vision clear,
your guidance is forever here.**

8. Divine Director, shatter the energetic matrix that prevents people from seeing that democracies require that we develop a sense of connection between us. That connection is our basic or essential humanity.

Divine Director, vision one,
I see that I AM God's own Sun,
with your direction so Divine,
I am now letting my light shine.

**Divine Director, send the light,
from blindness clear my inner sight,
my vision free, my vision clear,
your guidance is forever here.**

9. Divine Director, shatter the energetic matrix that prevents people from seeing that all men and women are created equal, all of us are endowed from a higher authority with certain rights. All people have those rights. This is an expression in words of the basic humanity.

Divine Director, what a gift,
to be a part of Spirit's lift,
to raise mankind out of the night,
to bask in Spirit's loving sight.

**Divine Director, send the light,
from blindness clear my inner sight,
my vision free, my vision clear,
your guidance is forever here.**

Part 5

1. Divine Director, shatter the energetic matrix that prevents people from seeing that "do unto others what you want others to do to you," is an expression in words of the basic humanity.

> Divine Director, I now see,
> the world is unreality,
> in my heart I now truly feel,
> the Spirit is all that is real.

> **Divine Director, send the light,**
> **from blindness clear my inner sight,**
> **my vision free, my vision clear,**
> **your guidance is forever here.**

2. Divine Director, shatter the energetic matrix that prevents people from seeing that when we feel compassion for others and want to do something to relieve the suffering of others, this is because we have that sense of basic humanity.

> Divine Director, vision give,
> in clarity I want to live,
> I now behold my plan Divine,
> the plan that is uniquely mine.

> **Divine Director, send the light,**
> **from blindness clear my inner sight,**
> **my vision free, my vision clear,**
> **your guidance is forever here.**

3. Divine Director, shatter the energetic matrix that prevents people from seeing that what works against this basic humanity is the fanatical mindset that divides humanity into separate groups that are not just separated by degree, but are separated in a fundamental way that makes it possible to dehumanize one group.

Divine Director, show in me,
the ego games, and set me free,
help me escape the ego's cage,
to help bring in the golden age.

**Divine Director, send the light,
from blindness clear my inner sight,
my vision free, my vision clear,
your guidance is forever here.**

4. Divine Director, shatter the energetic matrix that prevents people from seeing that when democracies emerged, there was a tremendous shift in the collective awareness. There were shock waves radiating through the collective emotional, mental and identity bodies.

Divine Director, I'm with you,
my vision one, no longer two,
as karma's veil you do disperse,
I see a whole new universe.

**Divine Director, send the light,
from blindness clear my inner sight,
my vision free, my vision clear,
your guidance is forever here.**

5. Divine Director, shatter the energetic matrix that prevents people from seeing that people saw tremendous hope and opportunity in not having to live their entire lives in a fixed station determined by their birth, but where they could do something to improve their station in life.

Divine Director, I go up,
electric light now fills my cup,
consume in me all shadows old,
bestow on me a vision bold.

**Divine Director, send the light,
from blindness clear my inner sight,
my vision free, my vision clear,
your guidance is forever here.**

6. Divine Director, shatter the energetic matrix that prevents people from seeing that the basis for democracy was the equal opportunity based on our own efforts. There was suddenly a new sense of equality.

Divine Director, heart of gold,
my sacred labor I unfold,
o blessed Guru, I now see,
where my own plan is taking me.

Divine Director, send the light,
from blindness clear my inner sight,
my vision free, my vision clear,
your guidance is forever here.

7. Divine Director, shatter the energetic matrix that prevents people from seeing that the basis for democracy is this sense of equality, based on the basic humanity. All people share in this essential humanity, therefore all people have rights, all people have a right to be here.

Divine Director, by your grace,
in grander scheme I find my place,
my individual flame I see,
uniqueness God has given me.

Divine Director, send the light,
from blindness clear my inner sight,
my vision free, my vision clear,
your guidance is forever here.

8. Divine Director, shatter the energetic matrix that prevents people from seeing that all people are just people, human beings. We cannot divide humanity into separate groups, say one is superior, one is inferior, one is right, the other group is bad and they can be killed.

Divine Director, vision one,
I see that I AM God's own Sun,
with your direction so Divine,
I am now letting my light shine.

**Divine Director, send the light,
from blindness clear my inner sight,
my vision free, my vision clear,
your guidance is forever here.**

9. Divine Director, shatter the energetic matrix that prevents people from seeing that at the identity level, it is the division of human beings into separate groups that starts fanaticism.

Divine Director, what a gift,
to be a part of Spirit's lift,
to raise mankind out of the night,
to bask in Spirit's loving sight.

**Divine Director, send the light,
from blindness clear my inner sight,
my vision free, my vision clear,
your guidance is forever here.**

Sealing

In the name of the I AM THAT I AM, I accept that Archangel Michael, Astrea and Shiva form an impenetrable shield around myself and all constructive people, sealing us from all fear-based energies in all four octaves. I accept that the Light of God is consuming and transforming all fear-based energies that make up the dark forces working against ending the era of fanaticism on earth!

27 | INVOKING APPRECIATION FOR TRUE EQUALITY (PART 2)

In the name of the I AM THAT I AM, Jesus Christ, I use the authority that I have as a being in embodiment on earth to call upon the Divine Director to reinforce my calls and use my chakras to project the statements in this invocation into the collective consciousness and awaken people to the fact that fanatics divide human beings into two groups and that this will always create conflict. Awaken people to the reality that we are spiritual beings and that we can co-create a new future by working with the ascended masters. I especially call for …

[Make your own calls here.]

Part 1

1. Divine Director, shatter the energetic matrix that prevents people from seeing that one aspect of fanaticism is based on hatred and anger in the emotional body.

Divine Director, I now see,
the world is unreality,
in my heart I now truly feel,
the Spirit is all that is real.

**Divine Director, send the light,
from blindness clear my inner sight,
my vision free, my vision clear,
your guidance is forever here.**

2. Divine Director, shatter the energetic matrix that prevents people from seeing that one aspect of fanaticism is driven by these "isms," these beliefs in the mental body.

Divine Director, vision give,
in clarity I want to live,
I now behold my plan Divine,
the plan that is uniquely mine.

**Divine Director, send the light,
from blindness clear my inner sight,
my vision free, my vision clear,
your guidance is forever here.**

3. Divine Director, shatter the energetic matrix that prevents people from seeing that the most fundamental aspect of fanaticism is the division in the identity body between those who are super-humans and those who are sub-humans.

Divine Director, show in me,
the ego games, and set me free,
help me escape the ego's cage,
to help bring in the golden age.

**Divine Director, send the light,
from blindness clear my inner sight,
my vision free, my vision clear,
your guidance is forever here.**

4. Divine Director, shatter the energetic matrix that prevents people from seeing that our democracies had a period where there was more of a sense of equality. In later decades, we have gone in the opposite direction and there is a growing inequality.

> Divine Director, I'm with you,
> my vision one, no longer two,
> as karma's veil you do disperse,
> I see a whole new universe.

> **Divine Director, send the light,**
> **from blindness clear my inner sight,**
> **my vision free, my vision clear,**
> **your guidance is forever here.**

5. Divine Director, shatter the energetic matrix that prevents people from seeing that there is the emergence of a very rich and privileged elite. They have become an elite through money, creating a clear division of the population of democratic nations between the very rich and the majority of the population who are not really poor, but who are nowhere near the rich elite.

> Divine Director, I go up,
> electric light now fills my cup,
> consume in me all shadows old,
> bestow on me a vision bold.

> **Divine Director, send the light,**
> **from blindness clear my inner sight,**
> **my vision free, my vision clear,**
> **your guidance is forever here.**

6. Divine Director, shatter the energetic matrix that prevents people from seeing that this division is a danger sign for democracy. It is a potential threat to democracy because it moves back towards the feudal societies where instead of a few people owning the land, a few people own the financial system.

Divine Director, heart of gold,
my sacred labor I unfold,
o blessed Guru, I now see,
where my own plan is taking me.

**Divine Director, send the light,
from blindness clear my inner sight,
my vision free, my vision clear,
your guidance is forever here.**

7. Divine Director, shatter the energetic matrix that prevents people from seeing that this ensures that the majority of the population can only stay at the level of working people, those who have to do actual work to make a living, whereas the elite make their money off of their money. The money makes more money, and this keeps going indefinitely.

Divine Director, by your grace,
in grander scheme I find my place,
my individual flame I see,
uniqueness God has given me.

**Divine Director, send the light,
from blindness clear my inner sight,
my vision free, my vision clear,
your guidance is forever here.**

8. Divine Director, shatter the energetic matrix that prevents people from seeing that after 9/11 in 2001 we have seen the emergence of a new type of anti-Muslim fundamentalists in the West. Those who are against terrorists, those who are the extreme right wing, from the Neo-Nazis to the more conservative people who want to shut out immigrants, close the borders, close the societies.

Divine Director, vision one,
I see that I AM God's own Sun,
with your direction so Divine,
I am now letting my light shine.

**Divine Director, send the light,
from blindness clear my inner sight,
my vision free, my vision clear,
your guidance is forever here.**

9. Divine Director, shatter the energetic matrix that prevents people from seeing that the key to survival is diversification. This new movement works directly against diversification.

Divine Director, what a gift,
to be a part of Spirit's lift,
to raise mankind out of the night,
to bask in Spirit's loving sight.

**Divine Director, send the light,
from blindness clear my inner sight,
my vision free, my vision clear,
your guidance is forever here.**

Part 2

1. Divine Director, shatter the energetic matrix that prevents people from seeing that the modern democracies have become more open and tolerant, but certain people cannot accept this so they have become more polarized against it.

Divine Director, I now see,
the world is unreality,
in my heart I now truly feel,
the Spirit is all that is real.

**Divine Director, send the light,
from blindness clear my inner sight,
my vision free, my vision clear,
your guidance is forever here.**

2. Divine Director, shatter the energetic matrix that prevents people from seeing that this is another danger sign where we see that these people are going into the same fanatical mindset as the Muslim extremists that they are so afraid of—without being willing to see this because of cognitive dissonance.

Divine Director, vision give,
in clarity I want to live,
I now behold my plan Divine,
the plan that is uniquely mine.

**Divine Director, send the light,
from blindness clear my inner sight,
my vision free, my vision clear,
your guidance is forever here.**

3. Divine Director, shatter the energetic matrix that prevents people from seeing that this is a danger sign in democracy. It is a sign that the modern democracies have started losing the basic connection that we are all equal, that we all have the same basic humanity, and therefore have the same rights and deserve the same opportunity.

Divine Director, show in me,
the ego games, and set me free,
help me escape the ego's cage,
to help bring in the golden age.

**Divine Director, send the light,
from blindness clear my inner sight,
my vision free, my vision clear,
your guidance is forever here.**

4. Divine Director, shatter the energetic matrix that prevents people from seeing that a few beings have developed a sense of identity as being set apart from all other beings. They see themselves as being superior to human beings, as belonging to an elite.

Divine Director, I'm with you,
my vision one, no longer two,

as karma's veil you do disperse,
I see a whole new universe.

Divine Director, send the light,
from blindness clear my inner sight,
my vision free, my vision clear,
your guidance is forever here.

5. Divine Director, shatter the energetic matrix that prevents people from seeing that the elite, some of them in physical embodiment, some of them in the emotional, mental and identity realm, see themselves as being fundamentally different from all other beings on earth.

Divine Director, I go up,
electric light now fills my cup,
consume in me all shadows old,
bestow on me a vision bold.

Divine Director, send the light,
from blindness clear my inner sight,
my vision free, my vision clear,
your guidance is forever here.

6. Divine Director, shatter the energetic matrix that prevents people from seeing that the elite believe they are in a fundamental way superior to human beings. They do not consider themselves human beings. An example is Hitler and the dream of the Aryan race, the super race.

Divine Director, heart of gold,
my sacred labor I unfold,
o blessed Guru, I now see,
where my own plan is taking me.

Divine Director, send the light,
from blindness clear my inner sight,
my vision free, my vision clear,
your guidance is forever here.

7. Divine Director, shatter the energetic matrix that prevents people from seeing that the elite do not consider themselves to be human beings as others. They think it is their right to look at human beings as chess pieces that can be moved around or knocked over at will. They think that humanity is just a playground for them to outplay their desire for power.

Divine Director, by your grace,
in grander scheme I find my place,
my individual flame I see,
uniqueness God has given me.

**Divine Director, send the light,
from blindness clear my inner sight,
my vision free, my vision clear,
your guidance is forever here.**

8. Divine Director, shatter the energetic matrix that prevents people from seeing that we cannot explain the cause of fanaticism unless we recognize that there is a certain group of beings who see themselves as being fundamentally different from human beings.

Divine Director, vision one,
I see that I AM God's own Sun,
with your direction so Divine,
I am now letting my light shine.

**Divine Director, send the light,
from blindness clear my inner sight,
my vision free, my vision clear,
your guidance is forever here.**

9. Divine Director, shatter the energetic matrix that prevents people from seeing that the elite see human beings as being lower than themselves. They have absolutely no empathy, no sense of connection. They have no sense of essential humanity. They have no pity, no mercy upon human beings.

Divine Director, what a gift,
to be a part of Spirit's lift,

to raise mankind out of the night,
to bask in Spirit's loving sight.

**Divine Director, send the light,
from blindness clear my inner sight,
my vision free, my vision clear,
your guidance is forever here.**

Part 3

1. Divine Director, shatter the energetic matrix that prevents people from seeing that the elite have no compunctions about starting a war that kills millions of human beings. If they had been able to, they would have started the Third World War, fought with nuclear weapons, that might have killed hundreds of millions of people.

Divine Director, I now see,
the world is unreality,
in my heart I now truly feel,
the Spirit is all that is real.

**Divine Director, send the light,
from blindness clear my inner sight,
my vision free, my vision clear,
your guidance is forever here.**

2. Divine Director, shatter the energetic matrix that prevents people from seeing that the elite have absolutely no pity, no empathy with the suffering of human beings. We cannot explain fanaticism, we cannot explain the presence of evil, without recognizing this.

Divine Director, vision give,
in clarity I want to live,
I now behold my plan Divine,
the plan that is uniquely mine.

Divine Director, send the light,
from blindness clear my inner sight,
my vision free, my vision clear,
your guidance is forever here.

3. Divine Director, shatter the energetic matrix that prevents people from seeing that these elite beings *are not* in a fundamentally different category. They *see themselves* as being in a fundamentally different category.

Divine Director, show in me,
the ego games, and set me free,
help me escape the ego's cage,
to help bring in the golden age.

Divine Director, send the light,
from blindness clear my inner sight,
my vision free, my vision clear,
your guidance is forever here.

4. Divine Director, shatter the energetic matrix that prevents people from seeing that we need to recognize the presence of these elite beings, recognize how they are working, without going into the fanatical mindset of judging them as being fundamentally different and because they are evil, it is justified to kill them.

Divine Director, I'm with you,
my vision one, no longer two,
as karma's veil you do disperse,
I see a whole new universe.

Divine Director, send the light,
from blindness clear my inner sight,
my vision free, my vision clear,
your guidance is forever here.

5. Divine Director, shatter the energetic matrix that prevents people from seeing that it is necessary to know that there is a certain group of beings who do not have any empathy for the suffering of humanity, who are willing to inflict suffering for their own ends.

Divine Director, I go up,
electric light now fills my cup,
consume in me all shadows old,
bestow on me a vision bold.

**Divine Director, send the light,
from blindness clear my inner sight,
my vision free, my vision clear,
your guidance is forever here.**

6. Divine Director, shatter the energetic matrix that prevents people from seeing that it is necessary to see this so that we can avoid becoming tools for them. It is not constructive to go into the fanatical mindset where we think that because these people are evil, it is justified to kill them.

Divine Director, heart of gold,
my sacred labor I unfold,
o blessed Guru, I now see,
where my own plan is taking me.

**Divine Director, send the light,
from blindness clear my inner sight,
my vision free, my vision clear,
your guidance is forever here.**

7. Divine Director, shatter the energetic matrix that prevents people from seeing that it was necessary to out-picture this extreme evil as the only way people could learn the lessons in the School of *very* Hard Knocks. Given the state of the planet, humanity had to see this out-pictured.

Divine Director, by your grace,
in grander scheme I find my place,
my individual flame I see,
uniqueness God has given me.

**Divine Director, send the light,
from blindness clear my inner sight,
my vision free, my vision clear,
your guidance is forever here.**

8. Divine Director, shatter the energetic matrix that prevents people from seeing that we do not need to remain in the School of Hard Knocks. We can transcend it, but the only people who can do this are those in the modern democracies who have risen to a higher level of spiritual development and maturity.

Divine Director, vision one,
I see that I AM God's own Sun,
with your direction so Divine,
I am now letting my light shine.

**Divine Director, send the light,
from blindness clear my inner sight,
my vision free, my vision clear,
your guidance is forever here.**

9. Divine Director, shatter the energetic matrix that prevents people from seeing that as a result of rising to a higher level of spiritual maturity, we have also gained a sense of the basic humanity.

Divine Director, what a gift,
to be a part of Spirit's lift,
to raise mankind out of the night,
to bask in Spirit's loving sight.

**Divine Director, send the light,
from blindness clear my inner sight,
my vision free, my vision clear,
your guidance is forever here.**

Part 4

1. Divine Director, shatter the energetic matrix that prevents people from seeing that we are facing the delicate challenge of realizing the fallen beings exist, but we avoid going into any kind of negative, angry, judgmental state of mind about them.

Divine Director, I now see,
the world is unreality,
in my heart I now truly feel,
the Spirit is all that is real.

Divine Director, send the light,
from blindness clear my inner sight,
my vision free, my vision clear,
your guidance is forever here.

2. Divine Director, shatter the energetic matrix that prevents people from seeing that instead of fighting the elite beings, we can call for the judgment of Christ upon them and leave the judgment to the ascended masters.

Divine Director, vision give,
in clarity I want to live,
I now behold my plan Divine,
the plan that is uniquely mine.

Divine Director, send the light,
from blindness clear my inner sight,
my vision free, my vision clear,
your guidance is forever here.

3. Divine Director, I call for the judgment of Christ upon the fallen beings in the identity, mental, emotional and physical realm who are behind fanaticism.

Divine Director, show in me,
the ego games, and set me free,
help me escape the ego's cage,
to help bring in the golden age.

Divine Director, send the light,
from blindness clear my inner sight,
my vision free, my vision clear,
your guidance is forever here.

4. Divine Director, I call for the removal of these dark forces so that the rest of humanity can become free from the blinding influence of these dark forces.

Divine Director, I'm with you,
my vision one, no longer two,
as karma's veil you do disperse,
I see a whole new universe.

**Divine Director, send the light,
from blindness clear my inner sight,
my vision free, my vision clear,
your guidance is forever here.**

5. Divine Director, I call for the judgment of Christ upon the fallen beings who have distorted people's minds by pulling them into supporting these "isms," these epic causes that cause people to be blinded by the mechanism in the mental body where there is a veil that prevents them from seeing their cognitive dissonance.

Divine Director, I go up,
electric light now fills my cup,
consume in me all shadows old,
bestow on me a vision bold.

**Divine Director, send the light,
from blindness clear my inner sight,
my vision free, my vision clear,
your guidance is forever here.**

6. Divine Director, I call for the judgment of Christ upon the fallen beings who have tricked people time and time again.

Divine Director, heart of gold,
my sacred labor I unfold,
o blessed Guru, I now see,
where my own plan is taking me.

**Divine Director, send the light,
from blindness clear my inner sight,
my vision free, my vision clear,
your guidance is forever here.**

7. Divine Director, shatter the energetic matrix that prevents people from seeing that there must be certain types of human beings who have a particular agenda, an agenda that always leads to conflict, warfare and suffering.

Divine Director, by your grace,
in grander scheme I find my place,
my individual flame I see,
uniqueness God has given me.

**Divine Director, send the light,
from blindness clear my inner sight,
my vision free, my vision clear,
your guidance is forever here.**

8. Divine Director, shatter the energetic matrix that prevents people from seeing that a few narcissists or psychopaths that have no empathy for the suffering of others have created so much suffering in history.

Divine Director, vision one,
I see that I AM God's own Sun,
with your direction so Divine,
I am now letting my light shine.

**Divine Director, send the light,
from blindness clear my inner sight,
my vision free, my vision clear,
your guidance is forever here.**

9. Divine Director, shatter the energetic matrix that prevents people from seeing that they have done this because they managed to take normal human beings and pull them into doing the dirty work for them, pull them into serving their epic causes.

Divine Director, what a gift,
to be a part of Spirit's lift,
to raise mankind out of the night,
to bask in Spirit's loving sight.

**Divine Director, send the light,
from blindness clear my inner sight,
my vision free, my vision clear,
your guidance is forever here.**

Part 5

1. Divine Director, shatter the energetic matrix that prevents people from seeing that throughout history, people have been seduced by these epic causes, such as medieval Christians who thought it was epically important to make all human beings members of the Catholic religion.

Divine Director, I now see,
the world is unreality,
in my heart I now truly feel,
the Spirit is all that is real.

**Divine Director, send the light,
from blindness clear my inner sight,
my vision free, my vision clear,
your guidance is forever here.**

2. Divine Director, shatter the energetic matrix that prevents people from seeing that there has been a tendency throughout history for the emergence of a small power elite who have had this mindset of defining certain epic causes and then pulling people into supporting a very aggressive militant action to promote this cause by killing all those people who stand in the way.

Divine Director, vision give,
in clarity I want to live,

I now behold my plan Divine,
the plan that is uniquely mine.

**Divine Director, send the light,
from blindness clear my inner sight,
my vision free, my vision clear,
your guidance is forever here.**

3. Divine Director, shatter the energetic matrix that prevents people from seeing that the elite have accomplished this by dividing humanity into at least two groups. There are us, we are the superior, we are those who are right, then there are the scapegoats, they are inferior. They are not even really human. We are not really killing our own species by killing them because they are subhuman.

Divine Director, show in me,
the ego games, and set me free,
help me escape the ego's cage,
to help bring in the golden age.

**Divine Director, send the light,
from blindness clear my inner sight,
my vision free, my vision clear,
your guidance is forever here.**

4. Divine Director, shatter the energetic matrix that prevents people from seeing that at the mental level the elite have defined an epic cause. We must spread Christianity around the world. We must spread communism around the world because it is a historical necessity. We must do this, we must do that.

Divine Director, I'm with you,
my vision one, no longer two,
as karma's veil you do disperse,
I see a whole new universe.

**Divine Director, send the light,
from blindness clear my inner sight,**

my vision free, my vision clear,
your guidance is forever here.

5. Divine Director, shatter the energetic matrix that prevents people from seeing that all of these epic causes that have been defined have pulled people into becoming *fan*s of an *ism,* thereby going into *fanaticism.*

Divine Director, I go up,
electric light now fills my cup,
consume in me all shadows old,
bestow on me a vision bold.

Divine Director, send the light,
from blindness clear my inner sight,
my vision free, my vision clear,
your guidance is forever here.

6. Divine Director, shatter the energetic matrix that prevents people from seeing that the elite have been experts in whipping up certain emotions in an entire population of anger and hatred that causes them to direct the frustrations they have against another group of people.

Divine Director, heart of gold,
my sacred labor I unfold,
o blessed Guru, I now see,
where my own plan is taking me.

Divine Director, send the light,
from blindness clear my inner sight,
my vision free, my vision clear,
your guidance is forever here.

7. Divine Director, shatter the energetic matrix that prevents people from seeing that when people are angry enough, they cannot see that what they are doing is not rational, is against their professed beliefs or their sense of humanity. They are taken over by anger and they have an outlet for their anger: Kill the scapegoats.

Divine Director, by your grace,
in grander scheme I find my place,
my individual flame I see,
uniqueness God has given me.

**Divine Director, send the light,
from blindness clear my inner sight,
my vision free, my vision clear,
your guidance is forever here.**

8. Divine Director, I call for the judgment of Christ upon the fallen beings who have used fanaticism to create all of these atrocities. I call for them to be removed so they cannot affect the future of this planet.

Divine Director, vision one,
I see that I AM God's own Sun,
with your direction so Divine,
I am now letting my light shine.

**Divine Director, send the light,
from blindness clear my inner sight,
my vision free, my vision clear,
your guidance is forever here.**

9. Divine Director, I call for the judgment of Christ upon all human beings who are trapped in the fanatical mindset so they will receive an opportunity to see it and to see how to free themselves and their societies from it.

Divine Director, what a gift,
to be a part of Spirit's lift,
to raise mankind out of the night,
to bask in Spirit's loving sight.

**Divine Director, send the light,
from blindness clear my inner sight,
my vision free, my vision clear,
your guidance is forever here.**

Sealing

In the name of the I AM THAT I AM, I accept that Archangel Michael, Astrea and Shiva form an impenetrable shield around myself and all constructive people, sealing us from all fear-based energies in all four octaves. I accept that the Light of God is consuming and transforming all fear-based energies that make up the dark forces working against ending the era of fanaticism on earth!

28 | THE MOST SUBTLE ASPECT OF FANATICISM

I AM the Ascended Master Gautama Buddha. Sometimes people say that you save the best for last. In our case, we have saved the most difficult for last, in the sense that what I will try to expound upon in this discourse is the most subtle, the most difficult to grasp, aspect of fanaticism.

The question I will begin with is to have you look at the many, many people, both today and throughout history, who have gone into this fanatical mindset. They have defined some kind of cause based on some kind of worldview, some kind of "ism," some kind of religion. They have been absolutely convinced that they were right, that their viewpoint had some absolute truth or some absolute authority, being given by God himself, or whatever people have used to give their viewpoint the particular sense of authority that made them feel it was epically important to get the world to conform to their viewpoint. Even in many cases, to the point where they were willing to kill other people and felt that it was justified by God that they killed these other people.

How is it possible that people can be so convinced about this? We have said before that today you can look back at some of the beliefs people had in previous ages and you clearly see the limitations of them. Therefore, you should be able to project that in your own time here, many people have these absolutist viewpoints and it is likely that in times to come, they will be seen as also being incomplete or primitive. It will be obvious to people why they are not absolute viewpoints, whereas to the people who are now trapped in the fanatical mindset, they are completely unable to see that their viewpoint is not absolute.

How is it possible that human beings can take a viewpoint that truly is not absolute but they elevate it to the status of being absolute? This is something that very few people, at least in the western world, have considered. You can see that if the democratic nations are to really move beyond this era of fanaticism that has dominated the earth for all of known history, then they need to come to an understanding of how this can be. How is it possible that human beings can convince themselves that an illusion is an absolute truth, that an incomplete understanding or view is some ultimate, final understanding?

Thinking an illusion is an absolute truth

If you look at western philosophers, going back to Aristotle and Plato and all the ones in between, very few have actually even considered the cause of this. I gave a teaching 2,500 years ago that can at least be a starting point. It is to be found in the Dhammapada today and it is the concept of the pairs—that there are always two pairs, two opposites, what we today call two dualistic polarities. I also gave the concept of the Four Noble Truths and the idea that life is suffering, that there is a Sea of Samsara that causes suffering. What I really wanted to say with these concepts, but which was difficult to express in words so long ago, was that the reason so many people experience life as suffering is that they have gone into a particular state of consciousness. This state of consciousness is dominated by these pairs of dualistic opposites. It is this state of consciousness that causes suffering, but how does it cause suffering? Well, it causes suffering because it causes people to go into a state of illusion.

Now, we may say that if you have a car, this is a particular piece of technology that is developed to make your life easier. It is developed in order to make it easier for you to get from point A to point B, however long the distance is. If the car is working well and if you are operating it correctly, using your car will be an easy experience—a comfortable, pleasant experience that will get you from point A to point B. However, if you are not operating your car correctly because you are in a state of ignorance of how the car actually functions, then your car can give you a very frustrating experience. If, as we said, you put the car in reverse and expect it to go forward, then it can be rather frustrating to get to work at rush hour. If you are driving backwards against the currents of all the other cars, then it is not going to be a whole lot of fun to try to get to work on time.

The reality here is that the earth, the material universe, can be considered as a piece of machinery. I am not saying it *is* a piece of machinery but for the sake of analogy, it can be considered as a piece of machinery, a piece of technology. We have talked before about the earth being a reality simulator. The earth is a piece of technology, it is designed to work a certain way. Now, you know that your car may not always function the way it is designed to do, but I can assure you that the material universe, planet earth, the physical realm, always works the way it is intended to work, the way it is designed to work. In other words, there is no fault possible on the part of the machinery.

I know that there are many, many people who have come up with the idea that something has gone wrong with God's plan for the universe. They have used this to justify the fanatical mindset because these people have to help God make his universe work by killing other people. Regardless, I am telling you the absolute fact here: There is nothing wrong with the machinery on earth. It works the way it was designed to do. It is just like a computer, it can only operate based on its programming, it cannot deviate from the programming. Nothing has gone wrong here. The earth works the way it was designed to work.

Operating the earth from a state of ignorance

Why is it that people suffer on earth? It is because they are trying to operate the machinery of the earth from a state of ignorance. They are not operating the machinery the way it was designed to work, they are going against the basic design principles as we have described. For example, going against the very biological principles that you can observe by looking at the history of how species have evolved. It is attempting to go against the basic principles of the machinery, operating the machinery in a way it was not designed to operate. This is what causes suffering. This is what causes friction. This is what causes you not to get the results you want to get from the machinery.

This is a simple analogy. We can then build on it and say: "Well, what is it that has caused people to operate the machinery in a different way than it was intended?" It is that they have gone into a state of ignorance about how the machinery works. They do not understand how the machine works, they do not know which buttons to push. Therefore, they are pushing the wrong buttons and the machinery cannot give them the result they want. Why are they pushing the wrong buttons? Because they have gone into, not only a state of ignorance but this particular state of consciousness where they are actually doing the opposite of what the machinery is designed to do. They have gone into this state of what we call the dualistic state of consciousness that is dominated by two opposite polarities.

As a result of this, we could say that the machinery is designed to work a certain way. This is what I called the Middle Way. It is not the midpoint between two extremes, but there is a certain way the machine is designed to work and if you understand that, your experience of being on earth will not be frustrated.

Somewhere in what we might call the Middle Way, there is the correct workings of the machinery. The duality consciousness causes people to go towards two extremes. Again, the Middle Way is not the midpoint between the extremes but the extremes pull people away from the Middle Way. When you are pulled towards one extreme, you are adopting a mental image of how the machine is supposed to work according to your image. You think you know how the machine is supposed to work but you do not understand how the machine actually works. Your dualistic polarity (the pair towards which you have been polarized and including the other dualistic polarity), they do not give you a correct understanding of how the machine operates. Whether you are in this extreme, *this* dualistic polarity, or the *other* dualistic polarity, you are pulled away from a clear vision of how the machine actually operates.

Those seeking to deceive humankind

What is the characteristic of this dualistic state of consciousness? Naturally, you who are ascended master students know that we have given many teachings on this, but for the completeness of this book and the tools, I wish to give you at least some basic understanding of this. This is where it can be difficult to understand this without realizing that there is a certain consciousness, a certain type of beings, who are deliberately trying to deceive human beings in order to be able to control them. The reason it is important to understand this is that otherwise people tend to think (as many people do think) something has gone wrong with the machinery.

There must be a flaw in the design. Some cosmic accident happened and God's intent was not fulfilled. That is why we now have to help God combat the devil by killing the people who are doing the works of the devil. Or you can even have materialists who think there is some kind of flaw in the design of nature. Therefore, they need to do genetic experiments and genetic mutations to improve the body. Or they need to help evolution along by purifying the species of these unfortunate elements. That is why you have the whole concept of Eugenics and selective breeding and purifying the race through the concentration camps and so on.

You see that, whether you are religious, whether you have a materialistic approach or a political approach, you can find ways to justify killing others if you think something has gone wrong. The only way to really free yourself from this idea that something has gone wrong with the actual workings of the machinery, is to realize that there are some beings who have an aggressive intent to pull humanity into these dualistic extremes.

You realize that it is not by accident that people have gone into the extremes, it is by design. Not necessarily intelligent design, I would rather call it *un*intelligent design, but definitely there is an aggressive intent to pull people into these dualistic polarities that causes the fanatical mindset.

Of course, this raises the question of why? We have given teachings on this that I do not want to go into here because I simply want to make an observation of human history and see that there has always been a small elite of people who are attempting to control and manipulate the broad population. This is an observation that anyone with a neutral approach can make from just looking at history. There is an intent to manipulate. It was not an accident that people stepped into duality. It is the result of a direct manipulation.

This means you can now realize that, even though people who are pulled into a dualistic polarity believe it is an absolute truth, it is truly an illusion. It is a lie. In many cases, it is a deliberate lie that is created in order (in many cases) to set one group of people in conflict with another group of people. If you actually look at history, you will see that in all cases where you have had these kinds of epic battles, epic conflicts, epic causes (such as the Nazi cause, to again use an obvious example here from Europe) you have had this dynamic that the people who were promoting the cause were claiming that it was all done for a beneficial purpose. There was a reason why the Jews had to be killed and it was to benefit the human race or some other cause, some *epic* cause.

No epic cause is ever true

Now, as we have said, all of these epic causes that people have defined throughout the ages, if they go to the point where they cause people to kill each other, this goes against your biological instincts. You do not naturally kill members of your own species. This shows that all of these epic causes are actually out of touch with how the machinery works. As we said, the process of evolution can be seen as a very long process of experimentation that has gradually clarified what actually works, what actually allows the species to survive. This demonstrates how the machine actually works. Any cause that causes people to kill each other, goes against the basic design of the machinery. Therefore, it is proven to be an illusion. Anything that causes people to kill each other can only be based on an illusion because it goes against nature itself. It even goes against human nature when you understand what human nature is, as opposed to the fallen nature.

How is it then possible to define such an epic cause? Well, you do that by using the duality consciousness—what I called ignorance. Ignorance, not in the sense that you do not know, but that you have an incomplete understanding that you think is complete, that you think is absolute. What is the main characteristic of this dualistic consciousness? It is that it is selective. When you go into this state of consciousness, it is like putting on (to give you the simplest example) a pair of colored glasses. You know that these glasses distort your vision by, for example, excluding a certain type of light. You may wear a certain color glasses and the sky looks purple because the glasses filter out a certain type of light. If you did not have a frame of reference by having seen the sky without the glasses, you might believe the sky is purple, but you know it is not. When you go into the duality consciousness, it is like putting on a pair of colored glasses. What you see is a distorted vision. You do not realize it is distorted or limited. You do not realize that something has been excluded. You think you have the complete vision of life.

The duality consciousness is selective because there are certain things you can see and there are certain things that are filtered out that you cannot see. When you have this selective vision (which we could also call a *relative* vision because it is relative to your vantage point, the perspective you have from where you are), then there are certain things you just cannot see. You cannot see how the machine actually operates. You cannot see, for example, that all human beings on earth are connected at the energetic level, that you are all connected through this collective energy field. Whether it is an emotional, a mental or an identity level field, there is a collective field that connects all people. What you do to others, will affect the whole. You are part of that whole, therefore what you do to others will affect yourself.

The machine is designed to give people growth

When you go into the state of duality, you cannot see that you are connected to everybody else. You begin to see yourself as a separate individual. In most cases, you think you belong to a particular group that is separated from a particular other group or from the rest of humanity.

We could say that the machinery on earth is designed based on the absolute fact, the absolute reality, that all life is one, that you are all connected through this collective energy field. Therefore, what is best for you as an individual is to do something that raises the whole. This is how the machine is designed to work. This is how the machine actually works.

When you go into the duality consciousness, you lose this vision. Now, you start thinking that just as human bodies are separate, human minds are also separate, human *beings* are separate You think that what you observe at the physical level is the ultimate reality. This is how life works. The way life works at the physical level is the way it works everywhere. You may even deny that there is anything beyond the physical level, as materialists do.

You think that, for example, you can observe at the physical level: "Oh, I can kill that other person's physical body but my body still stays alive. It doesn't affect me that I kill that other person." That is why you come to believe that you are separate beings and you can do something to others and get away with it. It does not affect yourself.

Is this true? Is this correct? Well, it is of course an illusion, and because it is an illusion, because you are trying to operate the machinery on earth in a way that it is not designed to operate, then the machinery can only give you suffering. It can only cause suffering. How does it cause suffering? Well, let us first look at how the machine is designed to work.

The machine is designed to give all human beings on earth a positive, joyous experience. What makes you have a positive experience? It is that you feel that you are not limited, you are not restricted. You are free to grow. You are free to transcend yourself. In the way that the machine is designed to work, it is possible for seven billion individuals to be in embodiment on this planet at the same time but they do not feel they are restricted by each other. They do not feel they are in conflict with each other. Each human being sees that: "The real purpose of my life is to expand my individual consciousness. That expansion of my individual consciousness is not restricted by anybody else. However, I am connected to everybody else. When I live my life in a way that gives me personal growth, without hindering the growth of other people (perhaps I even use my experience to help other people grow), then we all grow together and then we all have that positive experience of constantly growing, constantly transcending ourselves."

We have said that if you look at biological evolution, you must conclude from a neutral observation that there is a driving force behind the evolution that causes life to grow, to constantly transcend itself. This is the basic drive in human psychology. In order to have a positive life experience, you need to feel you are growing, you are expanding. What is it then that causes suffering? Well, it is when people first of all lose the awareness that the purpose of life is growth in awareness. Instead, they are pulled away from that realization, that experience. They are pulled into thinking that they are static beings, they are pulled into adopting a sense of identity: "I am a human being and this is what it means to be a human being, this is what I *can* and *cannot* do." Then, as a result of this they are also pulled into focusing very much on the outer situation.

Your growth depends on your inner conditions

When you go into the duality consciousness, you lose the awareness that you can transcend your own state of consciousness. You think that your state of consciousness does not depend entirely on your inner conditions and your own choices, your state of consciousness depends on outer conditions. The extreme example of this, the extreme outplaying of this consciousness, is Materialism, which claims that human consciousness is a product of the material processes in the brain. In other words, there is no consciousness separate from matter. What has happened in this process is that you (who are not a material being, your mind is not a material being) have been blinded by the dualistic consciousness into thinking that you are either a material being or at least that your state of mind, your happiness, is defined by material conditions.

In the original design of the machinery, the material conditions on earth are simply tools that are designed to facilitate your growth in consciousness.

When you go into the state of duality, you start seeing yourself as a separate being, meaning you are separated from the process of life. Instead of seeing material conditions as tools to promote your growth, you begin to think that material conditions limit you, even define you, certainly define what you *can* and *cannot* do on earth. You do not think you can change or transcend the material conditions that are here on earth right now. You think they are defined by something, whether it be a remote God in the sky or some natural law, over which you have no influence, over which humankind at large has no influence. This is what happens when you see yourself as a separate being. You are separated from your own higher self, therefore you do not have the direct experience that there is more to your being than what you experience at the conscious level. Therefore, you forget that you have the possibility to expand your consciousness until you establish oneness with your higher self, and therefore you are not affected by any conditions on earth. Instead, you think you are separated from the flow of life, the process of life, the process of transcendence, you are defined by matter, you are limited by matter. When you step into duality, you experience that you are limited by matter because you see yourself as separated from matter.

Consciousness is cause, matter is effect

When you are not in duality, when you are not in ignorance, you realize that (as we have said) matter is a form of energy. Energy is vibration, the connection between matter and energy is that thoughts are a form of energy. Therefore, thoughts can affect the energy that makes up matter and ultimately affect matter. You therefore realize that you can actually change the conditions, humankind can change the conditions, on earth through their consciousness. You can even come to realize that after humankind fell into duality, they have changed the original design and made the earth more dense. You realize here that you lose the awareness of reality: That consciousness is cause and matter is effect, consciousness is the primary and matter is secondary.

Now, you begin to think that because you are separated from matter, you cannot influence matter with your consciousness, you experience that you cannot influence matter with your consciousness. This is not reality, this is because you have gained an incorrect vision of how the machine operates. Now, instead of pushing the right buttons, you are pushing all the wrong buttons. Therefore, your experience is correct: You cannot change matter with the mind. This does not mean that mind cannot change matter. It means that the dualistic mind cannot change matter. When you go into this state of duality, you can no longer change matter and therefore, as long as you are in the dualistic state of mind, you are limited by matter. You are potentially (depending on how deeply you go into duality) defined by matter.

When you step into this mindset of seeing yourself as a separate being (you are separated from your source, your higher self, you are separated from matter), well, naturally you also then experience that you are separated from other human beings. It is when you see yourself as separated from other human beings that there will inevitably be tension, conflicts of interest between you and other people. This will inevitably create suffering. Instead of people all having the same goal and all moving in the same direction (namely self-transcendence towards higher states of consciousness) and all pursuing their individual growth without limiting others, you now have people having all kinds of different individual goals, wanting to go in all kinds of separate directions. Therefore, you have a state that could very well be described as chaos, people are going in all these different directions. Each person, each man is an island, each one is going towards a separate goal. Depending on how deeply they are trapped in the illusions of duality, they may feel that they have a perfect right to pursue their individual goals regardless of the consequences that it has for other people.

You can see how this is the original cause of human suffering. You see yourself as separate beings, you no longer have an awareness of your connection, of any common goal, of any purpose for life. You are not seeing how the machine is designed to facilitate your experience and therefore, instead of having a *fulfilling* experience, you are having a *frustrating* experience. This is the Sea of Samsara, this is suffering.

From innocent ignorance to aggressive ignorance

Now, this is not fanaticism. Because in a sense we could say that the initial stage of going into duality and separation is what we might call "innocent ignorance." You are just unaware now of your connection to other people, your connection to your higher self. You no longer see it because you have put on these glasses that filter out that connection and only allows you to see yourself as a separate being. Therefore, you are going your own way, everybody else is doing the same thing and you are all running around in a chaotic manner, just like you see in, for example, an anthill where (even though the ants are actually coordinated) to you it looks completely chaotic. This has nothing to do with fanaticism—it is just ignorance of how the machinery works.

Fanaticism comes in when you take duality further towards the extreme. This is where you now, instead of just being ignorant of how the machine works, you start formulating a theory, an idea, an ism, a religion where you attempt to define how the machine *should* work, how you want the machine to work. Now, instead of being *innocently* ignorant, you become *aggressively* ignorant. Because now you are actually saying to yourself: "I don't want to be suffering." But you are not aware that the only true way to escape suffering is to change your own state of consciousness.

The only way to truly escape suffering is to again free yourself from duality so you are not seeing yourself as a separate being. The only way to feel fulfilled as a human being is to be connected to your higher self, to be connected to the flow of life so you are transcending yourself. Now, you could still do this on earth even as chaotic as the planet is. That is why, from the beginning of time, there has always been a mystical path for those who were able to find it. A few people, going back to the beginning, have found it and walked it, and you can walk it as an individual.

Those who go further and further into duality, they cannot see self-transcendence as a way to get what they actually want. They are saying: "I don't want to have a frustrating experience. How can I have a better experience? Well, I don't have the physical power to do it myself, I need other people." This is what is behind the entire mindset where certain people now go into this aggressive state of mind where they want to manipulate and control other people so that these other people will conform to their vision and therefore give them a less frustrating experience.

You can see it outpictured in the feudal societies of Europe where the noblemen sat in their castles and had a more pleasant lifestyle than the peasants because the peasants were doing all the hard work. The noblemen were just reaping the rewards of the peasants' labor. This was the start, we might say, of the more aggressive form of ignorance, the more aggressive form of duality. You can see this going back very, very far in many societies where there was the emergence of a privileged elite. They were not necessarily maliciously manipulating people. They were not necessarily manipulating people into killing each other. They were manipulating other people to do the work for them so that they could have a more comfortable, affluent, privileged lifestyle. This was, we might say, the more innocent beginnings of fanaticism. It was not really necessarily fanaticism but it set the stage for fanaticism.

Ideas that gave birth to fanaticism

If you actually look at the earth before the advent, the incarnation, of fallen beings, before there were any fallen beings associated with the earth, you still saw that humankind had gone into duality. You still saw that certain people started to set themselves up as a privileged elite because they wanted a more comfortable, pleasant lifestyle. They got that lifestyle by getting other people to work for them.

Now, this was something that could not be done by physical power. One nobleman does not have the physical power to force five hundred peasants to work for him. In order to get this done, they needed to have some kind of idea, some kind of philosophy, some kind of ism that caused these other people to work for the elite. Back in prehistoric times there were various versions of this. You can even see some of it in historical times, but you really only saw this take the turn that you see today after the fallen beings began to embody on the planet.

What you see in the fallen beings is that in many cases they do set themselves up as a privileged elite when they are in physical embodiment but this is not actually what drives them. They are actually not so concerned about having a pleasant lifestyle. At least, having a comfortable lifestyle is not enough for them. They have some kind of agenda that goes beyond just their comfortability. They have what we call an epic agenda and the epic agenda is the extreme outcome of the dualistic mindset. Basically, we could say (to use the analogy I have used here) that the machinery of planet earth (the physical octave, or even the entire physical universe), is designed to work a certain way.

Human beings on earth, before the fallen beings came here, were ignorant. They had become ignorant of how the machine actually works. The fallen beings, well, they are also ignorant of how the machine works, but they have now used the dualistic mindset to set themselves up where they believe that they can take the dualistic mindset and they can take it towards one dualistic extreme. They can elevate that dualistic extreme into an absolute truth. Then, they can project that on the machinery and they can say: "This is how the machine *should* have been working all along. This is how it *should* have been designed to work." In other words, at first you are just ignorant of how the machine works and therefore you create suffering. When you take this to the logical extreme, you start judging how the machine *should* have been designed, you start finding fault with the design of the machine and in some cases even with the designer of the machine.

You realize there must have been a designer, whether you call it God or something else. Now, you start thinking that because you have elevated one dualistic extreme (which is basically an illusion, but you have elevated it to an absolute truth), therefore, you can judge that the designer of the machine made a mistake and should not have designed it that way. It should have been designed in another way. This is what leads to this ultimate epic cause where now you see certain beings on earth who create this epic idea and now they seek to first persuade people to accept their epic idea. If you look at history, you will see that it has always been impossible for them to get all people on earth to accept the idea. Therefore, they take the next step of saying that those people who will not accept the epic idea should be killed because the epic idea defines a goal that should be manifest on earth, a change that should be manifest. Those people who will not accept that idea are working against that goal and therefore it is justified that they be killed so that the goal can be manifest. This is truly the essence of fanaticism and the fanatical mindset.

Why any "truth" has an opposite

Although this is a teaching that you cannot expect the general public to begin to understand, there are actually people who are ready to begin to see this in a more universal version than what we have given you previously in our teachings. They may not be able to recognize ascended masters or fallen beings but they can certainly make observations and see that there is this epic mindset, and that some people tend to promote this epic mindset.

What is it that makes these epic causes seem plausible to people? It is again that the duality consciousness focuses on one aspect of reality, elevates this to being the complete understanding of reality, and therefore defines that all different understandings are wrong in an epic way. Therefore, the people who hold these other ideas are wrong in an epic way and should be killed.

Now, why is it that even these very aggressive beings can never persuade everybody to accept their dualistic idea? Well, it is because in duality, nothing can exist alone. If you go back throughout history, you will see that there has been a dream among human beings to find the ultimate truth, the one truth, the absolute truth. This is because you still have some subconscious memory that there is an ultimate truth. But the ultimate truth is in the correct understanding of how the machine works and how it was designed to work. *That* is the truth.

When you step into duality, you cannot see that truth. You can come to see it again by raising yourself above duality, but you can never see it in duality. In duality, there is never one truth because in duality you are moving towards one polarity, one extreme. In moving towards that extreme, you are moving away from the opposite extreme.

In other words, as I said 2,500 years ago with the pairs, they come into being as pairs, the dualistic polarities. It is never so that you have one polarity that comes into being first and then the other comes later. They come into being simultaneously and this means that, as some people start converting other people to believing in one dualistic polarity, it is inevitable that other people will start believing in the opposite dualistic polarity. Therefore, you can never through persuasion convince everybody of one truth.

Why is that? Because when you have a pair of dualistic polarities, there is no ultimate argument that validates one and invalidates the other. There is no ultimate argument possible in dualistic polarities. It is so, my beloved, that if you are not in duality, you can clearly see that none of the two polarities is true. It is not so that one is absolutely true and the other is absolutely wrong. When you are not in duality, you see that they are both wrong in the sense that they are both illusions. Right and wrong does not really apply when you are not in duality, but you see that they are both illusions.

There is no absolute argument, no objective truth, no objective reality that could be discovered. There is no ultimate revelation from God that can validate a dualistic polarity. What makes it seem valid? Well, it is that you are moving in consciousness into the polarity. You are putting on the glasses. You are drinking the Kool-Aid. When you put on the glasses of one dualistic polarity, you see only what validates that polarity and the glasses filter out anything that invalidates it. You might be able to see these other arguments, but you see them as invalid. Of course, those who are in the opposite dualistic polarity, they have another pair of glasses so everything that these people see as valid, the other group sees as invalid and vice versa. *That* is why, after humankind descended into duality, there could never ever be consensus where everybody believed in the same religion or the same belief system.

The alternative to duality

When Jesus said: "Go ye into all the world and make all people my disciples," he did not mean to go into the world and convert them to one dualistic polarity, such as a particular outer religion, even if it was based on his teachings. What he really came to show was that there is an alternative to the dualistic state of consciousness, namely the Christ consciousness or what I called enlightenment. He wanted his disciples (that hopefully had glimpsed and experienced the Christ consciousness) to convert all other people to realize that there is an alternative to duality.

This is what I wanted 2,500 years ago and it is what all true spiritual teachers throughout the ages have wanted for people—just to set them free, to demonstrate that there is an alternative to duality because duality can only cause suffering. The only way to escape suffering is to transcend duality, to go beyond duality.

Now, what is it that those who are manipulating humankind are saying? They are saying there is actually a way to escape suffering in duality and it is defined by our epic philosophy. This defines how the machinery should work and if you follow this, then you will escape suffering and we will have this wonderful utopia manifest on earth. However, this requires that all people accept this belief system. Obviously those other people are not accepting it. So how are we going to manifest this wonderful kingdom on earth? Well, we have to kill those other people.

Now, of course attempting to kill other people—well they are not likely to just lie down and wait for you to kill them so this inevitably creates a struggle. You can see how, when you look at the reality of this, it is not difficult for people to actually go through one of these shifts we have talked about, and realize that although these epic causes (and there are many examples of them throughout history) always promise that we will escape suffering, it is precisely because they lead to conflict between groups of people that they actually reinforce suffering.

Suffering is not natural or inevitable

When you look with the current level of understanding of life, you may say: "There are certain conditions on earth that are natural conditions that we can't do anything about." As we said, everything is a result of consciousness. Nevertheless, what people believe right now is that there are certain natural conditions that we humans cannot do anything about and some of these natural conditions cause various forms of suffering. You could say then that this is something we cannot do anything about, but then you can certainly very easily come to see that throughout history these "natural" forms of suffering are not even the ones that have caused the most human suffering.

What has caused the most human suffering is man-made conflicts that have been (all of them) driven by these epic causes. The epic mindset, this tendency to define epic causes that requires you to force or kill other people, *that* is actually the single cause of most of the suffering you see on earth.

Then, people can start wondering: "Well, how can we then escape that? How can we escape this state of consciousness that has caused so much suffering?" This is where again there is a potential that people in the democratic nations can come to see: "Why do we have democracies? Well, isn't it because we have moved away from believing in these epic causes? Therefore, we have actually moved into starting to go beyond the illusion that we are all separate beings." The epic cause only seems plausible when you think you are separate. This is the only reason you can believe that you can diminish suffering by killing other people, that you can create an ideal state on earth by killing other people.

What is democracy an expression of? It is that many people have started moving beyond the more extreme aspects of the duality consciousness and started to see that there is some state of connection between people. Democracy is based on some realization that we are all in the same boat. Therefore, we need to look at what is best for the whole, what is best for the largest number of people, instead of just a small elite or a particular group. We cannot allow the interests of one small group to override the interests of the general population.

You can see that the advent of democracy proves that humankind has started to move beyond the dualistic state of consciousness and specifically the epic mindset. It is not actually impossible for you to call forth a shift where in the beginning just a few people (as has already happened to some degree) start to see that there is something here, there is some kind of consciousness that blinds people, there is some kind of consciousness that is the cause of human conflict. When people begin to see this, it can come to that point where it starts spreading and more and more people begin to see it, and suddenly they see that the emperors of duality have nothing on, these epic causes have nothing on.

Again, you can say: "Well, the radical Muslims are obviously in the epic mindset. They think that it is epically important that they spread Islam around the world, and that this is the will of Allah. How are we going to change them?" This is again where you need to hold the vision that democracies prove that people have begun to see that all people are connected somehow, and therefore you are connected to these Muslim extremists. When you raise your own consciousness in the democratic nations, you will pull up on the whole and it will gradually shift the equation.

The control game to prevent change

As an example, let us take the Muslim nations in the Middle East. If you could see it from the ascended perspective, you could see that there is tremendous tension in these societies. You could actually come to see, if you look at history, that every time there has been one of these extreme manifestations of fanaticism, it is because of what we have called fallen beings, the very aggressive beings that seek to control humankind. They are making a desperate attempt to maintain control. The reason they are doing this is that they can see that they are in danger of losing control because the collective consciousness has been raised so that a majority of the people are close to the point where they will no longer believe the illusion that has allowed them to be controlled.

Now, you see in the Muslim world that there is a growing tension, because we are getting close to that point where a majority of the people in Muslim nations are breaking free of the illusion of the extreme, the fundamentalist, interpretation of Islam, the Sharia law. They are beginning to question it, and, at least in their own minds, they no longer believe in it. Therefore, they are becoming more and more reluctant to submit to this very controlled society, this very divided society with a clearly privileged elite that the population cannot touch. The fallen beings know that they are getting closer and closer to losing control. That is why they have launched this, quite frankly desperate and not very intelligent, attempt to create these radical Muslim fundamentalist movements that do all kinds of chaotic things.

If you accept these ideas in the West, you can actually look at this, you can see that clearly many people in the West see how primitive it is. Then, you can realize that if you turn the dial of your consciousness just a little bit, you can see that this is actually a sign that a breakthrough is very close to happening because otherwise there would not be such a clearly unbalanced, desperate attempt.

Muslim terrorism is not really directed at the West, the West is just a scapegoat. The real purpose behind Muslim fundamentalism is actually to maintain control over the population in Muslim countries. The West is just a distraction to draw people's attention away from their internal tensions and the need to change their own societies.

The German population before Hitler was close to breaking through to a new level, as we said. The fallen beings managed to use Hitler to divert their attention so that instead of changing German society in a fundamental way, they directed all their frustration and willingness to change toward the Jews as the scapegoat. They thought they could solve their problems by changing the scapegoat or killing the scapegoat. This is exactly what is happening in Muslim countries right now. This is exactly what has been happening throughout the ages.

You can go back to the feudal times in Europe, you can see how many wars were created that were simply distractions to prevent an overthrow of the basic system. You can even see how wars were created as a distraction to prevent people from escaping the control of the Catholic church. Therefore, you can see that if you look at world history, the deeper underlying cause of many wars, in fact most wars, has been this mechanism. There have been those beings who have had control of a population but over time they cannot continue to maintain their control, precisely because people begin to see the illusions of this dualistic polarity that has been used to justify the control. Just as you saw that the Catholic doctrines, the completely distorted view of Jesus' teachings, were used to justify these very rigid medieval societies, you saw that there came a point where people gradually started doubting or questioning Catholic doctrine.

Then, you can see that the fallen beings created various conflicts, various wars, such as the Crusades (as the obvious example) to divert people away from the need for internal change where people again were misled into thinking that they could change their situation by changing other people, by forcing other people, by killing other people.

Duality causes internal suffering

Do you see the picture that begins to emerge here? To go back to my analogy, the material universe is a machine that is perfectly designed to give all people on earth a positive experience without suffering. The way the machine is designed is that you get a positive experience by changing yourself and by working to raise the whole, helping other people to change themselves. When you go into duality, you lose the awareness of how the machine is designed to work. You experience from the very beginning that you are suffering and now you begin to think that the way to escape suffering is not to change yourself but to change other people, to force other people.

When you go into duality, you actually have a state of internal suffering, you cannot be in duality without suffering psychologically. Once you step into the duality consciousness, there is a division in your psyche that pulls you in different directions. You are, as Jesus said: "A house divided against itself." This causes internal psychological suffering.

When you are in duality, you cannot see that you could transcend yourself, you could escape the suffering by working on yourself. Therefore, you are pulled into thinking that your suffering is not caused by *internal* factors, it is caused by *external* factors, including other people. The way to escape suffering is to change other people and since they will not change voluntarily, it is justified to force them.

Do you see? If you look throughout the ages, you can see that some people have not been willing to kill other people but other people have. Why is it that some people come to the extreme where they are willing to kill other people? Well, it is because their internal suffering has become so intense that they can barely stand it. They are becoming desperate to escape their internal suffering. That is why they are willing to go to this extreme measure of forcing or even killing other human beings.

Of course, they do this because they have been deceived by an epic cause that says that if they kill other people, they will diminish their suffering. The reality that you can see throughout history is that this has never worked because as soon as you start physically forcing or killing other people, you only increase your suffering.

Democracy is based on not forcing others

Therefore, it is possible that people in democratic nations can make this shift of suddenly seeing what is the basis of democratic societies, namely, that we cannot diminish suffering in the world through force and by forcing others. How can we then create a society that has less suffering? By creating a society where all men, all human beings, are seen as being equal and having equal rights. Therefore, no individual or no group of people have a right to force others. This is the basic principle of democracy. One group of people does not have a right to force another group of people because people have a right to live without force. That is why you have seen the democratic nations create societies where there is less suffering, there is less conflict, there is less force. We might say there is less physical suffering in the democratic nations. Greater abundance, greater material affluence, equals less physical suffering.

Increased mental problems is a measure of success

What have we talked about of the increase in mental problems and mental illness? What does that demonstrate? It demonstrates that even though democratic societies have completed one part of the process of creating less physical suffering, they have not sufficiently started the other part of the process, which is to create less internal, less psychological, suffering.

The very fact that you see an increase in psychological problems, and people who are willing to acknowledge their psychological problems, actually demonstrates how successful you have been. As we talked about with Maslow's pyramid of needs, when you have an intense physical suffering, you cannot really worry about your psychology. It is perfectly natural that when you create societies where people's entire attention is not put into just physical survival and combating physical forms of suffering, it is only natural and logical that they are freed up, their attention is freed up, to focus on the internal suffering.

Therefore, the next logical step in the evolution of democracy is to focus on helping people overcome the internal suffering. How do you do this? Well, not through a materialistic approach to psychology but by acknowledging that throughout the ages there has been, in various forms, these mystical paths where people have been offered a way to escape duality. It is not a matter of western democracies now going back to Buddhism and accepting Buddhism. It is even not a matter of them accepting some mystical form of Christianity. It is a matter of realizing that certainly there is a version of this path beyond duality that is suitable for modern western democracies, or modern democracies anywhere on the planet.

It is just a matter of developing this, finding this so that you can help people escape that suffering. As more and more people in the democratic nations begin to escape the dualistic mindset, then you will see that there will be less of an external threat against the democratic nations from those people who are still in the dualistic mindset. What Jesus actually meant, the deeper meaning of what Jesus said with "turn the other cheek," is that if you turn the other cheek and continue to turn the other cheek, then there will come a point where you will no longer be attacked because the aggression of the attacker will be turned back upon themselves.

The mistake made after 9/11

What actually happened after 9/11 when America started this crusade to go into Muslim nations with armed forces? This actually postponed this process. If the West had been willing to turn the other cheek, then you would have already seen that the tension in Muslim societies would *not* have been diverted towards attacking the West. It would have resulted in civil wars that would have started the process of overthrowing the fundamentalist Islamic group. In other words, the aggression in Muslim nations could not have been channeled against the West, if the West had turned the other cheek. It would have therefore been directed against themselves. This would have led to an undeniable change, as you to some degree have already seen in some of these nations.

This is again just a matter of observing life and realizing that what Jesus said, what I said about coming into Nirvana and walking the Middle Way, is simply a way to escape duality. The Middle Way is beyond duality. When you recognize this, you realize that we are describing a general principle of, not necessarily nature but certainly how the universe works. This is how the universe works. When you accept this, you bring yourself and your society into alignment with how the machine actually works. That is how you can start creating societies where people do not see themselves as separate. They see that there is a goal for their lives, which is to raise their consciousness, even transcend a certain lower state of consciousness but then continue growing in consciousness. If this is the main goal for society, where nobody is seeking to limit each other, then there is almost no end to the material affluence and the material progress that such a society can see.

What you have seen in the rise of affluence in many modern nations in the last hundred years is just the tip of the iceberg of what could actually happen. You could have Golden Age societies that you cannot even imagine today. When you stop fighting amongst each other, stop fighting internally, you stop fighting against the machine and instead, start looking at: "How is the machine actually designed? Could it be that we have had the machine in reverse? If we put it in a forward gear, we will suddenly start going forward. Could it be that simple?" And it *is* that simple.

Working with, not against, the universe

It is only the epic mindset, the epic causes, that complicates everything. There are certain beings that deliberately want to deceive and want to confuse by making everything seem so incredibly complicated. Your car may seem like a very complicated device but it is very, very simple. If you want to go forward, put it in a forward gear. Do not put it in reverse and expect that you can go forward. How simple is that? Life works exactly the same way. Put your mind in a forward gear and your entire society will go forward. What could be more simple?

Can people trapped in duality see this? Absolutely not because they think they have an absolute truth that is far more complex and that requires them to, not find out how the machine works and then push the right buttons. No, their quest is to change the machine.

Again, go back to this consciousness that people have today (even though it is not correct), the belief that there are certain natural conditions that you cannot change. Well, what is best for you? To find out how the machine actually works and then work with the machine? Or to try to change the machine? Would it be possible for people to change the orbit of the earth around the sun? Imagine you had a civilization where all people in that civilization directed all of their efforts, all of their mental efforts, towards that one cause of changing the earth's orbit around the sun. Would you consider this a productive use of people's time and energy? Obviously, it would be ridiculous. Then, look at how many civilizations throughout history have had some epic belief where they were actually attempting to change the way the universe works. You can see that there was no chance whatsoever that they could have been successful.

What the universe is really designed to do

I know this has been a long discourse already, my beloved, but surely, if it has already been too long, what does it matter that it is a little bit more too long? This brings us to consider: Well, if the machine is actually designed to give people a positive experience, how come they can go into suffering? How come it is possible? This means that if we step back from this, we realize that what I have said is actually not the full understanding. The machine is not really designed to give you a *positive* experience. It can very well give you, it is designed in such a way that you can have an entirely positive experience. The deeper reality is that the machine is designed to give you *any* experience you want. That is why people can go into duality.

In order to have an uplifting experience, you have to see yourself as connected to the machine, to your higher self, to other people. When you are in that connected state of consciousness, you can have an entirely positive experience. What if people do not want a positive experience? They want a different experience. Well, they can have that by going into the consciousness of duality where now they see themselves as separate beings.

Of course, when you think about this logically, if there is the possibility of having an uplifting, positive experience, what can be different from that? What is the alternative to a positive experience? Well, it is an experience of suffering, right? There is a state of no suffering and there is a state of suffering. You can have the experience of not suffering or you can have the experience of suffering.

How do you have the experience of suffering? You go into duality. You see yourself as a separate being and *that* is how you suffer. You suffer internally. You suffer externally. What is the machine designed to do? Well, it is designed in such a way that people are allowed to go into suffering. Unfortunately, the very mechanics of how the machine has to be designed, based on free will, is that once you go into duality, the illusion of duality becomes self-reinforcing.

Duality is a self-reinforcing illusion

What have I explained? You have two dualistic polarities. If you move towards one polarity, what you are seeing is what validates the polarity. You are not seeing, or you are seeing as false, what questions the polarity. This is how duality becomes a self-reinforcing process, a self-reinforcing, a self-perpetuating illusion. Once you are in duality, you have a limited view. You can only use logic. You still have a logical mental mind but there is a limit to how you can use that mental mind.

That is what other masters have talked about that enables people to stay in the fanatical mindset. At the intellectual level, in their mental bodies, there is a veil. They cannot see. When you have two dualistic polarities, there is a veil between them that prevents you from seeing both at the same time. Therefore, you cannot see both as valid. Or rather, you cannot see that they are both limited, they are both illusions. You cannot see this at the same time. There is simply a limit, once you are inside the box of duality, to how you can use logic and reason.

That is why it is, from an ascended perspective, completely unrealistic when modern scientists, materialists, think they can know everything through reason. It is a complete blind alley when Aristotle thought (and instead of considering the ideal forms in a higher realm, like Plato talked about) you could know everything about how the material universe works by looking at the material universe, taking a reductionist approach, looking at smaller units. His philosophy was an expression of duality, separation.

When you are not in separation, you look at the whole. When you go into separation, you only look at the parts. You cannot see the whole. You cannot see the forest for the trees. You are looking at it from the vantage point of being a separate individual and therefore you think everything in the universe can be understood as being made up of separate components. You cannot see that although you can talk about components of a whole, what really is the cause of everything is the whole, the workings of the whole. There are no separate components. There are components, but they are not separate. There are parts in the machine but they are not separate. They are all *part* of the machine, they are not *apart* from the machine. In duality, you think that you are apart from everything. Therefore, you can never use reason to escape duality. It cannot be done.

The way out of duality

What is the way out? Well, there are two ways out or rather there is only one. It is that people begin to go beyond reason and they use their intuitive faculties. Now, in this day and age we have explained that if you go into duality (where your four lower bodies, your outer self, the outer self that you use to interact with the world is divided), you are a house divided against yourself. Even though you are in this state, you still have a part of your being that we call the Conscious You, which is not divided, it cannot be divided.

Therefore, if you can switch away from the divisions, you can experience an alternative to the dualistic state of consciousness. You can experience what we have called pure awareness or a neutral state of mind. What I, in a sense, called enlightenment as the Buddha, this is what you can experience. Jesus called it Christ consciousness, other spiritual teachers have called it other things. The name does not matter. You have the ability to go into this neutral state of mind where you experience. You are not reasoning. You are not believing. You are not arguing. You *experience* that there is something outside of duality.

This gives you a frame of reference that now allows you to look at the dualistic beliefs and begin to see what you cannot see from inside the mental box. You begin to see the limitations. You begin to see the contradictions. That is how you can overcome the cognitive dissonance. This is what we might call an intuitive approach. You are not reasoning with the linear mind, with the logical mind. You are not coming up with some kind of theory. You are just going into neutral and experiencing that there is something outside of this dualistic chaos, this Sea of Samsara. Beyond all the chaos of the Sea of Samsara there is silence, there is quietness.

What is it going to take to bring a person to the point where he or she is willing to pull their attention away from the dualistic mind that is always seeking to change the world? What is it going to take? Well, as we have said, people (once they go into duality) must have a certain number of experiences in the School of Hard Knocks. They simply must experience a certain amount of suffering before they come to that point where they have had enough of suffering and they have experienced (over several lifetimes, which is why reincarnation is so important) that following these epic causes simply does not work.

Therefore, they come to that point where they say: "Could it be that if I want to escape suffering, I need to change something *inside* of myself, instead of changing something *outside* of myself? After all, where is the suffering occurring? Is it not occurring inside my own mind? Is it not in my mind that I am suffering? So is it really logical that I can only escape the suffering by changing something outside of my mind? Couldn't it be that the real way to escape suffering is to change something inside my mind?" *That* is when they become open and that is when they can have an experience of some kind that there is something beyond the dualistic mind and the reasoning of the dualistic mind, the arguing back and forth.

A new human right to internal freedom

That is when they can start the path that I called the Eight-Fold Path. It has been called many other things. You could come up with a version that is perfectly neutral for the modern democracies, a path where you systematically change your consciousness and you escape these illusions, this sense of separation, that causes all human suffering. It is possible, my beloved, that people can come to grasp this. Right now, there is a tension that has been built in the collective consciousness. You can see, when you look at the whole field of alternative or New Age spirituality, how there are already many people out there who have grasped versions of this, elements of this, and there is a tension that has been built.

In fact, you could again look at the militant atheist who launched such an aggressive attack against religion a few years ago, and see this as another desperate attempt to maintain the control over people's mindset that the materialist paradigm has given to the fallen beings now for a long time. The tension has already been building, and your calls can be just that final drop that causes the glass to overflow and now there is no holding back the shift to a new level of awareness. A new awareness, a new paradigm, a new worldview that can take the modern democracies to the next logical stage in their development where they focus on minimizing the internal suffering, the psychological suffering, of their people.

You could actually define a new human right. So far, you have focused on that people have a right to live without any *external* force limiting them. Likewise, people have a right to live without having any *internal* force limiting them. This therefore, is the next logical step in the evolution of humanity, and the nations who can take that step are clearly the modern democracies.

With this I have completed the delivery I wanted to give you and I can only express my gratitude for your willingness to endure such a long release. Really, we found it important to complete the message about fanaticism that we want to put out there so that it can be complete enough that it can actually have the desired effect. It can form a machine that has all the buttons that you need in order to get the result that you want: A new world that has transcended the era of fanaticism.

29 | INVOKING A NEW AWARENESS OF DUALITY (PART 1)

In the name of the I AM THAT I AM, Jesus Christ, I use the authority that I have as a being in embodiment on earth to call upon Gautama Buddha to reinforce my calls and use my chakras to project the statements in this invocation into the collective consciousness and awaken people to the reality of how the dualistic mindset has distorted life on earth. Awaken people to the reality that we are spiritual beings and that we can co-create a new future by working with the ascended masters. I especially call for …

[Make your own calls here.]

Part 1

1. Gautama Buddha, shatter the energetic matrix that prevents people from seeing that fanatics are absolutely convinced that they are right, that their viewpoint has some absolute truth or some absolute authority.

Gautama, show my mental state
that does give rise to love and hate,

your exposé I do endure,
so my perception will be pure.

**Gautama, Flame of Cosmic Peace,
unruly thoughts do hereby cease,
we radiate from you and me
the peace to still Samsara's Sea.**

2. Gautama Buddha, shatter the energetic matrix that prevents people from seeing that we can look back at some of the beliefs people had in previous ages and we clearly see the limitations of them.

Gautama, in your Flame of Peace,
the struggling self I now release,
the Buddha Nature I now see,
it is the core of you and me.

**Gautama, Flame of Cosmic Peace,
unruly thoughts do hereby cease,
we radiate from you and me
the peace to still Samsara's Sea.**

3. Gautama Buddha, shatter the energetic matrix that prevents people from seeing that in our own time, many people have these absolutist viewpoints and it is likely that in times to come, they will be seen as also being incomplete or primitive.

Gautama, I am one with thee,
Mara's demons do now flee,
your Presence like a soothing balm,
my mind and senses ever calm.

**Gautama, Flame of Cosmic Peace,
unruly thoughts do hereby cease,
we radiate from you and me
the peace to still Samsara's Sea.**

4. Gautama Buddha, shatter the energetic matrix that prevents people from seeing that in the future it will be obvious to people why they are

not absolute viewpoints whereas to the people who are now trapped in the fanatical mindset, they are completely unable to see that their viewpoint is not absolute.

Gautama, I now take the vow,
to live in the eternal now,
with you I do transcend all time,
to live in present so sublime.

Gautama, Flame of Cosmic Peace,
unruly thoughts do hereby cease,
we radiate from you and me
the peace to still Samsara's Sea.

5. Gautama Buddha, shatter the energetic matrix that prevents people from seeing that we need to understand how we can take a viewpoint that truly is not absolute but we elevate it to the status of being absolute.

Gautama, I have no desire,
to nothing earthly I aspire,
in non-attachment I now rest,
passing Mara's subtle test.

Gautama, Flame of Cosmic Peace,
unruly thoughts do hereby cease,
we radiate from you and me
the peace to still Samsara's Sea.

6. Gautama Buddha, shatter the energetic matrix that prevents people from seeing that if the democratic nations are to really move beyond the era of fanaticism that has dominated earth for all of known history, we need to understand how it is possible that we can convince ourselves that an illusion is an absolute truth.

Gautama, I melt into you,
my mind is one, no longer two,
immersed in your resplendent glow,
Nirvana is all that I know.

Gautama, Flame of Cosmic Peace,
unruly thoughts do hereby cease,
we radiate from you and me
the peace to still Samsara's Sea.

7. Gautama Buddha, shatter the energetic matrix that prevents people from seeing that the reason so many people experience life as suffering is that they have gone into a state of consciousness that is dominated by pairs of dualistic opposites.

Gautama, in your timeless space,
I am immersed in Cosmic Grace,
I know the God beyond all form,
to world I will no more conform.

Gautama, Flame of Cosmic Peace,
unruly thoughts do hereby cease,
we radiate from you and me
the peace to still Samsara's Sea.

8. Gautama Buddha, shatter the energetic matrix that prevents people from seeing that this state of consciousness causes suffering because it causes people to go into a state of illusion.

Gautama, I am now awake,
I clearly see what is at stake,
and thus I claim my sacred right
to be on earth the Buddhic Light.

Gautama, Flame of Cosmic Peace,
unruly thoughts do hereby cease,
we radiate from you and me
the peace to still Samsara's Sea.

9. Gautama Buddha, shatter the energetic matrix that prevents people from seeing that the earth, the material universe, can be considered as a piece of technology that is designed to work a certain way.

Gautama, with your thunderbolt,
we give the earth a mighty jolt,
I know that some will understand,
and join the Buddha's timeless band.

Gautama, Flame of Cosmic Peace,
unruly thoughts do hereby cease,
we radiate from you and me
the peace to still Samsara's Sea.

Part 2

1. Gautama Buddha, shatter the energetic matrix that prevents people from seeing that the material universe always works the way it is intended to work, the way it is designed to work. There is no fault possible on the part of the machinery.

Gautama, show my mental state
that does give rise to love and hate,
your exposé I do endure,
so my perception will be pure.

Gautama, Flame of Cosmic Peace,
unruly thoughts do hereby cease,
we radiate from you and me
the peace to still Samsara's Sea.

2. Gautama Buddha, shatter the energetic matrix that prevents people from seeing that many people have accepted the idea that something has gone wrong with God's plan for the universe. They have used this to justify the fanatical mindset because these people have to help God make his universe work by killing other people.

Gautama, in your Flame of Peace,
the struggling self I now release,
the Buddha Nature I now see,
it is the core of you and me.

Gautama, Flame of Cosmic Peace,
unruly thoughts do hereby cease,
we radiate from you and me
the peace to still Samsara's Sea.

3. Gautama Buddha, shatter the energetic matrix that prevents people from seeing that it is an absolute fact that there is nothing wrong with the machinery on earth. It works the way it was designed to do.

Gautama, I am one with thee,
Mara's demons do now flee,
your Presence like a soothing balm,
my mind and senses ever calm.

Gautama, Flame of Cosmic Peace,
unruly thoughts do hereby cease,
we radiate from you and me
the peace to still Samsara's Sea.

4. Gautama Buddha, shatter the energetic matrix that prevents people from seeing that the earth is just like a computer, it can only operate based on its programming, it cannot deviate from the programming. Nothing has gone wrong here. The earth works the way it was designed to work.

Gautama, I now take the vow,
to live in the eternal now,
with you I do transcend all time,
to live in present so sublime.

Gautama, Flame of Cosmic Peace,
unruly thoughts do hereby cease,
we radiate from you and me
the peace to still Samsara's Sea.

5. Gautama Buddha, shatter the energetic matrix that prevents people from seeing that people suffer on earth because they are trying to operate the machinery of the earth from a state of ignorance. They are not operating the machinery the way it was designed to work, they are going against the basic design principles.

Gautama, I have no desire,
to nothing earthly I aspire,
in non-attachment I now rest,
passing Mara's subtle test.

**Gautama, Flame of Cosmic Peace,
unruly thoughts do hereby cease,
we radiate from you and me
the peace to still Samsara's Sea.**

6. Gautama Buddha, shatter the energetic matrix that prevents people from seeing that operating the machinery in a way it was not designed to operate is what causes suffering. This is what causes friction. This is what causes us *not* to get the results we want to get from the machinery.

Gautama, I melt into you,
my mind is one, no longer two,
immersed in your resplendent glow,
Nirvana is all that I know.

**Gautama, Flame of Cosmic Peace,
unruly thoughts do hereby cease,
we radiate from you and me
the peace to still Samsara's Sea.**

7. Gautama Buddha, shatter the energetic matrix that prevents people from seeing that what has caused us to operate the machinery in a different way than it was intended is that we have gone into a state of ignorance about how the machinery works.

Gautama, in your timeless space,
I am immersed in Cosmic Grace,
I know the God beyond all form,
to world I will no more conform.

**Gautama, Flame of Cosmic Peace,
unruly thoughts do hereby cease,
we radiate from you and me
the peace to still Samsara's Sea.**

8. Gautama Buddha, shatter the energetic matrix that prevents people from seeing that we do not understand how the machine works, we do not know which buttons to push. Therefore, we are pushing the wrong buttons and the machinery cannot give us the result we want.

Gautama, I am now awake,
I clearly see what is at stake,
and thus I claim my sacred right
to be on earth the Buddhic Light.

Gautama, Flame of Cosmic Peace,
unruly thoughts do hereby cease,
we radiate from you and me
the peace to still Samsara's Sea.

9. Gautama Buddha, shatter the energetic matrix that prevents people from seeing that we are pushing the wrong buttons because we have gone into this particular state of consciousness, the dualistic state of consciousness, that is dominated by two opposite polarities.

Gautama, with your thunderbolt,
we give the earth a mighty jolt,
I know that some will understand,
and join the Buddha's timeless band.

Gautama, Flame of Cosmic Peace,
unruly thoughts do hereby cease,
we radiate from you and me
the peace to still Samsara's Sea.

Part 3

1. Gautama Buddha, shatter the energetic matrix that prevents people from seeing that the machine is designed to work a certain way and if we understand that, our experience of being on earth will not be frustrated.

Gautama, show my mental state
that does give rise to love and hate,
your exposé I do endure,
so my perception will be pure.

Gautama, Flame of Cosmic Peace,
unruly thoughts do hereby cease,
we radiate from you and me
the peace to still Samsara's Sea.

2. Gautama Buddha, shatter the energetic matrix that prevents people from seeing that the Middle Way is the correct workings of the machinery. The duality consciousness causes people to go towards two extremes.

Gautama, in your Flame of Peace,
the struggling self I now release,
the Buddha Nature I now see,
it is the core of you and me.

Gautama, Flame of Cosmic Peace,
unruly thoughts do hereby cease,
we radiate from you and me
the peace to still Samsara's Sea.

3. Gautama Buddha, shatter the energetic matrix that prevents people from seeing that the Middle Way is not the midpoint between the extremes but the extremes pull people away from the Middle Way.

Gautama, I am one with thee,
Mara's demons do now flee,
your Presence like a soothing balm,
my mind and senses ever calm.

Gautama, Flame of Cosmic Peace,
unruly thoughts do hereby cease,
we radiate from you and me
the peace to still Samsara's Sea.

4. Gautama Buddha, shatter the energetic matrix that prevents people from seeing that when we are pulled towards one extreme, we are adopting a mental image of how the machine is supposed to work according to our image.

Gautama, I now take the vow,
to live in the eternal now,
with you I do transcend all time,
to live in present so sublime.

Gautama, Flame of Cosmic Peace,
unruly thoughts do hereby cease,
we radiate from you and me
the peace to still Samsara's Sea.

5. Gautama Buddha, shatter the energetic matrix that prevents people from seeing that we think we know how the machine is supposed to work but we do not understand how the machine actually works.

Gautama, I have no desire,
to nothing earthly I aspire,
in non-attachment I now rest,
passing Mara's subtle test.

Gautama, Flame of Cosmic Peace,
unruly thoughts do hereby cease,
we radiate from you and me
the peace to still Samsara's Sea.

6. Gautama Buddha, shatter the energetic matrix that prevents people from seeing that the dualistic polarity towards which we have been polarized does not give us a correct understanding of how the machine operates.

Gautama, I melt into you,
my mind is one, no longer two,
immersed in your resplendent glow,
Nirvana is all that I know.

Gautama, Flame of Cosmic Peace,
unruly thoughts do hereby cease,
we radiate from you and me
the peace to still Samsara's Sea.

7. Gautama Buddha, shatter the energetic matrix that prevents people from seeing that whether we are in this extreme, this dualistic polarity, or the other dualistic polarity, we are pulled away from a clear vision of how the machine actually operates.

Gautama, in your timeless space,
I am immersed in Cosmic Grace,
I know the God beyond all form,
to world I will no more conform.

Gautama, Flame of Cosmic Peace,
unruly thoughts do hereby cease,
we radiate from you and me
the peace to still Samsara's Sea.

8. Gautama Buddha, shatter the energetic matrix that prevents people from seeing that there is a certain consciousness, a certain type of beings, who are deliberately trying to deceive human beings in order to be able to control us.

Gautama, I am now awake,
I clearly see what is at stake,
and thus I claim my sacred right
to be on earth the Buddhic Light.

Gautama, Flame of Cosmic Peace,
unruly thoughts do hereby cease,
we radiate from you and me
the peace to still Samsara's Sea.

9. Gautama Buddha, shatter the energetic matrix that prevents people from seeing that whether we are religious, whether we have a materialistic approach or a political approach, we can find ways to justify killing others if we think something has gone wrong.

Gautama, with your thunderbolt,
we give the earth a mighty jolt,
I know that some will understand,
and join the Buddha's timeless band.

**Gautama, Flame of Cosmic Peace,
unruly thoughts do hereby cease,
we radiate from you and me
the peace to still Samsara's Sea.**

Part 4

1. Gautama Buddha, shatter the energetic matrix that prevents people from seeing that the only way to free ourselves from the idea that something has gone wrong with the workings of the machinery, is to realize that there are some beings who have an aggressive intent to pull humanity into these dualistic extremes.

Gautama, show my mental state
that does give rise to love and hate,
your exposé I do endure,
so my perception will be pure.

**Gautama, Flame of Cosmic Peace,
unruly thoughts do hereby cease,
we radiate from you and me
the peace to still Samsara's Sea.**

2. Gautama Buddha, shatter the energetic matrix that prevents people from seeing that it is not by accident that people have gone into the extremes, it is by design. Not necessarily intelligent design, but unintelligent design. There is an aggressive intent to pull people into these dualistic polarities that causes the fanatical mindset.

Gautama, in your Flame of Peace,
the struggling self I now release,

the Buddha Nature I now see,
it is the core of you and me.

**Gautama, Flame of Cosmic Peace,
unruly thoughts do hereby cease,
we radiate from you and me
the peace to still Samsara's Sea.**

3. Gautama Buddha, shatter the energetic matrix that prevents people from seeing that human history shows that there has always been a small elite of people who are attempting to control and manipulate the broad population.

Gautama, I am one with thee,
Mara's demons do now flee,
your Presence like a soothing balm,
my mind and senses ever calm.

**Gautama, Flame of Cosmic Peace,
unruly thoughts do hereby cease,
we radiate from you and me
the peace to still Samsara's Sea.**

4. Gautama Buddha, shatter the energetic matrix that prevents people from seeing that there is an intent to manipulate. It was not an accident that we stepped into duality. It is the result of a direct manipulation.

Gautama, I now take the vow,
to live in the eternal now,
with you I do transcend all time,
to live in present so sublime.

**Gautama, Flame of Cosmic Peace,
unruly thoughts do hereby cease,
we radiate from you and me
the peace to still Samsara's Sea.**

5. Gautama Buddha, shatter the energetic matrix that prevents people from seeing that even though people who are pulled into a dualistic polarity believe it is an absolute truth, it is truly an illusion. It is a lie.

> Gautama, I have no desire,
> to nothing earthly I aspire,
> in non-attachment I now rest,
> passing Mara's subtle test.
>
> **Gautama, Flame of Cosmic Peace,**
> **unruly thoughts do hereby cease,**
> **we radiate from you and me**
> **the peace to still Samsara's Sea.**

6. Gautama Buddha, shatter the energetic matrix that prevents people from seeing that in many cases, it is a deliberate lie that is created in order to set one group of people in conflict with another group of people.

> Gautama, I melt into you,
> my mind is one, no longer two,
> immersed in your resplendent glow,
> Nirvana is all that I know.
>
> **Gautama, Flame of Cosmic Peace,**
> **unruly thoughts do hereby cease,**
> **we radiate from you and me**
> **the peace to still Samsara's Sea.**

7. Gautama Buddha, shatter the energetic matrix that prevents people from seeing that in all cases where we have had these kinds of epic battles, epic conflicts, epic causes, the people who were promoting the cause were claiming that it was all done for a beneficial purpose.

> Gautama, in your timeless space,
> I am immersed in Cosmic Grace,
> I know the God beyond all form,
> to world I will no more conform.

Gautama, Flame of Cosmic Peace,
unruly thoughts do hereby cease,
we radiate from you and me
the peace to still Samsara's Sea.

8. Gautama Buddha, shatter the energetic matrix that prevents people from seeing that all of the epic causes that people have defined throughout the ages, if they go to the point where they cause people to kill each other, this goes against our biological instincts.

Gautama, I am now awake,
I clearly see what is at stake,
and thus I claim my sacred right
to be on earth the Buddhic Light.

Gautama, Flame of Cosmic Peace,
unruly thoughts do hereby cease,
we radiate from you and me
the peace to still Samsara's Sea.

9. Gautama Buddha, shatter the energetic matrix that prevents people from seeing that all of these epic causes are out of touch with how the machinery works. Any cause that causes people to kill each other, goes against the basic design of the machinery. Therefore, it is proven to be an illusion.

Gautama, with your thunderbolt,
we give the earth a mighty jolt,
I know that some will understand,
and join the Buddha's timeless band.

Gautama, Flame of Cosmic Peace,
unruly thoughts do hereby cease,
we radiate from you and me
the peace to still Samsara's Sea.

Part 5

1. Gautama Buddha, shatter the energetic matrix that prevents people from seeing that anything that causes people to kill each other can only be based on an illusion because it goes against nature itself. It even goes against human nature, as opposed to the nature of the elite.

> Gautama, show my mental state
> that does give rise to love and hate,
> your exposé I do endure,
> so my perception will be pure.

> **Gautama, Flame of Cosmic Peace,**
> **unruly thoughts do hereby cease,**
> **we radiate from you and me**
> **the peace to still Samsara's Sea.**

2. Gautama Buddha, shatter the energetic matrix that prevents people from seeing that the elite defines an epic cause by using the duality consciousness.

> Gautama, in your Flame of Peace,
> the struggling self I now release,
> the Buddha Nature I now see,
> it is the core of you and me.

> **Gautama, Flame of Cosmic Peace,**
> **unruly thoughts do hereby cease,**
> **we radiate from you and me**
> **the peace to still Samsara's Sea.**

3. Gautama Buddha, shatter the energetic matrix that prevents people from seeing that duality is ignorance, not in the sense that we do not know, but that we have an incomplete understanding that we think is complete, that we think is absolute.

> Gautama, I am one with thee,
> Mara's demons do now flee,

your Presence like a soothing balm,
my mind and senses ever calm.

**Gautama, Flame of Cosmic Peace,
unruly thoughts do hereby cease,
we radiate from you and me
the peace to still Samsara's Sea.**

4. Gautama Buddha, shatter the energetic matrix that prevents people from seeing that the main characteristic of the dualistic consciousness is that it is selective. It is like wearing colored glasses.

Gautama, I now take the vow,
to live in the eternal now,
with you I do transcend all time,
to live in present so sublime.

**Gautama, Flame of Cosmic Peace,
unruly thoughts do hereby cease,
we radiate from you and me
the peace to still Samsara's Sea.**

5. Gautama Buddha, shatter the energetic matrix that prevents people from seeing that what we see through duality is a distorted vision but we do not realize it is distorted or limited. We do not realize that something has been excluded. We think we have the complete vision of life.

Gautama, I have no desire,
to nothing earthly I aspire,
in non-attachment I now rest,
passing Mara's subtle test.

**Gautama, Flame of Cosmic Peace,
unruly thoughts do hereby cease,
we radiate from you and me
the peace to still Samsara's Sea.**

6. Gautama Buddha, shatter the energetic matrix that prevents people from seeing that the duality consciousness is selective because there are

certain things we can see and there are certain things that are filtered out that we cannot see.

> Gautama, I melt into you,
> my mind is one, no longer two,
> immersed in your resplendent glow,
> Nirvana is all that I know.

> **Gautama, Flame of Cosmic Peace,**
> **unruly thoughts do hereby cease,**
> **we radiate from you and me**
> **the peace to still Samsara's Sea.**

7. Gautama Buddha, shatter the energetic matrix that prevents people from seeing that when we have this selective vision, then there are certain things we cannot see. We cannot see how the machine actually operates.

> Gautama, in your timeless space,
> I am immersed in Cosmic Grace,
> I know the God beyond all form,
> to world I will no more conform.

> **Gautama, Flame of Cosmic Peace,**
> **unruly thoughts do hereby cease,**
> **we radiate from you and me**
> **the peace to still Samsara's Sea.**

8. Gautama Buddha, shatter the energetic matrix that prevents people from seeing that we cannot see that all human beings on earth are connected at the energetic level, that we are all connected through this collective energy field.

> Gautama, I am now awake,
> I clearly see what is at stake,
> and thus I claim my sacred right
> to be on earth the Buddhic Light.

> **Gautama, Flame of Cosmic Peace,**
> **unruly thoughts do hereby cease,**

**we radiate from you and me
the peace to still Samsara's Sea.**

9. Gautama Buddha, shatter the energetic matrix that prevents people from seeing that whether it is an emotional, a mental or an identity level field, there is a collective field that connects all people. What we do to others, will affect the whole. We are part of that whole, therefore what we do to others will affect ourselves.

Gautama, with your thunderbolt,
we give the earth a mighty jolt,
I know that some will understand,
and join the Buddha's timeless band.

**Gautama, Flame of Cosmic Peace,
unruly thoughts do hereby cease,
we radiate from you and me
the peace to still Samsara's Sea.**

Sealing

In the name of the I AM THAT I AM, I accept that Archangel Michael, Astrea and Shiva form an impenetrable shield around myself and all constructive people, sealing us from all fear-based energies in all four octaves. I accept that the Light of God is consuming and transforming all fear-based energies that make up the dark forces working against ending the era of fanaticism on earth!

30 | INVOKING A NEW AWARENESS OF DUALITY (PART 2)

In the name of the I AM THAT I AM, Jesus Christ, I use the authority that I have as a being in embodiment on earth to call upon Gautama Buddha to reinforce my calls and use my chakras to project the statements in this invocation into the collective consciousness and awaken people to the reality of how the dualistic mindset has distorted life on earth. Awaken people to the reality that we are spiritual beings and that we can co-create a new future by working with the ascended masters. I especially call for ...

[Make your own calls here.]

Part 1

1. Gautama Buddha, shatter the energetic matrix that prevents people from seeing that in duality, we see ourselves as separate individuals. We think we belong to a particular group that is separated from a particular other group or from the rest of humanity.

Gautama, show my mental state
that does give rise to love and hate,
your exposé I do endure,
so my perception will be pure.

Gautama, Flame of Cosmic Peace,
unruly thoughts do hereby cease,
we radiate from you and me
the peace to still Samsara's Sea.

2. Gautama Buddha, shatter the energetic matrix that prevents people from seeing that the machinery on earth is designed based on the absolute fact that all life is one, that we are all connected through this collective energy field.

Gautama, in your Flame of Peace,
the struggling self I now release,
the Buddha Nature I now see,
it is the core of you and me.

Gautama, Flame of Cosmic Peace,
unruly thoughts do hereby cease,
we radiate from you and me
the peace to still Samsara's Sea.

3. Gautama Buddha, shatter the energetic matrix that prevents people from seeing that what is best for an individual is to do something that raises the whole. This is how the machine is designed to work. This is how the machine actually works.

Gautama, I am one with thee,
Mara's demons do now flee,
your Presence like a soothing balm,
my mind and senses ever calm.

Gautama, Flame of Cosmic Peace,
unruly thoughts do hereby cease,
we radiate from you and me
the peace to still Samsara's Sea.

4. Gautama Buddha, shatter the energetic matrix that prevents people from seeing that in the duality consciousness we start thinking that just as human bodies are separate, human minds are also separate, human *beings* are separate.

Gautama, I now take the vow,
to live in the eternal now,
with you I do transcend all time,
to live in present so sublime.

Gautama, Flame of Cosmic Peace,
unruly thoughts do hereby cease,
we radiate from you and me
the peace to still Samsara's Sea.

5. Gautama Buddha, shatter the energetic matrix that prevents people from seeing that we think what we observe at the physical level is the ultimate reality. This is how life works. The way life works at the physical level is the way it works everywhere.

Gautama, I have no desire,
to nothing earthly I aspire,
in non-attachment I now rest,
passing Mara's subtle test.

Gautama, Flame of Cosmic Peace,
unruly thoughts do hereby cease,
we radiate from you and me
the peace to still Samsara's Sea.

6. Gautama Buddha, shatter the energetic matrix that prevents people from seeing that we think we can kill another person's physical body but our bodies stay alive. That is why we come to believe that we are separate beings and we can do something to others and get away with it.

Gautama, I melt into you,
my mind is one, no longer two,
immersed in your resplendent glow,
Nirvana is all that I know.

Gautama, Flame of Cosmic Peace,
unruly thoughts do hereby cease,
we radiate from you and me
the peace to still Samsara's Sea.

7. Gautama Buddha, shatter the energetic matrix that prevents people from seeing that this is an illusion, and because it is an illusion, because we are trying to operate the machinery in a way it is not designed to operate, then the machinery can only give us suffering.

Gautama, in your timeless space,
I am immersed in Cosmic Grace,
I know the God beyond all form,
to world I will no more conform.

Gautama, Flame of Cosmic Peace,
unruly thoughts do hereby cease,
we radiate from you and me
the peace to still Samsara's Sea.

8. Gautama Buddha, shatter the energetic matrix that prevents people from seeing that the machine is designed to give all human beings on earth a positive, joyous experience. What makes us have a positive experience is that we feel that we are not limited, we are not restricted. We are free to grow.

Gautama, I am now awake,
I clearly see what is at stake,
and thus I claim my sacred right
to be on earth the Buddhic Light.

Gautama, Flame of Cosmic Peace,
unruly thoughts do hereby cease,
we radiate from you and me
the peace to still Samsara's Sea.

9. Gautama Buddha, shatter the energetic matrix that prevents people from seeing that in the way the machine is designed to work, it is possible for seven billion individuals to be in embodiment on this planet at the

same time but they do not feel they are restricted by each other. They do not feel they are in conflict with each other.

Gautama, with your thunderbolt,
we give the earth a mighty jolt,
I know that some will understand,
and join the Buddha's timeless band.

**Gautama, Flame of Cosmic Peace,
unruly thoughts do hereby cease,
we radiate from you and me
the peace to still Samsara's Sea.**

Part 2

1. Gautama Buddha, shatter the energetic matrix that prevents people from seeing that the real purpose of our lives is to expand our individual consciousness. That expansion of individual consciousness is not restricted by anybody else.

Gautama, show my mental state
that does give rise to love and hate,
your exposé I do endure,
so my perception will be pure.

**Gautama, Flame of Cosmic Peace,
unruly thoughts do hereby cease,
we radiate from you and me
the peace to still Samsara's Sea.**

2. Gautama Buddha, shatter the energetic matrix that prevents people from seeing that when we live our lives in a way that gives us personal growth, without hindering the growth of other people, then we all grow together and then we all have that positive experience.

Gautama, in your Flame of Peace,
the struggling self I now release,

the Buddha Nature I now see,
it is the core of you and me.

**Gautama, Flame of Cosmic Peace,
unruly thoughts do hereby cease,
we radiate from you and me
the peace to still Samsara's Sea.**

3. Gautama Buddha, shatter the energetic matrix that prevents people from seeing that there is a driving force behind the evolution that causes life to grow, to constantly transcend itself. This is the basic drive in human psychology.

Gautama, I am one with thee,
Mara's demons do now flee,
your Presence like a soothing balm,
my mind and senses ever calm.

**Gautama, Flame of Cosmic Peace,
unruly thoughts do hereby cease,
we radiate from you and me
the peace to still Samsara's Sea.**

4. Gautama Buddha, shatter the energetic matrix that prevents people from seeing that in order to have a positive life experience, we need to feel we are growing. What causes suffering is when people lose the knowledge that the purpose of life is growth in awareness.

Gautama, I now take the vow,
to live in the eternal now,
with you I do transcend all time,
to live in present so sublime.

**Gautama, Flame of Cosmic Peace,
unruly thoughts do hereby cease,
we radiate from you and me
the peace to still Samsara's Sea.**

5. Gautama Buddha, shatter the energetic matrix that prevents people from seeing that we are pulled into thinking that we are static beings: "I am a human being and this is what it means to be a human being, this is what I *can* and *cannot* do."

Gautama, I have no desire,
to nothing earthly I aspire,
in non-attachment I now rest,
passing Mara's subtle test.

Gautama, Flame of Cosmic Peace,
unruly thoughts do hereby cease,
we radiate from you and me
the peace to still Samsara's Sea.

6. Gautama Buddha, shatter the energetic matrix that prevents people from seeing that when we go into the duality consciousness, we lose the awareness that we can transcend our own state of consciousness.

Gautama, I melt into you,
my mind is one, no longer two,
immersed in your resplendent glow,
Nirvana is all that I know.

Gautama, Flame of Cosmic Peace,
unruly thoughts do hereby cease,
we radiate from you and me
the peace to still Samsara's Sea.

7. Gautama Buddha, shatter the energetic matrix that prevents people from seeing that we think our state of consciousness does not depend entirely on our inner conditions and our own choices, our state of consciousness depends on outer conditions.

Gautama, in your timeless space,
I am immersed in Cosmic Grace,
I know the God beyond all form,
to world I will no more conform.

Gautama, Flame of Cosmic Peace,
unruly thoughts do hereby cease,
we radiate from you and me
the peace to still Samsara's Sea.

8. Gautama Buddha, shatter the energetic matrix that prevents people from seeing that the extreme outplaying of this consciousness is Materialism, which claims that human consciousness is a product of the material processes in the brain.

Gautama, I am now awake,
I clearly see what is at stake,
and thus I claim my sacred right
to be on earth the Buddhic Light.

Gautama, Flame of Cosmic Peace,
unruly thoughts do hereby cease,
we radiate from you and me
the peace to still Samsara's Sea.

9. Gautama Buddha, shatter the energetic matrix that prevents people from seeing that we are not material beings, our minds are not material beings, but we have been blinded by the dualistic consciousness into thinking that we are either material beings or at least that our state of mind, our happiness, is defined by material conditions.

Gautama, with your thunderbolt,
we give the earth a mighty jolt,
I know that some will understand,
and join the Buddha's timeless band.

Gautama, Flame of Cosmic Peace,
unruly thoughts do hereby cease,
we radiate from you and me
the peace to still Samsara's Sea.

Part 3

1. Gautama Buddha, shatter the energetic matrix that prevents people from seeing that in the original design of the machinery, the material conditions on earth are tools for facilitating our growth in consciousness.

> Gautama, show my mental state
> that does give rise to love and hate,
> your exposé I do endure,
> so my perception will be pure.

> **Gautama, Flame of Cosmic Peace,**
> **unruly thoughts do hereby cease,**
> **we radiate from you and me**
> **the peace to still Samsara's Sea.**

2. Gautama Buddha, shatter the energetic matrix that prevents people from seeing that when we go into duality, we start seeing ourselves as separate beings, meaning we are separated from the process of life.

> Gautama, in your Flame of Peace,
> the struggling self I now release,
> the Buddha Nature I now see,
> it is the core of you and me.

> **Gautama, Flame of Cosmic Peace,**
> **unruly thoughts do hereby cease,**
> **we radiate from you and me**
> **the peace to still Samsara's Sea.**

3. Gautama Buddha, shatter the energetic matrix that prevents people from seeing that instead of viewing material conditions as tools to promote our growth, we begin to think that material conditions limit us, even define us, certainly define what we *can* and *cannot* do on earth.

> Gautama, I am one with thee,
> Mara's demons do now flee,

your Presence like a soothing balm,
my mind and senses ever calm.

**Gautama, Flame of Cosmic Peace,
unruly thoughts do hereby cease,
we radiate from you and me
the peace to still Samsara's Sea.**

4. Gautama Buddha, shatter the energetic matrix that prevents people from seeing that we do not think we can change or transcend the material conditions that are here on earth right now. We think they are defined by something, whether it be a remote God in the sky or some natural law, over which we have no influence.

Gautama, I now take the vow,
to live in the eternal now,
with you I do transcend all time,
to live in present so sublime.

**Gautama, Flame of Cosmic Peace,
unruly thoughts do hereby cease,
we radiate from you and me
the peace to still Samsara's Sea.**

5. Gautama Buddha, shatter the energetic matrix that prevents people from seeing that we are separated from our own higher selves, therefore we do not have the direct experience that there is more to our beings than what we experience at the conscious level.

Gautama, I have no desire,
to nothing earthly I aspire,
in non-attachment I now rest,
passing Mara's subtle test.

**Gautama, Flame of Cosmic Peace,
unruly thoughts do hereby cease,
we radiate from you and me
the peace to still Samsara's Sea.**

6. Gautama Buddha, shatter the energetic matrix that prevents people from seeing that we forget we have the possibility to expand our consciousness until we establish oneness with our higher selves, and therefore we are not affected by any conditions on earth.

> Gautama, I melt into you,
> my mind is one, no longer two,
> immersed in your resplendent glow,
> Nirvana is all that I know.

> **Gautama, Flame of Cosmic Peace,**
> **unruly thoughts do hereby cease,**
> **we radiate from you and me**
> **the peace to still Samsara's Sea.**

7. Gautama Buddha, shatter the energetic matrix that prevents people from seeing that we think we are separated from the flow of life, the process of life, the process of transcendence. We are defined by matter, we are limited by matter.

> Gautama, in your timeless space,
> I am immersed in Cosmic Grace,
> I know the God beyond all form,
> to world I will no more conform.

> **Gautama, Flame of Cosmic Peace,**
> **unruly thoughts do hereby cease,**
> **we radiate from you and me**
> **the peace to still Samsara's Sea.**

8. Gautama Buddha, shatter the energetic matrix that prevents people from seeing that when we step into duality, we experience that we are limited by matter because we see ourselves as separated from matter.

> Gautama, I am now awake,
> I clearly see what is at stake,
> and thus I claim my sacred right
> to be on earth the Buddhic Light.

Gautama, Flame of Cosmic Peace,
unruly thoughts do hereby cease,
we radiate from you and me
the peace to still Samsara's Sea.

9. Gautama Buddha, shatter the energetic matrix that prevents people from seeing that when we are not in duality, we realize that matter is a form of energy. The connection between matter and energy is that thoughts are a form of energy. Therefore, thought can affect the energy that makes up matter and ultimately affect matter.

Gautama, with your thunderbolt,
we give the earth a mighty jolt,
I know that some will understand,
and join the Buddha's timeless band.

Gautama, Flame of Cosmic Peace,
unruly thoughts do hereby cease,
we radiate from you and me
the peace to still Samsara's Sea.

Part 4

1. Gautama Buddha, shatter the energetic matrix that prevents people from seeing that humankind can change the conditions on earth through our consciousness.

Gautama, show my mental state
that does give rise to love and hate,
your exposé I do endure,
so my perception will be pure.

Gautama, Flame of Cosmic Peace,
unruly thoughts do hereby cease,
we radiate from you and me
the peace to still Samsara's Sea.

2. Gautama Buddha, shatter the energetic matrix that prevents people from seeing that after humankind fell into duality, we have changed the original design and made the earth more dense.

> Gautama, in your Flame of Peace,
> the struggling self I now release,
> the Buddha Nature I now see,
> it is the core of you and me.

> **Gautama, Flame of Cosmic Peace,**
> **unruly thoughts do hereby cease,**
> **we radiate from you and me**
> **the peace to still Samsara's Sea.**

3. Gautama Buddha, shatter the energetic matrix that prevents people from seeing that consciousness is cause and matter is effect, consciousness is the primary and matter is secondary.

> Gautama, I am one with thee,
> Mara's demons do now flee,
> your Presence like a soothing balm,
> my mind and senses ever calm.

> **Gautama, Flame of Cosmic Peace,**
> **unruly thoughts do hereby cease,**
> **we radiate from you and me**
> **the peace to still Samsara's Sea.**

4. Gautama Buddha, shatter the energetic matrix that prevents people from seeing that in duality we think that because we are separated from matter, we cannot influence matter with our consciousness. We experience that we cannot influence matter with our consciousness.

> Gautama, I now take the vow,
> to live in the eternal now,
> with you I do transcend all time,
> to live in present so sublime.

Gautama, Flame of Cosmic Peace,
unruly thoughts do hereby cease,
we radiate from you and me
the peace to still Samsara's Sea.

5. Gautama Buddha, shatter the energetic matrix that prevents people from seeing that this is because we have gained an incorrect vision of how the machine operates. Instead of pushing the right buttons, we are pushing all the wrong buttons.

Gautama, I have no desire,
to nothing earthly I aspire,
in non-attachment I now rest,
passing Mara's subtle test.

Gautama, Flame of Cosmic Peace,
unruly thoughts do hereby cease,
we radiate from you and me
the peace to still Samsara's Sea.

6. Gautama Buddha, shatter the energetic matrix that prevents people from seeing that our experience is correct, we cannot change matter with the mind. This does not mean that mind cannot change matter. It means that the dualistic mind cannot change matter.

Gautama, I melt into you,
my mind is one, no longer two,
immersed in your resplendent glow,
Nirvana is all that I know.

Gautama, Flame of Cosmic Peace,
unruly thoughts do hereby cease,
we radiate from you and me
the peace to still Samsara's Sea.

7. Gautama Buddha, shatter the energetic matrix that prevents people from seeing that when we go into duality, we can no longer change matter and therefore, as long as we are in the dualistic state of mind, we are limited by matter.

Gautama, in your timeless space,
I am immersed in Cosmic Grace,
I know the God beyond all form,
to world I will no more conform.

Gautama, Flame of Cosmic Peace,
unruly thoughts do hereby cease,
we radiate from you and me
the peace to still Samsara's Sea.

8. Gautama Buddha, shatter the energetic matrix that prevents people from seeing that when we step into this mindset of seeing ourselves as separate beings, we also experience that we are separated from other human beings.

Gautama, I am now awake,
I clearly see what is at stake,
and thus I claim my sacred right
to be on earth the Buddhic Light.

Gautama, Flame of Cosmic Peace,
unruly thoughts do hereby cease,
we radiate from you and me
the peace to still Samsara's Sea.

9. Gautama Buddha, shatter the energetic matrix that prevents people from seeing that it is when we see ourselves as separated from other human beings that there will inevitably be tension, conflicts of interest between us and other people. This will inevitably create suffering.

Gautama, with your thunderbolt,
we give the earth a mighty jolt,
I know that some will understand,
and join the Buddha's timeless band.

Gautama, Flame of Cosmic Peace,
unruly thoughts do hereby cease,
we radiate from you and me
the peace to still Samsara's Sea.

Part 5

1. Gautama Buddha, shatter the energetic matrix that prevents people from seeing that instead of people having the same goal of self-transcendence, people are having all kinds of different individual goals, wanting to go in all kinds of separate directions.

> Gautama, show my mental state
> that does give rise to love and hate,
> your exposé I do endure,
> so my perception will be pure.

> **Gautama, Flame of Cosmic Peace,**
> **unruly thoughts do hereby cease,**
> **we radiate from you and me**
> **the peace to still Samsara's Sea.**

2. Gautama Buddha, shatter the energetic matrix that prevents people from seeing that this is a state of chaos. Depending on how deeply we are trapped in the illusions of duality, we may feel that we have a right to pursue our individual goals regardless of the consequences that it has for other people.

> Gautama, in your Flame of Peace,
> the struggling self I now release,
> the Buddha Nature I now see,
> it is the core of you and me.

> **Gautama, Flame of Cosmic Peace,**
> **unruly thoughts do hereby cease,**
> **we radiate from you and me**
> **the peace to still Samsara's Sea.**

3. Gautama Buddha, shatter the energetic matrix that prevents people from seeing that this is the original cause of human suffering. We see ourselves as separate beings and go in different directions.

Gautama, I am one with thee,
Mara's demons do now flee,
your Presence like a soothing balm,
my mind and senses ever calm.

**Gautama, Flame of Cosmic Peace,
unruly thoughts do hereby cease,
we radiate from you and me
the peace to still Samsara's Sea.**

4. Gautama Buddha, shatter the energetic matrix that prevents people from seeing that we are not seeing how the machine is designed to facilitate our experience and therefore, instead of having a *fulfilling* experience, we are having a *frustrating* experience. This is the Sea of Samsara, this is suffering.

Gautama, I now take the vow,
to live in the eternal now,
with you I do transcend all time,
to live in present so sublime.

**Gautama, Flame of Cosmic Peace,
unruly thoughts do hereby cease,
we radiate from you and me
the peace to still Samsara's Sea.**

5. Gautama Buddha, shatter the energetic matrix that prevents people from seeing that this is not fanaticism. The initial stage of going into duality and separation is "innocent ignorance." We are unaware of our connection to other people, our connection to our higher selves.

Gautama, I have no desire,
to nothing earthly I aspire,
in non-attachment I now rest,
passing Mara's subtle test.

**Gautama, Flame of Cosmic Peace,
unruly thoughts do hereby cease,
we radiate from you and me
the peace to still Samsara's Sea.**

6. Gautama Buddha, shatter the energetic matrix that prevents people from seeing that fanaticism comes in when we take duality further towards the extreme. This is where, instead of just being ignorant of how the machine works, we start formulating a theory, an idea, an ism, a religion where we attempt to define how the machine *should* work.

Gautama, I melt into you,
my mind is one, no longer two,
immersed in your resplendent glow,
Nirvana is all that I know.

Gautama, Flame of Cosmic Peace,
unruly thoughts do hereby cease,
we radiate from you and me
the peace to still Samsara's Sea.

7. Gautama Buddha, shatter the energetic matrix that prevents people from seeing that instead of being *innocently* ignorant, we become *aggressively* ignorant. We do not want to suffer, but we are not aware that the only true way to escape suffering is to change our own state of consciousness.

Gautama, in your timeless space,
I am immersed in Cosmic Grace,
I know the God beyond all form,
to world I will no more conform.

Gautama, Flame of Cosmic Peace,
unruly thoughts do hereby cease,
we radiate from you and me
the peace to still Samsara's Sea.

8. Gautama Buddha, shatter the energetic matrix that prevents people from seeing that the only way to truly escape suffering is to free ourselves from duality so we are not seeing ourselves as separate beings.

Gautama, I am now awake,
I clearly see what is at stake,
and thus I claim my sacred right
to be on earth the Buddhic Light.

**Gautama, Flame of Cosmic Peace,
unruly thoughts do hereby cease,
we radiate from you and me
the peace to still Samsara's Sea.**

9. Gautama Buddha, shatter the energetic matrix that prevents people from seeing that the only way to feel fulfilled as a human being is to be connected to our higher selves, to be connected to the flow of life so we are transcending ourselves.

Gautama, with your thunderbolt,
we give the earth a mighty jolt,
I know that some will understand,
and join the Buddha's timeless band.

**Gautama, Flame of Cosmic Peace,
unruly thoughts do hereby cease,
we radiate from you and me
the peace to still Samsara's Sea.**

Sealing

In the name of the I AM THAT I AM, I accept that Archangel Michael, Astrea and Shiva form an impenetrable shield around myself and all constructive people, sealing us from all fear-based energies in all four octaves. I accept that the Light of God is consuming and transforming all fear-based energies that make up the dark forces working against ending the era of fanaticism on earth!

31 | INVOKING A NEW AWARENESS OF DUALITY (PART 3)

In the name of the I AM THAT I AM, Jesus Christ, I use the authority that I have as a being in embodiment on earth to call upon Gautama Buddha to reinforce my calls and use my chakras to project the statements in this invocation into the collective consciousness and awaken people to the reality of how the dualistic mindset has distorted life on earth. Awaken people to the reality that we are spiritual beings and that we can co-create a new future by working with the ascended masters. I especially call for …

[Make your own calls here.]

Part 1

1. Gautama Buddha, shatter the energetic matrix that prevents people from seeing that when we go into duality, we cannot see self-transcendence as a way to get what we actually want.

> Gautama, show my mental state
> that does give rise to love and hate,

your exposé I do endure,
so my perception will be pure.

**Gautama, Flame of Cosmic Peace,
unruly thoughts do hereby cease,
we radiate from you and me
the peace to still Samsara's Sea.**

2. Gautama Buddha, shatter the energetic matrix that prevents people from seeing that in duality we think we do not have the physical power to get a better experience by ourselves, so we need other people.

Gautama, in your Flame of Peace,
the struggling self I now release,
the Buddha Nature I now see,
it is the core of you and me.

**Gautama, Flame of Cosmic Peace,
unruly thoughts do hereby cease,
we radiate from you and me
the peace to still Samsara's Sea.**

3. Gautama Buddha, shatter the energetic matrix that prevents people from seeing that duality creates the mindset where certain people go into this aggressive state of mind, where they want to manipulate and control other people, so that these other people will conform to their vision and therefore give them a less frustrating experience.

Gautama, I am one with thee,
Mara's demons do now flee,
your Presence like a soothing balm,
my mind and senses ever calm.

**Gautama, Flame of Cosmic Peace,
unruly thoughts do hereby cease,
we radiate from you and me
the peace to still Samsara's Sea.**

4. Gautama Buddha, shatter the energetic matrix that prevents people from seeing that in the feudal societies of Europe the noblemen had a more pleasant lifestyle than the peasants because the peasants were doing all the hard work. The noblemen were reaping the rewards of the peasants' labor.

Gautama, I now take the vow,
to live in the eternal now,
with you I do transcend all time,
to live in present so sublime.

Gautama, Flame of Cosmic Peace,
unruly thoughts do hereby cease,
we radiate from you and me
the peace to still Samsara's Sea.

5. Gautama Buddha, shatter the energetic matrix that prevents people from seeing that this is the aggressive form of ignorance. In many societies we see the emergence of a privileged elite.

Gautama, I have no desire,
to nothing earthly I aspire,
in non-attachment I now rest,
passing Mara's subtle test.

Gautama, Flame of Cosmic Peace,
unruly thoughts do hereby cease,
we radiate from you and me
the peace to still Samsara's Sea.

6. Gautama Buddha, shatter the energetic matrix that prevents people from seeing that the elite were manipulating other people to do the work for them so that they could have a more comfortable, affluent, privileged lifestyle. This was not necessarily fanaticism but it set the stage for fanaticism.

Gautama, I melt into you,
my mind is one, no longer two,
immersed in your resplendent glow,
Nirvana is all that I know.

Gautama, Flame of Cosmic Peace,
unruly thoughts do hereby cease,
we radiate from you and me
the peace to still Samsara's Sea.

7. Gautama Buddha, shatter the energetic matrix that prevents people from seeing that this was something that could not be done by physical power. In order to get this done, the elite needed some kind of idea, some kind of philosophy, some kind of ism that caused these other people to work for the elite.

Gautama, in your timeless space,
I am immersed in Cosmic Grace,
I know the God beyond all form,
to world I will no more conform.

Gautama, Flame of Cosmic Peace,
unruly thoughts do hereby cease,
we radiate from you and me
the peace to still Samsara's Sea.

8. Gautama Buddha, shatter the energetic matrix that prevents people from seeing that this manipulation became more severe after the fallen beings began to embody on the planet.

Gautama, I am now awake,
I clearly see what is at stake,
and thus I claim my sacred right
to be on earth the Buddhic Light.

Gautama, Flame of Cosmic Peace,
unruly thoughts do hereby cease,
we radiate from you and me
the peace to still Samsara's Sea.

9. Gautama Buddha, shatter the energetic matrix that prevents people from seeing that the fallen beings do set themselves up as a privileged elite but this is not what drives them. They have an agenda that goes beyond their comfortability.

Gautama, with your thunderbolt,
we give the earth a mighty jolt,
I know that some will understand,
and join the Buddha's timeless band.

Gautama, Flame of Cosmic Peace,
unruly thoughts do hereby cease,
we radiate from you and me
the peace to still Samsara's Sea.

Part 2

1. Gautama Buddha, shatter the energetic matrix that prevents people from seeing that the fallen beings have an epic agenda and the epic agenda is the extreme outcome of the dualistic mindset.

Gautama, show my mental state
that does give rise to love and hate,
your exposé I do endure,
so my perception will be pure.

Gautama, Flame of Cosmic Peace,
unruly thoughts do hereby cease,
we radiate from you and me
the peace to still Samsara's Sea.

2. Gautama Buddha, shatter the energetic matrix that prevents people from seeing that the machinery of planet earth is designed to work a certain way. Before the fallen beings came here, people had become ignorant of how the machine actually works.

Gautama, in your Flame of Peace,
the struggling self I now release,
the Buddha Nature I now see,
it is the core of you and me.

**Gautama, Flame of Cosmic Peace,
unruly thoughts do hereby cease,
we radiate from you and me
the peace to still Samsara's Sea.**

3. Gautama Buddha, shatter the energetic matrix that prevents people from seeing that the fallen beings are also ignorant of how the machine works, but they believe they can elevate one dualistic extreme into an absolute truth.

Gautama, I am one with thee,
Mara's demons do now flee,
your Presence like a soothing balm,
my mind and senses ever calm.

**Gautama, Flame of Cosmic Peace,
unruly thoughts do hereby cease,
we radiate from you and me
the peace to still Samsara's Sea.**

4. Gautama Buddha, shatter the energetic matrix that prevents people from seeing that the fallen beings project their idea on the machinery and say: "This is how the machine *should* have been working all along. This is how it *should* have been designed to work."

Gautama, I now take the vow,
to live in the eternal now,
with you I do transcend all time,
to live in present so sublime.

**Gautama, Flame of Cosmic Peace,
unruly thoughts do hereby cease,
we radiate from you and me
the peace to still Samsara's Sea.**

5. Gautama Buddha, shatter the energetic matrix that prevents people from seeing that at first, people are just ignorant of how the machine works and therefore they create suffering. The logical extreme is that we start judging how the machine *should* have been designed. We start finding fault with

the design of the machine and in some cases even with the designer of the machine.

Gautama, I have no desire,
to nothing earthly I aspire,
in non-attachment I now rest,
passing Mara's subtle test.

**Gautama, Flame of Cosmic Peace,
unruly thoughts do hereby cease,
we radiate from you and me
the peace to still Samsara's Sea.**

6. Gautama Buddha, shatter the energetic matrix that prevents people from seeing that when we think we have elevated one dualistic extreme to an absolute truth, we can judge that the designer of the machine made a mistake and should not have designed it that way.

Gautama, I melt into you,
my mind is one, no longer two,
immersed in your resplendent glow,
Nirvana is all that I know.

**Gautama, Flame of Cosmic Peace,
unruly thoughts do hereby cease,
we radiate from you and me
the peace to still Samsara's Sea.**

7. Gautama Buddha, shatter the energetic matrix that prevents people from seeing that this leads to this ultimate epic cause where some people seek to persuade others to accept their epic idea. It has always been impossible to get all people on earth to accept one idea.

Gautama, in your timeless space,
I am immersed in Cosmic Grace,
I know the God beyond all form,
to world I will no more conform.

**Gautama, Flame of Cosmic Peace,
unruly thoughts do hereby cease,
we radiate from you and me
the peace to still Samsara's Sea.**

8. Gautama Buddha, shatter the energetic matrix that prevents people from seeing that as the next step, these people think that those people who will not accept the epic idea should be killed because the epic idea defines a goal that should be manifest on earth.

Gautama, I am now awake,
I clearly see what is at stake,
and thus I claim my sacred right
to be on earth the Buddhic Light.

**Gautama, Flame of Cosmic Peace,
unruly thoughts do hereby cease,
we radiate from you and me
the peace to still Samsara's Sea.**

9. Gautama Buddha, shatter the energetic matrix that prevents people from seeing that fanatics think that those people who will not accept the idea, are working against the goal and therefore it is justified that they be killed so that the goal can be manifest. This is the essence of fanaticism and the fanatical mindset.

Gautama, with your thunderbolt,
we give the earth a mighty jolt,
I know that some will understand,
and join the Buddha's timeless band.

**Gautama, Flame of Cosmic Peace,
unruly thoughts do hereby cease,
we radiate from you and me
the peace to still Samsara's Sea.**

Part 3

1. Gautama Buddha, shatter the energetic matrix that prevents people from seeing that what makes these epic causes seem plausible to people is that the duality consciousness focuses on one aspect of reality and elevates this to being the complete understanding of reality.

> Gautama, show my mental state
> that does give rise to love and hate,
> your exposé I do endure,
> so my perception will be pure.

> **Gautama, Flame of Cosmic Peace,**
> **unruly thoughts do hereby cease,**
> **we radiate from you and me**
> **the peace to still Samsara's Sea.**

2. Gautama Buddha, shatter the energetic matrix that prevents people from seeing that duality defines that all different understandings are wrong in an epic way. Therefore, the people who hold these other ideas are wrong in an epic way and should be killed.

> Gautama, in your Flame of Peace,
> the struggling self I now release,
> the Buddha Nature I now see,
> it is the core of you and me.

> **Gautama, Flame of Cosmic Peace,**
> **unruly thoughts do hereby cease,**
> **we radiate from you and me**
> **the peace to still Samsara's Sea.**

3. Gautama Buddha, shatter the energetic matrix that prevents people from seeing that in duality, nothing can exist alone, there are always two opposites. There is no ultimate truth, except for the correct understanding of how the machine works and how it was designed to work.

Gautama, I am one with thee,
Mara's demons do now flee,
your Presence like a soothing balm,
my mind and senses ever calm.

**Gautama, Flame of Cosmic Peace,
unruly thoughts do hereby cease,
we radiate from you and me
the peace to still Samsara's Sea.**

4. Gautama Buddha, shatter the energetic matrix that prevents people from seeing that when we step into duality, we cannot see that truth. We can come to see it again by raising ourselves above duality, but we can never see it in duality.

Gautama, I now take the vow,
to live in the eternal now,
with you I do transcend all time,
to live in present so sublime.

**Gautama, Flame of Cosmic Peace,
unruly thoughts do hereby cease,
we radiate from you and me
the peace to still Samsara's Sea.**

5. Gautama Buddha, shatter the energetic matrix that prevents people from seeing that in duality, there is never one truth because in duality we are moving towards one polarity, one extreme. In moving towards that extreme, we are moving away from the opposite extreme.

Gautama, I have no desire,
to nothing earthly I aspire,
in non-attachment I now rest,
passing Mara's subtle test.

**Gautama, Flame of Cosmic Peace,
unruly thoughts do hereby cease,
we radiate from you and me
the peace to still Samsara's Sea.**

6. Gautama Buddha, shatter the energetic matrix that prevents people from seeing that dualistic ideas come into being as pairs. We never have one polarity that comes into being first and then the other comes later. They come into being simultaneously.

> Gautama, I melt into you,
> my mind is one, no longer two,
> immersed in your resplendent glow,
> Nirvana is all that I know.

> **Gautama, Flame of Cosmic Peace,**
> **unruly thoughts do hereby cease,**
> **we radiate from you and me**
> **the peace to still Samsara's Sea.**

7. Gautama Buddha, shatter the energetic matrix that prevents people from seeing that as some people start converting other people to believing in one dualistic polarity, it is inevitable that other people will start believing in the opposite dualistic polarity. Therefore, we can never through persuasion convince everybody of one truth.

> Gautama, in your timeless space,
> I am immersed in Cosmic Grace,
> I know the God beyond all form,
> to world I will no more conform.

> **Gautama, Flame of Cosmic Peace,**
> **unruly thoughts do hereby cease,**
> **we radiate from you and me**
> **the peace to still Samsara's Sea.**

8. Gautama Buddha, shatter the energetic matrix that prevents people from seeing that when we have a pair of dualistic polarities, there is no ultimate argument that validates one and invalidates the other. There is no ultimate argument possible in dualistic polarities.

> Gautama, I am now awake,
> I clearly see what is at stake,

and thus I claim my sacred right
to be on earth the Buddhic Light.

**Gautama, Flame of Cosmic Peace,
unruly thoughts do hereby cease,
we radiate from you and me
the peace to still Samsara's Sea.**

9. Gautama Buddha, shatter the energetic matrix that prevents people from seeing that if we are not in duality, we can see that none of the two polarities is true. It is not so that one is absolutely true and the other is absolutely wrong. When we are not in duality, we see that they are both illusions.

Gautama, with your thunderbolt,
we give the earth a mighty jolt,
I know that some will understand,
and join the Buddha's timeless band.

**Gautama, Flame of Cosmic Peace,
unruly thoughts do hereby cease,
we radiate from you and me
the peace to still Samsara's Sea.**

Part 4

1. Gautama Buddha, shatter the energetic matrix that prevents people from seeing that there is no absolute argument, no objective truth, no objective reality that could be discovered. There is no ultimate revelation from God that can validate a dualistic polarity.

Gautama, show my mental state
that does give rise to love and hate,
your exposé I do endure,
so my perception will be pure.

**Gautama, Flame of Cosmic Peace,
unruly thoughts do hereby cease,**

**we radiate from you and me
the peace to still Samsara's Sea.**

2. Gautama Buddha, shatter the energetic matrix that prevents people from seeing that what makes a polarity seem valid is that we are moving in consciousness into the polarity. We are putting on the glasses. We are drinking the Kool-Aid.

Gautama, in your Flame of Peace,
the struggling self I now release,
the Buddha Nature I now see,
it is the core of you and me.

**Gautama, Flame of Cosmic Peace,
unruly thoughts do hereby cease,
we radiate from you and me
the peace to still Samsara's Sea.**

3. Gautama Buddha, shatter the energetic matrix that prevents people from seeing that when we put on the glasses of one dualistic polarity, we see only what validates that polarity and the glasses filter out anything that invalidates it.

Gautama, I am one with thee,
Mara's demons do now flee,
your Presence like a soothing balm,
my mind and senses ever calm.

**Gautama, Flame of Cosmic Peace,
unruly thoughts do hereby cease,
we radiate from you and me
the peace to still Samsara's Sea.**

4. Gautama Buddha, shatter the energetic matrix that prevents people from seeing that those who are in the opposite dualistic polarity, they have another pair of glasses. *That* is why, after humankind descended into duality, there could never be consensus where everybody believed in the same religion or the same belief system.

Gautama, I now take the vow,
to live in the eternal now,
with you I do transcend all time,
to live in present so sublime.

**Gautama, Flame of Cosmic Peace,
unruly thoughts do hereby cease,
we radiate from you and me
the peace to still Samsara's Sea.**

5. Gautama Buddha, shatter the energetic matrix that prevents people from seeing that Jesus did not mean to convert all people to one dualistic polarity. He came to show that there is an alternative to the dualistic state of consciousness, namely the Christ consciousness or what the Buddha called enlightenment.

Gautama, I have no desire,
to nothing earthly I aspire,
in non-attachment I now rest,
passing Mara's subtle test.

**Gautama, Flame of Cosmic Peace,
unruly thoughts do hereby cease,
we radiate from you and me
the peace to still Samsara's Sea.**

6. Gautama Buddha, shatter the energetic matrix that prevents people from seeing that all spiritual teachers throughout the ages have wanted to set people free, and to demonstrate that there is an alternative to duality because duality can only cause suffering. The only way to escape suffering is to transcend duality.

Gautama, I melt into you,
my mind is one, no longer two,
immersed in your resplendent glow,
Nirvana is all that I know.

**Gautama, Flame of Cosmic Peace,
unruly thoughts do hereby cease,**

**we radiate from you and me
the peace to still Samsara's Sea.**

7. Gautama Buddha, shatter the energetic matrix that prevents people from seeing that those who are manipulating humankind are saying there is a way to escape suffering in duality and it is defined by their epic philosophy. This defines how the machinery should work and if you follow this, then you will escape suffering.

Gautama, in your timeless space,
I am immersed in Cosmic Grace,
I know the God beyond all form,
to world I will no more conform.

**Gautama, Flame of Cosmic Peace,
unruly thoughts do hereby cease,
we radiate from you and me
the peace to still Samsara's Sea.**

8. Gautama Buddha, shatter the energetic matrix that prevents people from seeing that this requires that all people accept this belief system. In order to manifest this wonderful kingdom on earth, we have to kill those who will not comply.

Gautama, I am now awake,
I clearly see what is at stake,
and thus I claim my sacred right
to be on earth the Buddhic Light.

**Gautama, Flame of Cosmic Peace,
unruly thoughts do hereby cease,
we radiate from you and me
the peace to still Samsara's Sea.**

9. Gautama Buddha, shatter the energetic matrix that prevents people from seeing that this inevitably creates a struggle. Although these epic causes always promise that we will escape suffering, it is precisely because they lead to conflict between groups of people that they reinforce suffering.

Gautama, with your thunderbolt,
we give the earth a mighty jolt,
I know that some will understand,
and join the Buddha's timeless band.

**Gautama, Flame of Cosmic Peace,
unruly thoughts do hereby cease,
we radiate from you and me
the peace to still Samsara's Sea.**

Part 5

1. Gautama Buddha, shatter the energetic matrix that prevents people from seeing that what has caused the most human suffering is man-made conflicts that have been driven by these epic causes.

Gautama, show my mental state
that does give rise to love and hate,
your exposé I do endure,
so my perception will be pure.

**Gautama, Flame of Cosmic Peace,
unruly thoughts do hereby cease,
we radiate from you and me
the peace to still Samsara's Sea.**

2. Gautama Buddha, shatter the energetic matrix that prevents people from seeing that the epic mindset, the tendency to define epic causes that require us to force or kill other people, *that* is actually the single cause of most of the suffering we see on earth.

Gautama, in your Flame of Peace,
the struggling self I now release,
the Buddha Nature I now see,
it is the core of you and me.

Gautama, Flame of Cosmic Peace,
unruly thoughts do hereby cease,
we radiate from you and me
the peace to still Samsara's Sea.

3. Gautama Buddha, shatter the energetic matrix that prevents people from seeing that we have democracies because we have moved away from believing in these epic causes. We have started to go beyond the illusion that we are separate beings.

Gautama, I am one with thee,
Mara's demons do now flee,
your Presence like a soothing balm,
my mind and senses ever calm.

Gautama, Flame of Cosmic Peace,
unruly thoughts do hereby cease,
we radiate from you and me
the peace to still Samsara's Sea.

4. Gautama Buddha, shatter the energetic matrix that prevents people from seeing that the epic cause only seems plausible when we think we are separate. That is why we can believe that we can diminish suffering by killing other people, that we can create an ideal state by killing other people.

Gautama, I now take the vow,
to live in the eternal now,
with you I do transcend all time,
to live in present so sublime.

Gautama, Flame of Cosmic Peace,
unruly thoughts do hereby cease,
we radiate from you and me
the peace to still Samsara's Sea.

5. Gautama Buddha, shatter the energetic matrix that prevents people from seeing that democracy is possible because many people have started moving beyond the more extreme aspects of the duality consciousness and started to see that there is some state of connection between people.

Gautama, I have no desire,
to nothing earthly I aspire,
in non-attachment I now rest,
passing Mara's subtle test.

Gautama, Flame of Cosmic Peace,
unruly thoughts do hereby cease,
we radiate from you and me
the peace to still Samsara's Sea.

6. Gautama Buddha, shatter the energetic matrix that prevents people from seeing that democracy is based on the realization that we need to look at what is best for the whole, what is best for the largest number of people instead of just a small elite or a particular group. We cannot allow the interests of one small group to override the interests of the general population.

Gautama, I melt into you,
my mind is one, no longer two,
immersed in your resplendent glow,
Nirvana is all that I know.

Gautama, Flame of Cosmic Peace,
unruly thoughts do hereby cease,
we radiate from you and me
the peace to still Samsara's Sea.

7. Gautama Buddha, shatter the energetic matrix that prevents people from seeing that the advent of democracy proves that humankind has started to move beyond the dualistic state of consciousness and specifically the epic mindset.

Gautama, in your timeless space,
I am immersed in Cosmic Grace,
I know the God beyond all form,
to world I will no more conform.

Gautama, Flame of Cosmic Peace,
unruly thoughts do hereby cease,

we radiate from you and me
the peace to still Samsara's Sea.

8. Gautama Buddha, shatter the energetic matrix that prevents people from seeing that there is some kind of consciousness that blinds people, there is some kind of consciousness that is the cause of human conflict. Help people see that the emperors of duality have nothing on, these epic causes have no reality.

Gautama, I am now awake,
I clearly see what is at stake,
and thus I claim my sacred right
to be on earth the Buddhic Light.

Gautama, Flame of Cosmic Peace,
unruly thoughts do hereby cease,
we radiate from you and me
the peace to still Samsara's Sea.

9. Gautama Buddha, shatter the energetic matrix that prevents people from seeing that democracies prove that people have begun to see that all people are connected, and therefore we are connected to the radical Muslim extremists. When we raise our own consciousness in the democratic nations, we will pull up on the whole and it will gradually shift the equation.

Gautama, with your thunderbolt,
we give the earth a mighty jolt,
I know that some will understand,
and join the Buddha's timeless band.

Gautama, Flame of Cosmic Peace,
unruly thoughts do hereby cease,
we radiate from you and me
the peace to still Samsara's Sea.

Part 6

1. Gautama Buddha, shatter the energetic matrix that prevents people from seeing that there is tremendous tension in Muslim societies. Every time there has been an extreme manifestation of fanaticism, it is because of the very aggressive beings that seek to control humankind.

Gautama, show my mental state
that does give rise to love and hate,
your exposé I do endure,
so my perception will be pure.

Gautama, Flame of Cosmic Peace,
unruly thoughts do hereby cease,
we radiate from you and me
the peace to still Samsara's Sea.

2. Gautama Buddha, shatter the energetic matrix that prevents people from seeing that these beings make a desperate attempt to maintain control because they can see that they are in danger of losing control.

Gautama, in your Flame of Peace,
the struggling self I now release,
the Buddha Nature I now see,
it is the core of you and me.

Gautama, Flame of Cosmic Peace,
unruly thoughts do hereby cease,
we radiate from you and me
the peace to still Samsara's Sea.

3. Gautama Buddha, shatter the energetic matrix that prevents people from seeing that the fallen beings are losing control because the collective consciousness is being raised, so that a majority of the people will no longer believe the illusion that has allowed them to be controlled.

Gautama, I am one with thee,
Mara's demons do now flee,

your Presence like a soothing balm,
my mind and senses ever calm.

Gautama, Flame of Cosmic Peace,
unruly thoughts do hereby cease,
we radiate from you and me
the peace to still Samsara's Sea.

4. Gautama Buddha, shatter the energetic matrix that prevents people in Muslim nations from breaking free of the illusion of the extreme, the fundamentalist, interpretation of Islam, the Sharia law.

Gautama, I now take the vow,
to live in the eternal now,
with you I do transcend all time,
to live in present so sublime.

Gautama, Flame of Cosmic Peace,
unruly thoughts do hereby cease,
we radiate from you and me
the peace to still Samsara's Sea.

5. Gautama Buddha, shatter the energetic matrix that prevents people from breaking free of this very controlled society, this very divided society with a clearly privileged elite that the population cannot touch.

Gautama, I have no desire,
to nothing earthly I aspire,
in non-attachment I now rest,
passing Mara's subtle test.

Gautama, Flame of Cosmic Peace,
unruly thoughts do hereby cease,
we radiate from you and me
the peace to still Samsara's Sea.

6. Gautama Buddha, shatter the energetic matrix that prevents people from seeing that the fallen beings know they are losing control, and that

is why they have launched this not very intelligent attempt to create these
radical Muslim fundamentalist movements that do chaotic things.

> Gautama, I melt into you,
> my mind is one, no longer two,
> immersed in your resplendent glow,
> Nirvana is all that I know.

> **Gautama, Flame of Cosmic Peace,**
> **unruly thoughts do hereby cease,**
> **we radiate from you and me**
> **the peace to still Samsara's Sea.**

7. Gautama Buddha, shatter the energetic matrix that prevents people
from seeing that this is actually a sign that a breakthrough is very close
to happening because otherwise there would not be such a clearly unbalanced, desperate attempt.

> Gautama, in your timeless space,
> I am immersed in Cosmic Grace,
> I know the God beyond all form,
> to world I will no more conform.

> **Gautama, Flame of Cosmic Peace,**
> **unruly thoughts do hereby cease,**
> **we radiate from you and me**
> **the peace to still Samsara's Sea.**

8. Gautama Buddha, shatter the energetic matrix that prevents people
from seeing that Muslim terrorism is not really directed at the West, the
West is just a scapegoat. The real purpose behind Muslim fundamentalism
is to maintain control over the population in Muslim countries.

> Gautama, I am now awake,
> I clearly see what is at stake,
> and thus I claim my sacred right
> to be on earth the Buddhic Light.

**Gautama, Flame of Cosmic Peace,
unruly thoughts do hereby cease,
we radiate from you and me
the peace to still Samsara's Sea.**

9. Gautama Buddha, shatter the energetic matrix that prevents people from seeing that the West is just a distraction to draw people's attention away from their internal tensions and the need to change their own societies.

Gautama, with your thunderbolt,
we give the earth a mighty jolt,
I know that some will understand,
and join the Buddha's timeless band.

**Gautama, Flame of Cosmic Peace,
unruly thoughts do hereby cease,
we radiate from you and me
the peace to still Samsara's Sea.**

Sealing

In the name of the I AM THAT I AM, I accept that Archangel Michael, Astrea and Shiva form an impenetrable shield around myself and all constructive people, sealing us from all fear-based energies in all four octaves. I accept that the Light of God is consuming and transforming all fear-based energies that make up the dark forces working against ending the era of fanaticism on earth!

32 | INVOKING A NEW AWARENESS OF DUALITY (PART 4)

In the name of the I AM THAT I AM, Jesus Christ, I use the authority that I have as a being in embodiment on earth to call upon Gautama Buddha to reinforce my calls and use my chakras to project the statements in this invocation into the collective consciousness and awaken people to the reality of how the dualistic mindset has distorted life on earth. Awaken people to the reality that we are spiritual beings and that we can co-create a new future by working with the ascended masters. I especially call for ...

[Make your own calls here.]

Part 1

1. Gautama Buddha, shatter the energetic matrix that prevents people from seeing that the deeper underlying cause of many wars has been this mechanism of attempting to maintain control by defining a scapegoat.

> Gautama, show my mental state
> that does give rise to love and hate,

your exposé I do endure,
so my perception will be pure.

Gautama, Flame of Cosmic Peace,
unruly thoughts do hereby cease,
we radiate from you and me
the peace to still Samsara's Sea.

2. Gautama Buddha, shatter the energetic matrix that prevents people from seeing that the fallen beings have created conflicts to divert people away from the need for internal change. People were misled into thinking that they could change their situation by changing other people, by forcing other people, by killing other people.

Gautama, in your Flame of Peace,
the struggling self I now release,
the Buddha Nature I now see,
it is the core of you and me.

Gautama, Flame of Cosmic Peace,
unruly thoughts do hereby cease,
we radiate from you and me
the peace to still Samsara's Sea.

3. Gautama Buddha, shatter the energetic matrix that prevents people from seeing that the material universe is a machine that is designed to give all people on earth a positive experience without suffering. We get a positive experience by changing ourselves and by working to raise the whole.

Gautama, I am one with thee,
Mara's demons do now flee,
your Presence like a soothing balm,
my mind and senses ever calm.

Gautama, Flame of Cosmic Peace,
unruly thoughts do hereby cease,
we radiate from you and me
the peace to still Samsara's Sea.

4. Gautama Buddha, shatter the energetic matrix that prevents people from seeing that when we go into duality, we lose the awareness of how the machine is designed to work.

Gautama, I now take the vow,
to live in the eternal now,
with you I do transcend all time,
to live in present so sublime.

Gautama, Flame of Cosmic Peace,
unruly thoughts do hereby cease,
we radiate from you and me
the peace to still Samsara's Sea.

5. Gautama Buddha, shatter the energetic matrix that prevents people from seeing that we experience that we are suffering and now we begin to think that the way to escape suffering is *not* to change ourselves but to change other people, to force other people.

Gautama, I have no desire,
to nothing earthly I aspire,
in non-attachment I now rest,
passing Mara's subtle test.

Gautama, Flame of Cosmic Peace,
unruly thoughts do hereby cease,
we radiate from you and me
the peace to still Samsara's Sea.

6. Gautama Buddha, shatter the energetic matrix that prevents people from seeing that in duality, we have a state of internal suffering, we cannot be in duality without suffering psychologically. There is a division in our psyches that pulls us in different directions.

Gautama, I melt into you,
my mind is one, no longer two,
immersed in your resplendent glow,
Nirvana is all that I know.

Gautama, Flame of Cosmic Peace,
unruly thoughts do hereby cease,
we radiate from you and me
the peace to still Samsara's Sea.

7. Gautama Buddha, shatter the energetic matrix that prevents people from seeing that when we are in duality, we cannot see that we could transcend ourselves, we could escape the suffering by working on ourselves.

Gautama, in your timeless space,
I am immersed in Cosmic Grace,
I know the God beyond all form,
to world I will no more conform.

Gautama, Flame of Cosmic Peace,
unruly thoughts do hereby cease,
we radiate from you and me
the peace to still Samsara's Sea.

8. Gautama Buddha, shatter the energetic matrix that prevents people from seeing that we are pulled into thinking that our suffering is not caused by *internal* factors, it is caused by *external* factors, including other people. The way to escape suffering is to change other people and since they will not change voluntarily, it is justified to force them.

Gautama, I am now awake,
I clearly see what is at stake,
and thus I claim my sacred right
to be on earth the Buddhic Light.

Gautama, Flame of Cosmic Peace,
unruly thoughts do hereby cease,
we radiate from you and me
the peace to still Samsara's Sea.

9. Gautama Buddha, shatter the energetic matrix that prevents people from seeing that throughout the ages some people have been willing to kill other people. This is because their internal suffering has become so intense

that they are desperate to escape it. They are willing to go to the extreme measure of forcing or killing other human beings.

> Gautama, with your thunderbolt,
> we give the earth a mighty jolt,
> I know that some will understand,
> and join the Buddha's timeless band.

> **Gautama, Flame of Cosmic Peace,**
> **unruly thoughts do hereby cease,**
> **we radiate from you and me**
> **the peace to still Samsara's Sea.**

Part 2

1. Gautama Buddha, shatter the energetic matrix that prevents people from seeing that they do this because they have been deceived by an epic cause that says that if they kill other people, they will diminish their suffering. This has never worked because as soon as we start forcing or killing other people, we only increase our suffering.

> Gautama, show my mental state
> that does give rise to love and hate,
> your exposé I do endure,
> so my perception will be pure.

> **Gautama, Flame of Cosmic Peace,**
> **unruly thoughts do hereby cease,**
> **we radiate from you and me**
> **the peace to still Samsara's Sea.**

2. Gautama Buddha, shatter the energetic matrix that prevents people from seeing that the basis of democratic societies is that we cannot diminish suffering in the world through force and by forcing others.

> Gautama, in your Flame of Peace,
> the struggling self I now release,

the Buddha Nature I now see,
it is the core of you and me.

**Gautama, Flame of Cosmic Peace,
unruly thoughts do hereby cease,
we radiate from you and me
the peace to still Samsara's Sea.**

3. Gautama Buddha, shatter the energetic matrix that prevents people from seeing that we can have a society that has less suffering by creating a society where all human beings are seen as being equal and having equal rights.

Gautama, I am one with thee,
Mara's demons do now flee,
your Presence like a soothing balm,
my mind and senses ever calm.

**Gautama, Flame of Cosmic Peace,
unruly thoughts do hereby cease,
we radiate from you and me
the peace to still Samsara's Sea.**

4. Gautama Buddha, shatter the energetic matrix that prevents people from seeing that no individual or no group of people have a right to force others. This is the basic principle of democracy. People have a right to live without force.

Gautama, I now take the vow,
to live in the eternal now,
with you I do transcend all time,
to live in present so sublime.

**Gautama, Flame of Cosmic Peace,
unruly thoughts do hereby cease,
we radiate from you and me
the peace to still Samsara's Sea.**

5. Gautama Buddha, shatter the energetic matrix that prevents people from seeing that in democratic nations there is less physical suffering. Greater abundance, greater material affluence equals less physical suffering.

Gautama, I have no desire,
to nothing earthly I aspire,
in non-attachment I now rest,
passing Mara's subtle test.

**Gautama, Flame of Cosmic Peace,
unruly thoughts do hereby cease,
we radiate from you and me
the peace to still Samsara's Sea.**

6. Gautama Buddha, shatter the energetic matrix that prevents people from seeing that the increase in mental problems demonstrates that even though democratic societies have created less physical suffering, we have not created less internal, less psychological, suffering.

Gautama, I melt into you,
my mind is one, no longer two,
immersed in your resplendent glow,
Nirvana is all that I know.

**Gautama, Flame of Cosmic Peace,
unruly thoughts do hereby cease,
we radiate from you and me
the peace to still Samsara's Sea.**

7. Gautama Buddha, shatter the energetic matrix that prevents people from seeing that the increase in psychological problems, where people are willing to acknowledge their psychological problems, actually demonstrates how successful we have been.

Gautama, in your timeless space,
I am immersed in Cosmic Grace,
I know the God beyond all form,
to world I will no more conform.

Gautama, Flame of Cosmic Peace,
unruly thoughts do hereby cease,
we radiate from you and me
the peace to still Samsara's Sea.

8. Gautama Buddha, shatter the energetic matrix that prevents people from seeing that it is perfectly natural that when we create societies where people's attention is not focused on physical forms of suffering, their attention is freed up to focus on the internal suffering.

Gautama, I am now awake,
I clearly see what is at stake,
and thus I claim my sacred right
to be on earth the Buddhic Light.

Gautama, Flame of Cosmic Peace,
unruly thoughts do hereby cease,
we radiate from you and me
the peace to still Samsara's Sea.

9. Gautama Buddha, shatter the energetic matrix that prevents people from seeing that the next logical step in the evolution of democracy is to focus on helping people overcome the internal suffering.

Gautama, with your thunderbolt,
we give the earth a mighty jolt,
I know that some will understand,
and join the Buddha's timeless band.

Gautama, Flame of Cosmic Peace,
unruly thoughts do hereby cease,
we radiate from you and me
the peace to still Samsara's Sea.

Part 3

1. Gautama Buddha, shatter the energetic matrix that prevents people from seeing that we cannot help people through a materialistic approach to psychology but by acknowledging that there is a mystical path whereby we can escape duality.

Gautama, show my mental state
that does give rise to love and hate,
your exposé I do endure,
so my perception will be pure.

Gautama, Flame of Cosmic Peace,
unruly thoughts do hereby cease,
we radiate from you and me
the peace to still Samsara's Sea.

2. Gautama Buddha, shatter the energetic matrix that prevents people from seeing that it is not a matter of western democracies accepting Buddhism or a mystical form of Christianity. It is a matter of realizing that there is a version of this path that is suitable for modern democracies.

Gautama, in your Flame of Peace,
the struggling self I now release,
the Buddha Nature I now see,
it is the core of you and me.

Gautama, Flame of Cosmic Peace,
unruly thoughts do hereby cease,
we radiate from you and me
the peace to still Samsara's Sea.

3. Gautama Buddha, shatter the energetic matrix that prevents people from seeing that as we, in the democratic nations, begin to escape the dualistic mindset, there will be less of an external threat against the democratic nations from those people who are still in the dualistic mindset.

Gautama, I am one with thee,
Mara's demons do now flee,
your Presence like a soothing balm,
my mind and senses ever calm.

Gautama, Flame of Cosmic Peace,
unruly thoughts do hereby cease,
we radiate from you and me
the peace to still Samsara's Sea.

4. Gautama Buddha, shatter the energetic matrix that prevents people from seeing that when we turn the other cheek and continue to turn the other cheek, there will come a point where we will no longer be attacked because the aggression of the attacker will be turned back upon themselves.

Gautama, I now take the vow,
to live in the eternal now,
with you I do transcend all time,
to live in present so sublime.

Gautama, Flame of Cosmic Peace,
unruly thoughts do hereby cease,
we radiate from you and me
the peace to still Samsara's Sea.

5. Gautama Buddha, shatter the energetic matrix that prevents people from seeing that if the West had been willing to turn the other cheek after 9/11, we would have already seen that the tension in Muslim societies would not have been diverted towards the West.

Gautama, I have no desire,
to nothing earthly I aspire,
in non-attachment I now rest,
passing Mara's subtle test.

Gautama, Flame of Cosmic Peace,
unruly thoughts do hereby cease,
we radiate from you and me
the peace to still Samsara's Sea.

6. Gautama Buddha, shatter the energetic matrix that prevents people from seeing that the tension would have resulted in civil wars that would have started the process of overthrowing the fundamentalist Islamic group.

Gautama, I melt into you,
my mind is one, no longer two,
immersed in your resplendent glow,
Nirvana is all that I know.

Gautama, Flame of Cosmic Peace,
unruly thoughts do hereby cease,
we radiate from you and me
the peace to still Samsara's Sea.

7. Gautama Buddha, shatter the energetic matrix that prevents people from seeing that the aggression in Muslim nations could not have been channeled against the West, if the West had turned the other cheek. It would have therefore been directed against themselves.

Gautama, in your timeless space,
I am immersed in Cosmic Grace,
I know the God beyond all form,
to world I will no more conform.

Gautama, Flame of Cosmic Peace,
unruly thoughts do hereby cease,
we radiate from you and me
the peace to still Samsara's Sea.

8. Gautama Buddha, shatter the energetic matrix that prevents people from seeing that by accepting how the machine actually works, we can create societies where we do not see ourselves as separate. We see that the goal is to raise our consciousness.

Gautama, I am now awake,
I clearly see what is at stake,
and thus I claim my sacred right
to be on earth the Buddhic Light.

Gautama, Flame of Cosmic Peace,
unruly thoughts do hereby cease,
we radiate from you and me
the peace to still Samsara's Sea.

9. Gautama Buddha, shatter the energetic matrix that prevents people from seeing that when raising consciousness is the main goal for society, there is almost no end to the material affluence and the material progress that such a society can see.

Gautama, with your thunderbolt,
we give the earth a mighty jolt,
I know that some will understand,
and join the Buddha's timeless band.

Gautama, Flame of Cosmic Peace,
unruly thoughts do hereby cease,
we radiate from you and me
the peace to still Samsara's Sea.

Part 4

1. Gautama Buddha, shatter the energetic matrix that prevents people from seeing that the epic mindset complicates everything. There are certain beings that deliberately want to deceive and want to confuse by making everything seem so incredibly complicated.

Gautama, show my mental state
that does give rise to love and hate,
your exposé I do endure,
so my perception will be pure.

Gautama, Flame of Cosmic Peace,
unruly thoughts do hereby cease,
we radiate from you and me
the peace to still Samsara's Sea.

2. Gautama Buddha, shatter the energetic matrix that prevents people from seeing that life is actually very simple. When we put our minds in a forward gear, our entire society will go forward.

> Gautama, in your Flame of Peace,
> the struggling self I now release,
> the Buddha Nature I now see,
> it is the core of you and me.

> **Gautama, Flame of Cosmic Peace,**
> **unruly thoughts do hereby cease,**
> **we radiate from you and me**
> **the peace to still Samsara's Sea.**

3. Gautama Buddha, shatter the energetic matrix that prevents people from seeing that what is best for us is to find out how the machine actually works and then work with the machine.

> Gautama, I am one with thee,
> Mara's demons do now flee,
> your Presence like a soothing balm,
> my mind and senses ever calm.

> **Gautama, Flame of Cosmic Peace,**
> **unruly thoughts do hereby cease,**
> **we radiate from you and me**
> **the peace to still Samsara's Sea.**

4. Gautama Buddha, shatter the energetic matrix that prevents people from seeing that we cannot change the orbit of the earth around the sun. Yet many civilizations have had some epic belief where they were attempting to change the way the universe works. There was no chance whatsoever that they could have been successful.

> Gautama, I now take the vow,
> to live in the eternal now,
> with you I do transcend all time,
> to live in present so sublime.

**Gautama, Flame of Cosmic Peace,
unruly thoughts do hereby cease,
we radiate from you and me
the peace to still Samsara's Sea.**

5. Gautama Buddha, shatter the energetic matrix that prevents people from seeing that the machine is not really designed to give us a *positive* experience. The deeper reality is that the machine is designed to give us *any* experience we want. That is why people can go into duality.

Gautama, I have no desire,
to nothing earthly I aspire,
in non-attachment I now rest,
passing Mara's subtle test.

**Gautama, Flame of Cosmic Peace,
unruly thoughts do hereby cease,
we radiate from you and me
the peace to still Samsara's Sea.**

6. Gautama Buddha, shatter the energetic matrix that prevents people from seeing that in order to have an uplifting experience, we have to see ourselves as connected to the machine, to our higher selves, to other people.

Gautama, I melt into you,
my mind is one, no longer two,
immersed in your resplendent glow,
Nirvana is all that I know.

**Gautama, Flame of Cosmic Peace,
unruly thoughts do hereby cease,
we radiate from you and me
the peace to still Samsara's Sea.**

7. Gautama Buddha, shatter the energetic matrix that prevents people from seeing that if people want a different experience, they can have that by going into the consciousness of duality where now they see themselves as separate beings.

Gautama, in your timeless space,
I am immersed in Cosmic Grace,
I know the God beyond all form,
to world I will no more conform.

Gautama, Flame of Cosmic Peace,
unruly thoughts do hereby cease,
we radiate from you and me
the peace to still Samsara's Sea.

8. Gautama Buddha, shatter the energetic matrix that prevents people from seeing that the alternative to a positive experience is an experience of suffering. There is a state of no suffering and there is a state of suffering. We can have the experience of no suffering or we can have the experience of suffering.

Gautama, I am now awake,
I clearly see what is at stake,
and thus I claim my sacred right
to be on earth the Buddhic Light.

Gautama, Flame of Cosmic Peace,
unruly thoughts do hereby cease,
we radiate from you and me
the peace to still Samsara's Sea.

9. Gautama Buddha, shatter the energetic matrix that prevents people from seeing that we have the experience of suffering by going into duality. We see ourselves as separate beings and *that* is how we suffer. We suffer internally. We suffer externally.

Gautama, with your thunderbolt,
we give the earth a mighty jolt,
I know that some will understand,
and join the Buddha's timeless band.

Gautama, Flame of Cosmic Peace,
unruly thoughts do hereby cease,

**we radiate from you and me
the peace to still Samsara's Sea.**

Part 5

1. Gautama Buddha, shatter the energetic matrix that prevents people from seeing that the machine is designed in such a way that people are allowed to go into suffering. The mechanics of how the machine has to be designed, based on free will, is that once we go into duality, the illusion of duality becomes self-reinforcing.

Gautama, show my mental state
that does give rise to love and hate,
your exposé I do endure,
so my perception will be pure.

**Gautama, Flame of Cosmic Peace,
unruly thoughts do hereby cease,
we radiate from you and me
the peace to still Samsara's Sea.**

2. Gautama Buddha, shatter the energetic matrix that prevents people from seeing that we have two dualistic polarities. If we move towards one polarity, what we are seeing is what validates the polarity. We are not seeing, or we are seeing as false, what questions the polarity.

Gautama, in your Flame of Peace,
the struggling self I now release,
the Buddha Nature I now see,
it is the core of you and me.

**Gautama, Flame of Cosmic Peace,
unruly thoughts do hereby cease,
we radiate from you and me
the peace to still Samsara's Sea.**

3. Gautama Buddha, shatter the energetic matrix that prevents people from seeing that this is how duality becomes a self-reinforcing process, a self-reinforcing, a self-perpetuating illusion. Once we are in duality, we have a limited view. We still have a logical mental mind but there is a limit to how we can use that mind.

Gautama, I am one with thee,
Mara's demons do now flee,
your Presence like a soothing balm,
my mind and senses ever calm.

Gautama, Flame of Cosmic Peace,
unruly thoughts do hereby cease,
we radiate from you and me
the peace to still Samsara's Sea.

4. Gautama Buddha, shatter the energetic matrix that prevents people from seeing that this is what enables people to stay in the fanatical mindset. At the intellectual level, in their mental bodies, there is a veil. They cannot see.

Gautama, I now take the vow,
to live in the eternal now,
with you I do transcend all time,
to live in present so sublime.

Gautama, Flame of Cosmic Peace,
unruly thoughts do hereby cease,
we radiate from you and me
the peace to still Samsara's Sea.

5. Gautama Buddha, shatter the energetic matrix that prevents people from seeing that when we have two dualistic polarities, there is a veil between them that prevents us from seeing both at the same time. We cannot see that they are both limited, they are both illusions.

Gautama, I have no desire,
to nothing earthly I aspire,
in non-attachment I now rest,
passing Mara's subtle test.

Gautama, Flame of Cosmic Peace,
unruly thoughts do hereby cease,
we radiate from you and me
the peace to still Samsara's Sea.

6. Gautama Buddha, shatter the energetic matrix that prevents people from seeing that once we are inside the box of duality, there is a limit to how we can use logic and reason. Yet we cannot know everything through reason.

Gautama, I melt into you,
my mind is one, no longer two,
immersed in your resplendent glow,
Nirvana is all that I know.

Gautama, Flame of Cosmic Peace,
unruly thoughts do hereby cease,
we radiate from you and me
the peace to still Samsara's Sea.

7. Gautama Buddha, shatter the energetic matrix that prevents people from seeing that it is a blind alley to think we can know everything about how the material universe works by looking at the material universe, taking a reductionist approach, looking at smaller units. Aristotle's philosophy was an expression of duality.

Gautama, in your timeless space,
I am immersed in Cosmic Grace,
I know the God beyond all form,
to world I will no more conform.

Gautama, Flame of Cosmic Peace,
unruly thoughts do hereby cease,
we radiate from you and me
the peace to still Samsara's Sea.

8. Gautama Buddha, shatter the energetic matrix that prevents people from seeing that when we are not in separation, we look at the whole. When we go into separation, we only look at the parts. We cannot see the whole, we cannot see the forest for the trees.

Gautama, I am now awake,
I clearly see what is at stake,
and thus I claim my sacred right
to be on earth the Buddhic Light.

Gautama, Flame of Cosmic Peace,
unruly thoughts do hereby cease,
we radiate from you and me
the peace to still Samsara's Sea.

9. Gautama Buddha, shatter the energetic matrix that prevents people from seeing that we are looking at life from the vantage point of being a separate individual and therefore we think everything in the universe can be understood as being made up of separate components.

Gautama, with your thunderbolt,
we give the earth a mighty jolt,
I know that some will understand,
and join the Buddha's timeless band.

Gautama, Flame of Cosmic Peace,
unruly thoughts do hereby cease,
we radiate from you and me
the peace to still Samsara's Sea.

Part 6

1. Gautama Buddha, shatter the energetic matrix that prevents people from seeing that we cannot see that although we can talk about components of a whole, what really is the cause of everything is the whole. There are no separate components.

Gautama, show my mental state
that does give rise to love and hate,
your exposé I do endure,
so my perception will be pure.

Gautama, Flame of Cosmic Peace,
unruly thoughts do hereby cease,
we radiate from you and me
the peace to still Samsara's Sea.

2. Gautama Buddha, shatter the energetic matrix that prevents people from seeing that we can never use reason to escape duality. The way out is to go beyond reason and use our intuitive faculties. We can switch away from the divisions and experience an alternative to the dualistic state of consciousness.

Gautama, in your Flame of Peace,
the struggling self I now release,
the Buddha Nature I now see,
it is the core of you and me.

Gautama, Flame of Cosmic Peace,
unruly thoughts do hereby cease,
we radiate from you and me
the peace to still Samsara's Sea.

3. Gautama Buddha, shatter the energetic matrix that prevents people from seeing that we have the ability to go into this neutral state of mind where we experience. We are not reasoning. We are not believing. We are not arguing. We *experience* that there is something outside of duality.

Gautama, I am one with thee,
Mara's demons do now flee,
your Presence like a soothing balm,
my mind and senses ever calm.

Gautama, Flame of Cosmic Peace,
unruly thoughts do hereby cease,
we radiate from you and me
the peace to still Samsara's Sea.

4. Gautama Buddha, shatter the energetic matrix that prevents people from seeing that this gives us a frame of reference that allows us to look

at the dualistic beliefs and begin to see what we cannot see from inside the mental box. We begin to see the limitations and contradictions.

Gautama, I now take the vow,
to live in the eternal now,
with you I do transcend all time,
to live in present so sublime.

Gautama, Flame of Cosmic Peace,
unruly thoughts do hereby cease,
we radiate from you and me
the peace to still Samsara's Sea.

5. Gautama Buddha, shatter the energetic matrix that prevents people from seeing that in the intuitive approach, we are not reasoning with the linear mind. We are not coming up with some kind of theory. We are going into neutral and experiencing that there is something outside of this dualistic chaos.

Gautama, I have no desire,
to nothing earthly I aspire,
in non-attachment I now rest,
passing Mara's subtle test.

Gautama, Flame of Cosmic Peace,
unruly thoughts do hereby cease,
we radiate from you and me
the peace to still Samsara's Sea.

6. Gautama Buddha, shatter the energetic matrix that prevents people from seeing that once we go into duality, we must experience a certain amount of suffering before we can see that if we want to escape suffering, we need to change something inside of ourselves, instead of changing something outside of ourselves.

Gautama, I melt into you,
my mind is one, no longer two,
immersed in your resplendent glow,
Nirvana is all that I know.

Gautama, Flame of Cosmic Peace,
unruly thoughts do hereby cease,
we radiate from you and me
the peace to still Samsara's Sea.

7. Gautama Buddha, shatter the energetic matrix that prevents people from seeing that there is a path where we systematically change our consciousness and escape the illusions, the sense of separation that causes all human suffering.

Gautama, in your timeless space,
I am immersed in Cosmic Grace,
I know the God beyond all form,
to world I will no more conform.

Gautama, Flame of Cosmic Peace,
unruly thoughts do hereby cease,
we radiate from you and me
the peace to still Samsara's Sea.

8. Gautama Buddha, shatter the energetic matrix that prevents people from seeing a new awareness, a new paradigm, a new worldview that can take the modern democracies to the next logical stage in our development, where we focus on minimizing internal suffering, the psychological suffering of our people.

Gautama, I am now awake,
I clearly see what is at stake,
and thus I claim my sacred right
to be on earth the Buddhic Light.

Gautama, Flame of Cosmic Peace,
unruly thoughts do hereby cease,
we radiate from you and me
the peace to still Samsara's Sea.

9. Gautama Buddha, shatter the energetic matrix that prevents people from seeing that this is a new human right. A democracy says that we have a right to live without any external force limiting us. We also have a right

to live without having any internal force limiting us. This is the next logical step in the evolution of humanity, and the nations who can take that step are clearly the modern democracies.

Gautama, with your thunderbolt,
we give the earth a mighty jolt,
I know that some will understand,
and join the Buddha's timeless band.

Gautama, Flame of Cosmic Peace,
unruly thoughts do hereby cease,
we radiate from you and me
the peace to still Samsara's Sea.

Sealing

In the name of the I AM THAT I AM, I accept that Archangel Michael, Astrea and Shiva form an impenetrable shield around myself and all constructive people, sealing us from all fear-based energies in all four octaves. I accept that the Light of God is consuming and transforming all fear-based energies that make up the dark forces working against ending the era of fanaticism on earth!

33 | USING A SPIRITUAL TEACHING TO ESCAPE FANATICISM

I AM the Ascended Master Mother Mary, and for this conference I am the Alpha and Omega, the beginning and the ending. I wish to give you a few closing remarks before I seal this conference. First of all, we have said before that when we have a conference, from the ascended realm we always see a high potential and a low potential for what could be accomplished during the conference. I want to assure you that even though some of you have felt the heaviness of the energy of the city, you have even exceeded the high potential that we saw for this conference. For this we are very grateful.

We congratulate you for your willingness, first of all, to be here, but also to look at yourselves, work with yourselves, talk amongst yourselves, and therefore make progress in many ways by sharing your experiences, by sharing your hearts and forming more of a bond than you normally have when you are not physically together. We are of course grateful for those on the broadcast as well who have also added your momentums to the momentum of the people who are physically present.

We consider this conference a success from any perspective, and we are grateful for your willingness to transcend yourselves. This is really what allows us to use your chakras and auras to broadcast this impulse into the collective consciousness. When a conference like this sets off a strong initial impulse, then it becomes easier for people, when the book comes out and the invocations are made, to continue that momentum and build upon it. This means that the goal we have, the long-term goal for this conference, can more easily be accomplished. The same of course we achieved in Korea, and we hope to achieve the same at the other conferences we are having.

Spiritual people and the fanatical mindset

I want to also give you a few remarks about the topic of how you as spiritual people can transcend the fanatical mindset. Although we have touched upon it before, I still want to go a little more into it. When you look at previous ascended master organizations, you will, if you are brutally honest, have to say that many of the people who were the students, the members, of these organizations were in the fanatical mindset. I am not saying that they were ready to kill somebody, but they were in the less aggressive, more benign aspects of the fanatical mindset. This can be seen in several different ways.

First of all, there was this very subtle culture of feeling superior. They thought, for example: "We have the highest teaching on the planet. The consequences must be that since we recognize this teaching, and so many other people don't, then we are the most advanced spiritual students on the planet." This is not necessarily the case. Nevertheless, even believing this and reinforcing that in an organization, can create this culture of superiority that is one aspect of the fanatical mindset.

The other aspect is that you see this tendency to create a standard for how a chela of the ascended masters should be, should behave, what kind of car they should drive, what color car, what color clothes, all of these outer things that you define a standard for. Once you have defined a standard, then you are always evaluating yourself and others based on the standard. This is what, not only in ascended master organizations but also in many spiritual and religious organizations (many other organizations) leads to this very judgmental culture, judgmental mindset, where everybody is always judging each other. Of course, this is an unpleasant environment to be in, and it causes a certain amount of tension, a certain amount of suffering, quite frankly.

Another aspect of this fanatical mindset is that people have a fear that the teachings could be proven wrong, that the messenger could make a mistake, that there could be a contradiction between one dictation and a later dictation, or between this organization and a previous organization, or between the spiritual teaching and scientific discoveries. You see that many, many people around the world have created this huge beast in the collective consciousness. It is of course part of the fanatical mindset where, when you accept that you have a certain idea that has some supreme authority or validity, you are always afraid: What if it was proven wrong? All of a sudden, the sense of security that you gained by accepting the idea would then be shattered, and you would plunge back into the state you were in before you accepted that viewpoint, maybe even a worse state. As you see with some people who have their faith destroyed, now they dare not believe in anything, and therefore they often sink into this doubt, agnosticism, depression, or even more severe mental illness, like schizophrenia.

Those who seek to destroy constructive ideas

What I want to give you here is some directions on how you can avoid this, or how you can move out of this collective pull and how you can see elements in your own consciousness. The reality here is that you are of course living on a planet that is ruled by the dualistic consciousness. There are fallen beings on the planet, and quite frankly if you have any constructive idea, you can be sure that there are fallen beings who will make an attempt to destroy that idea, to disprove it, to take the credibility of the people behind the idea, and this and that. It is simply something you can see from history that any positive constructive endeavor will be exposed to a certain amount of criticism. Because of this, and because this has been going on for so long, and because of this very aggressive intent of the fallen beings, there has been created this fear that whenever you have something positive, it could be destroyed.

You can see how ascended master students in previous dispensations had these fears that something could disprove their belief in the ascended masters' teachings. Some contradiction could creep up, the messenger could make a mistake, she could make a prediction that did not come true, or whatever you have. Over the years you have seen various people who have left the organization, stopped believing in the teachings because of some outer thing, some outer condition they had set up in their minds that was not fulfilled. The way to overcome this is partly to of course use the teachings on fanaticism, partly to use the teachings on the separate selves, because where does the fear come from? It comes from a separate self, but there is also a certain element of doubt here where you are still in a mindset where you are thinking in terms of right and wrong.

What I really want to point out to you is that when you step back from this entire phenomenon, you see that if you have a fear that the teaching you are following could be proven wrong, it shows that you still have some self that is in this dualistic mindset where it thinks in terms of right and wrong. In other words, you think that a teaching, if it is a valid teaching, should be true, it should be absolutely true, and therefore it should never be proven wrong. Do you not see that the more subtle attitude behind this is the essence of duality? There are always two opposites. You are still trapped in what the Buddha called the pairs. You are thinking in terms of right and wrong, true and false.

No teaching is meant to be absolute

The reality here, and we have attempted to explain this to you in the last couple of years, is that it has never been our goal to give a teaching that is absolute and therefore represents an absolute truth. It cannot be done, given the level of consciousness you have on planet earth and the way people use words based on the dualistic consciousness. Even we of the ascended masters cannot formulate a teaching in words that is an absolute teaching. We cannot create a teaching that, if you look at it from the linear mindset, could not be proven wrong by people in that linear mindset.

You can see this by just asking yourself a simple question: Why is it that more than 99% of the population on earth do not believe in ascended master teachings and in fact think you are crazy for following them? Well, it is because, as the Buddha explained about duality, they have stepped into a dualistic polarity. They have put on these glasses that filter out certain things, and therefore they cannot see the validity of an ascended master teaching. They think it is absolutely wrong. Why do *you* think it is right? Well, because you have stepped into some other mindset. You have put on another pair of glasses.

This is what we are pointing out: Many of the students in previous dispensations, when they came into the teaching, so to speak, put on a certain pair of glasses that made them now only see what validated the teaching and tend to ignore or push away what questioned the teaching.

What happened to some people was that they were in this mindset for a while, and then something happened that made them doubt the teaching. Suddenly, instead of pushing away their doubts, they decided to take a look at the doubts, and now they switched from this blind belief to an equally blind doubt. They switched from one extreme to the other. The very fact that this is a possibility, that people can switch from believing in a teaching to not believing in a teaching, shows that there is still a self that is in that dualistic mind where there are always two polarities: true and false, right and wrong.

What we have attempted to tell you is that when you shift beyond this state of consciousness, it is not a matter of whether the teaching is true or false, right or wrong, in an absolute linear sense. As I said earlier in a question and answer session, it is not constructive for you to take the teaching we are giving through this dispensation, use the linear mind to compare it to the teachings of previous dispensations and try to find contradictions. It just is not constructive because the linear mind cannot take you where the teaching is meant to take you. You take a given teaching, and you apply it for the purpose of shifting your consciousness, not for the purpose of seeing some absolute truth.

The purpose of a teaching is shifting consciousness

Do you understand? This is part of the fanatical mindset where the fallen beings have inserted this illusion that they use against people. When people start coming to the point where they realize that they have some illusions, then the fallen beings will try to say: "But the way to overcome your ignorance, your illusions, is to find an absolute truth. And when you find that outer expression of absolute truth, then you will be free from ignorance." This is dualistic. It is only in the dualistic mind there could be a concept of absolute truth. What we are really guiding you towards is realizing that it is not a matter of finding an outer truth. It is a matter of using an outer teaching as a tool to gain an inner experience. It is the inner experience that is true. It is the inner experience that is valid. It is the inner experience that shifts your consciousness.

We have seen people who took ascended master teachings and accepted with their outer minds that this represented an absolute truth. They studied the teachings faithfully, they became very adept in understanding the teaching intellectually, but it did not shift their consciousness. They could go on with this for decades and make very little progress. You can see the same phenomenon in any other religion where you have the scribes and the Pharisees who know the outer teaching and the outer law (all the rules, all the scriptures), but they have not shifted their consciousness.

We are not interested in you blindly following the teaching. We are not interested in you *believing* the teaching, thinking it is an absolute truth. We are interested in you looking at the teaching as a tool for giving you the inner experiences to shift your consciousness, and therefore you make progress. You have to become aware of the limitations of the outer, linear mind. There can come a point where you simply accept and you experience that the purpose of the teaching is to give you an inner experience that shifts your consciousness. Therefore, all of a sudden it is not so important that the outer teaching, the outer form of the teaching, is linear, absolutely consistent with previous teachings, or this or that. There comes a point where you are not even concerned about contradictions, for example, among spiritual teachings.

Have no outer loyalty to a teaching

One of the big weapons used by the fallen beings through scientific materialists is that the materialists would point out contradictions between different religious beliefs and then say, by using Aristotelian logic: "Well, here are two teachings that clearly contradict each other, so they can't both be true. Maybe none of them are true. Maybe all religion is just a hoax." When you step beyond that, you realize that there have, in the history of humankind, been many, many spiritual teachings. The mystical path, as Gautama said, has been taught in many different versions, many different contexts.

It is not constructive to ask: "Were some of them false? Was there only one that was the real one, and all the others were false?" No, they were all valid. They were all valid in the sense that they had teachings and tools that could help people shift their consciousness. If people took a particular mystical teaching and used it to shift their consciousness, then that was a valid teaching for them. They do not need to compare this to other teachings and try to find some superior teaching, or try to label other teachings as false. The form of the outer teaching is not what matters. What matters is: Does it help you shift your consciousness or does it not?

We have not created an organization with this absolutist belief that if you follow all the rules and regulations and teachings of this organization, you are guaranteed to make your ascension. You will only make your ascension by shifting your consciousness until you reach the 144th level and then let go of that final illusion. What does it take for you to let go of a certain illusion? It takes some kind of thing that stimulates the process whereby you see the illusion and let it go. This can be an outer teaching. We have attempted to give you teachings that can help you shift your consciousness, but we have never claimed, and we certainly do not see, that they will work equally well for all people. If you find that there is a certain other teaching that helps you shift your consciousness, by all means make use of that teaching. We are not in any way demanding loyalty to this teaching.

The messenger himself has moved beyond this desire to have anybody be loyal to him. He does not consider that you are *his* students, in the sense that he has any ownership over you. He does not want any loyalty from you if this is a hindrance on your own path. He wants you to go wherever you need to go and have the experiences you need to have to make maximum progress on your path. In a sense, you could say the messenger is not even afraid of you coming to the point where you have used the teachings he has brought forth to the point where you no longer need him or the teaching. In other words, he is not afraid of making himself obsolete.

You of course should have no outer loyalty. Your real loyalty is to your personal path and your progress on that path. The outer teachings are just tools to facilitate that progress. Whatever you feel you need, then you go there, you make use of it. This does not mean that you have to suddenly shift and label this teaching as false, or say the messenger is no longer in contact with the real masters, or this or that. You just say: "I need something else." You do not close the door because perhaps at some time in the future, you could need this teaching again.

True and false teachings

You are loyal to your own path in the sense that you are not thinking in terms of false and true. You are thinking in terms of usefulness, a very practical approach. Does a teaching help me grow? Does it help me shift my consciousness? Is it useful to me? You can see examples throughout history where people have followed a teaching that contained a great number of errors, but there were a few correct ideas in it. When I say errors, I mean errors that were deliberately inserted by the fallen beings to actively deceive people. But there were still a few statements in there that were true, and people were able to focus on the ones that were true and therefore shift their consciousness.

From a certain perspective, you could say that there are some teachings that are deliberately created by the fallen beings. They have a certain number of correct statements in them, statements that can help you shift your consciousness, but they are mixed in with other teachings that are designed to deceive people and keep you stuck at a certain level. You could say from an overall perspective that this teaching contains more *destructive* ideas than *constructive* ideas, and it is not a teaching we could recommend people to go into. Nevertheless, there are people who have been able to use even such a teaching. You see examples of people who have taken even the Catholic doctrines, as limited as they are, but still found a way to go within their hearts to transcend the outer teaching and attain such devotion to Jesus or myself that it has shifted their consciousness, and they have made progress.

Beyond the outer mind

What I am saying is this: If you still have any doubt about whether the teaching is true, if you still have any fear that it could be disproven, then realize that this comes from a separate self and make an effort to come to see that self and let it go. Then, you will find that your path will take on a much more joyful dimension where your intuition will work much better, because now you are not evaluating a teaching with the outer mind.

You are not feeling with the outer mind a certain loyalty to a particular teaching. Instead, you are flowing with your intuitive promptings, and you study whatever you feel prompted to study. You sometimes might read a whole book and just pick up one idea, but that idea helps you shift your consciousness. You might even come to a point where your intuition has been refined to where you can pick out a 500-page book from the shelf and open it up to one particular page. There is the one idea you needed to find in that book, and you do not have to read the rest of the book. What a time saver, which would give you much more time to check your e-mail and your text messages on your phone! So a win-win.

The point is this: In order for you to have the maximum impact on raising the planet out of the consciousness of fanaticism, you need to be willing to just look at yourself and see where you have these elements of fanaticism concerning the spiritual teaching you are following. Then, use these teachings I have given you, use the tools we have given you on the separate selves. Fear and doubt can only come from a separate self because the Conscious You has no fear of a particular teaching being proven wrong. It just neutrally observes, and it just neutrally evaluates what is useful, what is not useful. All of these other things then fade away. There is no saying whatsoever that once you have found this teaching, you have to follow it for the rest of your life or study it the same way as you have been doing so far.

There are, as we have said, levels of the path, and at certain times you need to approach the path a certain way. Then, you may come to a point where you need something different. This is again what the fanatical mindset will block because now you think with the outer mind that you are supposed to create some kind of standard for how you are going to behave for the rest of your life as a spiritual student. When you let go of this fanatical mindset and the fear of failure, the fear of making a mistake, the fear of being wrong, then you can flow with your intuition, and you go where you get the most benefit. You get the exact thing you need to take the next step on your path.

That might mean, for example, that you would find this teaching, and you would get certain ideas from it. Then, you would feel you needed something else so you go out there, find another teaching, practice that for some years. Then, you come back to this teaching, and now you can pick up something that you did not see the first time. There is absolutely nothing wrong in this process, so avoid this outer mind's fanatical approach, this sense of loyalty or this sense that you *should* absolutely follow this teaching.

Going beyond the need for security

In order to really avoid this, be willing to take the teachings we have given on fanaticism, about how it gives people a sense of security, how it gives people a sense of equilibrium. Then, look at yourselves and see: Have you developed or adopted a sense of security based on this teaching? Is there some sense in you that if you follow this teaching faithfully for the rest of your life, then you must be able to make your ascension?

If you are honest with yourself, you will see that we have never claimed that through this messenger. Where does that belief come from? It comes from a separate self that has this need for security, and it wants you to feel that because you have found this teaching, because you are following this teaching, now you are secure. Be willing to actually look at what we have said in the teaching. We have not encouraged this kind of security, especially in later years where we are giving you the teachings on the separate selves. We are actually saying there is no security in the outer teaching. There is no security in the outer practice. There is only security, a dynamic security, of constant self-transcendence where you continue to take step by step, walking higher on the 144 levels of consciousness until you shed that last illusion. That is the inner security, and when you can shift to this, your path becomes much more peaceful, much more joyful, because you know you cannot really go wrong.

May you pass every test

There was a concept in a previous ascended master organization that many situations in life were tests and that we of the ascended masters were constantly giving our chelas tests. Everybody was in this mindset of always evaluating: "What is the test? Have I failed my test?" There was a collective fear of failing your test. I am not telling you that this previous dispensation was wrong, but I am telling you that this is only valid at a certain level of consciousness. We would like all of you who are following this dispensation to rise above that, where you are not afraid of failing your tests because you know that you are always willing to see a higher understanding than what you have right now.

In a sense we could say: "What is the only test that we of the ascended masters have ever given?" It is always: "Are you willing to transcend your present level of consciousness?" In this previous dispensation they often thought that it was a matter of doing the right outer things, making the right choices in outer situations, but the real test is always that whenever you are facing some kind of issue, situation, problem, riddle, the only way to really solve it is not to solve it on an outer level that the outer mind can grasp, but to see that the situation represents a certain level of consciousness. The way to pass your test is to transcend that level of consciousness. This is how you can come to that level where you are no longer worrying about passing your test, failing your test. You are always open to looking for a higher understanding.

As the messenger said, he has no fixed opinions, he has no beliefs anymore, he has no knowledge in his mind that he considers absolute because he realizes that he is still in embodiment. He cannot see what we of the ascended masters can see. He has had enough contact with us that he realizes our consciousness is infinitely higher than what he can have while he is in physical embodiment.

No matter what idea he has, even if it is an idea given by the ascended masters, we of the ascended masters could always give him and you a different perspective, a higher understanding of the same idea. We could always give you an understanding where you saw, it was not that your previous idea was false, but that it was not the complete story. It was just part of a much greater picture.

There is no limit to how much of a greater picture you can come to see, but there is a limit to how much you can see while you are in embodiment. In order to see the full picture, you have to ascend. If you are in this mindset where you are not "grasping your ideas," as the Buddhists say, you are not holding on to any idea, not afraid of questioning any idea, you are not even afraid of an idea being proven wrong. How can an idea you have be proven wrong unless you at the same time see why the idea was wrong or limited and then see a better idea, a broader idea, and grow from it? You can get to that point where it is not a matter of right or wrong, true or false. You know that as long as you are willing to transcend your present level of consciousness, you cannot go wrong, you cannot make a mistake, you cannot fail your test.

With this, my beloved, we have given you everything we wanted to give you, including, we hope, our gratitude and our love, and therefore I simply seal you. I seal this conference in the Mother's love that I represent to planet earth. *May you pass every test.*

34 | INVOKING FREEDOM FROM SPIRITUAL FANATICISM

In the name of the I AM THAT I AM, Jesus Christ, I use the authority that I have as a being in embodiment on earth to call upon Mother Mary to reinforce my calls and use my chakras to project the statements in this invocation into the collective consciousness and awaken people to the need to overcome the subtle fanaticism in spiritual movements. Awaken people to the reality that we are spiritual beings and that we can co-create a new future by working with the ascended masters. I especially call for …

[Make your own calls here.]

Part 1

1. Mother Mary, shatter the energetic matrix that prevents spiritual people from seeing that many spiritual organizations are in the less aggressive, more benign aspects of the fanatical mindset.

O blessed Mary, Mother mine,
there is no greater love than thine,

as we are one in heart and mind,
my place in hierarchy I find.

O Mother Mary, generate,
the song that does accelerate,
the earth into a higher state,
all matter does now scintillate.

2. Mother Mary, shatter the energetic matrix that prevents spiritual people from seeing that many spiritual organizations have a subtle culture of feeling superior.

I came to earth from heaven sent,
as I am in embodiment,
I use Divine authority,
commanding you to set earth free.

O Mother Mary, generate,
the song that does accelerate,
the earth into a higher state,
all matter does now scintillate.

3. Mother Mary, shatter the energetic matrix that prevents spiritual people from seeing that if we believe we are very advanced because we recognize a certain spiritual teaching, it can create this culture of superiority that is one aspect of the fanatical mindset.

I call now in God's sacred name,
for you to use your Mother Flame,
to burn all fear-based energy,
restoring sacred harmony.

O Mother Mary, generate,
the song that does accelerate,
the earth into a higher state,
all matter does now scintillate.

4. Mother Mary, shatter the energetic matrix that prevents spiritual people from seeing that spiritual organizations have a tendency to create a standard for how a member should be and should behave.

Your sacred name I hereby praise,
collective consciousness you raise,
no more of fear and doubt and shame,
consume it with your Mother Flame.

**O Mother Mary, generate,
the song that does accelerate,
the earth into a higher state,
all matter does now scintillate.**

5. Mother Mary, shatter the energetic matrix that prevents spiritual people from seeing that once we have defined a standard, then we are always evaluating ourselves and others based on the standard.

All darkness from the earth you purge,
your light moves as a mighty surge,
no force of darkness can now stop,
the spiral that goes only up.

**O Mother Mary, generate,
the song that does accelerate,
the earth into a higher state,
all matter does now scintillate.**

6. Mother Mary, shatter the energetic matrix that prevents spiritual people from seeing that in many spiritual and religious organizations this leads to a very judgmental culture, a judgmental mindset, where everybody is always judging each other.

All elemental life you bless,
removing from them man-made stress,
the nature spirits are now free,
outpicturing Divine decree.

O Mother Mary, generate,
the song that does accelerate,
the earth into a higher state,
all matter does now scintillate.

7. Mother Mary, shatter the energetic matrix that prevents spiritual people from seeing that another aspect of the fanatical mindset is that people have a fear that the teachings could be proven wrong, that the leader could make a mistake, that there could be contradictions in the teaching.

I raise my voice and take my stand,
a stop to war I do command,
no more shall warring scar the earth,
a golden age is given birth.

O Mother Mary, generate,
the song that does accelerate,
the earth into a higher state,
all matter does now scintillate.

8. Mother Mary, shatter the energetic matrix that prevents spiritual people from seeing that part of the fanatical mindset is when we accept that we have a certain idea that has some supreme authority or validity, we are always afraid that it could be proven wrong.

As Mother Earth is free at last,
disasters belong to the past,
your Mother Light is so intense,
that matter is now far less dense.

O Mother Mary, generate,
the song that does accelerate,
the earth into a higher state,
all matter does now scintillate.

9. Mother Mary, shatter the energetic matrix that prevents spiritual people from seeing that the sense of security that we gained by accepting the idea would then be shattered, and we would plunge back into the state we were in before we accepted that viewpoint, maybe even a worse state.

In Mother Light the earth is pure,
the upward spiral will endure,
prosperity is now the norm,
God's vision manifest as form.

**O Mother Mary, generate,
the song that does accelerate,
the earth into a higher state,
all matter does now scintillate.**

Part 2

1. Mother Mary, shatter the energetic matrix that prevents spiritual people from seeing that some people who have their faith destroyed, dare not believe in anything, and they often sink into doubt, agnosticism, depression, or even more severe mental illness, like schizophrenia.

O blessed Mary, Mother mine,
there is no greater love than thine,
as we are one in heart and mind,
my place in hierarchy I find.

**O Mother Mary, generate,
the song that does accelerate,
the earth into a higher state,
all matter does now scintillate.**

2. Mother Mary, shatter the energetic matrix that prevents spiritual people from seeing that we are living on a planet that is ruled by the dualistic consciousness. There are fallen beings who will attempt to destroy any constructive idea, to disprove it or to destroy the credibility of the people behind the idea.

I came to earth from heaven sent,
as I am in embodiment,
I use Divine authority,
commanding you to set earth free.

**O Mother Mary, generate,
the song that does accelerate,
the earth into a higher state,
all matter does now scintillate.**

3. Mother Mary, shatter the energetic matrix that prevents spiritual people from seeing that any positive constructive endeavor will be exposed to a certain amount of criticism. This has created a fear that whenever we have something positive, it could be destroyed.

I call now in God's sacred name,
for you to use your Mother Flame,
to burn all fear-based energy,
restoring sacred harmony.

**O Mother Mary, generate,
the song that does accelerate,
the earth into a higher state,
all matter does now scintillate.**

4. Mother Mary, shatter the energetic matrix that prevents spiritual people from seeing that many people have left an organization, stopped believing in the teachings because of some outer thing, some outer condition they had set up in their minds that was not fulfilled.

Your sacred name I hereby praise,
collective consciousness you raise,
no more of fear and doubt and shame,
consume it with your Mother Flame.

**O Mother Mary, generate,
the song that does accelerate,
the earth into a higher state,
all matter does now scintillate.**

5. Mother Mary, shatter the energetic matrix that prevents spiritual people from seeing that the fear comes from a separate self, but there is also a certain element of doubt where we are in a mindset where we are thinking in terms of right and wrong.

All darkness from the earth you purge,
your light moves as a mighty surge,
no force of darkness can now stop,
the spiral that goes only up.

O Mother Mary, generate,
the song that does accelerate,
the earth into a higher state,
all matter does now scintillate.

6. Mother Mary, shatter the energetic matrix that prevents spiritual people from seeing that if we have a fear that the teaching we are following could be proven wrong, it shows that we still have some self that is in this dualistic mindset where it thinks in terms of right and wrong.

All elemental life you bless,
removing from them man-made stress,
the nature spirits are now free,
outpicturing Divine decree.

O Mother Mary, generate,
the song that does accelerate,
the earth into a higher state,
all matter does now scintillate.

7. Mother Mary, shatter the energetic matrix that prevents spiritual people from seeing that we think that a teaching, if it is a valid teaching, should be true. It should be absolutely true, and therefore it should never be proven wrong.

I raise my voice and take my stand,
a stop to war I do command,
no more shall warring scar the earth,
a golden age is given birth.

O Mother Mary, generate,
the song that does accelerate,
the earth into a higher state,
all matter does now scintillate.

8. Mother Mary, shatter the energetic matrix that prevents spiritual people from seeing that the more subtle attitude behind this is the essence of duality. There are always two opposites. We are still trapped in what the Buddha called the pairs. We are thinking in terms of right and wrong, true and false.

As Mother Earth is free at last,
disasters belong to the past,
your Mother Light is so intense,
that matter is now far less dense.

O Mother Mary, generate,
the song that does accelerate,
the earth into a higher state,
all matter does now scintillate.

9. Mother Mary, shatter the energetic matrix that prevents spiritual people from seeing that no spiritual teaching is absolute and therefore it does not represent an absolute truth. An absolute truth cannot be released, given the level of consciousness we have on planet earth and the way people use words based on the dualistic consciousness.

In Mother Light the earth is pure,
the upward spiral will endure,
prosperity is now the norm,
God's vision manifest as form.

O Mother Mary, generate,
the song that does accelerate,
the earth into a higher state,
all matter does now scintillate.

Part 3

1. Mother Mary, shatter the energetic matrix that prevents spiritual people from seeing that even the ascended masters cannot formulate a teaching

in words that is an absolute teaching. They cannot create a teaching that could not be proven "wrong" by people in the linear mindset.

> O blessed Mary, Mother mine,
> there is no greater love than thine,
> as we are one in heart and mind,
> my place in hierarchy I find.

> **O Mother Mary, generate,**
> **the song that does accelerate,**
> **the earth into a higher state,**
> **all matter does now scintillate.**

2. Mother Mary, shatter the energetic matrix that prevents spiritual people from seeing that many spiritual students, when they come into a teaching, put on a certain pair of glasses that makes them only see what validates the teaching, and they tend to ignore or push away what questions the teaching.

> I came to earth from heaven sent,
> as I am in embodiment,
> I use Divine authority,
> commanding you to set earth free.

> **O Mother Mary, generate,**
> **the song that does accelerate,**
> **the earth into a higher state,**
> **all matter does now scintillate.**

3. Mother Mary, shatter the energetic matrix that prevents spiritual people from seeing that some people have been in this mindset for a while, and then something happened that made them doubt the teaching.

> I call now in God's sacred name,
> for you to use your Mother Flame,
> to burn all fear-based energy,
> restoring sacred harmony.

O Mother Mary, generate,
the song that does accelerate,
the earth into a higher state,
all matter does now scintillate.

4. Mother Mary, shatter the energetic matrix that prevents spiritual people from seeing that instead of pushing away their doubts, they decided to take a look at the doubts, and now they switched from this blind belief to an equally blind doubt. They switched from one extreme to the other.

Your sacred name I hereby praise,
collective consciousness you raise,
no more of fear and doubt and shame,
consume it with your Mother Flame.

O Mother Mary, generate,
the song that does accelerate,
the earth into a higher state,
all matter does now scintillate.

5. Mother Mary, shatter the energetic matrix that prevents spiritual people from seeing that the very fact that people can switch from believing in a teaching to not believing in a teaching, shows that there is still a self that is in that dualistic mind where there are always two polarities: true and false, right and wrong.

All darkness from the earth you purge,
your light moves as a mighty surge,
no force of darkness can now stop,
the spiral that goes only up.

O Mother Mary, generate,
the song that does accelerate,
the earth into a higher state,
all matter does now scintillate.

6. Mother Mary, shatter the energetic matrix that prevents spiritual people from seeing that when we shift beyond this state of consciousness, it is

not a matter of whether the teaching is true or false, right or wrong, in an absolute linear sense.

> All elemental life you bless,
> removing from them man-made stress,
> the nature spirits are now free,
> outpicturing Divine decree.

> **O Mother Mary, generate,**
> **the song that does accelerate,**
> **the earth into a higher state,**
> **all matter does now scintillate.**

7. Mother Mary, shatter the energetic matrix that prevents spiritual people from seeing that it is not constructive to take one teaching and use the linear mind to compare it to another teaching.

> I raise my voice and take my stand,
> a stop to war I do command,
> no more shall warring scar the earth,
> a golden age is given birth.

> **O Mother Mary, generate,**
> **the song that does accelerate,**
> **the earth into a higher state,**
> **all matter does now scintillate.**

8. Mother Mary, shatter the energetic matrix that prevents spiritual people from seeing that this is not constructive because the linear mind cannot take us where the teaching is meant to take us. We take a given teaching, and we apply it for the purpose of shifting our consciousness, not for the purpose of seeing some absolute truth.

> As Mother Earth is free at last,
> disasters belong to the past,
> your Mother Light is so intense,
> that matter is now far less dense.

O Mother Mary, generate,
the song that does accelerate,
the earth into a higher state,
all matter does now scintillate.

9. Mother Mary, shatter the energetic matrix that prevents spiritual people from seeing that as part of the fanatical mindset, the fallen beings have inserted the illusion that the way to overcome ignorance is to find an absolute truth. And when we find that outer expression of absolute truth, then we will be free from ignorance.

In Mother Light the earth is pure,
the upward spiral will endure,
prosperity is now the norm,
God's vision manifest as form.

O Mother Mary, generate,
the song that does accelerate,
the earth into a higher state,
all matter does now scintillate.

Part 4

1. Mother Mary, shatter the energetic matrix that prevents spiritual people from seeing that only a dualistic mind can have a concept of absolute truth. It is not a matter of finding an outer truth.

O blessed Mary, Mother mine,
there is no greater love than thine,
as we are one in heart and mind,
my place in hierarchy I find.

O Mother Mary, generate,
the song that does accelerate,
the earth into a higher state,
all matter does now scintillate.

2. Mother Mary, shatter the energetic matrix that prevents spiritual people from seeing that it is a matter of using an outer teaching as a tool to gain an inner experience. It is the inner experience that is true. It is the inner experience that is valid. It is the inner experience that shifts our consciousness.

I came to earth from heaven sent,
as I am in embodiment,
I use Divine authority,
commanding you to set earth free.

O Mother Mary, generate,
the song that does accelerate,
the earth into a higher state,
all matter does now scintillate.

3. Mother Mary, shatter the energetic matrix that prevents spiritual people from seeing that it is possible to take a valid spiritual teaching and accept with the outer mind that this represents an absolute truth.

I call now in God's sacred name,
for you to use your Mother Flame,
to burn all fear-based energy,
restoring sacred harmony.

O Mother Mary, generate,
the song that does accelerate,
the earth into a higher state,
all matter does now scintillate.

4. Mother Mary, shatter the energetic matrix that prevents spiritual people from seeing that it is possible to study a teachings faithfully, and become adept in understanding the teaching intellectually, but without making a shift in consciousness.

Your sacred name I hereby praise,
collective consciousness you raise,
no more of fear and doubt and shame,
consume it with your Mother Flame.

O Mother Mary, generate,
the song that does accelerate,
the earth into a higher state,
all matter does now scintillate.

5. Mother Mary, shatter the energetic matrix that prevents spiritual people from seeing that any spiritual movement has the scribes and the Pharisees who know the outer teaching and the outer law, but they have not shifted their consciousness.

All darkness from the earth you purge,
your light moves as a mighty surge,
no force of darkness can now stop,
the spiral that goes only up.

O Mother Mary, generate,
the song that does accelerate,
the earth into a higher state,
all matter does now scintillate.

6. Mother Mary, shatter the energetic matrix that prevents spiritual people from seeing that the ascended masters are not interested in us blindly following a teaching. They want us to look at the teaching as a tool for giving us the inner experiences to shift our consciousness, and therefore we make progress.

All elemental life you bless,
removing from them man-made stress,
the nature spirits are now free,
outpicturing Divine decree.

O Mother Mary, generate,
the song that does accelerate,
the earth into a higher state,
all matter does now scintillate.

7. Mother Mary, shatter the energetic matrix that prevents spiritual people from accepting that the purpose of the teaching is to give us an inner experience that shifts our consciousness. Therefore, it is not so important that

the outer teaching, the outer form of the teaching, is linear and absolutely consistent with previous teachings.

> I raise my voice and take my stand,
> a stop to war I do command,
> no more shall warring scar the earth,
> a golden age is given birth.

> **O Mother Mary, generate,**
> **the song that does accelerate,**
> **the earth into a higher state,**
> **all matter does now scintillate.**

8. Mother Mary, shatter the energetic matrix that prevents spiritual people from seeing that there comes a point where we are not even concerned about contradictions within or among spiritual teachings.

> As Mother Earth is free at last,
> disasters belong to the past,
> your Mother Light is so intense,
> that matter is now far less dense.

> **O Mother Mary, generate,**
> **the song that does accelerate,**
> **the earth into a higher state,**
> **all matter does now scintillate.**

9. Mother Mary, shatter the energetic matrix that prevents spiritual people from seeing that one of the big weapons used by the fallen beings through scientific materialists is that they point out contradictions between different religious beliefs and then say this proves none of them are valid.

> In Mother Light the earth is pure,
> the upward spiral will endure,
> prosperity is now the norm,
> God's vision manifest as form.

> **O Mother Mary, generate,**
> **the song that does accelerate,**

**the earth into a higher state,
all matter does now scintillate.**

Part 5

1. Mother Mary, shatter the energetic matrix that prevents spiritual people from seeing that the mystical path for shifting consciousness has been taught in many different versions, in many different contexts. They were all valid in the sense that they had teachings and tools that could help people shift their consciousness.

O blessed Mary, Mother mine,
there is no greater love than thine,
as we are one in heart and mind,
my place in hierarchy I find.

**O Mother Mary, generate,
the song that does accelerate,
the earth into a higher state,
all matter does now scintillate.**

2. Mother Mary, shatter the energetic matrix that prevents spiritual people from seeing that if we take a particular mystical teaching and use it to shift our consciousness, then that is a valid teaching for us.

I came to earth from heaven sent,
as I am in embodiment,
I use Divine authority,
commanding you to set earth free.

**O Mother Mary, generate,
the song that does accelerate,
the earth into a higher state,
all matter does now scintillate.**

3. Mother Mary, shatter the energetic matrix that prevents spiritual people from seeing that we do not need to compare this to other teachings and

try to find some superior teaching, or try to label other teachings as false. The form of the outer teaching is not what matters. What matters is that it helps us shift our consciousness.

> I call now in God's sacred name,
> for you to use your Mother Flame,
> to burn all fear-based energy,
> restoring sacred harmony.

> **O Mother Mary, generate,**
> **the song that does accelerate,**
> **the earth into a higher state,**
> **all matter does now scintillate.**

4. Mother Mary, shatter the energetic matrix that prevents spiritual people from seeing that we will not make our ascension by following all the rules and teachings of an organization. We will only make our ascension by shifting our consciousness and letting go of all illusions.

> Your sacred name I hereby praise,
> collective consciousness you raise,
> no more of fear and doubt and shame,
> consume it with your Mother Flame.

> **O Mother Mary, generate,**
> **the song that does accelerate,**
> **the earth into a higher state,**
> **all matter does now scintillate.**

5. Mother Mary, shatter the energetic matrix that prevents spiritual people from seeing that in order to let go of a certain illusion, we need something that stimulates the process whereby we see the illusion and let it go. This can be an outer teaching.

> All darkness from the earth you purge,
> your light moves as a mighty surge,
> no force of darkness can now stop,
> the spiral that goes only up.

**O Mother Mary, generate,
the song that does accelerate,
the earth into a higher state,
all matter does now scintillate.**

6. Mother Mary, shatter the energetic matrix that prevents spiritual people from seeing that no spiritual teaching will work equally well for all people. We each need to find the teaching that helps us shift our consciousness. We do not need loyalty to a specific teaching.

All elemental life you bless,
removing from them man-made stress,
the nature spirits are now free,
outpicturing Divine decree.

**O Mother Mary, generate,
the song that does accelerate,
the earth into a higher state,
all matter does now scintillate.**

7. Mother Mary, shatter the energetic matrix that prevents spiritual people from seeing that our real loyalty is to our personal path and our progress on that path. The outer teachings are just tools to facilitate that progress.

I raise my voice and take my stand,
a stop to war I do command,
no more shall warring scar the earth,
a golden age is given birth.

**O Mother Mary, generate,
the song that does accelerate,
the earth into a higher state,
all matter does now scintillate.**

8. Mother Mary, shatter the energetic matrix that prevents spiritual people from seeing that we are loyal to our own path in the sense that we are not thinking in terms of false and true. We are thinking in terms of usefulness and take a practical approach.

As Mother Earth is free at last,
disasters belong to the past,
your Mother Light is so intense,
that matter is now far less dense.

O Mother Mary, generate,
the song that does accelerate,
the earth into a higher state,
all matter does now scintillate.

9. Mother Mary, shatter the energetic matrix that prevents spiritual people from seeing that if we have any doubt about whether a teaching is true, if we still have any fear that it could be disproven, then this comes from a separate self and we need to make an effort to come to see that self and let it go.

In Mother Light the earth is pure,
the upward spiral will endure,
prosperity is now the norm,
God's vision manifest as form.

O Mother Mary, generate,
the song that does accelerate,
the earth into a higher state,
all matter does now scintillate.

Part 6

1. Mother Mary, shatter the energetic matrix that prevents spiritual people from seeing that our path will then take on a more joyful dimension where our intuition will work much better, because now we are not evaluating a teaching with the outer mind.

O blessed Mary, Mother mine,
there is no greater love than thine,
as we are one in heart and mind,
my place in hierarchy I find.

**O Mother Mary, generate,
the song that does accelerate,
the earth into a higher state,
all matter does now scintillate.**

2. Mother Mary, shatter the energetic matrix that prevents spiritual people from seeing that we are not feeling with the outer mind loyalty to a particular teaching. Instead, we are flowing with our intuitive promptings, and we study whatever we feel prompted to study.

I came to earth from heaven sent,
as I am in embodiment,
I use Divine authority,
commanding you to set earth free.

**O Mother Mary, generate,
the song that does accelerate,
the earth into a higher state,
all matter does now scintillate.**

3. Mother Mary, shatter the energetic matrix that prevents spiritual people from seeing that in order for us to have the maximum impact on raising the planet out of the consciousness of fanaticism, we need to be willing to look at ourselves and see where we have these elements of fanaticism concerning the spiritual teaching we are following.

I call now in God's sacred name,
for you to use your Mother Flame,
to burn all fear-based energy,
restoring sacred harmony.

**O Mother Mary, generate,
the song that does accelerate,
the earth into a higher state,
all matter does now scintillate.**

4. Mother Mary, shatter the energetic matrix that prevents spiritual people from seeing that fear and doubt can only come from a separate self because the Conscious You has no fear of a particular teaching being

proven wrong. It just neutrally observes, and evaluates what is useful and what is not useful.

> Your sacred name I hereby praise,
> collective consciousness you raise,
> no more of fear and doubt and shame,
> consume it with your Mother Flame.

> **O Mother Mary, generate,**
> **the song that does accelerate,**
> **the earth into a higher state,**
> **all matter does now scintillate.**

5. Mother Mary, shatter the energetic matrix that prevents spiritual people from seeing that there is no saying that once we have found a certain teaching, we have to follow it for the rest of our lives or study it the same way as we have been doing so far.

> All darkness from the earth you purge,
> your light moves as a mighty surge,
> no force of darkness can now stop,
> the spiral that goes only up.

> **O Mother Mary, generate,**
> **the song that does accelerate,**
> **the earth into a higher state,**
> **all matter does now scintillate.**

6. Mother Mary, shatter the energetic matrix that prevents spiritual people from seeing that there are levels of the path, and at certain times we need to approach the path a certain way. Then, we may come to a point where we need something different.

> All elemental life you bless,
> removing from them man-made stress,
> the nature spirits are now free,
> outpicturing Divine decree.

**O Mother Mary, generate,
the song that does accelerate,
the earth into a higher state,
all matter does now scintillate.**

7. Mother Mary, shatter the energetic matrix that prevents spiritual people from seeing that the fanatical mindset will make us think with the outer mind that we are supposed to create a standard for how we are going to behave for the rest of our lives as spiritual students.

I raise my voice and take my stand,
a stop to war I do command,
no more shall warring scar the earth,
a golden age is given birth.

**O Mother Mary, generate,
the song that does accelerate,
the earth into a higher state,
all matter does now scintillate.**

8. Mother Mary, shatter the energetic matrix that prevents spiritual people from seeing that when we let go of this fanatical mindset and the fear of failure, the fear of making a mistake, the fear of being wrong, then we can flow with our intuition. We go where we get the most benefit. We get the exact thing we need in order to take the next step on our path.

As Mother Earth is free at last,
disasters belong to the past,
your Mother Light is so intense,
that matter is now far less dense.

**O Mother Mary, generate,
the song that does accelerate,
the earth into a higher state,
all matter does now scintillate.**

9. Mother Mary, shatter the energetic matrix that prevents spiritual people from seeing if we have developed or adopted a sense of security based on

a certain teaching. Is there a sense that if we follow this teaching faithfully for the rest of our lives, then we must be able to make our ascension?

> In Mother Light the earth is pure,
> the upward spiral will endure,
> prosperity is now the norm,
> God's vision manifest as form.

> **O Mother Mary, generate,**
> **the song that does accelerate,**
> **the earth into a higher state,**
> **all matter does now scintillate.**

Part 7

1. Mother Mary, shatter the energetic matrix that prevents spiritual people from seeing that this belief comes from a separate self that has this need for security, and it wants us to feel that because we have found this teaching, because we are following this teaching, now we are secure.

> O blessed Mary, Mother mine,
> there is no greater love than thine,
> as we are one in heart and mind,
> my place in hierarchy I find.

> **O Mother Mary, generate,**
> **the song that does accelerate,**
> **the earth into a higher state,**
> **all matter does now scintillate.**

2. Mother Mary, shatter the energetic matrix that prevents spiritual people from seeing that there is no security in the outer teaching, there is no security in the outer practice.

> I came to earth from heaven sent,
> as I am in embodiment,

I use Divine authority,
commanding you to set earth free.

**O Mother Mary, generate,
the song that does accelerate,
the earth into a higher state,
all matter does now scintillate.**

3. Mother Mary, shatter the energetic matrix that prevents spiritual people from seeing that there is only a dynamic security of constant self-transcendence where we continue to take step by step, walking higher on the 144 levels of consciousness until we shed that last illusion.

I call now in God's sacred name,
for you to use your Mother Flame,
to burn all fear-based energy,
restoring sacred harmony.

**O Mother Mary, generate,
the song that does accelerate,
the earth into a higher state,
all matter does now scintillate.**

4. Mother Mary, shatter the energetic matrix that prevents spiritual people from seeing that this is an inner security, and when we shift to this, our path becomes much more peaceful and joyful because we know we cannot really go wrong.

Your sacred name I hereby praise,
collective consciousness you raise,
no more of fear and doubt and shame,
consume it with your Mother Flame.

**O Mother Mary, generate,
the song that does accelerate,
the earth into a higher state,
all matter does now scintillate.**

5. Mother Mary, shatter the energetic matrix that prevents spiritual people from seeing that we cannot fail our tests when we are willing to see a higher understanding than what we have right now.

> All darkness from the earth you purge,
> your light moves as a mighty surge,
> no force of darkness can now stop,
> the spiral that goes only up.

> **O Mother Mary, generate,**
> **the song that does accelerate,**
> **the earth into a higher state,**
> **all matter does now scintillate.**

6. Mother Mary, shatter the energetic matrix that prevents spiritual people from seeing that the only test the ascended masters have ever given is: Are we willing to transcend our present level of consciousness?

> All elemental life you bless,
> removing from them man-made stress,
> the nature spirits are now free,
> outpicturing Divine decree.

> **O Mother Mary, generate,**
> **the song that does accelerate,**
> **the earth into a higher state,**
> **all matter does now scintillate.**

7. Mother Mary, shatter the energetic matrix that prevents spiritual people from seeing that it is not a matter of doing the right outer things, making the right choices in outer situations. The real test is always to see that any situation represents a certain level of consciousness.

> I raise my voice and take my stand,
> a stop to war I do command,
> no more shall warring scar the earth,
> a golden age is given birth.

O Mother Mary, generate,
the song that does accelerate,
the earth into a higher state,
all matter does now scintillate.

8. Mother Mary, shatter the energetic matrix that prevents spiritual people from seeing that the way to pass a test is to transcend that level of consciousness. We can come to see that our previous idea was not false, but that it was not the complete story. It was part of a much greater picture.

As Mother Earth is free at last,
disasters belong to the past,
your Mother Light is so intense,
that matter is now far less dense.

O Mother Mary, generate,
the song that does accelerate,
the earth into a higher state,
all matter does now scintillate.

9. Mother Mary, shatter the energetic matrix that prevents spiritual people from seeing that we need to adopt the mindset where we are not "grasping our ideas." As long as we are willing to transcend our present level of consciousness, we cannot go wrong, we cannot make a mistake, we cannot fail our test.

In Mother Light the earth is pure,
the upward spiral will endure,
prosperity is now the norm,
God's vision manifest as form.

O Mother Mary, generate,
the song that does accelerate,
the earth into a higher state,
all matter does now scintillate.

Sealing

In the name of the I AM THAT I AM, I accept that Archangel Michael, Astrea and Shiva form an impenetrable shield around myself and all constructive people, sealing us from all fear-based energies in all four octaves. I accept that the Light of God is consuming and transforming all fear-based energies that make up the dark forces working against ending the era of fanaticism on earth!